Dissertations in American Economic History

This is a volume in the Arno Press collection

Dissertations in American Economic History

Advisory Editor
Stuart Bruchey

Research Associate
Eleanor Bruchey

See last pages of this volume for a complete list of titles.

THE CURRENCY OF THE AMERICAN COLONIES 1700-1764
A Study in Colonial Finance and Imperial Relations

Leslie V. Brock

ARNO PRESS
A New York Times Company
New York — 1975

First publication in book form, Arno Press, 1975

Copyright © 1975 by Leslie V. Brock

DISSERTATIONS IN AMERICAN ECONOMIC HISTORY
ISBN for complete set: 0-405-07252-X
See last pages of this volume for titles.

Manufactured in the United States of America

Publisher's Note: Table XIV Part B and Figure X between pages 327 and 328 are omitted because they were based on too incomplete data to be of value.

Library of Congress Cataloging in Publication Data

Brock, Leslie V
    The currency of the American colonies, 1700-1764.

  (Dissertations in American economic history)
  Originally presented as the author's thesis, University of Michigan, 1941.
    Bibliography: p.
    1. Monetary policy--United States--History.
2. Great Britain--Colonies--America--Finance.
I. Title. II. Series.
HG508.B7 1975   332.4'973   75-2576
0-405-07257-0

PREFACE

The writing of this dissertation was an exercise in emancipating myself from the bias of the writers whose views on colonial paper currency prevailed at the time — writers such as Horace White, Charles J. Bullock, and Andrew MacF. Davis, who wrote either during the struggle against "the Free Silver Heresy," or in the afterglow of the final triumph of the gold standard in 1900. To them, inconvertible paper currency was evil *per se*. They drew their examples chiefly from New England during its worst period, 1700-1751, and were greatly influenced by the virulent contemporary attacks of Dr. William Douglass of Boston against the "fraudulent" depreciating paper currency of the period, by which debtors defrauded creditors. This view was echoed at the time of writing in the "farmer-debtor merchant-creditor" thesis of Curtis P. Nettels.

As research progressed, it became evident that such a simple, all-embracing explanation did not fit the facts, that paper currency issued in anticipation of taxes was often a necessary instrument of government finance, that issues on loan provided needed long-term private credit, and that both provided a medium of exchange; and that in some colonies, their paper for long periods enjoyed a *de facto* convertibility into specie at a fixed ratio. Moreover, it became apparent that the currency experience of the colonies varied greatly from one to another, and from period to period. Further, that depreciation had repercussions in the Mother Country, hence the need for a consideration of its effect upon imperial relations. These facts dictated the organization of the dissertation.

Since 1941, I have been working on a comprehensive history of "The Currency of the English Colonies in America, 1690-1775," all of which is now researched and much of it written. As a result, my understanding of the colonial currency has been both broadened and deepened. Only the realization that time may not be given me to finish the work has induced me to publish the dissertation, for although I could now add to its statistical precision and completeness, and fill in many details in the story, I still feel that in its main elements the story is told there.

Writing today on the scale of the dissertation, I would remove the occasional echoes of the older writers found in Chapter II, "Paper Currency . . . before 1751; New England," which, perforce, was written largely, although not exclusively, from secondary sources, and which I have now developed from the original sources. At this point attention is called to the more accurate compilations of the paper currency outstanding in New England, 1703-1751, in the Appendix. I still consider accurate information concerning the annual amount of paper, and, insofar as possible, the approximate amount of specie in circulation of prime importance. From the monetary point of view, whether the money supply was increasing or decreasing relatively to the needs of trade will, *ceteribus paribus,* explain much. Of course, all other available relevant facts must be considered, for other things may not remain equal.

Further, I now realize that the existing colonial price indices based upon the prices of a few commodities chiefly sold in foreign markets are in no way indicative of the general price level, and hence of the degree of the French and Indian War inflation and the subsequent deflation. Nor are exchange rates. In Pennsylvania, for example, from 1757 to 1762, the price index of 20 commodities increased by 24.6% and the exchange rate by 5.9%. But

Benjamin Franklin, returning to Philadelphia in November, 1762, after six years in England, found "the Expence of Living . . . greatly advanced, it is more than double in most Articles, and in some 'tis treble." The "Rent of old Houses, & Value of Land" had trebled. All "in great measure owing to the enormous Plenty of Money among us."[1] The above remarks should be borne in mind when reading the chapters on the French and Indian War period.

The foregoing observations apply particularly to the Massachusetts portion of Chapter VI (New England, 1751-1764) for two reasons: (1) because the annual amounts of outstanding Treasurer's Certificates given in Table IX are inaccurate; and (2) because the Certificates, which bore 5% annual interest, predominately represented negotiable securities issued in large denominations to lenders of specie and were held out of circulation for the interest, thus forming only a small or negligible part of the money supply. Consequently, the attempt in Figure VIII to relate the amount outstanding to the price index (based only on the price of molasses, rum, and fish) was misguided. A revised and accurate Table IX calculated from the Treasurers' Accounts, now available, is included in the Appendix.

During the writing of the dissertation, I received the generous aid of many persons, to whom I express my gratitude. I owe a special debt to my old Michigan mentor and friend, the late Professor Verner W. Crane, who suggested the subject to me and whose meticulous scholarship has proven an abiding inspiration. Finally, I must pay tribute to my wife, Frances Sutherland Brock, who aided me in so many ways during so many trying days.

February 1975 Leslie V. Brock
Caldwell, Idaho The College of Idaho

---

[1] To Richard Jackson, March 8, 1763, Franklin, *Papers* (Yale ed.), X, 209.

THE CURRENCY OF THE AMERICAN COLONIES
1700 - 1764

A Study in Colonial Finance and Imperial Relations

by

Leslie V. Brock

A dissertation submitted in partial fulfillment of the requirements for the degree of Doctor of Philosophy, in the University of Michigan

1941

CONTENTS

LIST OF TABLES.. v

LIST OF FIGURES...................................... vii

I. THE CURRENCY OF THE AMERICAN COLONIES BEFORE 1751: THE GENERAL PROBLEM; COIN; COMMODITY CURRENCY; TOBACCO NOTES................1

II. PAPER CURRENCY IN THE COLONIES BEFORE 1751: NEW ENGLAND.................................17

III. PAPER CURRENCY IN THE COLONIES BEFORE 1751: THE MIDDLE AND SOUTHERN COLONIES.............65

IV. EARLY ATTEMPTS AT IMPERIAL CONTROL OF COLONIAL CURRENCY: COIN..........................130

V. EARLY ATTEMPTS AT IMPERIAL CONTROL OF COLONIAL CURRENCY: BILLS OF CREDIT. THE CURRENCY ACT OF 1751........................168

VI. MASSACHUSETTS RETURNS TO SILVER. THE CURRENCY OF NEW ENGLAND, 1751-1764..............244

VII. THE CURRENCY OF NEW YORK, PENNSYLVANIA, DELAWARE, AND NEW JERSEY, 1750-1764.........335

VIII. THE CURRENCY OF MARYLAND, NORTH CAROLINA, SOUTH CAROLINA, AND GEORGIA, 1751-1764......412

IX. THE INTRODUCTION OF PAPER CURRENCY IN VIRGINIA; THE BRITISH AND SCOTTISH MERCHANTS' PROTESTS; THE CURRENCY ACT OF 1764..465

X. CONCLUSIONS..528

BIBLIOGRAPHY...564

APPENDIX.. 590

LIST OF TABLES

I.	RELATION OF COLONIAL MONEY TO STERLING, 1700, 1701, AND AFTER 1708	8
II.	PART A. NEW ENGLAND BILLS OF CREDIT OUTSTANDING: MASSACHUSETTS, 1721-1745	29-30
II.	PART B. NEW ENGLAND BILLS OF CREDIT OUTSTANDING, 1703-1751	29-30
III.	PRICE OF SILVER IN BOSTON, 1700-1753	29-30
IV.	NEW YORK BILLS OF CREDIT, 1709-1747	72-73
V.	PENNSYLVANIA BILLS OF CREDIT, ISSUED AND OUTSTANDING, 1723-1751	82-83
VI.	NEW JERSEY BILLS OF CREDIT, ISSUED AND OUTSTANDING	91-92
VII.	DELAWARE BILLS OF CREDIT, ISSUES, 1723-1746	97-98
VIII.	MARYLAND BILLS OF CREDIT, ON LOAN AND TOTAL IN CIRCULATION, 1733-1751	104-105
IX.	MASSACHUSETTS TREASURER'S CERTIFICATES, ISSUED, CANCELLED, AND OUTSTANDING, 1750-1772	274-275
X.	MASSACHUSETTS PARLIAMENTARY GRANTS, 1756-1769	281
XI.	NEW HAMPSHIRE NEW TENOR BILLS OF CREDIT, ISSUES, 1755-1757	301
XII.	NEW HAMPSHIRE STERLING BILLS OF CREDIT, ISSUES, 1758-1762	303
XIII.	CONNECTICUT LAWFUL MONEY ISSUES, 1755-1764	321
XIV.	PART A. RHODE ISLAND BILLS OF CREDIT, ISSUES, 1751-1762	327-328

LIST OF TABLES

(continued)

XV.	NEW YORK WAR ISSUES, 1755-1764	345-346
XVI.	NEW YORK BILLS OF CREDIT, EMITTED, CANCELLED, AND OUTSTANDING	345-346
XVII.	NEW YORK PARLIAMENTARY GRANTS (RECEIVED IN PROVINCE BY 1764)	348-349
XVIII.	PENNSYLVANIA WAR ISSUES, 1755-1764	386-387
XIX.	PENNSYLVANIA PAPER CURRENCY OUTSTANDING	386-387
XX.	PENNSYLVANIA PARLIAMENTARY GRANTS	390-391
XXI.	PART A. NEW JERSEY WAR ISSUES, 1755-1764	402-403
XXI.	PART B. NEW JERSEY BILLS OF CREDIT ON TAX FUNDS, 1753-1755	402-403
XXII.	NORTH CAROLINA BILLS OF CREDIT, ISSUES, 1748-1761	436-437
XXIII.	NORTH CAROLINA PROCLAMATION BILLS, ISSUED, CANCELLED, AND OUTSTANDING, 1748-1768	436-437
XXIV.	NORTH CAROLINA INTEREST NOTES, ISSUED, CANCELLED, AND OUTSTANDING, 1756-1766	436-437
XXV.	NORTH CAROLINA PAPER CURRENCY OUTSTANDING, 1748-1768	436-437
XXVI.	SOUTH CAROLINA PUBLIC ORDERS, 1751-1764	460-461
XXVII.	SOUTH CAROLINA PAPER CURRENCY OUTSTANDING, 1750-1774	460-461
XXVIII.	VIRGINIA BILLS OF CREDIT, WAR ISSUES, 1755-1762	475-476

LIST OF FIGURES

I. NEW ENGLAND CURRENCY, 1701-1750.................29-30

Ia. NEW ENGLAND CURRENCY, REVISED FIGURE, 1726-1750....................................29-30

II. BILLS OF CREDIT OUTSTANDING IN THE SEVERAL NEW ENGLAND COLONIES, 1700-1751....................................29-30

III. PRICE OF SILVER IN THE COLONIES, 1701-1750....................................29-30

IV. DIAGRAM SHOWING DISAPPEARANCE OF SILVER, INCREASE OF PROVINCIAL CURRENCY AND CORRESPONDING MOVEMENT OF SILVER RATE, 1700-1750 (AFTER ANDREW MC-FARLAND DAVIS)..............................29-30

V. PENNSYLVANIA BILLS OF CREDIT, 1723-1751........82-83

VI. NEW JERSEY BILLS OF CREDIT, 1709-1750..........91-92

VII. MARYLAND BILLS OF CREDIT, 1733-1751..........104-105

VIII. MASSACHUSETTS TREASURER'S CERTIFICATES, 1750-1774..................................274-275

IX. VALUE OF SPANISH MILLED DOLLAR IN RHODE ISLAND, CONNECTICUT, AND NEW HAMPSHIRE, 1750-1774........................317-318

X. RHODE ISLAND BILLS OF CREDIT, 1749-1765......327-328

XI. NEW YORK BILLS OF CREDIT, EXCHANGE RATES, AND PRICES, 1750-1774....................345-346

XII. PENNSYLVANIA BILLS OF CREDIT, EXCHANGE RATES, AND PRICES, 1750-1774.............386-387

XIII. NEW JERSEY BILLS OF CREDIT AND EXCHANGE RATES, 1750-1774..........................402-403

XIV. NORTH CAROLINA BILLS OF CREDIT, 1748-1769.......................................436-437

LIST OF FIGURES

(continued)

XV. SOUTH CAROLINA PAPER CURRENCY, 1750-
1769...................................460-461

XVI. VIRGINIA BILLS OF CREDIT (WAR ISSUES)
AND EXCHANGE RATES, 1755-1773..........475-476

APPENDIX

Table II (Revised) Part B. NEW ENGLAND BILLS OF CREDIT
    OUTSTANDING..591-593

Figure I (Revised)..594-595

Table IX (Revised). MASSACHUSETTS TREASURER'S CERTIFICATES
    (Lawful Money)..596

Figure VIII (Revised)..597

CONNECTICUT TABLE. BILLS OF CREDIT ISSUED ON TAXES, 1740-1751..598

Partial Errata..599-601

CHAPTER I

THE CURRENCY OF THE AMERICAN COLONIES BEFORE 1751: THE GENERAL PROBLEM; COIN; COMMODITY CURRENCY; TOBACCO NOTES

> Silver & Gold tis impossible for us to preserve without ruining the Mother Country by a disuse of her Manufactorys.
>
> -- John Watts, New York merchant, 1765.

WHEN THE FIRST English settlers came to the shores of America, their immediate problems were remote from those of a more highly developed economic order. The pressing problem was that of providing the necessaries of subsistence. But before long, when the settlements had taken root in the soil and the colonists of the various regions had begun to develop the economic activities best suited to their respective locations, they began to produce commodities for export. Trading centers developed at Boston, Newport, New York, Philadelphia, and Charlestown, through which the raw materials produced in the colonies were exchanged, directly or indirectly, for the manufactured products of the mother country, or the products of Southern Europe or the West Indies; and factors took up their abode on the rivers of Virginia and Maryland to facilitate the exchange of tobacco for the goods of England.

It may be said that in general trade needs a currency to serve as a unit of account, as a medium of exchange, and as a standard of deferred payments. But the need for a medium of exchange was less imperative in some trading colonies than in others: it was less when the trade with England was direct, and greater when the trade was indirect. In this respect, the Southern colonies were on a different footing than were the Middle colonies and New England. Virginia and Maryland paid for their importations of English goods directly by means of the tobacco they sent to the mother country. South Carolina accomplished the same result by her exportations of rice, hides, and indigo. The actual manner in which the transactions took place might take any of a variety of forms; but in any case the principle involved was the same. When, for example, tobacco was marketed in London through a commission merchant, the money accruing in his hands to the credit of the Virginia shipper created a fund upon which the Virginian could draw. He might, for instance, direct his London correspondent to purchase and ship him a bill of goods, charging his account for the amount of the invoice. Here nothing more than a bookkeeping transaction was involved. If, however, the Virginia planter wished to bring some of his funds home for investment on this side of the water, he did so by selling a sterling bill of exchange drawn upon his balance in the possession of his London correspondent. This bill was usually bought by some fellow Virginian who needed to make a remittance to England. The bill of exchange, in the nature of an order to pay sterling money directed to the London correspondent of the drawer of the bill, was forwarded to England by the purchaser to pay for his importation. When received in England it was presented to the drawee for payment, and the transaction was closed. In these ways exports to England paid for imports from England and no shipments of specie were involved.

Unlike the Southern colonies, the Middle and the Northern colonies did not produce commodities that furnished substantial direct returns to England. In consequence, these areas had to resort to a roundabout trade to acquire the products, bills of exchange, or specie with which to pay for their imports from the mother country. The Middle colonies sent their provisions to the West Indies in exchange for sugar, molasses, specie, or bills of exchange drawn on England; and with these paid for their importations from England. Similarly, the New England colonies carried their products -- fish, provisions, lumber, rum -- to the West Indies, Southern Europe, or even Africa, where they exchanged them for goods, slaves, specie, or bills of exchange that could be used either to make remittances directly to England, or, in the case of some goods and slaves, to carry on a further trade that would eventually provide commodities, specie, or bills of exchange that could be sent to the mother country.

For carrying on internal trade and industry, the need for a currency was greatest in the colonies where the division of labor was greatest, and greater in the free-labor colonies than in the slave-labor ones. Moreover, the credit habits of the people conditioned the need for a currency. In South Carolina, for example, where "pay, after twelve Months, was reckoned as ready Money,"[1] a planter could apply his crop in payment of his debt, and no money need change hands.

Throughout the colonial period the exportation of English sterling coin to the colonies was prohibited. The result was that there was never any appreciable amount of sterling coin in circulation in the colonies. The colonists did, however, keep their accounts in pounds, shillings, and pence. The accounts, at first kept in sterling values, later were kept in the currencies of the various colonies when these diverged from sterling.

---

1. Dr. William Douglass, "A Discourse Concerning the Currencies of the British Plantations in America," in Andrew McF. Davis (ed.), *Colonial Currency Reprints*, III, 337, quoting Sir Alexander Cumings, who wrote in 1729.

Such coin as there was in the colonies was derived from the West Indian and Southern European trade and was chiefly in the form of Spanish silver and, in lesser degree, Portuguese gold. There was also in circulation varying amounts of the coin of France, Holland, and the German Empire, as well as that of England.[2] It is a fundamental fact, however, that throughout the colonial period the colonies never succeeded in amassing an adequate supply of specie. This was due fundamentally to the fact that the balance of trade between the colonies, both north and south, and Great Britain was unfavorable. The result was that much of the specie that found its way into the colonies in the course of the West Indian or Southern European

---

2. The Spanish dollar (piece of eight), to be discussed below in the text, was the most important coin in circulation in the colonies. It was divided into four pesetas (usually called pistareens) or eight reales (frequently spoken of as bits).

Among the more important of the other silver coins in circulation were the old rix dollars of several states of the Holy Roman Empire; the lion or dog dollar of Holland; the French crown or silver louis; the Portuguese crusado; the ducatoon of Flanders; the three guilder piece of Holland; and the silver crowns, half crown, florin, shilling, and six-pence of England.

Among the gold coins were the Spanish pistole or doubloon; the Portuguese johannes, half-johannes, and moidore (moeda d'ouro, lit., coin of gold); and the English guinea, sovereign, and half-sovereign.

English copper pence and half-pence also circulated. Clarence P. Gould, Money and Transportation in Maryland, 1720-1765, 1915, pp. 21-25.

For the values of the various silver coins as determined by the Proclamation of Queen Anne (1704), see below, p. 135.

trade was swept off to England to redress the balance of trade with the mother country. An examination of the available trade figures between the tobacco colonies and the mother country for the years after 1696 might at first lead one to believe that in this region the balance with the mother country was favorable.[3] But when the invisible items -- freight, insurance, commission fees, interest -- are taken into account, the balance is against the colonies.[4] Much the same may be said in the case of South Carolina, although there were times when the balance was such as to permit the province to amass a considerable quantity of specie.

The impression one draws from the figures of trade between New England, New York, and Pennsylvania, on the one hand, and Great Britain on the other, is apt to be very different from his first impression of the trade of the Southern colonies. Here the imports from Britain are customarily four, five, or even ten times the value of the exports to Britain. But while this is a matter of the utmost importance, a recent authority, Professor Curtis P. Nettels, has concluded that the commercial position of these colonies with respect to Britain was

---

3. Emory R. Johnson, et al., History of Domestic and Foreign Commerce of the United States, 1915, I, 120-121.
4. Curtis P. Nettels, Roots of American Civilization, 1938, pp. 252-258, has an excellent discussion of the matter.

more favorable than that of their Southern neighbors. This was because the invisible items in the balance of payments of the Middle and the Northern colonies did not run so strongly against the colonies, and because the West Indian, Southern European, and African trade developed by the merchants of these regions provided them with returns to redress the balance with England. Nevertheless, specie was customarily drained away to England from all the colonies, north and south alike. This fact encouraged the colonies to adopt measures aimed at increasing their specie supply.

The chief element in the colonies' supply of coin was the Spanish dollar, or piece of eight, of which there were several varieties, the Peru or light piece of eight, and the heavy pieces, Mexico, pillar, and Seville. Intrinsically, the heavy piece, a coin of seventeen and a half pennyweight, was worth 4s. 6d. sterling.[6] The colonial assemblies, however, in order to retain the colony's supply of coin and to attract coin from other colonies raised the valuation to some figure in excess of its intrinsic worth. According to a contemporaneous compilation made by William Penn,

---

5. Ibid., p. 259.
6. Curtis P. Nettels, The Money Supply of the American Colonies before 1720, p. 180, citing C. O. 323/5, no. 48. Professor Nettels' book is the best treatment of the colonial currency during the early years.

heavy pieces of eight passed in 1700 for 6s. in Boston; 6s. 9d. in New York; 7s. 8d. in Jersey and Pennsylvania; 4s. 6d. in Maryland; and 5s. in Virginia.[7] Professor Nettels obtains slightly different figures by using the highest legal values placed upon the pieces of eight by the colonies in 1701.[8] Using the same method he has made a similar compilation for the year 1708.[9] The relation of colonial money to sterling according to Penn's statement and Professor Nettels' compilations is indicated in the following table:

TABLE I

Colony	Relation of colonial money to sterling		
	Compiled from Penn's figures 1700	Nettels' figures 1701	After 1708
New England	133:100	137:100	155:100
New York and East Jersey	150:100	155:100	155:100
Pennsylvania and West Jersey	173:100	181:100	178:100
South Carolina		161:100	161:100
Virginia	111:100	111:100	120:100
Maryland	100:100	No legal value	133:100

---

7. Mr. Penn's Suggestions respecting the Plantations, E. B. O'Callaghan (ed.), New York Colonial Documents, IV, 757.
8. Nettels, Money Supply, p. 241.
9. Ibid., p. 248.

The value of other coins was raised in proportion to that of the piece of eight. But at best the practice of enhancing the value of coin by legislative enactment was no more than a local and a temporary expedient. It obviously could not be applied successfully by all the colonies at once, and even if the neighboring colonies were considerate enough to allow a colony to draw away their coin without taking counter measures, yet even then the magic ceased to work as soon as the importation of coin into the colony applying the expedient had caused a price rise sufficient to equalize the purchasing power of the dollar there and elsewhere.[10]

A substitute for coin was found in the use of commodity money. Many of the staple commodities of the regions were, at one time or another, used as money. Frequently they were "rated" by an act of assembly, that is, given values in pounds, shillings, and pence at which they were to be received in public and private payments.[11] In other cases taxes were levied and debts contracted in the commodity itself. Tobacco in

---

10. See Nettels, Money Supply, pp. 232-233, for a discussion of this point.
11. The South Carolina act of July 23, 1687, will serve as an example of the acts rating commodities. It provided "that all debts, accounts, contracts, bargains and judgments, and executions thereupon ... which are not made expressly for silver or money or some other particular commodity att a certain price, shall and may bee paid and discharged by Corne att two shillings the bushel, Indian Pease at two shillings sixpence the bushel,

Virginia and Maryland is perhaps the most important example from the long list of commodities put to monetary uses. In the colonies where commodity currency was used it served both as a standard of value and as a medium of exchange. It did not prove satisfactory, however, in performing either function. "Its history is," as Professor Nettels has written, "a story of defects and complaints." "Whether commodity money was tendered in public or in private payments, there was a tendency for the payer to deliver his most inferior products."[12]

That such was the case in Virginia is evident from the statement of Governor Alexander Spotswood, who in 1713, referring to the payment of public dues in tobacco, wrote: "People have, for a long time, indulged themselves in the unjust opinion that the worst Trash they could make was good enough to discharge their public Debts."[13] To remedy this situation he pushed through the House of Burgesses an act[14] that provided for the storing of tobacco in public warehouses, where its quali-

---

English Pease at three shillings sixpence the bushel, Porke at twenty shillings per cwt., Beefe at twopence the pound, Tobacco at tw... pence the pound, Tarr at eight shillings the barrell." Thomas Cooper (ed.), Statutes at Large of South Carolina, II, 37.
    12. Nettels, Money Supply, pp. 210, 211.
    13. R. A. Brock (ed.), Letters of Alexander Spotswood, II, 61-62. Spotswood to Mr. Blathwayt, March 13, 1713/14.
    14. Only the title of the act is printed in William W. Hening (comp.), Statutes at Large of Virginia (1819 edition).

ty was inspected by agents appointed for that purpose. These officials issued tobacco notes in the nature of warehouse receipts against the tobacco so deposited. It was intended that these notes should, in Spotswood's words, "pass like bank bills," and be received in satisfaction of tobacco obligations.[15] The law, however, was short-lived, for it was repealed by the Privy Council on July 31, 1717.[16] The testimony concerning the popularity of the act during its short duration is conflicting. The sheriff of Essex County wrote in 1715 that "the peoples inclinations are so great against the Tobacco law that they have not meet me to pay their Dues, so that all are unpayed, Except some Smal Part of his Majesties." Moreover, they had given further manifestation of their dissatisfaction by burning one of the warehouses.[17] In 1717, however, upon the repeal of the law, the governor wrote that "the Country are almost Generally sensible of the loss of the Tobacco Law."[18] All of which probably means that the people

---

15. See Nettels, Money Supply, p. 214; also W. Z. Ripley, The Financial History of Virginia, 1893, pp. 146-148.
16. Calendar of State Papers, Colonial Series, America and West Indies, 1716-17, pp. 362-363. Hening, IV, 37, contains Spotswood's proclamation of repeal, dated Nov. 13, 1717.
17. Calendar of Virginia State Papers, I, 181. Leo: Tarent to ..., April 15, 1715.
18. Spotswood, Letters, II, 263. Spotswood to the Lords of Trade, February 27, 1717/18.

accustomed to pay their public dues in "trash" thought harshly of the law, and those that had the government's interest at heart or were disinterested thought well of it.

In any event, Virginia in 1730 enacted a law similar to that disallowed in 1717. It provided that all tobacco for the payment "of any public or private debt or contract" was to be brought to a public warehouse of the county in which it had been grown. There it was inspected and inspectors' notes issued in exchange for it. These notes were to have a local circulation, being made a legal tender "in all tobacco paiments whatsoever" within the county of their origin, "or in any other county next adjacent ..., and not separated therefrom by any of the great rivers" or by Chesapeake Bay. Moreover, it was declared that "nothing should be accounted a lawful tender, to discharge any debt, contract, or duty, paible in tobacco, unless paiment ... be tendered in inspectors Notes."[19] The notes upon presentation were redeemed by the inspectors from tobacco of the kind called for by the note. Tobacco held against such notes was called transfer tobacco. In contradistinction to it was crop tobacco, which was tobacco deposited in a warehouse to await export, and not to be

---

19. Hening, IV, c. iii, 3 and 4 George II, p. 251-252, 256.

used for the payment of debts. "Crop notes" were issued against individual hogsheads of such tobacco. These notes were recognized by the act of 1754 amending and extending the act of 1730.[20] It appears at first not to have been the intention of the Burgesses that the crop notes should pass in satisfaction of tobacco debts. But the custom of using them for this purpose developed and appears to have been recognized by the General Tobacco Law of 1742,[21] which consolidated in one act all former legislation concerning tobacco. Provision was also made for the exchange at the warehouse of one kind of note for the other. The currency of the notes of this period came to be limited to eighteen months. Tobacco held against transfer notes and not claimed was sold before the fall of the year following that in which the crop had been made. Holders of notes against the tobacco sold were indemnified out of the funds received from its sale.

The commodity currency of the colonies reached its highest development in the tobacco notes of Virginia, and their importance to the Virginia economy is more readily understood when it is recalled that during this

---

20. *Ibid.*, IV, c. 1, 8 George II, p. 388.
21. *Ibid.*, V, c. 1, 15 George II, p. 134, sections xvi and xix. The statutes as printed in Hening do not make this matter entirely clear. Perhaps an intermediary statute has been omitted from the compilation.

period taxes, duties, court fees, and the salaries of the clergy were all paid in tobacco. The system perfected by the various tobacco acts passed after 1730 lasted until 1775,[22] with the exception of an interval during the French and Indian War. It seems on the whole to have provided a fairly satisfactory currency for the needs of Virginia's rural economy, although, since the value of the notes fluctuated with the price of tobacco, it did not provide a stable monetary medium. During ordinary years these fluctuations were not violent; and the long-time fluctuations were moderate in comparison with the fluctuations of the currency in some of the less restrained paper money colonies. Nevertheless, in years when the crop failed the value of the tobacco notes fluctuated more than did the bills of credit of any of the colonies in a similar period. This phenomenon led to attempts in the late 'fifties to commute tobacco debts to currency debts at a figure less than the market price of tobacco. None the less, it is probably true that the development of a paper currency based upon Virginia's staple commodity retarded the introduction of bills of credit within her borders. She was the last of the thirteen colonies to

---

22. W. Z. Ripley, The Financial History of Virginia, p. 15. Chapter vi of this work contains an accurate account of the tobacco notes.

public charges.[24] In 1747 Maryland adopted the Virginia system requiring all tobacco to be delivered to public warehouses, where it was inspected and the owner at his option given a nontransferable receipt or transfer notes. These notes, as in Virginia, were locally receivable in payment of tobacco obligations, and it was provided that no tobacco debts should be satisfied except by the tender of transfer notes. This system continued in operation until the close of the colonial period.[25]

North Carolina likewise adopted the system in 1754 and extended it to include other commodities in 1764.[26]

---

24. Ibid., p. 52.
25. Ibid., pp. 58-59.
26. Laws of N. C., 1754 (c. ix), State Records of North Carolina, XXIII, 402-417; Laws of N. C., 1764 (c. v), ibid., pp. 639-654.

have recourse to this medium, and did not adopt it until the exigencies of the last intercolonial war forced her to it in the year 1755.

Maryland also from a very early period made use of tobacco currency. "Though never declared so, it was in fact the official money of the province. All levies -- parish, county, and provincial -- all fines and court charges, and all ecclesiastical and official fees were regularly assessed in tobacco."[23] It was also widely used in commerce. Merchants' accounts were frequently kept in tobacco, and the planter during the winter season delivered tobacco from his crop in payment of his account. All the difficulties and abuses that attended the use of tobacco currency in Virginia were experienced in Maryland. Moreover, the problem was complicated by the fact that as time progressed certain areas of Maryland turned from tobacco to grain. The farmers in these areas found it difficult to pay their tobacco dues. Complaints began to reach the legislature, and in 1733, chiefly because of the accumulation of such complaints, the colony issued its first paper currency, and paper at the rate of ten shillings per hundred pounds of tobacco was made receivable for

---

23. Clarence P. Gould, Money and Transportation in Maryland, 1720-1765, p. 48. Chapter III contains an excellent analysis of the Maryland tobacco currency.

CHAPTER II

PAPER CURRENCY IN THE COLONIES BEFORE 1751: NEW ENGLAND

> I was at making the first bills of credit [in Massachusetts] in the year 1690. They were not made for want of money; but for want of Money in the Treasury.
>
> -- Judge Sewall in 1712.

THE DISTINCTIVE CONTRIBUTION of the American colonies to financial and monetary practice was a paper currency issued under governmental auspices. Such currency originated in the thirteen colonies near the close of the seventeenth century, and throughout the colonial period they served as experimental laboratories for its development.[1] The issuing of paper currency in the colonies "came as the culmination of financial practices long in vogue."[2] The promissory notes of individuals, upon endorsement, had enjoyed a limited circulation from hand to hand. Bills of exchange had likewise passed current. When a colony borrowed, it gave its notes, which frequently circulated. The colonial treasurers issued their notes in anticipation of taxes, and these notes were sometimes passed from hand to hand

---

1. Curtis P. Nettels, *The Money Supply of the American Colonies before 1720*, 1934, p. 205.
2. *Ibid.*, p. 250.

before they found their way back into the treasury. Early bank schemes were broached, wherein it was proposed that a group of individuals issue notes against their property and agree to accept them in their dealings one with another. Virtually all of these private schemes, however, came to naught, either through want of vitality or because they were suppressed by law. It remained for the colonial legislatures themselves to embark upon the issuance of "bills of credit," as the paper currency of the time was called.

In the course of developments, bills of credit came to be issued on two bases: on the credit of the colony supported by tax funds, and on loan. Massachusetts in 1690 was the first colony to issue bills on the credit of the colony,[3] and South Carolina in 1712, if the abortive attempt of Barbados in 1706 be neglected, was the first colony to put out bills on loan.[4] As the first method evolved it became customary to strike off the bills of credit, declare them a legal tender in both public and private transactions, and pay them out to the public creditors. At the time of issuance, provision was usually made for calling in the bills. For

---

3. The Massachusetts Act is printed in Andrew McF. Davis, Currency and Banking in Massachusetts Bay, Part I, Currency, 1901, pp. 10-11.
4. The South Carolina Bank Act of 1712 is printed in Statutes at Large of South Carolina, Vol. IX.

example, a tax would be levied for the five years next ensuing, from the proceeds of which one-fifth of the bills were to be retired annually. The tax would be paid into the treasury partly in bills and partly in coin, if there were coin in circulation. The coin so received would then be exchanged for an equivalent of the outstanding bills, and the whole sum of bills thus drawn in would be cancelled and burned under the superintendence of a committee of the assembly appointed for the purpose. This was the way the scheme worked at its best. In actual practice, however, the legislature sometimes failed at the time of issue to provide taxes for the retirement of the bills, or it happened that the taxes so provided proved inadequate. Moreover, even when adequate taxes were levied, the sums arising therefrom were not infrequently diverted to other uses, and the bills, when received in the treasury, were re-emitted. In certain colonies, and particularly in the early days of paper currency, these re-emissions were often accompanied by fresh issues. It was in this way that large sums became outstanding at one time. The result was that the currency depreciated in value.

By the second method of issue, the legislature established a "loan office" and struck off a sum in bills, likewise declaring them a legal tender. It was the duty of the commissioners of the loan office to place the bills out on loan in limited sums on adequate security, which was usually in the form of a mortgage on landed property. It was customary to require the property to be of double the value of the loan. Interest on the loan was payable annually, and, beginning either immediately or after a period of years, the principal was repaid in equal annual installments running over eight or ten years. Such issues served three purposes: (1) in an age when private banks were unknown they supplied individuals with the credit necessary for acquiring and improving land; (2) the interest payments contributed to the public revenue; and (3) the bills, while outstanding, supplied a medium of exchange.

Much has been made by historians and economists of the defects of the colonial paper currency and of the depreciation that it underwent. These defects have been dwelt upon to such an extent, and the admittedly grave abuses of some of the colonies at certain times in their history have so frequently been imputed to all the colonies during their entire history, that to reach any true understanding of the currency problem during colonial times, one first finds it necessary to disencumber his mind of prejudices unconsciously imbibed. Truly did a Pennsylvania governor, writing in 1753, observe that the bills of credit of the colonies have suffered by the "too general and undistinguished complaints" to which they have been subjected.[5] In approaching the problem of the colonial currency, one will do well to seek to distinguish the problems of one colony from those of another. When he does this, he will soon realize that in the factors affecting the currency problem, and in currency practices, the various colonies were frequently more dissimilar than similar. With this in view it will perhaps be well to attempt a short résumé of paper currency in each of the thirteen colonies before 1751. Insofar as it is possible from the evidence available, the role of specie will also be given attention.

As has already been indicated, recourse was first had to paper currency in Massachusetts, where the sum of ₤7,000 was emitted in 1690. The immediate occasion was the failure of the expedition under Sir William Phips against Quebec. "The government," writes Thomas Thomas Hutchinson, a later governor of the colony, in his History of Massachusetts Bay,[6] "was utterly unprepared for the return of the forces. They seem to have presumed, not only upon success, but upon the

---

5. James Hamilton to the Pennsylvania Assembly, January 26, 1753. Pennsylvania Archives, Eighth Series, Votes and Proceedings of the House of Representatives of the Province of Pennsylvania, IV, 3551.
6. Thomas Hutchinson, The History of the Colony and Province of Massachusetts-Bay (Mayo edition, 1936), I, 340-341.

enemy's treasure to bear the charge of the expedition. The soldiers were upon the point of mutiny for want of their wages. It was utterly impracticable to raise, in a few days, such a sum of money as would be necessary. An act was passed for levying the sum, but the men could not stay until it should be brought into the treasury. The extreme difficulty, to which the government was thus reduced, was the occasion of the first bills of credit ever issued in the colonies, as a substitute in the place of money." The soldiers received their pay in bills of credit, which were "to be received, for payment of the tax which was to be levied, and all other payments in the treasury." "But," Hutchinson continues, "the bills would not command money, nor any commodity at money price. Sir William Phips, it is said, exchanged a large sum, at par, in order to give them credit." The soldiers in general, however, "were great sufferers, and could get no more than twelve or fourteen shillings in the pound." The next year provision was made for receiving the bills in tax payments to the treasury at a five per cent advance. As the time for paying in the taxes approached, the bills "became better than money." The course of events that followed is accurately indicated by Hutchinson when he says,

> The government, encouraged by the restoration of the credit of their bills, afterwards issued others for charges of government. They obtained good credit at

the time of their being issued. The charges of government were paid in this manner from year to year. Whilst the sum was small, silver continued the measure, and bills continued their value. When the charges of government encreased, after the second expedition to Canada in 1711, the bills likewise encreased,[7] and in the same or greater proportion the silver and gold were sent out of the country. There being a cry of scarcity of money in 1714, the government caused 50,000 l. to be issued,

which were put out on loan to the inhabitants of the colony. In 1716 the additional sum of Ł100,000 was emitted and placed on loan.

The course of events in Massachusetts during these years is instructive, for here first became evident the pattern that events were to follow in other colonies. Because of this, it may be well to give some space to their analysis. As may be seen from Figure I it has been estimated that there were Ł200,000 of silver in circulation in New England in 1700. By 1713 this sum had been reduced to Ł130,000, and by 1718 according to some statements, or by 1726 according to others, there was none remaining.[8] The amount of bills of credit

---

7. In 1711 Massachusetts issued Ł50,000 in bills of credit, which were lent to the merchants that were providing supplies for a contemplated expedition against Quebec. These bills were to be redeemed within two years from the funds supplied by bills of exchange drawn by the agents of the British government. Nettels, Money Supply, p. 258 n; Andrew McF. Davis (ed.), Colonial Currency Reprints, IV, 211. It appears to have been this issue that started the value of Massachusetts currency on its downward course with respect to silver. See Figure I.

8. See Davis, I. The estimates for the years 1700, 1713, and 1718 are taken from Davis's graph

outstanding in Massachusetts on May first of each year increased from ₤5,000 in 1703 to ₤70,000 in 1709, even though, on the average, about ₤20,000 of bills were retired each year during the period. This, it will be remembered, was during Queen Anne's War. The sums emitted were to meet the increased expenses of government occasioned by that struggle. The closing years of the war were ones of even greater endeavor, with expenditures correspondingly increased. In consequence, the bills of credit outstanding were increased to ₤235,500 by May 1, 1713. During this period, which was marked by increased unfavorable trade balances with England, silver had been shipped out of the country in payment for English merchandise, and its place taken by the accumulating bills of credit. The price of silver did

---

(frontispiece, Vol. I), concerning which he says, pp. 389-390, "the delineation of the disappearance of silver is based upon the statement of one of the pamphleteers of the day as to the amount of silver required for the trade of New England, and the assertion of Dr. Douglass that there were 219,000 oz. still remaining in circulation in 1713, which had entirely disappeared in 1718." The author of the important "Enquiry Into the State of the Bills of Credit Of the Province of Massachusetts-Bay ..." (1743), Colonial Currency Reprints, IV, 157, "That the Silver and Gold Currency ... decreas'd more and more every year, and about the year 1726 quite vanish'd, and coin'd Silver and Gold became from that Time mere merchandize." In many ways this statement fits better the observable facts than the one that specie had vanished by 1718.

The disappearance of silver throughout New England was practically simultaneous, as will be explained later.

not rise, and, conversely, the bills of credit depreciate , as a result of these phenomena until after the issuance of the Ŀ50,000 lent to the merchants in 1711. The earlier rise in the price of silver from 7*s*. to 8*s*. the ounce that occurred in 1705 does not seem to have been connected with the issuance of bills of credit; more probably it resulted from the merchants arbitrarily raising the value at which they would receive silver coin, with a view to drawing silver into the province.[9]

The conclusion of the war brought problems no less than the struggle itself. With the ending of hostilities, the occasion for issuing sizeable sums in bills of credit was at an end. Thus whatever stimulus there had been to business activity by the constant emission of ever larger sums in bills was withdrawn. Moreover, to add to the complexities of the situation, the bills of credit outstanding were in the course of being retired by the annual tax levied for that purpose. In these factors -- the end of wartime activity and expenditures, and the prospect of a contracting circulating medium -- were the elements of impending depression. It is not remarkable, therefore, that during the next year (1714) "a cry of scarcity of money" was heard.[10] A cry in which the commercial element in the

---

9. See the discussion of this quite general practice in chapters i and iv.
10. This complaint is to be met with time and

province joined, for as Cotton Mather, writing at the time, reported, the "Gentlemen of Business" of the province considered the number and value of the bills of credit remaining in circulation as "no more than a <u>Spratt in a Whale Belly</u>." The amount bore "little Proportion to the Business of the Country, and [the] People [were] plunged into inexpressible Difficulties."[11]

As has been indicated, the difficulty was met by issuing bills of credit on loan. Fifty thousand pounds were authorized in 1714 and one hundred thousand pounds in 1716.[12] The act of 1714 put out the bills on landed

---

again during the colonial period. It probably more often meant that "times were hard," than that there was an actual scarcity of the circulating medium, although the two phenomena, as in this case, are frequently related.

    11. Cotton Mather to Sir Peter King, Boston, December 22, 1714. Massachusetts Historical Society, <u>Collections</u> (seventh series), VIII, 295-297.
    The question at the time was not whether a new issue of bills of credit should be forthcoming to maintain the circulating medium. All appear to have agreed that an issue was necessary. The question was whether the issue should be put out by a group of private individuals (chiefly merchants) or by the provincial government.

    12. <u>Acts and Resolves of Massachusetts Bay</u>, I, 750-751, contains the act of November 4, 1714. <u>Ibid.</u>, II, 61-62, has that of December 4, 1716.
    The preambles of these acts are illuminating. That of the act of 1714 reads:
Whereas the publick bills of credit on this province, which have so long and happily supported this his majesty's government in the long and expensive war with the French and Indians in our neighborhood, for defraying the necessary charges thereof, in the defence of his majesty's subjects and interest in this as well as the neighbouring provinces and colonies (and the preventing the inconveniences that may arise to the province

security to individuals for five years at an annual interest of five per cent. During these years one-fifth of the principal was to be repaid annually. The act

---

by and private projection for providing any other medium of exchange), and served as a medium of commerce in the business and trade of this province, greatly facilitating payments for goods imported from Great Britain and other places, are now grown very scarce, and few of them passing in proportion to the great demand of the same, whereby the affairs of the government are very much hindered, the payment of the publick debts and taxes retarded and in great measure rendered impracticable, and the trade and business of this province, both at home and abroad, is greatly obstructed, to the great discouragement and distress of the province... Be it enacted &c....

That of the act of 1716:

Whereas, by reason of a long and expensive war which his majesty's good subjects of this province have been lately engaged in for their own necessary defence, and of some very chargeable expeditions undertaken against the French of Canada and other places, by royal orders from her late majesty, there is an heavy debt now lying on the publick; and whereas all the silver money which formerly made payments in trade to be easy, is now sent into Great Britain to make returns for part of what is owing there, and the bills of credit on the province, being yearly called in, are now grown very scarce, and few of them passing in proportion to the great demand there is for the same; to the intent, therefore, that there be relief under these present difficulties, and that the husbandry, fishery and other trade and commerce of the province be encouraged and promoted... Be it enacted &c....

The preambles give a fairly clear picture of the course of events and of the reaction of the legislature thereto. The first one recognized that the emission of bills of credit had made it possible to export the colony's stock of silver, "thereby greatly facilitating payments for goods imported from Great Britain." The bills, however, had now grown scarce. The second preamble, two years later, indicates a realization that the silver of the colony was greatly diminished, and that the bills of credit, "being yearly called in," no longer took its place. The simple logic of the situation seemed to indicate a fresh emission.

of 1716 provided for similar loans for a period of ten years. At the expiration of the ten year period, the whole of the principal sum became due. In addition to the loans of 1714 and 1716, Massachusetts made two other emissions of bills on loans during the colonial period, one for the sum of Ł50,000 in 1721,[13] and another for Ł60,000 in 1728.[14] These later loans were issued on a basis different from that of the earlier ones. The sums struck were apportioned among the various towns according to the proportion that each town contributed to the province taxes. The towns were to lend the sums so received, the interest accruing to be used for their benefit. A province tax was levied to draw in the bills. Those of 1721 were to be retired in five annual installments, the first due May 31, 1726, and the last on the same date, 1730. The bills of 1728 were to be retired by a similar tax in six annual payments over the years 1734 to 1739.

During these years there were also issued annual sums in bills on taxes to meet the yearly cost of government. On the other hand, the tax acts of past years were annually retiring substantial sums. In some years these retirements exceeded the new issues, in others, they fell short of them. The amount of bills

---

13. *Ibid.*, II, 189-194. Passed March 31, 1721.
14. *Ibid.*, II, 470-477. Passed February 20, 1727/

in circulation in Massachusetts during the period can conveniently be followed in Table II and in graphic form in Figure II.

The effect of the later issues upon the price of silver was different from that of the earlier ones. Before 1710 the sums outstanding in bills were small relatively to the amount of silver in circulation. In 1709 there was perhaps as much silver in circulation as there were bills. As long as this was true, silver in quantities sufficient to make remittances to England came into the hands of merchants in the ordinary course of trade. After 1710, however, the situation changed. Bills were emitted in larger quantities. Moreover, silver left the colony at a more rapid rate, for these were years during which the balance of trade with England was extremely unfavorable. Reference to Figure I, will serve to emphasize this fact. The result was, that as the demand for silver for making payments abroad grew, and as the supply of the metal within this colony dwindled and fewer and fewer silver coins came into the hands of the merchants in the ordinary course of trade, those that needed it to make remittances to Britain began to bid one against the other for it, and its price rose. The existence of a stock of silver in a colony served to retard the rise of the price of the metal even in the face of a substantial increase in the sums outstanding in bills of credit. As soon as the stock was exhausted, the rise became more rapid, as can be seen by reference to Figure I. The only silver available for export after the stock was exhausted was that imported in the course of trade with Southern Europe and the West Indies.

Perhaps one other aspect of the matter should be noted. New issues of bills of credit in excess of retirements created purchasing power. This added purchasing power increased demand. Part, at least, of the increased demand was for English goods. This caused increased importations and larger unfavorable balances of trade, which in turn increased the demand for silver to meet these adverse balances. The price of silver and sterling exchange rose together; and as exchange rose, the price of English goods in terms of colonial currency likewise rose. The effect upon domestic prices of increases in purchasing power arising from issues of bills of credit was more direct. The receivers of the bills entered the market and bid prices up directly. In the case of commodities produced largely for export, a rise in sterling exchange was soon translated into a higher price for these commodities measured in colonial currency.

This analysis of the conditions that existed and of the forces that were at play in Massachusetts has

TABLE II

Part A

INVALID
See
APPENDIX
Table II, Part B
(Revised)
Massachusetts

NEW ENGLAND BILLS OF CREDIT OUTSTANDING

MASSACHUSETTS

Year	Within Periods £	Beyond Periods £	Total £
1721	267,500		267,500
1722	268,300	18,306	286,606
1723	297,300	36,612	333,912
1724	320,300	54,918	375,218
1725	350,700	73,224	423,924
1726	391,000	91,531	482,531
1727	376,300	109,837	486,137
1728	324,300	128,143	452,443
1729	321,300	146,449	467,749
1730	311,300	164,755[x]	476,055
1731	294,300	185,310	479,610
1732	294,500	205,866	500,366
1733	268,500	226,422	494,922
1734	326,700	246,977	573,677
1735	309,400	267,532	576,932
1736	290,400	288,087	578,487
1737	279,300	308,644	587,944
1738	279,400	329,199	608,599
1739	243,000	349,754	592,754
1740	205,500	370,309	575,809
1741	190,400	390,864[x]	581,264
1742	283,400	324,198	607,598
1743	314,300	258,469[x]	572,769
1744	304,800	129,235	434,035
1745	543,800	0[x]	543,800

[x] "An Enquiry Into the State of the Bills of Credit of ... Massachusetts-Bay" (1743), Colonial Currency Reprints, IV, 160-161, 191. The author says the figures are taken "from the Accounts of the Province Treasurer given in from Year to Year." Intervening years by interpolation. The author anticipates all bills beyond their periods being retired by 1744. The indications are that this was probably not done before 1745.

TABLE II

Part B

Superseded
APPENDIX
Table II, Part B
(Revised)

NEW ENGLAND BILLS OF CREDIT OUTSTANDING

Year	Mass.	R. I.	Conn.	N. H.	Total	Including Boston Merchants' Notes
	₤	₤	₤	₤	₤	₤
1703	5,090				5,090	
1704	25,500				25,500	
1705	35,500				35,500	
1706	31,500				31,500	
1707	49,500				49,500	
1708	59,500				59,500	
1709	69,500			3,000	72,500	
1710	115,500	7,000	13,738	5,500	141,738	
1711	137,500	13,300	18,687	7,500	176,987	
1712	232,500	13,300	23,638	8,000	277,437	
1713	235,500	13,300	24,177	8,000	280,977	
1714	227,500	12,198	22,876	9,200	271,774	
1715	244,500	51,898	22,490	8,200	327,088	
1716	205,500	51,898	23,681	8,200	289,279	
1717	284,500	50,176	20,433	23,200	378,309	
1718	261,500	48,762	20,080	22,300	352,642	
1719	240,500	47,611	19,822	22,300	330,233	
1720	229,500	46,753	17,828	21,336	315,417	
1721	267,500	86,498	17,487	20,148	391,633	
1722	286,606	85,812	17,499	24,948	414,865	
1723	333,912	87,170	16,832	24,627	462,541	
1724	375,218	86,263	14,662	26,001	502,145	
1725	423,924	85,394	12,198	26,624	548,140	
1726	482,531	131,434	7,975	27,684	649,624	
1727	486,137	116,443	10,274	28,585	641,439	
1728	452,443	153,870	9,220	28,585	644,118	
1729	467,749	145,334	6,738	25,477	645,298	
1730	476,055	138,726	4,381	26,777	645,939	
1731	479,610	190,528	4,667	26,777	701,582	
1732	500,366	184,147	2,554	25,466	712,533	

(continued)

TABLE II

Part B

(continued)

Superseded
APPENDIX
Table II, Part B
(Revised)

Year	Mass.	R. I.	Conn.	N. H.	Total	Including Boston Merchants' Notes
	₤	₤	₤	₤	₤	₤
1733	494,922	280,201	52,024	24,449	827,147	937,147
1734	573,677	278,268	51,688	23,431	927,064	1,037,064
1735	576,932	269,253	48,362	22,408	916,955	1,026,955
1736	578,487	257,738	43,720	21,408	901,353	978,353
1737	587,944	275,696	45,244	26,945	935,829	1,012,829
1738	608,599	351,427	39,600	22,611	1,022,237	1,099,237
1739	592,754	331,283	34,100	22,611	980,748	1,024,748
1740	575,809	417,283	70,100	23,414	1,086,606	1,130,606
1741	581,264	429,283	64,100	23,414	1,098,061	1,142,061
1742	607,198	415,283	61,100	40,962	1,124,943	1,168,943
1743	572,769	401,283	60,100	143,030	1,177,182	
1744	434,035	547,283	132,000	137,771	1,121,854	
1745	543,800	562,283	293,000	243,943	1,643,026	
1746	1,445,400	587,283	387,000	482,110	2,901,793	
1747	1,973,400	627,283	529,800	471,893	3,602,376	
1748	2,135,300	548,558	509,500	466,380	3,659,738	
1749	2,119,800	518,558	487,500	464,555	3,590,413	
1750	1,819,800		465,000	462,730		
1751			400,000	460,905		

Source: For a discussion of the bases on which these figures rest, see the text and footnotes, chapter ii.

TABLE III

PRICE OF SILVER IN BOSTON

(shillings per ounce)

Year							Year						
1700	7						1727	16					
1701	7						1728	16/6	17	18			
1702	7						1729	19	19/6	20	21	22	
1703	7						1730	21	20	19			
1704	7						1731	18/6	19				
1705	8						1732	19/6	20	20/6			
1706	8						1733	21	21/6	22	22/6	23	
1707	8						1734	24	25	26	26/6	27	
1708	8						1735	27/6					
1709	8						1736	27	26/6				
1710	8						1737	26/6	27				
1711	8/4						1738	27/6	28				
1712	8/6						1739	29	29/6	29			
1713	8/6						1740	28/6	29	28	29		
1714	9						1741	28/6	28				
1715	9						1742	28	27/6	28/6	29		
1716	10						1743	30	32				
1717	10						1744	32	33	34			
1718	11						1745	35	36	37			
1719	12						1746	37	38	40	45	48	50
1720	12/4						1747	53	55	58	60	58	
1721	12/4	13	13/6				1748	58	56	55	57	55	56
1722	14	14/6						58	56				
1723	14/6	15	15/6				1749	56	58	60	58		
1724	16	16/6					1750	56	55	54	50		
1725	16	15					1751	50					
1726	16						1752	50					
							1753	50					

Data taken from the books of Jacob Hurd and Thomas Edwards, goldsmiths. Frank B. Dexter (ed.), <u>Extracts from the Itineraries and other Miscellanies of Ezra Stiles</u>, ... 1755-1794 ..., pp. 7-8.

This series of prices is fuller than any collected by Andrew McF. Davis in his <u>Currency and Banking in Massachusetts Bay</u>.

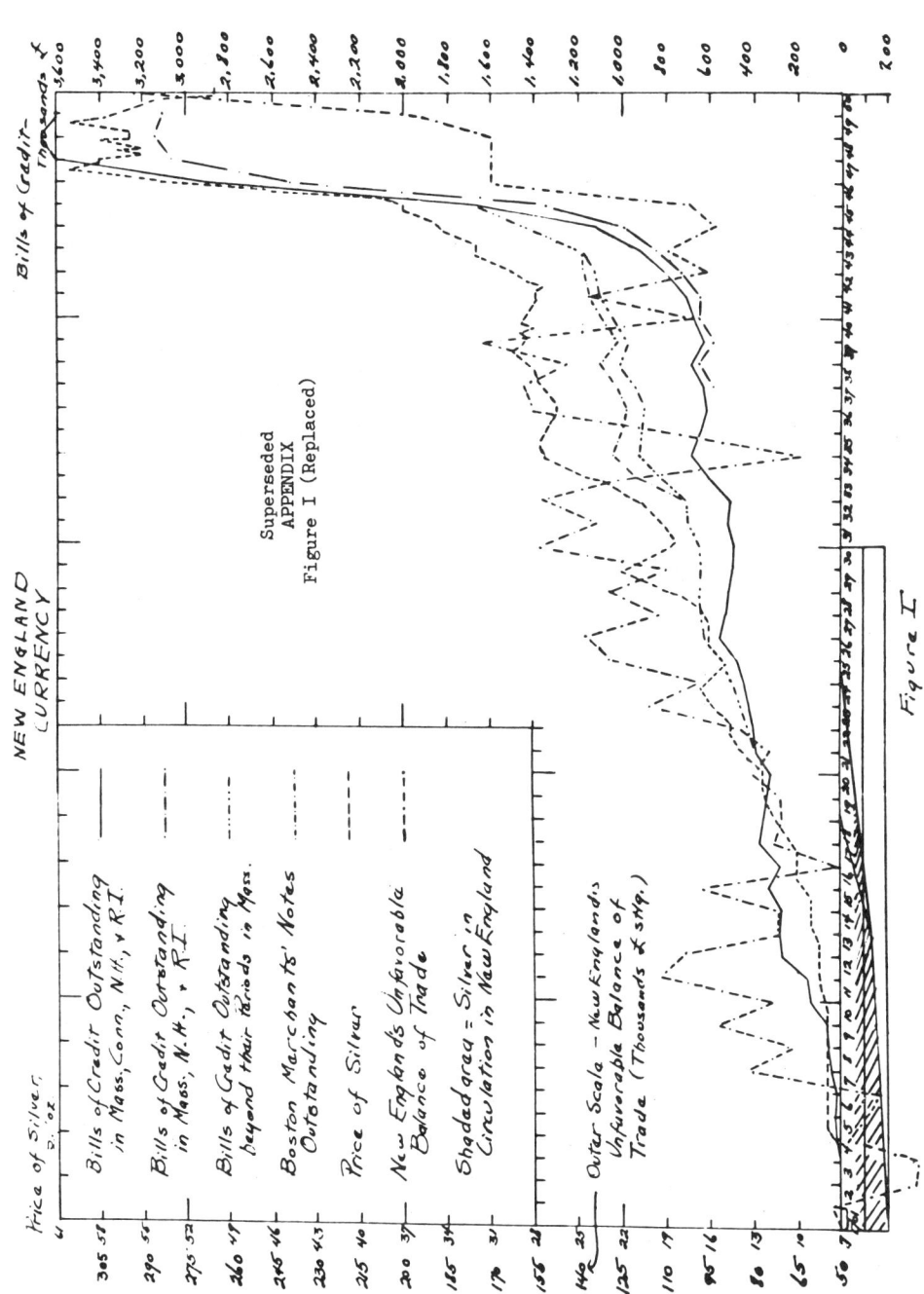

Figure I

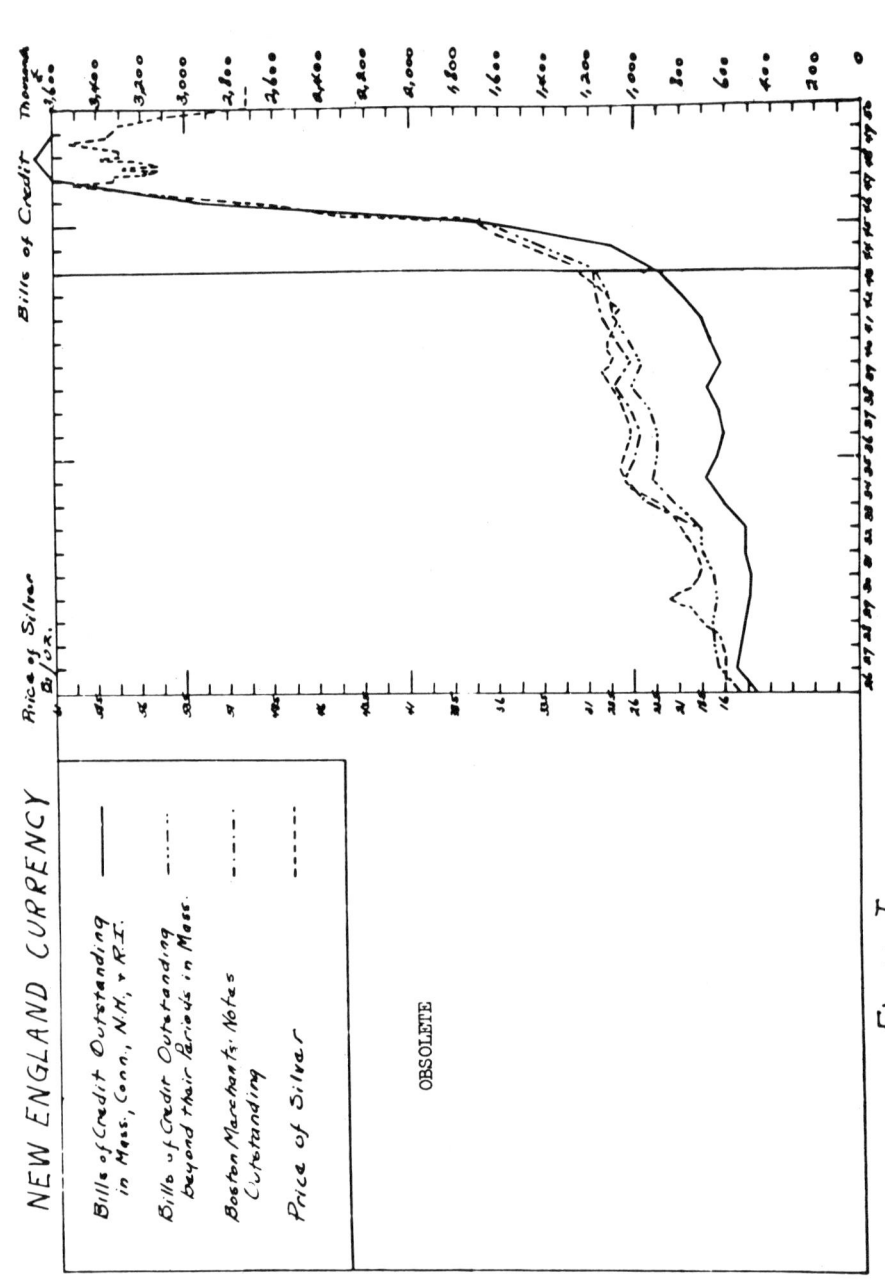

Figure Ia

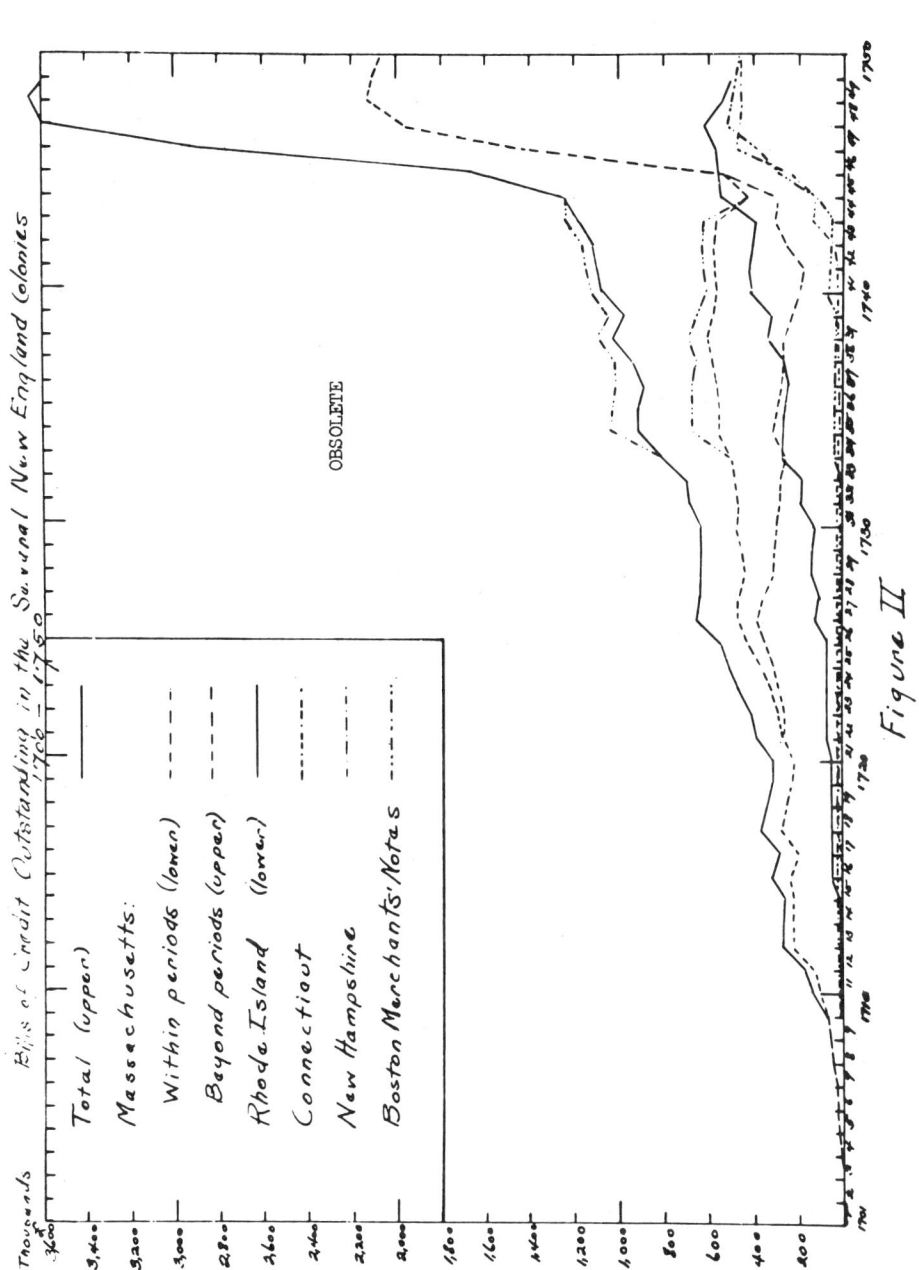

Figure II

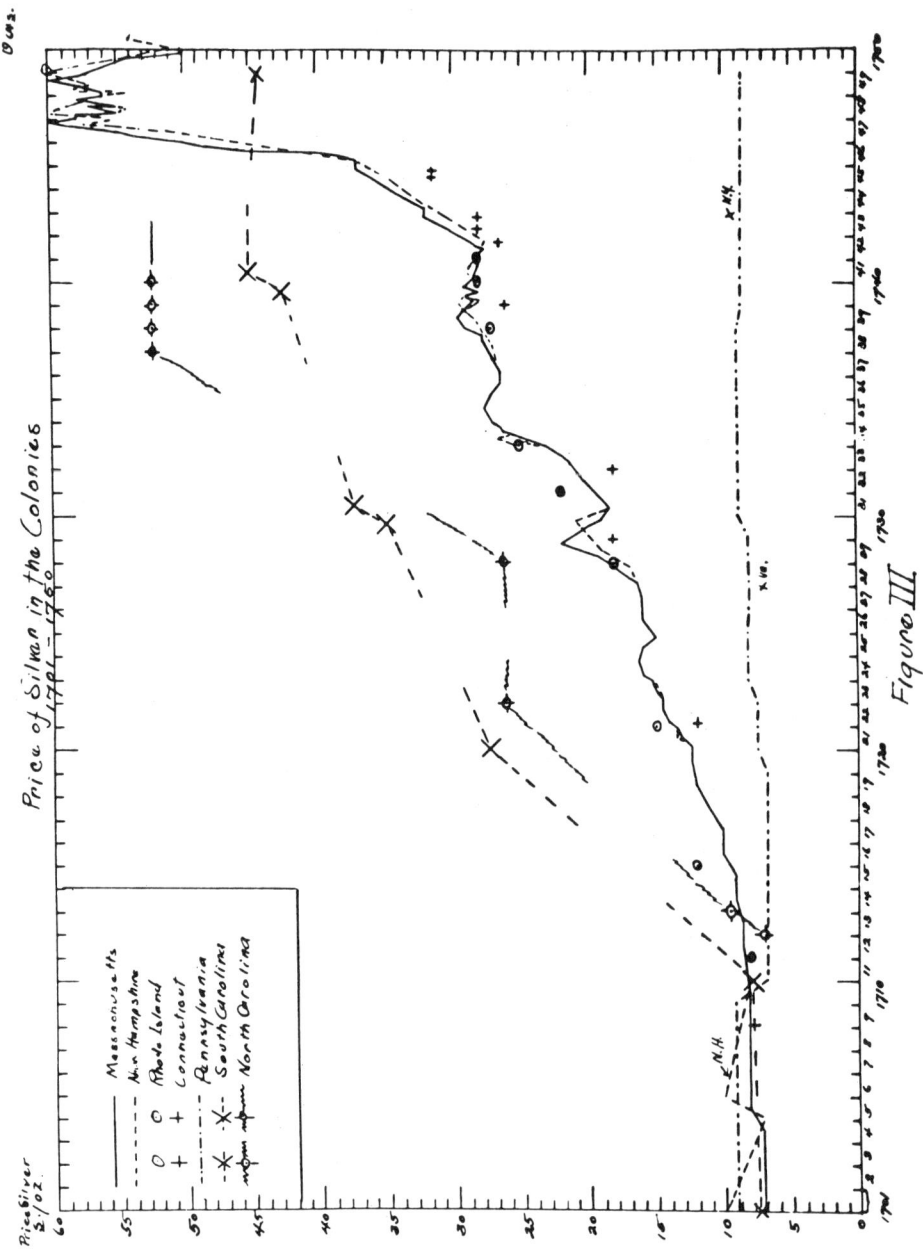
Figure III

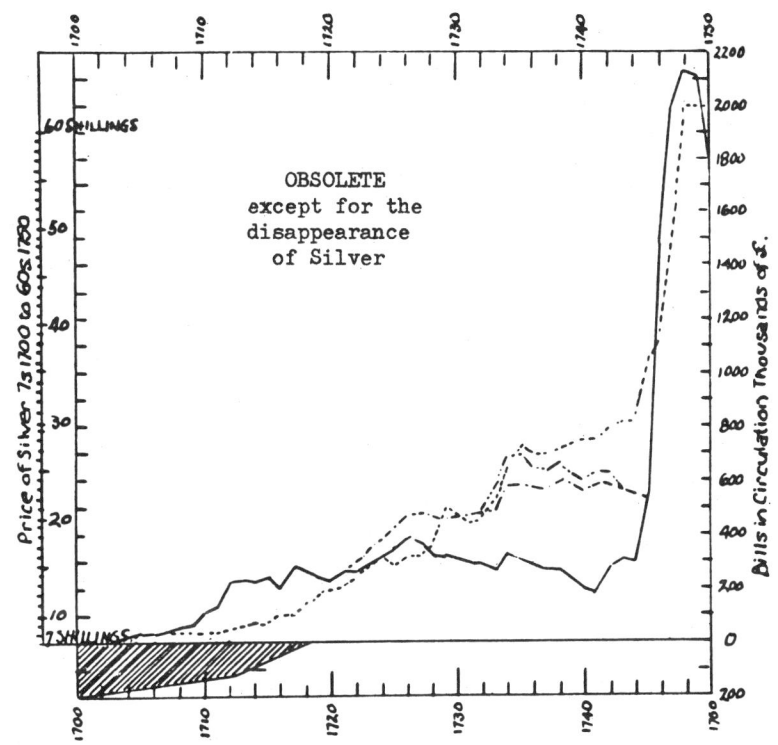

Figure IV

been developed in some detail because it indicates the factors for which one should be on the lookout when he examines elsewhere the behavior of prices and exchange as they are affected by issues of bills of credit. In general it may be said that, ceteris paribus, paper currency depreciated in reverse proportion to the relation that it bore to the amount of silver or gold in circulation in a colony at the time it was issued. It will be found helpful to bear this fact in mind when one looks for the reasons why the issues of some colonies depreciated more rapidly than did those of others.

The Massachusetts bills of credit outstanding in each year have been calculated by Andrew McFarland Davis.[15] His method of calculation was to add to the sum outstanding at the beginning of any year the amount issued during the year and then subtract the amount that should be retired during the year according to the provisions of the various tax acts.[16] While such a method may be the best that the data in certain cases will permit, it is accurate only if the taxes are collected promptly and the bills are retired at the end of their stipulated periods. Until about 1721 retirements in Massachusetts seem to have been made promptly. During

---

15. Currency and Banking in Massachusetts Bay, I, 443 (Appendix E).
16. Ibid., p. 386.

the two decades that followed, however, retirements lagged, with the result that increasing sums were from year to year outstanding beyond their periods.[17]

According to Davis's calculations there were ₤229,500 in bills of credit outstanding in Massachusetts in 1720 on loan and on taxes. Thence the amount increased from year to year until in 1726 there were ₤391,000 in circulation. The trend was then downward with the single exception of the year 1733-1734 until the year 1741, when there were but ₤190,000 extant.[18] When, however, the sums annually outstanding beyond their periods are taken into account, the picture assumes a different aspect. After 1721 the annual retirements began to fall behind the provisions of the tax acts. By 1730 it appears that there were no less than ₤164,755 in bills outstanding beyond their periods. When this sum is added to the ₤311,300 outstanding within their periods, the total sum is seen to be ₤476,055. During the next decade retirements lagged even farther behind statutory requirements, and by 1741 the bills outstanding beyond their periods had increased to ₤390,864. This increase was somewhat balanced, however, by the fact that during the same period, the bills out-

---

17. "An Enquiry Into the State of the Bills of Credit Of the Province of Massachusetts-Bay ..." (1743), Colonial Currency Reprints, IV, 160-161, 191.
18. Davis, Currency and Banking, I, 443.

standing within their periods had decreased to ₤190,400. The total sum outstanding was therefore ₤581,264. The accumulation of bills beyond their periods had been caused largely by delinquencies in the collection of taxes. With the arrival of Governor William Shirley steps were taken to force the collection of the taxes and by the fall of 1743 the bills outstanding beyond their periods had been reduced to ₤258,469 and measures were in operation to retire the whole amount by May of the next year.[19]

But no sooner were the province bills of credit outstanding beyond their periods called in, than they were supplanted by new issues occasioned by the outbreak of war with the French. In 1744 there were outstanding ₤304,800 in bills within their periods. By 1748 the war issues had increased this amount to ₤2,135,300 in old tenor values, a figure almost seven times that of 1744. These gigantic sums were issued to finance the expeditions against the French in Acadia. This was the

---

19. The amounts outstanding beyond their periods are taken from "An Enquiry ...," Colonial Currency Reprints, IV, 160-161, 191. The author of this anonymous pamphlet states that the figures are taken from the "Accounts of the Province Treasurers given in from Year to Year to the General Court" (p. 160).

The sums outstanding beyond their periods for the years for which the data are available, and for the intervening years by interpolation, may be followed in Table II. These sums have also been plotted in Figures I, Ia, and II.

period of Massachusetts' "great inflation." By 1749 the price of silver was double what it had been in 1743. Currency measured in this commodity had lost half its value in six years. This is the period of Massachusetts monetary history most often recalled by those intent upon pointing out the horrors of paper money. It might, however, serve to set the period in a truer perspective if one observed that the depreciation of the Massachusetts currency during King George's War was no greater than the rise of prices in the United States during and after the World War.[20]

The return of peace brought to a close an epoch in Massachusetts monetary history. The province resolved to return to a silver currency. To this end an act passed January 28, 1749,[21] provided for the importation in foreign silver of the sum granted by Parliament to reimburse the province for its wartime expenditures. During the years following March 31, 1750, the bills of credit of the colony were redeemed at the ratio of seven and one-half shillings old tenor for one shilling silver. The Spanish milled dollar (piece of eight) of

---

20. *Statistical Abstract of the United States*, 1936, p. 299. Wholesale commodity prices, as indicated by the index of the Bureau of Labor Statistics, rose from an average of 68.1 for the year 1914 to 158.4 for the year 1920.

21. *Acts and Resolves of Massachusetts Bay*, III, 430-441.

full weight, which was now the most important element in the colony's currency, was valued at six shillings.[22]

So far the discussion has concerned Massachusetts alone. Massachusetts, however, was but one of the colonies that made up New England, even though the most important; and such was the economic inter-relationship of the New England colonies, that the currency of New England should be considered as a unit during the period before 1751. Following closely upon the heels of Massachusetts, Connecticut and New Hampshire in 1709 and Rhode Island in 1710 began to issue bills of credit to meet the expenses of government. As the years passed these issues increased. But their circulation was not confined to the colonies that begot them. In the course of trade they soon found their way into the neighboring colonies. In fact, the bills of the several New England colonies customarily, although not always, passed current in all the rest at a uniform value.[23] They depreciated together, as may be seen

---

22. The consideration of the conversion of the bills of credit under the act of 1749 belongs more properly to a later period and will be discussed in chapter vi.

23. Dr. William Douglass, in his Discourse (1740), says that the "promiscuous Currency in the four Governments of New England, that is one Colony giving a Currency to the enormous Paper Credit Emissions of the other Colonies, has the same Effect as if that Colony did emit Bills of its own...." In Davis, Colonial Currency Reprints, III, 320.
    Hutchinson, III, 289, speaking of 1733,

by reference to the rise in the price of silver in each of the colonies indicated in Figure III.

The other New England colonies emitted their first issues just before the Massachusetts bills began to depreciate. The early issues of Rhode Island, Connecticut, and New Hampshire were small, both absolutely and when compared with the Massachusetts issues. This fact may be appreciated by reference to Figure II; and, as is evident from Figure III, when depreciation began,

---

says: "Many people wished to see the bills of each government current within the limits of such government only," thus indicating that they had a wider circulation.

Governor Talcott of Connecticut wrote in 1740 to the Board of Trade: "I must beg leave to refer your lordships to the account you shall receive from [Massachusetts] for the value of gold and silver yearly as compared with our paper currency, that Province governing in the affair of exchange between us and England, and our paper bills always passing at an equal value with the bills of that Province." New Haven Historical Society, Papers, I, 47.

A report of a committee of the Rhode Island Assembly in 1749 contains the following: "What hath been the case with Rhode Island bills, hath also been the common fate of all paper bills issued by the other colonies of New England; they having been all emitted at near equal value, and have always passed at par with one another, and... have equally sunk in their value." Rhode Island Colonial Records, V, 284.

The Massachusetts act of 1749 to provide for the conversion of the Massachusetts bills into silver, in providing drastic penalties for passing the bills of the adjoining colonies, recites: "Bills of credit have been the only medium of trade within this government for many years past, and the bills of Connecticut, New Hampshire, and Rhode Island, have passed promiscuously with the bills of this government...." Acts and Resolves of Massachusetts-Bay, III, 435.

Other and similar statements might be cited.

they began to depreciate together. The bills of Massachusetts and New Hampshire fell in value together and occupied the middle position. Those of Rhode Island soon led the way, the price of silver there rising in advance of the price in Massachusetts and New Hampshire. The Connecticut bills, being smallest in amount, lagged in depreciation. None the less, since the new emissions of one colony soon came to be diffused throughout the others, the trend of depreciation in all the colonies was closely parallel.

Of all the thirteen colonies, Rhode Island probably sinned most in her abuses of paper money. She was a small colony, in population as well as in area. While she numbered slightly more people than New Hampshire during the period between 1710 and 1750, she had but a third the population of Connecticut, which in turn numbered only a third or a half the population of her larger neighbor, Massachusetts.[24] Yet after 1725, the

---

24. The following estimates of the population of the New England colonies are taken from Evarts B. Greene and Virginia D. Harrington, <u>American Population before the Federal Census of 1790</u>, 1932, passim.

Colony	Year	Population	Year	Population
Massachusetts	1712	75,000	1750	200,000
Rhode Island	1708	7,000	1748	34,000
Connecticut	1710	25,000	1750	90,000
New Hampshire	1709	5,000	1750	30,000

amount of Rhode Island bills of credit outstanding climbed steadily until by the beginning of King George's War (1744) her issues equalled those of Massachusetts.[25]

Most of the Rhode Island bills were issued on loan, although liberal sums were from time to time issued on taxes. In all, during the period before 1751, the colony emitted on loan nine "banks," as they were called. The total issues amounted to ₤820,000 in old tenor values.[26] The effect of these emissions upon the currency outstanding can be conveniently followed by reference to Figure II. The loans were let out on mortgages, to be repaid over a term of years. The first "bank" of ₤40,000 in 1715 was to be repaid after ten years. In the meantime a second "bank" of ₤40,000 was emitted in

---

25. In 1744 there were about six times as many bills outstanding per capita in Rhode Island as in Massachusetts.

26.

Table of Rhode Island emissions on loan.
Rhode Island
"Banks"

Bank	Year	Sums in Old Tenor	Bank	Year	Sums in Old Tenor
1	1715	₤ 40,000	6	1738	₤ 100,000
2	1721	₤ 40,000	7	1740	₤ 80,000
3	1728	₤ 40,000	8	1744	₤ 160,000
4	1731	₤ 60,000	9	1750	₤ 200,000
5	1733	₤ 100,000	Total		₤ 820,000

The emission of 1740 was issued as ₤20,000 new tenor; that of 1744, as ₤40,000 new tenor. One shilling N.T. equalled four shillings O.T. The issue of 1750 was in a second new tenor. ₤137 10s. of it equalled ₤275 N.T.; ₤1,100 O.T.; or ₤100 sterling.

1721 for a period of five years. When the first bank became due in 1726, payment was postponed until 1728, when, beginning with that year, the principal was to be paid in ten annual installments.[27] Later loans appear to have followed this plan, the sums were put out for ten years, then repaid in equal annual installments over another ten.[28]

Rhode Islanders professed to believe in the sovereign restorative powers of issues of bills of credit whenever trade or industry languished -- so much so, in fact, that Governor Richard Ward could write to the Board of Trade in 1741: "In short, if this colony be in any respect happy and flourishing, it is paper money, and a right application of it, that hath rendered us so."[29] There were, however, those that dissented from such a sanguine view. The fact that Rhode Island bills circulated widely in the other colonies permitted her to levy tribute on her neighbors. Hutchinson records that "in 1733 there was a general complaint throughout the four governments of New-England of the unusual scarcity of money." Royal instructions, he pointed out, prevented Massachusetts and New Hampshire from author-

---

27. Report of Gov. Richard Ward to B.T., Jan. 9, 1741, Rhode Island Colonial Records, V, 8-9.
28. Report of the Assembly, Feb. 27, 1750; ibid., V, 283-284.
29. Ibid., V, 12. Ward to B.T., Jan. 9, 1741.

izing additional issues; and "Connecticut, although under no restraint [from royal instructions], yet, consisting of more husbandmen and fewer traders than the rest, did not so much feel the want of money." Rhode Island, however, likewise being unrestrained, took advantage of the opportunity to issue ₤100,000 on loan to her inhabitants, who, as Hutchinson complains, immediately had it "in their power to add ₤100,000 to their trading stock from the horses, sheep, lumber, fish, &c. of the Massachusetts inhabitants."[30] This is no doubt an exaggeration. Some of the bills would remain at home, and others would circulate in Connecticut,[31] so that the full weight of the emission would not fall upon Massachusetts. Nevertheless, the proportion of Rhode Island bills that circulated in Massachusetts was

---

30. Hutchinson, II, 288-289. Hutchinson's memory failed him as to the behavior of Connecticut, for in 1733 she emitted her first bills on loan, putting out the sum of ₤50,000. Massachusetts during the next year, 1734, also put out a sizeable sum on taxes.
    Hutchinson's point with respect to Rhode Island, however, stands.
31. The circulation of Rhode Island bills in New Hampshire seems to have been slight, although some few probably circulated there. Edward Scott wrote from Newport in 1750 to a London correspondent: "With the Province of New Hampshire we [Rhode Island] have very little Intercourse or Connection." None the less, New Hampshire bills passed in private transactions in Rhode Island, although they were not received in the treasury. Edward Scott to Alexander Grant, Newport, R. I., Sept. 14, 1750. Board of Trade Papers, Proprieties, XVIII, R. I. Transcripts in Historical Society of Pennsylvania.

high. A little later it was estimated that as many as five-sixths of the Rhode Island bills were absorbed by Massachusetts.[32]

The charge was frequently made by the opponents of paper money that throughout the colonies all the assemblies that issued bills of credit were debtor assemblies[33] -- an accusation easier to make than to support. The accusation, however does appear to apply with full force to Rhode Island. It was made contemporaneously by substantial citizens, and fits well the course of events in the colony. In 1750 a group of seventy-two Rhode Island citizens petitioned the king, asking that the colony be restrained from adding the sum of £50,000 in bills of credit of a new tenor -- a sum that would have nearly doubled the colony's currency. They represented "that the landholders of the colony, having generally mortgaged their farms, or plantations, as a security for the bills of credit they have taken upon

---

32. Speech of Governor Shirley to the Massachusetts General Court, February 9, 1743. He estimated also that more than one-half of the Connecticut bills circulated in Massachusetts. *Colonial Currency Reprints*, IV, 202.

33. "I have observed, that all our Paper-Money making assemblies have been legislatures of debtors, the representatives of people who from incogenitancy, idleness, and profuseness, have been under a necessity of mortgaging their lands." William Douglass, *A Summary, Historical and Political, of the First Planting, Progress, Improvements, and Present State of the British Settlements in North-America* (London, 1755), I, 310.

loan, have found it in their interest to multiply such bills, that they may depreciate and lessen in value, and which they have recourse to, as a legal expedient of wiping away their debts without labor: whereby," the memorial continues, "the laudable spirit of industry is greatly extinguished...'.'[34] Some of the petitioners also wrote privately to the same effect.[35]

Moreover, the mode of the emission of the "banks" seems to have added a further incentive to multiplying issues. It appears that as a result of influence one became a "sharer" in a new emission. These sharers received bills for the period of ten years at five per cent annual interest. After the expiration of this period, they paid back the principal in ten annual installments without interest. The sharers lent out the money they received "in their own & neighbouring Colonies" at ten per cent annual interest for the twenty years. In this way, every pound lent yielded the sharer a net return of ₤1 10s. over the twenty year period. Furthermore, it was possible for a sharer to reap an immediate return by selling for a "ready money premium" his privilege of participating in a loan. It

---

34. Petition to the King, Newport, R. I., Sept. 4, 1750. R.I. Col. Rec., V, 312.
35. Edward Scott to Alexander Grant, Newport, R. I., Sept. 14, 1750. Board of Trade Papers, Prop., XVIII. Transcripts in Historical Society of Pennsylvania.

is said that the premium was thirty-five per cent for the loan of 1738,[36] that is, the right to £100 of the loan could be sold for £35 cash.

It is no wonder that with the circumstances that obtained in Rhode Island, the colony persisted in her "otherwise mindedness" concerning paper money until Parliament laid a restraining hand upon her in 1751. In 1750 despite strong protests from many of her own citizens she emitted her Ninth Bank of £25,000, equivalent to £200,000 old tenor.[37]

Of the New England colonies, Connecticut used bills of credit the most judiciously. Reference to Figure II will make it clear that, until the period of King George's War, her emissions were quite modest. Although she did issue sizeable sums during that struggle, the amounts were smaller than those of her neighbors, save New Hampshire.[38] In fact, her record was such

---

36. Douglass, "Discourse," *Colonial Currency Reprints*, III, 317-318.

37. Henry Phillips, Jr., *Historical Sketches of the Paper Currency of the American Colonies*, 1865, I, 97-189, contains, "A Brief Account of Emissions of Paper Money made by the Colony of Rhode Island," by Elisha R. Potter. The same account somewhat amplified, and illustrated with reproductions of the various bills of credit, appears as "Some Account of the Bills of Credit or Paper Money of Rhode Island," by Elisha R. Potter and Sidney S. Rider, in *Rhode Island Historical Tracts*, No. 8, 1880.

38. The sums outstanding in Connecticut and New Hampshire roughly parallel each other for the years 1742 to 1750. It should be remembered, however, that the population of Connecticut during this period was

that even the Boston physician and writer on currency, Dr. William Douglass, the implacable foe of all paper currency, was forced to admit in 1740, that "Connecticut, a Charter Colony of industrious Husbandmen" had "with much Prudence emitted only small Quantities of Bills." He was further of the opinion at that time that silver would have continued there at eight shillings the ounce as it did in New York, had it not been for the fact her people gave "Currency to the publick Bills of their Bretheren, in the neighbouring Colonies of New England."[39] Even after Connecticut had had her fling during the war, Douglass could write in 1750: "Connecticut continues honest."[40]

Beginning in 1709,[41] Connecticut began to issue small sums in bills upon tax funds to meet the annual expenditures of government. The sums outstanding on this basis for the period prior to 1740 reached their apex in 1713, when there were slightly in excess of ₤24,000 in circulation. From then on the trend was downward until in the 'thirties the average was under ₤3,000. In 1733 the colony emitted ₤50,000 on loan,

---

perhaps three times that of New Hampshire.
39. Douglass, "Discourse," Colonial Currency Reprints, III, 319.
40. Douglass, A Summary of the British Settlements in North America, II, 192n.
41. Colonial Records of Connecticut, 1706-1716, pp. 111-112.

of which ₤33,600 were outstanding at the close of 1739. The total sum outstanding in the colony in 1737 was, in round numbers, ₤45,000.[42] In 1740 Connecticut issued her second and last bills on loan, emitting the sum of ₤22,000 new tenor, equivalent to ₤77,000 in old tenor terms. From 1740 to 1746, inclusive, she put out the equivalent of ₤430,000 old tenor on taxes to meet the expenses of government, ₤398,000 of which were placed in circulation during the war years 1744-1746.[43] Concerning the amounts in circulation throughout the 'forties, it is difficult to arrive at satisfactory conclusions from the data available. It was reported that the sum of ₤340,000 old tenor was outstanding in 1751.[44] This appears to be exclusive of the amounts outstanding on the two loans. These amounts were reported to be ₤39,586, old tenor, in September, 1752. Making allowance for retirements during that year, there were perhaps ₤60,000 out on loan in 1751, or ₤400,000 outstanding on loan and taxes combined. The sums indi-

---

42. Gov. Joseph Talcott to the Board of Trade, Hartford, Conn., Jan. 12, 1739/40. Printed in Henry Bronson, "A Historical Account of Connecticut Currency, Continental Money, and the Finances of the Revolution," pp. 47-50, in New Haven Historical Society, Papers, I, with a pagination of its own (1865).

43. Report of Committee of Assembly, November, 1740, Bronson, pp. 57-58; draft of letter, Governor Jonathan Law to the Duke of Bedford, October, 1750, Connecticut Historical Society, Collections, XV, 435-437.

44. Report of a committee of Assembly on the condition of the Treasury, October, 1751. Bronson, p. 69.

Note 45 should be neglected. For corrections, see Errata, p. 46n.45, and Connecticut Table in Appendix.

cated on Figure II as outstanding for the various years after 1737 represent estimates derived from a consideration of the issues and the reports of the sums outstanding set out in the note below.[45] While no precise ac-

---

45. Draft of letter, Law to Bedford, October, 1750, gives the amount outstanding at that time, presumably on taxes, as ₤385,000 old tenor values. Conn. Hist. Soc., Collections, XV, 435-437.

As to the amounts out on loan, committee reports to the assembly give the following information:

Year	First Loan (O.T.)	Second Loan (N.T.)	(O.T. Equivalent. 1s. N.T. = 3s.6d. O.T.)	Total O.T.
1743, May	₤ 36,271	₤ 6,671	₤ 23,349	₤ 59,690
1747, June	55,887	24,687	86,405	142,292
1752, Sept.	666	11,120	38,920	39,586

"The loan mortgages had not been paid up in February, 1757, and the mortgagers were to be sued."

It appears from the figures above that during the war years the sums received on mortgage payments were relent. Interest payments must have been in arrears on both loans as the amounts outstanding are in each case in excess of the total authorized issue. Just how much of this sum represents interest due, and not bills relent, it is impossible to say. Bronson, p. 59.

The sum authorized by the second loan act in May, 1740, was equivalent to ₤77,000 old tenor. The emissions on tax, in old tenor figures, were:

1740, May,	₤ 4,000	1746, May	₤ 70,000
July	10,000	May	3,000
1744, Oct.	52,500	June	122,000
1745, Mar.	70,000		

The issues for 1740, both on loan and on taxes, are taken from "The Answer of the Governor and Company of Connecticut to the Board of Trade," November, 1740. Public Records of the Colony of Connecticut, VIII, pp. 357-359 (also in Bronson, pp. 57-58). The issues for the latter years are from draft of letter, Law to Bedford, October, 1750. Conn. Hist. Soc., Collections, XV, 435-437.

curacy is claimed for them, they will suggest roughly the bills in circulation during this period. The peak appears to have been reached in 1747, when there were perhaps ₤530,000 in old tenor values outstanding.

From this résumé it will be evident that Connecticut departed from her earlier conservative position and greatly increased her paper issues during the war years. Two-thirds of the sums, however, were issued to finance the colony's effort in the joint struggle.

The total sums issued in bills of credit by New Hampshire roughly parallel those of Connecticut over the forty years ending in 1750. But when one takes into consideration the fact that Connecticut could at the beginning of the period boast perhaps five times, and at the end, three times, the population of New Hampshire, the difference between the records of the two colonies becomes apparent. New Hampshire put out her first issue in 1709 for the purpose of meeting the expenses of the war with the French.[46] The sum was ₤3,000, and the bills were made receivable for taxes at five per cent advance. Other emissions followed. The sums outstanding during the first eight years never exceeded ₤9,200, the sum outstanding in 1714. In 1717,

---

46. Charles J. Bullock, The Monetary History of the United States, 1900, p. 207. In Part III of this study, chapters i and ii, is to be found a satisfactory account of the colonial issues of New Hampshire.

however, the colony "voted to issue ₤15,000 on loan for eleven years at ten per cent interest. The money was to be lent upon mortgages on land double the value of each loan, and the various towns were to receive shares proportioned to their quotas of the province taxes. The annual payments of ten per cent of the loan were to be burned in the presence of the assembly each year, and bills issued by other provinces were to be accepted in such payments only at five per cent discount."[47] This issue brought the sum of bills in circulation up to ₤23,200.[48] From this issue in 1717 until the year 1742, the sum in circulation was never greater than ₤28,585, nor less than ₤21,336. During the late 'thirties, Governor Jonathan Belcher, under instructions from home, exercised a restraining influence upon the legislature's desire to issue additional bills.[49] He was succeeded in 1741 by Governor Benning Wentworth, who was more friendly toward paper money. After ample provision had been made for his support, he promised

---

47. Bullock, pp. 211-212.
48. The sums in circulation in the various years are taken from Professor Bullock's calculations, *passim*. His method of ascertaining the amount outstanding at the end of each year is to add to the sum outstanding at the beginning of the year the new issues, and to subtract therefrom the sums in old bills burned during the year. This is without doubt the best method to ascertain the sums outstanding where the data permit its use.
49. Bullock, Part III, chap. i.

his "'hearty concurrence' in any measure that would 'expedite' the emission of a loan bank," then much desired by the legislature. The result of this bargain was the issuance of ₤4,720 in new tenor bills to be applied to the expenses of government, and ₤25,000, likewise new tenor, to be put out on loan.[50] These sums were equivalent to ₤18,880 and ₤100,000 old tenor, respectively. The loan money was not put into circulation until after the home authorities had assented to the act the next year.[51] In 1744 the outbreak of war brought occasion for new issues. By the end of 1746, the sum in circulation had reached ₤471,893 in old tenor values. Between that year and the end of 1751, nearly ₤11,000 had been retired, leaving ₤460,905 outstanding at the end of the period.

As has been stated earlier, the bills of New Hampshire circulated in the other New England colonies. New Hampshire was part of the hinterland of Boston, practically all of her trade with the outside world being carried on through that port. It was quite natural, therefore, that New Hampshire's bills soon found their way thither. As early as 1712 "New Hampshire deposited a certain quantity of her bills in Boston in order that they might be exchanged for worn and defaced

---

50. Bullock, p. 234.
51. Ibid., p. 235.

money."[52] Throughout the years they continued there. In 1741 a Massachusetts correspondent wrote: "We have in Massachusetts public bills of four Provinces at 29s. for an oz. of silver."[53] As New Hampshire bills had a common circulation with the bills of her New England neighbors, so they had a common depreciation -- a fact that has already been noted.[54] Until 1742, at least, she probably suffered from issues in Massachusetts and Rhode Island. After that date her contribution to the general outpouring of bills was not inconsiderable. None the less, taking into account the early period as well as the later one, it is probable that Dr. Douglass spoke too harshly when he characterized New Hampshire as "always inclinable to a depreciating fraudulent paper currency."[55]

So far we have been concerned with the paper issues of the New England governments. There were in addition several note issues of private associations during the period, one at least of which seems to have added materially to the bills in circulation. The first of these associations in point of time was the New Lon-

---

52. Bullock, p. 209, citing Joseph B. Felt, *A Historical Account of Massachusetts Currency*, 1839, p. 64. Felt relies upon an advertisement in the *Boston News Letter*.
53. Felt, p. 107.
54. See Figure III.
55. Douglass, *Summary*, II, 193n.

don Society for Trade and Commerce, which received a charter from the Connecticut legislature in May, 1732. The associators had petitioned for a charter as early as October, 1729. At that time, the petitioners, among other things, desired, as they phrased it, "That our Company may be allowed to emitt bills for currency upon our own credit, as we may see occasion at any time for promoting or maintaining our trade."[56] In this form the petition was refused. In 1732, however, as a result of an amended petition that apparently left out the obnoxious bills-of-credit clause, the society received its charter. But the real purpose of the society soon became evident. Its first step was to authorize the issuance of ₤50,000 in bills of credit. The bills were to be lent on landed security to the members of the society.

News of the activity of the society soon reached official ears. Governor Joseph Talcott, upon hearing of the society's activities, issued a proclamation against the bills, alleging their issuance to be contrary to the peace of the crown, and summoned a special session of the legislature to consider the matter. The legislature determined against the legality of the bills and annulled the company's charter. It appeared that

---

56. Davis, II, 105.

perhaps ₤15,000 of the bills had been put into actual circulation. The legislature, upon considering the manner in which the bills of the society could be withdrawn with the least confusion, determined to issue ₤50,000 of colony bills upon loan. Of these bills a number sufficient to retire the society's bills were lent to the borrowing members of the society, who exchanged the bills of the society for them. The mortgages that had been given as security for the society's bills were then transferred to the colony, and became the security for the colony's bills.[57] Since the notes of the society were replaced by those of the colony, one does not need to take separate account of them in determining the amount of bills in circulation.

The case of the Massachusetts Merchants' Notes, however, was different. In 1733, Rhode Island emitted ₤100,000 on loan. The merchants of Boston, fearing, so they alleged, that a large part of the issue would gravitate to that city and would depreciate the currency, agreed among themselves not to receive the Rhode Island bills in trade, and, to meet the need for a medium, issued their own notes on a silver basis. In all, ₤110,000 were issued and put out on loan. The notes were redeemable in silver at 19s. the ounce, three-

---

57. Davis, II, 106-121.

tenths at the end of six years, and the remaining four-tenths at the end of ten years.[58] The notes seem to have circulated during their respective periods and to have maintained their value. A writer in 1741 stated that they continued to be "punctually paid in gold and silver as they [became] due, and [were then] 33 *per cent.* better than Province Bills."[59]

The Merchants' Notes made a sizeable addition to the Massachusetts paper currency. The sums outstanding have been plotted as an addition to the New England currency curve in Figures I and Ia, and as an addition to both the Massachusetts and New England curves in Figure II. By consulting these figures one may obtain some notion of the importance of these private notes in relation to the public bills.

Neglecting the apparently abortive effort of certain New Hampshire merchants in 1734 to issue notes in imitation of the Boston Merchants' Notes of the preceding year,[60] the remaining private note-issuing ventures of the period were those of the Massachusetts Land Bank and the Massachusetts Silver Bank, both of which were organized in the year 1740. The Land Bank

---

58. Davis, II, 122-125.
59. "A letter to ... Merchant in London," [Boston], 1741 (attributed to Dr. Douglass), Colonial Currency Reprints, IV, 70-71.
60. Davis, II, 125-129; Bullock, pp. 223-224.

seems to have been fostered by the Bostonian, John Coleman, whose interest in such schemes dates back to 1714. The Bank planned to issue ₤150,000 of its notes and lend them to its members on mortgage at three per cent annual interest. The principal was to be repaid in twenty annual installments. Payments of principal and interest were to be made in the notes of the Bank or in certain commodities.[61] It appears that notes to the sum of ₤47,282 2s. 10d. were issued to the several directors and partners of the company.[62] But the life of the Bank was short. Its foes succeeded in 1741 in having Parliament adopt an act to suppress it.[63] By June, 1742, "upwards of ₤32,500" of the notes issued had been drawn in, leaving no more than ₤15,000 in circulation. It was some years, however, before the affairs of the Bank were wound up, and its suppression caused very considerable repercussions in Massachusetts politics, for those interested in it were both numerous and influential.[64]

As the Rhode Island issue of bills on landed se-

---

61. Davis, II, 130-133.
62. "An Account of the Rise ... of ... the Land-Bank ... and the Silver Scheme ...," 1744, Colonial Currency Reprints, IV, 303. Felt, p. 111, says that by September, 1741, ₤49,250 of the notes of the Land Bank had been struck off. Of these the treasurer had issued ₤35,582, and the directors were employing ₤4,067 in trade.
63. 14 George II, c. 37.
64. Davis, II, chaps. vii, ix, x, xi, and xii.

curity in 1733 had brought into existence the Boston Merchants' Notes of the same year, so the Land Bank gave rise to a similar antidote, the Silver Bank. A group of associators pledged themselves not to receive the notes of the Land Bank, and proposed an issue of Ł120,000 of their own notes. These notes were to run for fifteen years, at the end of which time they were to be redeemed in silver at the rate of twenty shillings per ounce. The associators promised to receive them in trade according to a sliding scale of value. In 1741 they were to be received at the rate of 28s. 4d. the ounce of silver; in 1742, at the rate of 27s. 9d. the ounce; and so on, each year their value in silver rising 7d. the ounce, until in 1755 twenty shillings should equal an ounce of silver. It was also agreed to exchange the silver bills for common current notes on the basis of the scale of appreciation indicated above. The bills were to be lent on mortgage, the borrowers obligating themselves to pay in annually the sum of eighty-seven and one-half ounces of silver, or six ounces of gold, for every Ł100 of the notes borrowed. During the first thirteen years, however, these annual payments might be tendered in certain commodities, which were then sold by the directors for gold or silver.[65] Like the Land Bank, the Silver Bank fell

---

65. "Articles of the Silver Bank," Davis, II,

under the ban of Parliament. In June, 1742, it was reported that the association had emitted ₤120,000 in notes, but of these ₤69,361 12<u>s</u>. 6<u>d</u>. had been recalled, leaving ₤50,638 7<u>s</u>. 6<u>d</u>. in circulation.[66]

Temporarily the notes of both the Land Bank and the Silver Bank doubtless had some effect upon prices. The fact that they were soon suppressed, however, makes it possible to leave them out of account without doing too great violence to the facts.

One other question remains for discussion before we leave New England, that of the relation of the rise in the price of silver to increases in the amount of bills in credit in circulation. Andrew McFarland Davis examined this relationship. His method was to plot the amount of bills of credit outstanding in Massachusetts against the price of silver.[67] Davis's graph is reproduced as Figure IV. Reference to it will reveal that from 1728 to 1741, with the exception of the year 1734, the trend of the Massachusetts currency curve was downward, while the silver curve continued to rise. In explanation of this phenomenon, Davis observed that since the years that witnessed a decrease in Massachusetts bills were the years during which Rhode Island

---

Appendix C, pp. 277-286.
    66. Felt, p. 114.
    67. Davis, I, frontispiece.

was multiplying her issues (see Figure II), the continued rise in the price of silver was occasioned by the issues of the smaller colony. In consequence, he concluded that Massachusetts was "suffering vicariously for the sins of Rhode Island."[68] But the issues of Rhode Island, although an important factor, must not be charged with full responsibility for the continued rise in the price of silver during this period. If one computes the amount of bills outstanding in New England as a whole by adding to Davis's computations for Massachusetts the amounts outstanding in the other New England colonies, and then plots bills outstanding against the price of silver, he will find that the gap between the currency curve and the silver curve still persists. Obviously, since the Rhode Island issues are now taken into account in plotting the currency curve, their omission cannot be urged as the reason for the divergence of the curves, and one is forced to search for a further explanation. There are two, or perhaps three, additional factors that must be considered. In the first place, Davis's method of computation of the sums outstanding in Massachusetts, assuming as it does that retirements were made promptly in accordance with the provisions of the tax acts, fails to take into account

---

68. *Ibid.,* 392.

the sizeable sums outstanding beyond their periods because of the tardiness with which the tax acts were executed. Moreover, no account is taken of the not inconsiderable issue of Boston Merchants' Notes. Secondly, there are technical defects in Davis's method of constructing and interpreting his graph. And, thirdly, it seems probable that New England's unfavorable balance of trade, or, more accurately, fluctuations in the demand for and supply of bills of exchange and silver to meet it, may supply the explanation for some of the shorter aberrations in the silver curve.

As regards the first of these factors, if the Massachusetts bills outstanding beyond their periods, together with the Merchants' Notes, are plotted as additions to the Massachusetts currency curve in Davis's graph (Figure IV) and to the New England currency curve in Figure I, it will be seen that the divergence between the currency and silver curves on both graphs will be lessened: that for New England as a whole by about one-half; and, strangely enough, that for Massachusetts during a considerable part of the period is eliminated entirely.

The remaining divergence of the two curves in the New England graph (Figure I), which is the important one, is largely accounted for by certain technical considerations concerning the construction and interpretation of the graph. The technically involved nature of these considerations makes it advisable, perhaps, to confine their discussion to the footnote below.[69] But

---

69. The formula indicating the relation of the amount of currency in circulation and the price level is that developed by Irving Fisher in his The Purchasing Power of Money, 1911. It may be used here in its simpler form, MV equals PT; where M is the amount of currency in circulation; V, its velocity or rate of turnover; P, the average of prices over a given period of time; and T, the physical volume of transactions, i.e., the number of things exchanged for money (whose prices go into the make-up of P) times the number of times each is exchanged for money within the period of time taken.

First let us assume that V remains constant. Then, if T likewise remains constant, increases in M will occasion proportionate increases in P. If, however, T increases at a uniform rate, say doubling over a period of ten years, and over the same period M quadruples, P but doubles. (MV equals PT, or, P equals MV/T. Assume at the beginning that M, V, and T each equals 1. Then P equals 1. After ten years of uniform increase, M equals 4, and T equals 2. Now P equals $\frac{4 \times 1}{2}$ or 2.) If we plot two curves, one representing changes in M; the other, changes in P; and so choose our scales that in the first and last years the two curves coincide, they will, under our assumptions, coincide throughout. If, however, the rate of change in M or in T varies from year to year, the two curves will diverge.

In the light of the foregoing, let us examine Figure I. (And the same analysis may be applied to Davis's graph, Figure IV.) It is immediately obvious that the rate of increase in M is not uniform, else the curve representing the bills of credit in circulation would be a straight line. In fact, not only does the currency curve fail to rise at a uniform rate, but there are years when it falls. During some years the curve rises sharply, throughout 1733 and 1734 and during the war years 1744-1747, for example. One would then expect a divergence in the curves. Moreover, there is reason to believe that the increase in T was not uniform throughout all periods.

The facts are such, however, that the graph may be broken into sections within which our assumptions

if the analysis undertaken there be correct, the objections can largely be removed by plotting a new graph such as that in Figure I<u>a</u>. Here it will be seen that there is, in their general aspects, a close correspondence between the currency and silver curves. Increases in the bills of credit outstanding occasioned rises in the price of silver, and, by and large, these rises, within the periods into which the graph has been divided, bore a fixed ratio to increases in the bills of credit outstanding.

It will be noted, however, that in the first of the two periods into which Figure I<u>a</u> has been broken, there are smaller periods during which the silver curve does not move with the currency curve. From a price of 16<u>s</u>. the ounce in 1727 the value of silver moved sharply upward until it had reached 22<u>s</u>. by the close of 1729.

---

are roughly approximated. In the first place, P depends upon the total amount of money, paper and coin together, that is in circulation. It appears certain that by 1726, if not earlier, New England's stock of silver had been exhausted. After this time what little of the metal was imported was immediately shipped off to make remittances to Great Britain. We may, then, without great violence to the facts, assume that after 1726 M closely approximated the amount of bills of credit in circulation. If we neglect the period before 1726 and break the remaining years into two periods, 1726-1743, and 1744-1749, we have periods within which the rate of change of both M and T is much more nearly uniform, than when we consider the whole period, or even that from 1726 on, as a single period. It will be seen that within each period the M and P curves tend to coincide closely. During the first period both M and P roughly double, and during the second, M trebles, while P doubles.

With the opening of the next year, the trend was reversed, and by early in the year 1731 the price had fallen to 18s. 6d. During the entire period of rise and fall, however, the amount of money in circulation remained practically constant. Again toward the close of the period it is observed that during 1741 and the first half of 1742 the silver curve fell despite the fact that the currency curve was rising.

These phenomena may find their explanation in changes in the demand for silver for returns to Great Britain occasioned by fluctuations in the unfavorableness of New England's balance of trade with the mother country. Contemporaneously, it was frequently urged that it was the unfavorableness of the balance of trade with Britain that caused the colonial bills of credit to depreciate.[70] Over an extended period, however,

---

70. For example, a committee of the Rhode Island Assembly in 1750 argued: "The reason of the great depreciation observable in the bills issued by this colony, is, because the inhabitants of New England constantly consume a much greater quantity of British manufactures than their exports are able to pay for; which makes such a continual demand for gold, silver and bills of exchange, to make remittances with, that the merchants, to procure them, are always bidding one upon another, and thereby daily sink the value of paper bills, with which they purchase them." R. I. Col. Rec., V, 284.
    The anonymous author of the "Enquiry," 1743, Colonial Currency Reprints, IV, 195-196, getting the cart before the horse, views the unfavorable balance as the "primary" cause of depreciation and the increase in bills as a "secondary" cause. "The Increase or Decrease of the Quantity of Bills of Credit," he further observes, "can't affect the Price of Silver and Gold and Bills of

the rôle of the unfavorable balance appears to have been mediative rather than causal. The causal factor was the increase in the amount of bills of credit in circulation. The effect of new emissions of bills upon the price of silver has already been discussed.[71] New issues created purchasing power; imports from Britain increased, and with them, the unfavorable balance of trade; the larger unfavorable balance increased the demand for bills of exchange and silver to make payments to Britain; and the price of both bills of exchange and silver were bid up. Other factors than new issues, however, might, over short periods at least, affect the demand for and the supply of bills of exchange and silver. A temporary failure of the supply of the commodities relied upon to furnish returns increased the demand for bills of exchange and silver for remittances to Britain and caused them to rise in price (together). Likewise, a failure of the West Indian trade lessened both the supply of bills of exchange and silver from that important source. This diminution in supply caused a rise in the price of exchange and silver. Conversely,

---

Exchange any further, than as it checks or enlarges the Trade ... with Great-Britain, from whence arise the annual Demands for Silver and Gold and Bills of Exchange to pay off the Ballance, which is ever in favour of the latter." In this passage he glimpses the fact that new issues of bills may enlarge the unfavorable balance. Despite this, however, he is still inclined to confuse causal and mediative factors.

71. *Vide* *supra,* p. 30.

increases in the supply of bills of exchange or silver relatively to the demand for them to make payments abroad caused their price to fall. Fluctuations from these causes, however, appear to have been of short duration, either because they tended to set in operation corrective forces, or because of the revival of those branches of trade, the failure of which had occasioned a dearth of other returns. As to the corrective forces, a rise in the price of (sterling) exchange and silver caused a rise in the price of British goods measured in colonial currency. This tended to check the demand for further importations, thus lessening the unfavorable balance with the mother country. This in turn lessened the demand for returns, and, <u>ceteris paribus,</u> exchange and silver fell in value.

It appears probable that the sharp rise and subsequent fall in the price of silver during the years 1728-1731 resulted from the operation of factors of the kind just discussed.[71a] Moreover, the fall in the price of silver in 1741 and 1742 in the face of increases in the amount of currency outstanding, was probably occasioned by the fact that for the years 1740, 1741, and 1742, the balance of trade with Britain was much less unfavorable than it had been throughout the years immediately preceding. Changes in the unfavorableness of the balance may be followed in Figures <u>I</u> and <u>Ia.</u>

[71a.] See end of chapter, p. 64a.

During the war years 1744-1747 both the currency and silver curves rose together precipitately. Thence until late in 1750 silver fluctuated between 60*s.* and 50*s.* the ounce, finally settling at the latter figure, which approximated the value set upon silver by the Massachusetts redemption act of 1749.

The year 1751 marks the end of an era in the currency history of New England. The "great inflation" had run its course during the years of the late war; Massachusetts was in the process of returning to a silver standard; and other of the New England colonies were, in part at least, following her example. But more important, the restraining hand of the British Parliament had been laid upon the currency practices of New England. Henceforth, no loan issues of any kind were to be permitted, and no legal tender bills were to be issued on tax funds. Such non-legal tender bills as might be issued to meet the ordinary expenses of government were limited to a circulation of two years; in cases of wartime emergency, the limit was five years. It was within the confines of these restraints imposed by the Currency Act of 1751 that New England was forced to solve the serious problems of the next period of her history -- that of the French and Indian War.

71a. The following passage from Dr. Douglass bears out the explanation advanced in the text for the fluctuation of the price of silver in 1728-1730. He says: "In New England, as in all other trading Countries, from some particular Accident and Circumstances, there happened at Times, some small fluctuations in Exchange, without any Regard to Emissions of Paper Money. At all Times, when Returns in Ship Building, Whale Oil and Fins, Naval Stores &c. turn out well at Home; Silver and Exchange here suffer a small fall: at other Times when these prove bad Returns, Silver and Exchange rise a small Matter; the most noted Instance was A. 1729, when the usual Returns to Great Britain turned to bad Account; the Merchants from Home, directed their Factors here, to make Remittances in Silver or Exchange only, and at any Rate; together with an Agency from this Province and that of Connecticut, fitted out with a Silver Supply; Silver rose very considerably, but after a few Months fell again to the former Price." Douglass, "Discourse," Colonial Currency Reprints, III, 332.

CHAPTER III

PAPER CURRENCY IN THE COLONIES BEFORE 1751: THE MIDDLE AND SOUTHERN COLONIES

What he [the governor of Pennsylvania] was pleased to do in Favour of the Currency, the great Necessity and most pressing Importunities of the Inhabitants moved him, and the Assemblies of those Times (according to the Examples of the neighboring Provinces, whose Cash and Product (as well as ours) falling short to make immediate Remittances to England for the Goods which were wanted) did think fit to fall upon the Expedient of Paper Bills, to pass among ourselves, having not Cash enough to carry on our domestick Affairs and Commerce: And likewise the Value of Lands and Country Product, being brought so low by the Scarcity of Money, and Decay of Trade, that many Families were likely to be ruined; Besides, [t]here was no Means left to support Government but by an Excise, and taxing the Importation of Liquors, which cumber'd our Ports, and hindered Trade, and yet fell short of answering the Publick Exigencies.

These and many more Inconveniencies are now removed; the Administration of Government well supported, without clogging the Importations; our Ports clear, Trade revived, and the honest Debtors rescued from the Oppressions of their Creditors; the Value of our Country Product advanced, and the Ship-wrights (some of whom, before this Currency was struck, having left the Country for want of Work, and those that stay'd having little to do) are since returned, and come into full Employment at their Trade; so that many stately Vessels have been built, and more upon the Stocks, and several Iron-works are carried on; which, with divers other Instances of the Advantage this Currency has been to the Publick, as well as to those, who, both in City and Country, must have been ruined without it, we think may abundantly attone for this Part of the Governor's Conduct.

-- Address of the House of Representatives of the Province of Pennsylvania to the Descendents of the late Honourable Proprietary, William Penn, Esq., December 7, 1725, relative to the introduction of bills of credit in that province in 1723.

MUCH IN THE early currency history of the Middle and Southern colonies is in sharp contrast to events in New England. Now and then, however, similarities present themselves. The chief distinguishing feature was that, generally speaking, outside of New England the paper currency of each of the colonies ran its separate course. Although the currency policy of at least one of the Middle colonies, that of New Jersey, was influenced by the policies of her larger neighbors, New York and Pennsylvania, it is true that in no case were the fortunes of one colony bound up with those of another to the extent that this was true in New England. On the other hand, the story of the introduction of bills of credit in South Carolina, the colony on the southern frontier, bears many similarities to that in Massachusetts on the northern frontier.

New York began to issue bills of credit in 1709 to finance her wartime activities. In that year the colony passed three separate acts emitting a total of ₤13,000. In 1711 an additional ₤10,000 were placed in circulation. These sums were issued on taxes levied on the real and personal estates of the inhabitants of the colony. The issues of 1709 were to be retired by the close of 1713, and the issue of 1711 was to be retired over the years 1714 to 1718, inclusive. The issues were all made a legal tender between man and man, and the taxes levied to retire them were to be paid in the bills. The bills of 1709 originally bore interest, being receivable at the treasury at an advance. All interest on the bills, however, was terminated by an act passed in November, 1710.[1] The bills issued by the acts referred to were all declared equal in value to silver at the rate of eight shillings per ounce. It appears impossible to determine precisely the extent to which these bills were retired at the end of their periods. The issues of 1709 were probably retired fairly promptly, as is evidenced by the fact that their currency was never extended beyond the periods established by the original acts. The same is probably true of the greater part of the emission of 1711, even though some few of the bills of this year were not cancelled until 1750.

In 1714, to meet the debts of the colony hanging over from the war, a further issue of bills of credit in the amount of ₤27,680 was authorized. The bills were not, however, placed in circulation until after

---

1. The various acts may be found in Colonial Laws of New York, I. The acts authorizing the emission of bills are: c. 190 (June 8, 1709), ₤5,000; c. 204 (Nov. 1, 1709), ₤4,000; c. 207 (Nov. 12, 1709), ₤4,000; c. 231 (July 26, 1711). The acts levying taxes to retire the foregoing emissions are respectively: c. 186 (May 24, 1709); c. 191 (June 21, 1709); c. 206 (Nov. 12, 1709); c. 227 (July 26, 1711). The act terminating the interest on the issues of 1709 is c. 222 (Nov. 25, 1710).

news had been received of the confirmation of the act by the English authorities the next year. The bills of this issue were to be current for twenty-one years. Over this period the receipts of the excise on all strong liquors retailed in the colony were annually to be applied to their retirement. The sums arising from this source, however, proved insufficient to cancel the bills during the period. By 1734 only ₤2,274 7s. had been cancelled, leaving ₤25,405 13s. still outstanding.[2] In consequence, their currency was extended to 1739; and for similar reasons, the period was later lengthened until 1757.[3]

During the course of the next few years additional sums were needed, with the result that in 1715 bills to the amount of ₤6,000 were issued, this time to be retired over the next five years from the proceeds of certain custom duties levied at the time.[4] In 1717 the excise for the years 1734-1739 was anticipated, and ₤16,607 were issued.[5] Apparently some of these bills were cancelled before 1734 in lieu of those of 1714, which were also on the excise, for by the close of 1734,

---

2. New York Assembly Journal, 1691-1765, 1765, II, 424.
3. Colonial Laws of New York, I, c., 280 (the act of 1714); II, c. 631, and III, c. 676 (the continuing acts).
4. Ibid., II, c. 292.
5. Ibid., c. 347.

£4,702 11s. had been sunk, leaving £11,904 9s. in circulation. The total of the two issues of "long bills," as the issues of 1714 and 1717 were called, remaining in circulation at the end of 1734 was £37,310 2s.[6]

In 1720, £2,000 were emitted to be retired by 1726 from the custom duties.[7] In 1723, £2,140 and in 1724, £6,630 were issued on taxes on real and personal estates. The last of these bills were to be retired in 1728.[8] The issue of 1724 brought the total amount issued by the colony during its first fifteen years of paper money up to £84,057. Of this sum there were perhaps £56,000 still in circulation at the close of 1724.

During the ten years after the emission of 1724 there were no new issues, although on three separate occasions the legislature authorized the striking of the sum of £3,000 in new bills to be exchanged for the worn and torn bills of earlier issues whose periods of currency had not expired.[9] In 1734, however, the colony, fearing that war would break out, resolved to put its fortifications in a state of preparedness, and to finance the effort emitted £12,000 to be retired by 1744 from the revenues arising from certain custom and

---

6. *New York Assembly Journal*, II, 424.
7. *Colonial Laws of New York*, II, c. 396.
8. Ibid., c. 437 and c. 447.
9. Ibid., c. 450 (act of 1724); c. 492 (act of 1726); and c. 551 (act of 1730).

tonnage duties.[10] It appears, however, that none of the bills were retired during the period originally contemplated.

During the period before 1751, all the New York issues save one were issued in anticipation of taxes. The exception was the bills placed in circulation by the loan act of 1737,[11] under which an emission of ₤48,350 was authorized, ₤40,000 of which were to be placed out on loan. The remaining ₤8,350 were issued to meet the expenses of government and were all but a trifling sum to be retired from the interest payments on the loans. The preamble of the act urged that "the Decay of Trade & other Difficulties" had caused a large deficiency in the funds granted for the support of government and that there was "Likewise a great want for a Medium ... to Revive the Commerce Trade and Navigation of the ... Colony and to promote the Improvement and Settlement thereof." The lieutenant governor, writing home just after the passage of the act, testified that paper money "was much wanted" by the people at the time.[12] The act allocated the loan funds among

---

10. Ibid., c. 625.
11. Ibid., c. 666. There is a discussion of the act in Richard A. Lester, "Currency Issues to Overcome Depression in Delaware, New Jersey, New York, and Maryland, 1715-37," in Journal of Political Economy, XLVII (April, 1939), 199-208.
12. New York Colonial Documents, VI, 110-111. Lieut.-Gov. Clarke to the Duke of Bedford, New York,

the several counties of the colony and provided for the establishment of a loan office in each. Loans were to be made to individuals in sums of from ₺25 to ₺100 upon the security of "Lands[,] Lotts[,] Houses or other valuable Improvements" of double the value of the loan. The loans were to run for twelve years from April, 1738, and bore interest at five per cent. One-fourth of the principal was to be repaid in April, 1747, and a similar sum in April of each of the three succeeding years. Late in 1743 the loan period was extended for four years in order that the revenue arising from the interest might be prolonged.[13]

Following the loan act, there was a nine year period during which there were no new issues, although in 1739 an issue of ₺10,000 was authorized to provide new bills to be issued in exchange for worn bills of 1714 and 1717. At the same time the currency of these bills was prolonged until 1757, and the excise, upon which fund they had been issued, was similarly extended. The outbreak of war with the French, however, called for new issues. In 1746 the sums of ₺13,000 and ₺40,000 were authorized, and during the next year an additional issue of ₺28,000 was placed in circulation. Provision was made for the retirement of the bills

---

December 17, 1737.
   13. _Colonial Laws of New York_, III, c. 745.

during the ensuing years by taxes levied on the real and personal estates of the people of the colony.

The year 1747 is the first for which we are able to arrive at the precise number of bills in circulation. There was outstanding at the close of that year the sum of Ł189,601.[14] The total issues (exclusive of exchange issues) prior to that time had amounted to Ł225,425, so that over the period it appears that Ł35,824 had been cancelled. It should be remembered, however, that the retirement periods of the war issues were yet in the future. In 1748 effective provision was made for the cancellation of the bills of the various issues from the taxes levied for the purpose, and, as the records indicate, retirements were henceforth much more punctual.[15]

Throughout the period there seems always to have been a stock of gold and silver in circulation. The data concerning the price of silver for the period are scanty. The few quotations available are given in the

---

14. In 1762 a committee of the assembly went over the accounts of the treasurer from 1713 to that time. As a result there appears in the Assembly Journal a state of the sums cancelled and remaining in circulation of each of the issues beginning with that of 1714.
    As a result of the act of 1748 (next note), the sums burned during each year begin to appear in the Journal of that year. From these data we are able to arrive at the amount of bills in circulation at the close of 1747. New York Assembly Journal, II, 696 et passim.
15. Colonial Laws of New York, III, c. 861.

TABLE IV

NEW YORK BILLS OF CREDIT

Year	Issued ₤	Outstanding in 1747 ₤	Cancelled by end of 1747 ₤	Funds	Ref.: CLNY.
1709	5,000		5,000	Taxes, 1709, 1710	I, c. 190
1709	4,000		4,000	Taxes, 1712	I, c. 204
1709	4,000		4,000	Taxes, 1713	I, c. 207
1711	10,000	946	9,054	Taxes, retire ₤2,000 annually 1714-18.	I, c. 231
1714	27,680	16,722	10,957	On the excise, 21 yrs. through 1734; extd. 1739, 1757.	I, c. 280
1715	6,000	137	5,863	Retire ₤1,200 annually 1716-1720 on duties.	I, c. 292
1717	16,607	7,634	8,972	On the excise, 1735-39, inc. Extended.	I, c. 347
1720	2,000	1,834	166	Until 1726 on duties	II, c. 396
1723	2,140	356	1,783	Taxes on estates, real and personal. Retire ₤714 annually 1724-26.	II, c. 437
1724	6,630))- 3,963)))	3,963	5,667	Taxes on estates, real and personal. Retire ₤1,657 annually 1725-28.	II, c. 447

(continued)

TABLE IV

(continued)

Year	Issued £	Outstanding in 1747 £	Cancelled by end of 1747 £	Funds	Ref.: CLNY.
1724	3,000)			Exchange issue	II, c. 450
1726	3,000	1,836	1,164	Exchange issue	II, c. 492
1730	4,803	4,803		Exchange issue	II, c. 551
1734	12,000	12,000		To 1744	II, c. 625
1737	48,368	48,368		£40,000 on loan £ 8,368 for use of colony	II, c. 666
1739	10,000	10,000		Exchange issue	III, c. 676
1746	13,000	13,000		Taxes, estates, real and personal, 1746-48, inc.	III, c. 825
1746	40,000	40,000		Taxes, estates, real and personal, 1749-56, inc.	III, c. 832
1747	28,000	28,000		Taxes, estates, real and personal, 1748-55, inc.	III, c. 854
	£246,228	£189,601	£56,626		

note below,[16] and are plotted in Figure III. They indicate some tendency for the bills to depreciate, measured in this commodity, as their quantity increased, although the depreciation between the first issue and the beginning of King George's War appears never to have been more than 16 per cent. The price data for these early years are likewise few. The trend of wholesale prices from 1720, the first year for which figures are available, to 1745 was downward, although shorter periods reversed the trend. As a whole there seems to be no very close correspondence between prices and the amount of bills outstanding.[17] A factor that retarded depreciation was the fact that during the period the population and trade of the colony were rapidly increasing. By the end of the period the population was perhaps three times what it had been in 1709, the year of the first issue; and trade, if the commerce carried on with Great Britain is any index, had increased by the same proportion.[18]

16. PRICE OF SILVER IN NEW YORK

Year	Price/Oz.	Year	Price/Oz.	Year	Price/Oz.
1701	6/10 1/2	1717	8/6	1740	9/
1702	6/10 1/2	1722	8/3 to		8/10
1710	8/		8/9	1743	9/
1716	8/	1739	9/3		9/2

17. Arthur H. Cole, Wholesale Commodity Prices in the United States, 1700-1861, 1938, I, Chart 5, p. 14; Appendix B, Table 39, p. 120.

All in all, the history of the paper currency of New York during the period is the history of its use rather than its abuse. Issues were moderate and were confined to legitimate ends. There appears never to have been a large debtor element bent upon depreciation for depreciation's sake. The administration of the paper currency, although inefficient in the beginning, improved in the later years, so that after 1748 it was fairly efficient.

In the currency history of Pennsylvania, one finds similarities, yet great differences, in comparison with New York. The currencies of the two colonies were similar in that they were issued in moderate quantities and retained their values; but they were largely different in the causes that called forth the issues, and

---

18. Greene and Harrington, American Population before 1790, pp. 90-91.

Year	Population	Year	Population
1703	20,749	1731	50,289
1712	28,000	1746	61,589
1715	31,000	1749	73,448
1723	40,564		

Emory R. Johnson, et al., History of Domestic and Foreign Commerce of the United States, 1915, I, 120-121.

The average of the foreign trade with Great Britain for the five years centered about 1709, was Ŀ41,890 annually. That of the five years centered about 1746, was Ŀ121,537, indicating an increase of not quite three times over the period.

in the forms that the issues took. During Queen Anne's War, when so many other colonies had recourse to bills of credit, Pennsylvania refrained, partly because she was situated farther from the theater of action than her northern neighbors, but more perhaps because the Quakers, averse to war as they were, dominated the government. Her initial issue in the year 1723 was an effort to relieve the province from the disastrous effects of the economic depression that had set in in 1720.

Pennsylvania's balance of trade with England was unfavorable,[19] and in consequence it was necessary to export gold and silver to settle accounts. These metals were acquired chiefly from the colony's trade with the West Indies.[20] The economic situation in the early 'twenties that led to the issue of 1723 is graphically portrayed in the following extract from a letter of the Pennsylvania Assembly to the Board of Trade in 1726:

> ... By the general Damp that was given to Trade in the Year 1720, and the great Fall of our Produce about the same Time, we were in the Years 1721 and 1722, so effectually drained of our Coin, which, for want of other Returns, was generally ship'd off to Britain, that

---

19. Ibid.
20. Pennsylvania Assembly to the Board of Trade, Philadelphia, December 10, 1726, Votes and Proceedings of the House of Representatives of the Province of Pennsylvania (Penna. Archives, 8th series), III, 1828.
    See also the excellent discussion of Pennsylvania's economy in the letter of Lt. Gov. Sir William Keith to Board of Trade, December 18, 1722. Calendar of State Papers, America and West Indies, 1722-1723, #390.

the Inhabitants of every Degree were reduced to the greatest Straits; Debts could not be discharged, nor Payments be made; the Rents of Houses fell, many whereof were deserted; and the Value of Lands and Improvements sunk considerably; Families who had lived well could scarce find Means to purchase necessary Provisions for their Support; and ... both Artificers and Traders were obliged to quit the Country, in Search of Employment and Sustenance elsewhere: But, above all, our Shipbuilding, by which the most advantageous Returns for Britain had been made, was so generally declined, that our Yards appeared almost empty, and all Trade discouraged ...

In the year 1722-3, the Governor and Assembly ..., moved by the Petitions and Complaints of great Numbers of the Inhabitants of each County, thought themselves obliged to take into their serious Consideration the distressed Circumstances and Sufferings of the People, through that extreme Want of some Kind of Currency for Pay, Divers expedients were thought of to remedy the Grievances; and particularly the Proposal to make the Produce of our Country a lawful Tender in Payments, was considered; but being found too bulky, and soon subject to decay was rejected: They were therefore, after a most serious Search, fully convinced there was no other safe Method left than the Scheme that, upon the maturest Deliberation, they fell into; which was to strike a Quantity of Bills of Credit, to be emitted out of a Provincial Bank, on the Security of real Estates in Fee-simple, to be pledged in double the Value of the Sum lent. And accordingly Bills were in that Manner issued for Fifteen Thousand Pounds of our American Money. These Bills being emitted, their Effect very sensibly appeared, in giving new Life to Business, and raising the Country in some measure, from its languishing State. 21

The expedient of seeking relief by the issuance of paper currency was not without its opponents. The merchants of the colony vigorously opposed the issue, and presented their case fully to the legislature.[22] Nor was the argument confined to the legislative halls. The

---

21. Penna. Votes, III, 1828. The petitions referred to are noted in ibid., II, 1461-1467.
22. Ibid., II, 1469-1472, 1481-1484, 1486-1496.

way had first been prepared by the pamphleteers.[23] The merchants in their addresses to the assembly demonstrated considerable familiarity with English monetary history and the fate of the currency experiments in the other colonies. They recalled the fate of bills of credit in South Carolina and New England. At that time the price of silver in South Carolina was 30_s._ per ounce, and in New England, 15_s._, indicating that the paper of those colonies was worth but twenty-three per cent and forty-seven per cent, respectively, of its former value. Moreover, the opponents of a paper issue pointed out that even in New York, which had been cited by the proponents of the scheme as a colony in which paper currency had maintained its credit, sterling exchange had risen in 1717 upon the paper emission of that year from fifty per cent advance the preceeding year, to sixty-five per cent after the issue.[24]

The assembly seems to have been guilty of no exaggeration when it stated that only after "the maturest Deliberation" did it decide upon the paper currency scheme adopted. The plan was well conceived at the beginning, even though experience later dictated certain changes.

---

23. See Richard A. Lester, "Currency Issues to Overcome Depressions in Pennsylvania, 1723 and 1729," Journal of Political Economy, XLVI, No. 3 (June, 1938), pp. 324-375, and the references there cited.
24. Penna. Votes, I, 1491.

the issues were moderate, and, what appears even more remarkable in the light of early experiences elsewhere, the scheme was well administered from the beginning.

The original issuing act [25] authorized the striking of ₤15,000 "current money of America," according to the Act of Parliament of 6th. Anne. ₤11,000 of the sum were to be lent to the inhabitants of the colony on land security of double the value of the loan for a period of eight years at five per cent interest. The principal was to be repaid in eight equal annual installments, and the sums so paid in were to be retired. Individuals might borrow sums ranging from ₤12 10s. to ₤100. Of the remaining ₤4,000 authorized, ₤2,500 were lent to the provincial treasurer, to be repaid over an eight year period from the receipts of the excise and certain duties, and ₤1,500 were divided among the counties of Philadelphia, Bucks, and Chester, to be repaid from taxes. The interest arising from the loans was at the disposal of the assembly for governmental uses.

It soon appeared that an issue of ₤15,000 was not sufficient to supply the need for a circulating medium. The result was that an additional ₤30,000 were authorized in December of the same year.[26] Of the sum,

---

25. *Statutes at Large of Pennsylvania,* III, c. 261. Passed March 2, 1722/3.
26. *Ibid.,* c. 275. Passed Dec. 21, 1723.

₤26,500 were to be lent out for twelve years, repayable in equal annual installments. The remaining ₤3,500 were for governmental use and were to be repaid from taxes.[27]

The new issue seems to have supplied the need for a medium of trade and debtor relief. Business revived and the experiment appeared a success.[28] Relief, however, was purchased not without some depreciation of the currency. Measured by the rise in sterling exchange, the currency had depreciated nine per cent by 1725,[29] and over the same period the prices of twenty wholesale

---

27. ₤1,300 to the provincial treasurer; ₤1,000 to Philadelphia County; ₤600 to the City of Philadelphia; ₤400 to Chester County; ₤200 to Bucks County.

28. Lester, *passim.*

29.
EXCHANGE RATE ON LONDON: NUMBER OF PENNSYLVANIA POUNDS FOR ₤100 STERLING (Silver par = 133 1/3)

Date or Period	Exchange Rate	Date or Period	Exchange Rate
November, 1721	143.0	October, 1725	153.33 and 155.33
November, 1722	137.5		
July, 1723	137.5	May, October and December,	
September, 1723	143.0		
December, 1723	135.33 and 136.33	1727	150.0
		1728	150.0
July, 1724	143.0	1729	150.0
September, October, and November, 1724	148.5 and 149.5	1730	151.7
		1731	153.1
		1732	161.1
		1733	165.0
First three quarters of 1725	148.5 and 149.5		

Lester, p. 351.

commodities had risen thirty-one per cent.[30] Part, at least, of the price rise may more aptly be thought of as the result of reflation, rather than of inflation.

As the annual payments on the loans began to be received and burned at the loan office, it soon appeared that a new currency shortage was impending. The sum of ₤6,110 had been withdrawn from circulation in this manner by March, 1726. At that time the legislature resolved to prevent further contraction by relending all future payments on the principal of existing loans.[31] At the same time the currency of all bills then outstanding was extended until 1736, and ₤10,000 in new bills were ordered to be exchanged for the worn bills of earlier issues.

In 1729 the province again felt the heavy hand of depression, and again recourse was had to a paper issue. After some agitation for an issue of ₤50,000,[32] the more moderate sum of ₤30,000 was agreed upon.[33] Of

---

30. Anne Bezanson, et al., Prices in Colonial Pennsylvania, 1935, Appendix, Table 11, p. 425.
31. Penna. Statutes, IV, c. 289. Passed Mar. 5, 1725/6.
32. Penna. Votes, III, 1906-1975, passim.
33. Penna. Statutes, IV, c. 300. Passed May 10, 1729. This act, as were the earlier ones, was the subject of considerable public discussion, and it was on this occasion that Benjamin Franklin, aged twenty-three, entered the lists as a defender of paper money. See his "A Modest Inquiry into the Nature and Necessity of a Paper Currency," Albert H. Smyth (ed.), Writings of Benjamin Franklin, II, 133-155.

the amount authorized, ₤26,000 were to be placed on loan in sums from ₤12 10s. to ₤300 for sixteen years on the now familiar terms. The remaining ₤4,000 were for the use of government.[34] Again the experiment seems to have resulted in a trade revival.[35] This time, however, there was no immediate rise in exchange and prices continued stable.[36] "The prosperity resulting from the ... issue ..., however, lasted only about a year. In 1730, Pennsylvania had 'the greatest crop that ever was raised' there, while at the same time there was then 'no demand in Europe' for wheat, or likely to be in the near future."[37]

Faced with this renewed slump in trade, the legislature in 1731 provided for the continuing and relending of all bills as they were repaid.[38] As a result, the sum in circulation remained constant at ₤68,890 until 1739. In that year all outstanding bills were reprinted and re-emitted, and an additional ₤6,110 were placed in

---

34. *Penna. Statutes*, IV, c. 300. ₤1,000 was lent to the provincial treasurer, to be repaid ₤100 annually out of the interest money; ₤1,000 to the City of Philadelphia for an almshouse, to be repaid from a tax; and ₤2,000 to a commission for erecting a building in Philadelphia for the use of the House of Representatives to be repaid ₤200 annually out of the interest money.
35. Lester, pp. 365-369.
36. Benzanson, Appendix, Table 11, p. 425; and Table 17, p. 431.
37. Lester, p. 366.
38. *Penna. Statutes*, IV, c. 319. Passed Feb. 6, 1730/1.

circulation, bringing the total sum up to ₤80,000.[39]
The new issue was to be lent for sixteen years in sums from ₤12 to ₤100. Payments on principal received before October 15, 1749, were to be relent for "the residue" of the sixteen year period, i.e., until October 15, 1755. In 1746, the old issues were extended until October 15, 1762, and all sums received on payments of principal before October 15, 1756, were to be relent for the residue of the period.[40]

In 1746 Pennsylvania made its first wartime emission, when it granted the sum of ₤5,000 "to the King's use." The bills were to be retired annually over a ten year period from the receipts of the excise.[41]

After the initial issues of 1723, there appears no marked relationship between fluctuations in the amount of paper in circulation, and fluctuations in wholesale commodity prices and the rate of sterling exchange.

The war issue of 1746 brought to a close Pennsylvania's unique experiment with paper money. With the coming of the French and Indian War she was soon to be caught in the maelstrom of wartime finance. Until 1746, however, her issues had been dictated by purely economic considerations. Her currency had been expanded to meet

---

39. Ibid., c. 353. Passed May 19, 1739.
40. Ibid., c. 363. Passed March 7, 1745/6.
41. Ibid., c. 370. Passed June 24, 1746.

TABLE V

PENNSYLVANIA BILLS OF CREDIT

Year	Issued £	Outstanding £
1723	15,000	15,000
1724	30,000	44,915
1725		38,915
1726		38,890
1727		38,890
1728		38,890
1729	30,000	68,890
1730		68,890
1731		68,890
1732		68,890
1733		68,890
1734		68,890
1735		68,890
1736		68,890
1737		68,890
1738		68,890
1739	11,110	80,000
1740		80,000
1741		80,000
1742		80,000
1743		80,000
1744		80,000
1745		80,000
1746	5,000	85,000
1747		85,000
1748		85,000
1749		85,000
1750		84,500
1751		84,000

Source: Issuing acts, Penna. Statutes; redemptions, Penna. Votes.

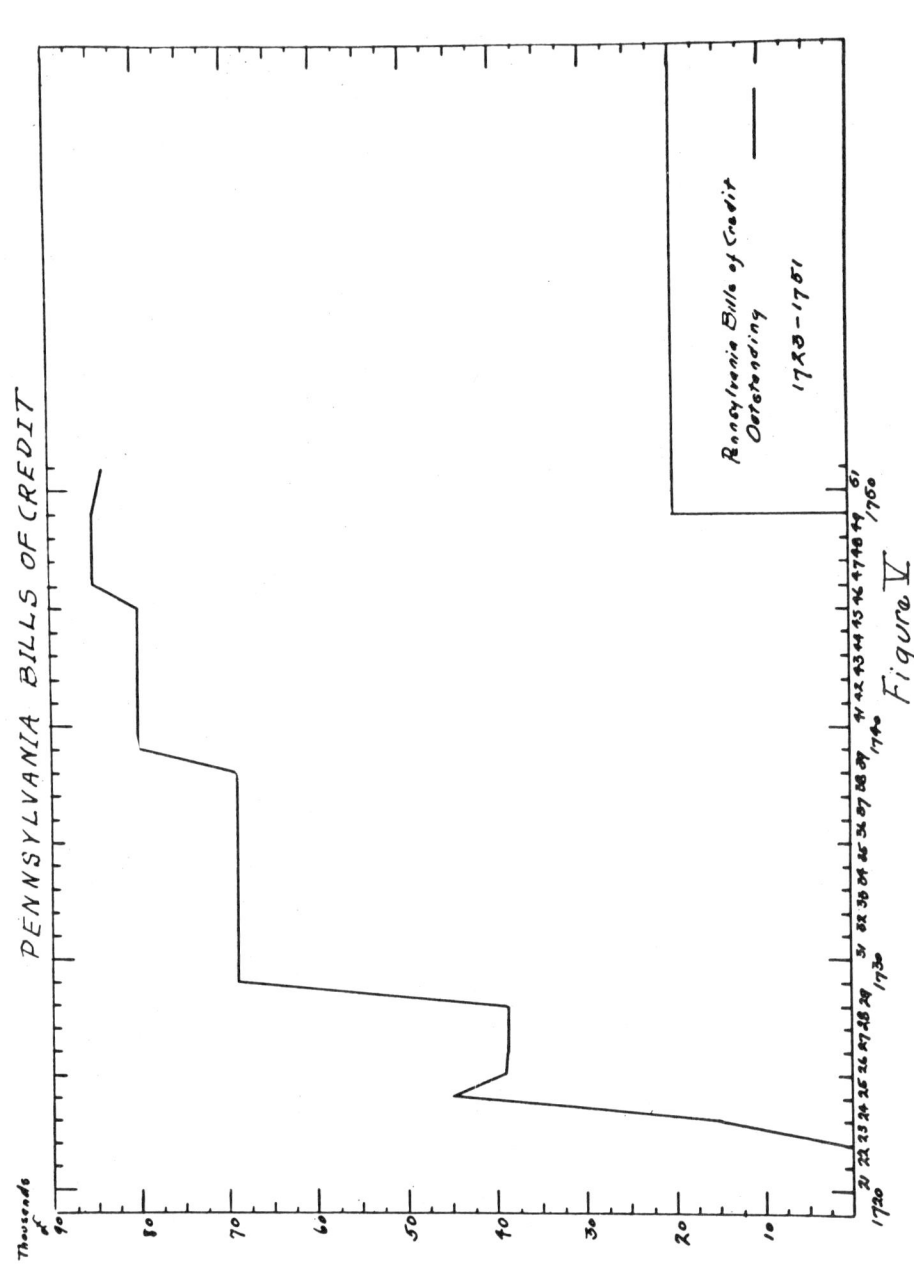

the needs of an expanding population and an increasing trade.[42] Nevertheless, it should not be forgotten that specie circulated side by side with paper. In 1749 the Assembly reported to the Board of Trade that at that time payments in the province were "chiefly in Gold and Silver."[43] The combination of a moderate supply of paper and an increasing stock of specie was a happy one. But, as a committee of the assembly observed, "the manner of issuing [the] Medium contributed no less to [its] happy Effects than the Medium itself." The loans "for a long Term, on easy Interest, and payable in yearly Quotas ... put it in the Power of many to purchase lands, and make Plantations," thereby aiding in the settlement and the development of the country.[44] At the same time the interest on the loans supplied the

---

42. A glance at the various contemporary guesses as to the number of people in Pennsylvania during this period collected in Greene and Harrington, *American Population before 1790*, pp. 114-115, will reconcile one to no more precise statement than that "population was increasing." See *Penna. Votes*, IV, 3515-3520, for a report of a committee of the Assembly on the subject, August 19, 1752.

The average of the foreign trade with Great Britain for the five years centered about 1723, the year of the first paper issues, was ₤35,152 annually. That of the five years centered about 1747 was ₤116,280. The trade of the latter period was about three and one-third times that of the former. Johnson, et. al., *Hist. of Dom. and For. Com. of the U. S.*, I, 120-121.

43. *Penna. Votes*, IV, 3284. The report of the Assembly to the Board of Trade relative to currency, dated November 23, 1739, is in ibid., III, 2521-2523. The report of 1749 is in ibid., IV, 3283-3284.

44. Ibid., IV, 3519.

colony with a substantial revenue, so that no taxes save the excise and custom duties were necessary.

During this period when Pennsylvania was as yet untroubled by effective proprietary instructions on the subject of currency, the exigencies of a war on her own frontiers, or parliamentary restrictions, she managed her paper currency admirably, administered it efficiently, and adapted it to the needs of a growing colony.[45]

Lying between Pennsylvania and New York was the colony of New Jersey. Having no port of her own, she was in many ways an economic appanage of her larger neighbors. The economy of East Jersey was bound up with that of New York; and the economy of West Jersey, with that of Pennsylvania. The importance of this relationship will become increasingly apparent as the story of New Jersey's currency develops.

As was the case in so many other colonies, the expeditions against Canada in 1709 and 1711 provided the cause and the occasion for New Jersey's first paper issues. In the former year, £3,000 were put out on taxes, and in the latter, £5,000 more were placed in circulation on a similar foundation.[46] The issue of

---

45. Even Dr. Douglass acknowledged "the good management of [Pennsylvania's] paper loan office." Douglass, Summary, II, 335.
46. Edwin P. Tanner, The Province of New Jersey, 1664-1738, 1908, p. 539. Chapter X, which is devoted to "Financial Affairs," contains an account of the bills of

1709 seems to have been attended with some irregularity, which caused reluctance on the part of the merchants to accept the bills. This irregularity was corrected before the issue of 1711 was emitted,[47] and the bills of both issues gained a currency. In 1714 the further sum of ₤4,670 was put out on taxes to pay the debts of the government.[48] The bills were to be retired over a period of ten years.

The three issues growing out of the war introduced paper currency into New Jersey. And it seems a correct judgment that "the bills of credit undeniably filled a need in supplying the province with a currency."[49] It is impossible to follow the retirements of the early issues with precise accuracy. There were possibly ₤1,000 still in circulation in 1723.[50] Perhaps by 1725 they had passed from circulation. It is enough to know

---

credit for the period covered. Donald L. Kemmerer, Path to Freedom, The Struggle for Self-Government in Colonial New Jersey, 1703-1776, 1940, stresses the role of currency issues in the history of the colony.

New Jersey Archives (1st series), III, 468, Lieut. Gov. Richard Ingoldesby, New York, July 5, 1709; ibid., XV, 106-108, contains the report of a committee of council to the Board of Trade, December 4, 1739. This report contains a list of the issues up to that time.

47. Tanner, p. 541.
48. Tanner, p. 544. The act was entitled "An Act for the Currency of Bills of Credit up to 11,675 ounces of plate." The bills were issued at the rate of 8s. per oz. of silver plate. Hence 11,675 oz. of plate were equal to ₤4,670.
49. Ibid., p. 542.
50. Kemmerer, p. 121.

that in the early 'twenties the colony's scanty currency was in the process of extinction. The depression that descended upon Pennsylvania in 1720 was also felt in New Jersey. As has already been indicated, Pennsylvania's answer to the "decay of trade" of this period had been the issuance in the year 1723 of ₤45,000 on loan. As had been the case in Pennsylvania, there arose a great public clamor in New Jersey for a paper issue. After the Pennsylvania issues of 1723 the arguments for a similar issue in New Jersey were all the more compelling. They grew out of New Jersey's economic dependence upon New York and Pennsylvania, both of which were now paper money colonies. There was little or no specie in the colony,[51] nor was there any way of obtaining the metals. Governor William Burnet well described the situation at this time when he wrote:

> ... this Province having little or no Shipping or foreign Trade but relying wholly on Husbandry and raising Stock, are obliged to sell it to the neighbouring great Markets of New York and Philadelphia in both which places there is a paper Currency and where the Merchants will pay the New Jersey People in nothing but paper Bills, that they may save all their Gold and Silver, to send home to England for Goods, as this is

---

51. Gov. Burnet wrote in 1724, that, while the annual charge of government in the colony was only ₤800, "there was so little Silver of any sort in the Country, that the People were forced to cut their Spanish Gold into small bits and sometimes their earrings" to pay this small sum in taxes. Burnet to the Board of Trade, New York, May 12, 1724, *N. J. Archives* (1st series), V, 87.

the constant practice.[52]

It appears that about ₤20,000 of Pennsylvania and New York bills were soon found in circulation in New Jersey.[53] They furnished the only currency, and were not a legal tender either for taxes or in private payments, and were often refused for both purposes.[54] The only remedy seemed to be, either to endow the bills of the neighbouring colonies with the legal tender quality, or to emit an issue of New Jersey bills to "circulate" the colony's trade. To adopt the first course was equivalent to giving Pennsylvania and New York the power to levy tribute on New Jersey to the extent that their bills circulated within her limits. The only satisfactory expedient, therefore, seemed to be an issue of New Jersey bills.

The result was that early in 1724 the legislature passed an act for emitting ₤40,000, which was to be a

---

52. Ibid., 87. Burnet's letter cited in the preceding note.
53. "It is Esteemed that above 1/4 of the Exportation of New York is of the Groath of Jersey & that No Less of the Exportation of Pensilvania is also of the Groath of Jersey for all which they before this Act [the New Jersey Act of 1724] received No other Cash but their paper money and the quantity of Paper Currency in New Jersey Pensilvania and New York being Nearby in proportion to the Exportation of their own produce ... ." "Further Reasons for the Act pass'd in New Jersey in 172[4] ... [by James Alexander]," transmitted by Burnet in his letter cited above. Ibid., 96.
54. Burnet to the Board of Trade, May 12, 1724. Ibid., 87.

legal tender between man and man, and in tax payments. Of the sum, ₤36,000 were to be placed out on loan for a twelve year period at five per cent interest. The loans were to be secured by mortgages on land worth at least double the amount of the loan. The interest was payable annually, and the principal was to be repaid in twelve annual installments, the bills being destroyed as they came in. During each of the first ten years eight and one-half per cent of the loan was to be repaid, and during each of the last two years, seven and one-half per cent. It was first contemplated that the money arising from the interest payments should, after deducting the expenses of operating the loan offices, be applied to retire the bills. Soon, however, the interest money was appropriated to the support of government.[55] The remaining ₤4,000 were used to meet the expenses of government and were to be retired by a tax over the four years next ensuing.[56]

The bills relieved the currency stringency in New Jersey, and soon gained a currency in New York, and ap-

---

55. Ibid., pp. 98-99.
56. Tanner, pp. 545-548, contains a detailed digest of the act. See also N. J. Archives (1st series), V, 90-91, 98-99. This and subsequent loan acts are discussed in Lester's article, "Currency Issues to Overcome Depressions in Delaware, New Jersey, New York, and Maryland, 1715-37," loc. cit., pp. 188-199. Donald M. Kemmerer treats "The Colonial Loan-Office System in New Jersey," Journal of Political Economy, XLVII (December, 1939), 867-874.

parently also in Pennsylvania. In the former colony they soon became currency at 7s. New Jersey currency for 6s. New York currency, and a little later began to be preferred to the currency of New York at that rate.[57] And from Perth Amboy it was reported in 1726 that New Jersey and Pennsylvania currency were of equal value.[58]

The retirement of ₤4,060 annually during the first four years drastically contracted the circulating medium. It should be remembered also that the last of the wartime issues appear to have been withdrawn during this period. The legislature, when it reprinted all outstanding bills in 1728, set the amount in circulation at ₤24,760.[59] This indicates a contraction of something over forty per cent in four years. Such a contraction in the currency tended to have a depressing effect upon trade. The currency was further contracted at the rate of ₤3,060 annually during the years after 1728. It is not surprising, therefore, that a demand arose for a new issue on loan, and in 1730 the sum of ₤20,000 was authorized.[60] The act, however, contained a suspending

---

57. "Certificate of the New York Merchants," December 1, 1726. N. J. Archives (1st series), V, 153.
58. "Certificate of Perth Amboy Merchants of the Value of New Jersey Bills," December 19, 1726. Ibid., pp. 154-155.
59. Tanner, p. 550; N. J. Archives (1st series), XIV, 389. The act received the governor's assent, February 10, 1727/8.
60. Tanner, p. 551; N. J. Archives (1st series), XIV, 438. The bill received the governor's assent, July 8, 1730.

clause, and it was not until 1733, after notice of the royal confirmation had been received, that the bills were issued.[61] The new bills were to be put out on loan for a period of sixteen years, one-sixteenth of the principal to be repaid annually. During the first eight years of the period, however, the principal payments received were to be relent for the remainder of the sixteen year period. During the last eight years one-eighth of the amount of the issue was to be retired annually. The other features of the act were similar to those of the act of 1724.[62]

News of the confirmation of the act of 1730 encouraged the authorization in 1733 of an additional issue of ₤40,000 on similar terms.[63] This act likewise contained a suspending clause. It was confirmed in 1735, but the bills were not placed in circulation until 1737. This issue brought the amount of bills in circulation up to ₤60,000.

There were no further loan issues during the period. There were, however, five separate issues placed in circulation to meet extraordinary demands of government.

---

61. Tanner, p. 553; Report of Council to the Board of Trade, December 4, 1740, N. J. Archives (1st series), XV, 107.
62. Tanner, p. 552.
63. Ibid., pp. 553-554. N. J. Archives (1st series), XIV, 501. The act received the governor's assent, August 16, 1733. Ibid., XIV, 545-546.

In 1740, ₤2,000 were emitted "to provision and transport troops for an intended expedition to the West Indies."[64] The sum was to be retired from the interest money arising under the loan acts.[65] During the war years 1746 and 1747, a total of ₤15,850 was emitted to finance New Jersey's contribution to the expedition against Canada.[66] In 1749 these issues were still outstanding, as was also the issue of 1740, and the total sum in circulation was nearly ₤37,800.[67]

The emergency issues did not satisfy the demand of the people for paper money. Throughout the period of the 'forties the assembly persistently pressed for an additional emission of ₤40,000 on loan, only to have the proposal negatived by the governor, the council, or the authorities in England.[68]

The dependency of New Jersey on her larger neighbors,

---

64. Edgar J. Fisher, New Jersey as a Royal Province, 1738-1766, 1911, p. 291. This work takes up the story where Tanner leaves off. Chap. ix, "The Financial System," has a section on bills of credit.
65. N. J. Archives (1st series), VII, 358. State of the Paper Currency, Perth Amboy, October 20, 1749.
66. Fisher, p. 295; N. J. Archives (1st series), VII, 358-359. The sums were: ₤4,000 (act of June 1, 1746); ₤10,000 (act of June 1, 1746), to be retired out of the reimbursement money to be received from Parliament, supplemented, if necessary, from the interest money; ₤850 (act of November 1, 1746), to be retired out of the interest money; ₤1,000 (act of May 8, 1747), likewise to be retired from the interest money.
67. N. J. Archives (1st series), VII, 359.
68. Fisher, pp. 290-294.

New York and Pennsylvania, continued throughout the period. As had been the case in 1723, so in 1741 little specie was to be had. In the latter year Governor Lewis Morris wrote that what little gold and silver the people of New Jersey

> have (if any) comes from York or Pensilvania but chiefly from the last to purchase Wheat for their own Exportation and then passes at the Value it goes in Pensilvania with those who take it which are not many: the generality preferring the bills of credit current Amongst them whose Value they know to Silver and Gold which they do not; and few of them having need of remittances are not concern'd whether bills of Exchange be cheap or deare which may be one reason that the bills or what they call the Paper Money of this Province have not only retain'd but Encreas'd their Credit being now 12 1/2 P Cent better than those of the neighbouring Province of New York. 69

New Jersey currency seems to have been in demand

---

69. *N. J. Archives* (1st series), VI, 135. Gov. Morris to the Board of Trade, Trenton, August 16, 1741.

Dr. Douglass says of the New Jersey bills that after the emission of ₤40,000 in 1724, "their Bills became of less Value than those of New-York; but being yearly in good Faith, sunk, they became equal, and after some Years 2s. in the Pound better than New-York Bills. This is a Demonstration, that the Quantity of Paper Money increasing or faithfully decreasing, sinks or raises the value of it. -- A. 1733, was issued 20,000 l. more upon loan ...; this Emission fell their Bills to near Par with New-York. -- A. 1734, the first loan of A. 1724 being sunk, the Assembly enacted a 40,000 l. Loan, but was not issued till A. 1736[7], ... and passed scarce at Par with New-York; but upon the New-York Emission of 48,300 l. A. 1738, the Jersey Bills are 6d. in the Pound better than New-York Bills, and 1s. in the Pound better than those of Pensylvania." "Discourse," *Colonial Currency Reprints*, III, 322.

Douglass probably is correct insofar as the general movements of the value of the various currencies are concerned. Too much reliance, however, should not be put upon the precise accuracy of his figures.

TABLE VI

NEW JERSEY BILLS OF CREDIT

(calculated according to the terms of the issuing acts)

Year	Issued £	Outstanding £	Year	Issued £	Outstanding £
1709	3,000		1731		14,580
1710			1732		11,520
1711	5,000		1733	20,000	28,460
1712			1734		25,400
1713			1735		22,700
1714			1736		20,000
1715			1737	40,000	60,000
1716	4,670		1738		60,000
1717			1739		60,000
1718			1740	2,000	62,000
1719			1741		61,000
1720			1742		57,500
1721			1743		55,000
1722			1744		52,500
1723			1745		50,000
1724	40,000	40,000	1746	14,850	57,350
1725		35,940	1747	1,000	50,850
1726		30,880	1748		43,350
1727		27,820	1749		37,850
1728		23,760	1750		32,850
1729		20,700	1751		27,850
1730		17,640	1752		22,850

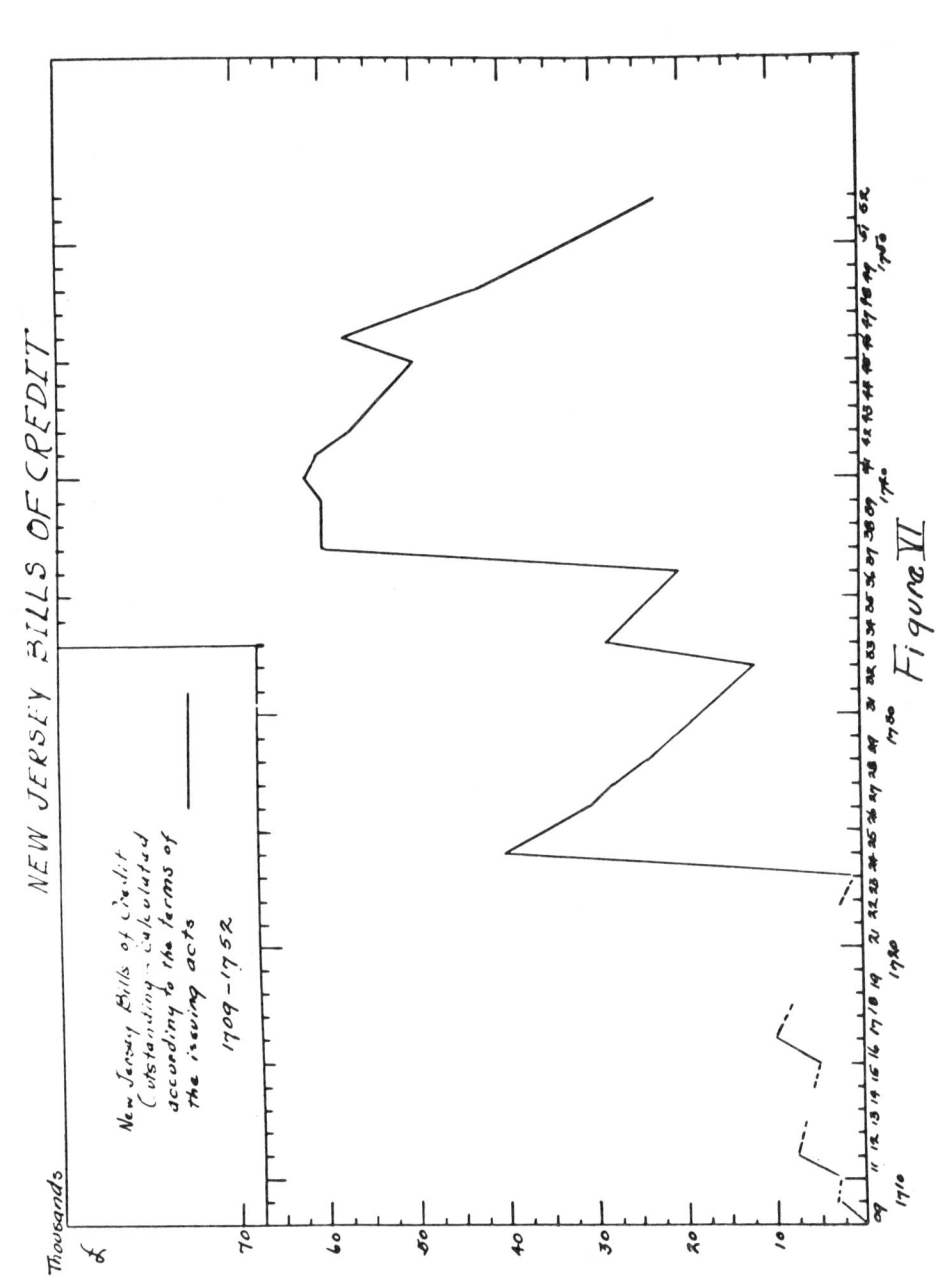

Figure VI

to settle balances between the colonies of New York and
Pennsylvania. This fact, by increasing the demand for
it, probably helped to maintain its value.[70]

It would be a mistake to reach the conclusion that
New Jersey managed her currency better than her neighbors
merely because her bills sometimes commanded a premium
in the currency of New York and Pennsylvania, which was,
partly at least, a result of the fact that the merchants
in these colonies at times bid up her bills as they vied
with one another for them to make intercolonial payments.
This is something for which New Jersey can scarcely claim
credit. The fact is that the currency her bills enjoyed
within the bounds of her neighbors doubtless permitted
her to issue larger sums without feeling the effects of

---

70. Dr. Douglass indicates this as a reason for the maintenance of the credit of the New Jersey bills, writing: "New-York Bills not being current in Pensylvania, and Pensylvania Bills not current in New-York; but Jersey Bills current in both, all Payments between New-York and Pensylvania are made in Jersey Bills." "Discourse," Colonial Currency Reprints, II, 322.

The fact the New Jersey bills were in demand for this purpose gave them the quality of bills of exchange. They tended to appreciate or depreciate in the currencies of New York and Pennsylvania depending on the nature of the balance of trade between these two colonies. See New York Historical Society, Collections, LXVII (1934), "The Letters and Papers of Cadwallader Colden ... 1715-1748," pp. 179, 197, 338, for examples of the use of New Jersey bills to make remittances from Pennsylvania to New York in the years 1725, 1731, and 1746.

In 1743 Colden wrote: "Jersey Bills of Proclamation frequently carry 1d in the shilling above ours that are struck at 8/ per ounce & sometimes a little more & sometimes less." Ibid., LXVII, 302.

depreciation than would have otherwise been possible.
New Jersey deserves credit for her own moderation,[71]
but at the same time she owes much to her fortunate
position and to the tutelage of Pennsylvania. She
probably managed her bills better than did New York,
but she did not have to raise sums proportionate to those
raised in New York for defensive purposes. Nor were her
loan issues as well conceived and managed as those of
Pennsylvania, and much that was good in them was modelled
after earlier Pennsylvania practices. By relending the
installments paid in to the loan office on the principal
of the loans, Pennsylvania kept the amount of bills in
circulation constant; and by extending old issues,
rather than calling them in and emitting new ones, that
colony probably avoided the temptation to put out ever
larger sums in new issues. While New Jersey did adopt
the relending principle in her acts of 1730 and 1734,
she never extended the currency of her loans, preferring
instead to retire them and put out new issues. Had she
not been restrained during the 'forties, one has no

---

71. Her emissions were never excessive when one considers her population, which was:

Year	Population	Year	Population
1715	22,500	1738	47,369
1726	32,442	1745	61,383

Greene and Harrington, <u>American Population before 1790</u>, p. 106.

means of knowing how far she would have gone in expanding her currency. Certain it is that there was a strong paper money sentiment among the people during these years.

None the less, a moderate amount of bills of credit seems to have been essential to New Jersey's prosperity during this period when no specie was to be had. The loans appear to have been well administered, and the interest money so long proved adequate to all the needs of government that in 1749 Lieutenant Governor Jonathan Belcher could write to the Board of Trade: "'Tis 17 Years since any Tax was raised on the People for Support of Government."[72]

The economy of Delaware was as closely bound up with that of Pennsylvania as was West Jersey's. The region, then under the Pennsylvania proprietors and their governor in Pennsylvania, but with a legislature of its own, was known throughout colonial times as the "Three Lower Counties." The depression that set in in 1720 enveloped alike both Pennsylvania and Delaware, and like her larger neighbor the smaller colony attempted to ameliorate conditions by paper issues. In April, 1723, the Delaware assembly authorized an emission of ₤5,000 at proclamation rates to be put on

---

72. Belcher to the Board of Trade, Burlington, N. J., April 21, 1749. *N. J. Archives* (1st series), VII, 246.

loan. The following November the additional sum of Ł6,000 was emitted on the same terms. These sums were to be lent out in amounts of from Ł12 to Ł60 on landed security of double the value of the loan. The loans were for a period of eight years and bore interest at five per cent. They were to be repaid in equal annual installments over the eight year period, and the principal sums paid in were to be burned. The annual interest payments were available for the uses of government.[73]

The experience of Delaware paralled that of Pennsylvania and New Jersey. The issues facilitated a revival of trade. But the provisions of the acts requiring that the bills should be retired as the principal of the loans was repaid had a deflationary effect. This was realized in 1726, by which time Ł2,750 of the issues of 1723 had been retired. Consequently an act was passed authorizing the relending, presumably for the remainder of the original period, of the bills that were received in the loan office from the annual repayments of principal. Obviously the relief granted by this measure was of but a temporary nature, as the requirements of the original acts would still bring in all the colony's bills in 1731. In 1729 the assembly sought to make provision against this by authorizing a new issue of Ł12,000

---

73. Richard S. Rodney, <u>Colonial Finances in Delaware,</u> 1928, pp. 17-19.

to be placed out on loan for a period of sixteen years. The loans were to be retired in equal annual installments over the whole period. Under this provision ₤3,750 of the issue of 1729 had been sunk by 1734. Presumably all the earlier issues had also been sunk by this time. In consequence, the sum left outstanding was only ₤8,250. The growth of the colony, the increase of its trade, and the yearly diminution in its paper currency indicated the necessity of a further emission, and an additional loan issue of ₤12,000 was sanctioned in 1734. In 1739 the sum reported in circulation was ₤17,250. As many of the old bills had by this time become worn and ragged, ₤6,000 in new bills were printed for exchange purposes.[74]

In 1740 the Delaware assembly directed that ₤1,000 of the exchange issues of the year before be appropriated to the support of the expedition to the West Indies. Provision was made for repaying the sum to the commissioners of the loan office from tax funds to be raised over a period of five years.[75]

In 1743 an issue of ₤6,100 was authorized, the nature of which is not altogether clear.[76] By 1746 it appears that ₤5,000 of former issues had been sunk, and

---

74. Ibid., pp. 19-25.
75. Ibid., p. 27.
76. Ibid.

that Ł20,000 were remaining in circulation. Provision was made to re-emit this sum on loan, and February 28, 1758, was set as the limit for the circulation of the bills authorized.[77]

The bills of credit circulating in Delaware at various times are tabulated in the note below.[78] It will be seen that the sums were at all times modest. Moreover, the loan office was well managed, and the terms of the acts adhered to. The bills appear to have maintained their value and gained at least a limited circulation in Pennsylvania. Sterling exchange was at 150 in terms of Delaware currency in 1730; at 134 1/2 in 1739; and at 159 in 1749.[79] The two latter quotations

---

77. "Report of the Committee of Assembly of the Lower Counties of the State of the Paper Currency," 1749, Pennsylvania Archives (1st series), V, 417-418. Copies of most of the emitting acts prior to this time appear not to exist. The report of 1749 cannot be relied upon as completely accurate. We are left in the dark as to many details, but the general picture is clear enough.

78. DELAWARE CURRENCY IN CIRCULATION

1723	Ł 11,000	1739	Ł 17,250
1727	8,250	1746	20,000
1734	20, 250		

Source: Lester, "Currency Issues to Overcome Depression in Delaware, New Jersey, New York, and Maryland, 1715-37," loc. cit., p. 185.
Francis Rawle, Ways and Means for the Inhabitants of Delaware to Become Rich, Philadelphia, 1725, gives much information and pertinent comment on the economic conditions existing in Delaware and Pennsylvania at the time of the introduction of paper currency. He also had an exceptionally clear understanding of money. Lester, pp. 184-185, quotes excerpts.

79. Lester, p. 186.

TABLE VII

DELAWARE BILLS OF CREDIT

Year	Issues £	Funds
1723 April	5,000	Loan
1723 November	6,000	Loan
1729	12,000	Loan
1734 (3/1/34)x	12,000	Loan
1739 (12/1/39)x	6,000	(Exchange issue) 1740 -- £1,000 of above issue granted to king's use to be retired from taxes over 5 years.
1743	6,100	Loan
1746 (2/28/46)x	20,000	Loan

x Bills dated.

Source: Richard S. Rodney, <u>Colonial Finances in Delaware,</u> pp. 17-27, 64.

are lower than quotations in Pennsylvania at the time.[80]

All the evidence points to the fact that Delaware's wisely managed paper currency provided a necessary circulating medium and in many ways contributed to the colony's economic well-being.

At an early date the province of Maryland, as has been indicated earlier, developed a commodity currency based upon her staple crop, tobacco. As the raising of grain in some sections of the province began to supplant the raising of tobacco, there arose a demand for a paper currency in which to pay taxes and fees theretofore levied and paid in tobacco. "Several years of agitation were necessary before an act for issuing the much-desired paper currency was passed."[81] The subject first came under discussion in the Lower House of Assembly in 1727, and was again broached in 1728, "but it was not until 1729 that the movement became really serious."[82] In that year Benedict Leonard Calvert appears to have expressed the prevailing opinion when he wrote:

> Money, or somewhat to answer its Current Effects in trade, is certainly much wanted here; wee may Barter between one Another our Staple Tobacco, but to Carry on

---

80. In 1739 sterling exchange was at 170 in Pennsylvania; and in 1749 at 172. Bezanson et al., *Prices in Colonial Pennsylvania*, pp. 431, 432.

81. Kathryn L. Behrens, *Paper Money in Maryland, 1727-1789*, 1923, p. 12. See also Clarence P. Gould, *Money and Transportation in Maryland, 1720-1765*, 1915, pp. 79-82.

82. Gould, pp. 79-80.

and Inlarge our trade Abroad, & to Invite Artificers, Shipwrights &c to settle amongst us, another species of Currency in payments Seems very desireable; New York, Pennsylvania &c are vastly improved in foreign Trade, as well as home Manufactures, by a Paper Currency; [which] in lieu of Specific Coin, ... Seems to give life, Expedition and Ease to trade and Commerce 83

Four years, however, were to elapse before the two houses of the legislature could agree upon a bill. Finally in 1733 an act was passed authorizing the emission of ₤90,000 "current Money of America, according to an Act of Parliament, made in the Sixth Year of the Reign of the late Queen Anne."[84]

The method for issuing the money and for supporting its value had certain unique features. In order that the bills of credit might "be the more useful to the Inhabitants of [the] Province, and the Circulation of them as speedy and diffuse as possible," thirty shillings were to be issued to every taxable, or, where the taxable was a servant or slave, to his master.[85] It appears that for this purpose ₤47,923 10s. were sent to the counties

---

83. Quoted in ibid., p. 79, from Calvert Papers, No. 2, pp. 69-71.

84. Archives of Maryland, XXXIX, 93; Gould, pp. 81-82.

Lester, "Currency Issues to Overcome Depression in Delaware, New Jersey, New York, and Maryland," loc. cit., pp. 208-215, discusses the act.

The increase in the proposed issues during these years is interesting. "The bills of 1729 and 1730 called for only ₤24,000 currency, that of 1731 was for ₤36,000, and that of 1732, for ₤72,000. The original bill of 1733 was also for ₤72,000; but in the conference committee, in order to provide a greater sum to be lent out at interest ... it was raised to ₤90,000 currency." Gould, pp. 82-83.

85. Archives of Maryland, XXXIX, 97.

for distribution.[86] Not quite all of it, however, was used for the purpose.[87] Certain specific appropriations were included in the act: £3,000 for a house for the governor; £500 to repair the public buildings in Annapolis; and £500 to each county for the erection of a jail. The remainder of the sum authorized was to be lent out upon mortgage on real or personal security of double or treble the value of the loan, according to the class of security given. The period was "for such Term as shall be agreed on, not exceeding Seven Years;" and the interest rate was four per cent. The interest was payable annually, and "the Principal at such Times, and in such Proportions," as were agreed upon within the seven year period.[88] The balance remaining unlent might be appropriated to meet the charges of government.

To support the credit of the bills, a tax of 1s. 3d. sterling was levied in bills of exchange on each hogshead of tobacco exported for a period of thirty-one years ending in September, 1764. The funds arising from this tax were to be transported to England, where they were lodged with commissioners, who were charged with investing them in the stock of the Bank of England. Between September 29, 1748, and March 29, 1749, all notes

---

86. Report of committee of the Upper House, April 19, 1735, ibid., XXXIX, 204.
87. Gould, p. 85n.
88. Archives of Maryland, XXXIX, 104-105.

outstanding were redeemable, one-third in sterling bills of exchange at the rate of £133 1/3 paper for £100 sterling, and two-thirds in new bills. At the end of the thirty-one year period, the remaining two-thirds of the notes were to be retired by redeeming them in sterling bills of exchange at the same rate.[89]

Apparently as a <u>quid pro quo</u> for the distribution of the thirty shillings in bills to the taxables of the province, every taxable that raised tobacco was required to burn 150 pounds of his trash tobacco annually during the next two years, and agents, who were paid for their services from the bills, were appointed to oversee the burning.[90]

The legal tender provisions of the act were so drawn that paper currency did not supplant tobacco money and "thus was defeated one of the chief objects for which paper currency had been issued."[91] This fact, by limiting the uses of the bills of credit, was no doubt a factor in their depreciation.

By April, 1735, £56,494 of the issue had been placed in circulation. Of the sum, £47,924 had been distributed to the taxables of the province, and £7,374

---

89. <u>Ibid.</u>, XXXIX, 105-109.
90. <u>Archives of Maryland</u>, XXXIX, 110-113.
91. Gould, p. 83. See the complicated legal tender provisions of the act, <u>Archives of Maryland</u>, XXXIX, 95-97.

had been placed on loan. The "journal of expenses," as the annual charges of government were called, for the years 1735, 1736, and 1737 were paid out of the bills remaining in the office. These sums, amounting altogether to ₤9,324, were in the nature of a loan to the province and were to be repaid out of tax funds. Chiefly as a result of these loans to the province, and of added loans to individuals, which now totaled ₤19,728, the amount of bills in circulation in the spring of 1740 had risen to ₤78,523. During the year 1740, the legislature again borrowed from the loan office, this time the sum of ₤5,747 to finance Maryland's share of the expedition to the West Indies. This sum was likewise to be repaid from taxes. The war loan of 1740 was chiefly responsible for bringing the amount of bills in circulation up to ₤83,444 by early 1741. For the next five years the sum outstanding hovered around this figure. In 1746 and 1747, however, the sum of ₤5,400 was borrowed from the loan office to finance Maryland's contribution to the expedition against Canada. The bills in circulation were now in excess of ₤85,000. As was customary, provision was made to repay this new loan to the province from funds raised by taxes.[92]

---

92. The various figures for the sums distributed, lent to individuals, and borrowed by the government are computed from the auditing committees reports in the Maryland Archives, "Journals of the Upper House," passim.

The amounts in circulation annually, as well as the sums on loan to individuals, for the entire period, 1733-1751, may conveniently be followed in Figure VII.

Over the years the 1s. 3d. tax on every hogshead of tobacco exported had proved more than adequate to accumulate a sufficient fund to redeem the required one-third of the bills of credit in 1748-1749. At this time Ł83,962 16s. of the old bills were burned, and in their place bills of exchange to the value of Ł20,990 14s. sterling (equal to Ł27,987 12s. currency at 133 1/3 per cent) and Ł55,975 4s. in new bills were paid out.[93] After this exchange there were some Ł62,000 in bills, new and old, in circulation.

Although the paper currency of Maryland appears to have been issued on sufficient funds and to have been well administered with respect to the loan features of the act, the bills did not maintain their value. They seem to have fallen in value almost immediately. By

---

93. *Archives* of *Maryland*, XLVI, 227, 529.
"Between 1734 and 1749 there were sent to the London agents bills of exchange for Ł28,907 sterling. This money was invested in bank-stock at premiums varying from 119 to 149 1/4. The semi-annual dividends on stock amounted to Ł7,697 sterling. The total amount of the funds on January 1, 1749, was Ł190 17s. sterling in cash and Ł24,000 in bank-stock, which had cost Ł32,977 10s. sterling, a total currency value of Ł44,223. Moreover, there was due the currency commission at this time Ł17,182 currency from well-secured private loans," making a grand total of Ł61,405 toward the redemption of the Ł90,000 issue. Gould, p. 95.

TABLE VIII

MARYLAND BILLS OF CREDIT

(Issue of 1733)

Year	On Loan £	Total in Circulation £
1733		
1734		
1735	7,374	56,495
1736	11,198	57,864
1737	16,160	69,856
1738		
1739	19,728	79,820
1740	18,627	78,523
1741	18,644	83,444
1742	17,924	82,072
1743		
1744	16,950	82,252
1745	18,067	83,058
1746		
1747	17,157	85,309
1748	17,479	86,040
1749		
1750	16,779	
1751	16,248	

Source: Committee reports, Maryland Archives.

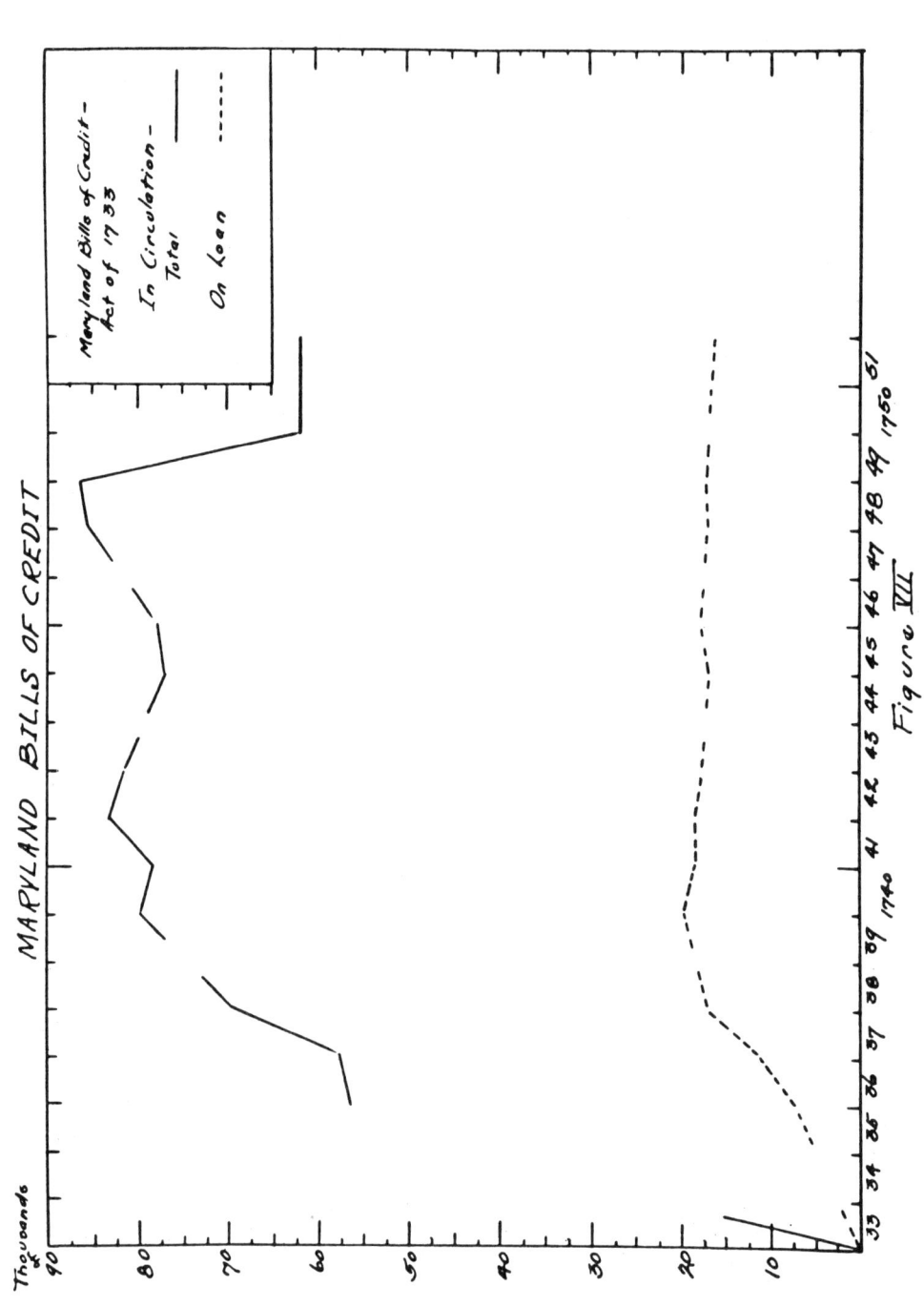

By 1739 exchange, formerly at 133 1/3, had risen to 200 and remained somewhere near that figure until the redemption of one-third of the bills in 1748-1749 brought it down to 133 1/3 again, that being the figure at which the old bills were converted into sterling. Exchange, however, did not hold at this level, and, although there were roughly one-third fewer bills of credit in circulation after the redemption, it rose rapidly, as high perhaps as 180. During the year "1752 exchange ranged from Ł155 to Ł160 paper to Ł100 sterling."[94]

Several factors appear to bear upon the problem of the depreciation. In the first place, the issue was larger than those placed in circulation at one time in the other Middle colonies. Moreover, it did not, to any great degree, supplant any other form of currency. Tobacco still passed current in the payment of fees and taxes. And specie, over the whole period, seems to have increased rather than diminished.[95] Furthermore, Maryland was an agricultural colony, with a large slave and indentured servant element in her population, rather than a free labor colony, where currency was needed for wages. From these considerations, it appears on the one hand that in Maryland paper had more monetary competitors than it did in the rest of the Middle colonies;

---

94. Gould, pp. 87-88, 96-99.
95. Ibid., p. 88.

and on the other, that the agricultural, indentured-servant, slave-labor economy of Maryland did not require so large a circulating medium as did the free-labor, commercial colonies to her immediate northward. After the retirement of one-third of her bills of credit in 1748-1749, it appears that she rapidly grew into her currency, and, although immediately after the retirement transactions were completed, exchange again rose, the long run trend was downward.[96]

Virginia issued no paper currency during the period. Not so, however, her southern neighbor, North Carolina. Throughout the period, North Carolina remained a small, poor, frontier colony. Concerning her, the Reverend

---

96. Gould, pp. 97-99.
The population figures for Maryland are as follows:

Year	Population
1715	22,500
1726	32,442
1738	47,369
1745	61,383

Greene and Harrington, American Population befor 1790, p. 136.

The figures of the trade of Maryland with England are lumped with those of Virginia. The balance for the two colonies was more or less favorable, although it is impossible to say how Maryland stood by herself. The apparently favorable position of the province in this respect may account for the fact that in none of the other colonies, where sterling exchange was more difficult to procure, was there ever an attempt to establish a fund in England. (Virginia is a later exception.)

See Johnson, et al., pp. 120-121, for the trade figures of Maryland and Virginia.

William Gordon wrote in 1709: "In this as in all other parts of the province, there is no money, every one buys and pays with their commodities, of which, corn, pork, pitch, and tar are the chief."[97] In 1715 the legislature passed a law regulating these and other commodities for payments in public and private transactions;[98] and in the same year, when it drew up a schedule of fees due the governor, it provided that the first four items were "to be paid in Pork or Silver."[99] The use of commodities for monetary purposes continued throughout the period "with very little Alteration"; and in North Carolina, as elsewhere, it had become "a stated rule, that of so many Commodities the worst sort were only paid."[100]

In 1715 the legislature rated "Lyon Dollars" at "three Bushalls of Inayan Corn and so proportionately for all other of the Rated Comoditys" and made them current "in all payments within [the] Province."[101] The object of the law, as a later governor explained it, was "to bring Dollars into the Country," but, he continues, "it never had that effect."[102] It appears certain that

---

97. Francis L. Hawks, History of North Carolina, 1858, II, 309.
98. State Records of North Carolina, XXIII, Law of North Carolina -- 1715, c. xl, pp. 54-55.
99. Ibid., XXIII, c. lviii, p. 83.
100. Colonial Records of North Carolina, IV, 920-921. Governor Gabriel Johnson to the Board of Trade, Edenton, April 4, 1749.
101. State Records of N. C., XXIII, Laws of North Carolina -- 1715, c. liv, p. 80.
102. Quoted in Charles J. Bullock, Essays on the

there was never any substantial amount of coin in the colony throughout the period.

In 1712 the first bills of credit were emitted. At that time the sum of ₤4,000 was placed in circulation on taxes in order to "defray the Charges of an Indian War then kindled" -- the Tuscarora War.[103] In the next year, 1713, an additional ₤8,000 were emitted for a like purpose. The bills of both issues appear to have borne interest, and to have been made a legal tender in all payments where rated commodities were receivable.[104] This second emission, we are told, "depreciated the value of the whole about 40 per cent."[105] By 1715 no part of the ₤12,000 placed in circulation by the two acts seems to have been retired. In that year ₤24,000 in new bills were authorized, ₤12,000 to be exchanged for those of the earlier issues, and ₤12,000 to be paid out to the creditors of the colony.[106] Possessors of the old bills were allowed two years interest on exchange. The new bills, however, did not bear interest. In 1715, to

---

Monetary History of the United States, 1900, p. 128. Part II of this study is devoted to "The Paper Currency of North Carolina." Chap. i covers the period 1712-1748.

103. Ibid., p. 129.
104. Ibid.
105. Col. Rec. of N.C., IV, 576. "An Account of the State of the paper currency of North Carolina from the first emission of any Bills of Credit to the year 1740."
106. The text of the act is in Col. Rec. of N. C., III, 177-179.

the end that the currency of "the Publick bills of Credit" might be encouraged, an act was passed raising the sum of £2,000 annually for so long as should be necessary to sink the bills then outstanding.[107] By 1722 half of the bills outstanding at the time of the adoption of the tax appear to have been retired, and £12,000 in new bills, to be exchanged for the old bills then outstanding, were voted.[108] The exchange act of 1722 so reduced the tax for calling in the bills that there appear to have been no further retirements.[109] In fact, the years 1715 to 1722 seem to have been the only ones within the period covered by this chapter in which North Carolina retired any of her bills from circulation. No precise data concerning the value of the bills during this period are available.[110] It appears certain, however, that after the exchange issue in 1722, exchange was at £500 currency to £100 sterling.[111]

There were no further issues until 1729, when the legislature established a loan office. At this time bills of credit to the amount of £40,000 were authorized, £30,000 of which were to be lent, and the remaining

---

107. *State Records of N. C.*, XXIII, Laws of 1715, c. lxii, pp. 90-92.
108. Bullock, p. 134.
109. *Ibid.*, pp. 134-135.
110. The citation that Bullock gives, p. 133, in support of his statement that in 1721 £250 currency equalled £100 sterling does not appear to substantiate the assertion.
111. *N. C. Col. Rec.*, IV, 576.

₤10,000 were to be exchanged for the old bills then in circulation.[112] The ₤30,000 were to be lent to the inhabitants of the colony on landed security for fifteen year periods at an annual interest of six and one-third per cent. The principal was to be repaid in equal annual installments.[113] The loan provisions of the act seem to have been laxly administered, for in 1734, when an accounting was had, the precinct treasurers were able to produce only one-tenth the sums that should have been repaid.[114] As the quit rents were in arrears, and "silver and Gold not being to be had," the legislature passed an act providing for the relending at six per cent of the payments received on the principal of the loans outstanding under the act of 1729. As a result of this provision, the full sum of ₤30,000 on loan was to remain in circulation until 1744. Moreover, at the same time there was issued on taxes the sum of ₤2,500 to pay the province debts and to defray the cost of the relending operation. The sum now in circulation was ₤54,500. As a result of this issue, sterling exchange soon rose

---

112. Ibid., IV, 576. There were really ₤12,000 in old bills circulating. The legislature, however, in providing only ₤10,000 to be exchanged assumed that ₤2,000 of the old bills had been lost.

113. Ibid., 576; Hugh Williamson, History of North Carolina, 1812, II, 282-287, where the provisions of the act are discussed in detail.

114. N. C. Col. Rec., IV, 179, "State of the present Currency in North Carolina," October 15, 1736.

115. Ibid., pp. 179-180.

to 1000.[116]

In the early 'forties the legislature was restrained by the governor from issuing additional sums in bills, and as the year of the expiration of the loan period drew near, that official urged that effective steps be taken to draw in the currency. In 1745, a tax was levied for the purpose, but it failed to bring any substantial sum into the treasury. Finally, recourse was had to replacing the old issues by bills of a new tenor, issued at the proclamation rate, i.e., 4s. currency equalled 3s. sterling. In the meantime, the Spanish from St. Augustine threatened, and there was demand for a new issue of bills of credit to finance the erection of forts. The result was the act of 1748, which authorized the issuance of Ł21,350 proclamation money. Of this sum, Ł6,000 were appropriated for the erection of four forts, and the sum remaining was to be used to retire the old bills of credit and pay the schedule of the colony's debts annexed to the act. The old bills were to be exchanged for the new bills at the rate of seven

---

116. Ibid., p. 577.
  Williamson gives the depreciation of the North Carolina bills, presumably relative to the value at which the bills were issued, as follows:

    1730 -------   3 1/2 to 1
    1735 -------   5   to 1
    1739 -------   7 1/2 to 1

  Williamson, II, 38-39.

and one-half to one. After the expiration of a year the old bills were no longer to pass current. To provide for the retirement of the issue, the act levied an annual tax of one shilling payable in "Gold, Silver, or Bills of Credit" on each taxable in the province.[117]

Since Ł7,000 of the new bills should have been sufficient to retire all the outstanding bills of the old issues, it appears that the issuing of the sum of Ł21,350 proclamation money authorized by the act of 1748 was equivalent to tripling the amount of bills in circulation. It is small wonder, therefore, that the new issue soon depreciated.[118]

The story of the North Carolina currency during this period is a discouraging one. With the exception of the years 1715 to 1722, no bills seem ever to have been retired by taxation. The loan office was badly managed. To make matters worse, North Carolina remained a barter colony. Until the law of 1748 provided for payment of taxes in gold, silver, or bills of credit, they had been payable in the rated commodities. The result was, as successive governors complained, that the taxes were paid in the commodity rated highest in proportion to its actual value, and of that commodity each person

---

117. Bullock, 147-148; N. C. State Records, XXIII, Laws of 1748, c. x, pp. 292-296.
118. Bullock, p. 157.

tendered his most inferior stock. It is small wonder, then, that the sums raised in taxes for the retirement of the outstanding bills were so frequently negligible. But the evil did not stop here. Taxes levied to meet the annual cost of government proved similarly unproductive. The colony fell into debt; and in order to pay the debt, a new issue of bills was emitted.

Another defect arose from the fact that rated commodities remained a legal tender in private transactions throughout the period. This limited the use of the bills of credit, and in limiting their use, hastened their depreciation. The matter, then, sums up to this. When the first bills were emitted there was no gold or silver in the colony to be displaced by them; nor was the barter currency supplanted by them. The result was that the bills were in a large measure superfluous, and in consequence fell in value.[119]

---

[119]. The idea can perhaps better be expressed by reference to the familiar formula: $MV = PT$, where M equals the amount of money in circulation, V its velocity, or rate of turnover, P the average of prices, and T the physical volume of transactions (the number of physical units exchanged x the number of times each is exchanged). V and T remaining constant, an increase in M may be expected to be followed by an increase in P. Or, to state the matter conversely, a fall in the value of a unit of M. Where silver and gold were in circulation in a colony at the time bills of credit were introduced, the result was usually an increased demand for goods, much of which was imported. This made the balance with England more unfavorable; exchange rose; and the merchants, who received paper in exchange for their goods, used the paper to buy gold and silver for remittance to

South Carolina was a frontier colony numbering perhaps 4,000 whites and 3,000 blacks in 1703, and 25,000 whites and 40,000 blacks in 1747.[120] Through her port of Charlestown she exported her agricultural products to England and the West Indies. Throughout the period rice was the staple, and in later years indigo became important. Hides were also a considerable item. Over the years, the balance of her trade with England was favorable.[121] Commodities apparently still passed current for money at the time of the first issue of paper in 1703, although there appear to have been some silver and

---

England. As a result of this increased demand for gold and silver, the price of the metal was bid up in terms of paper, or, conversely, paper depreciated. But as gold and silver left the country, M decreased. The result might be that soon M was little larger than it had been before the emissions of the bills of credit. Where this was the case, the bills of credit soon regained their value.

In a colony such as North Carolina, however, where there were no silver and gold to be displaced by the bills, and where the barter currency was in a large measure retained, the effect of the introduction of the bills was to increase M in proportion to the bills emitted. The result was higher prices, or conversely, a depreciated currency.

120. Greene and Harrington, American Population before 1790, pp. 172-175. The figures for her population follow:

Year	Whites	Blacks	Total
1703	4,150	3,000	7,150
1720	5,380	4,000	9,580
1724	14,000		
1747	25,000	40,000	65,000

121. Johnson, et al., pp. 120-121.

gold in the colony at that time, as well as later.[122]

The position of South Carolina on the "southern frontier" exposed her to the menace of the Spaniards in Florida and the French on the Gulf coast and on the Mississippi. Her expansion, both south and west, constantly brought her into contact with Spanish and later French Indians. As her traders, intent upon extending the sphere of their activities, penetrated the wilderness fastnesses, trade was opened with the more remote Indian tribes. After the settlement of the French in Louisiana in 1699 a keen rivalry for ascendency over the western tribes developed. Both the French and the Carolinians plied the arts of wilderness intrigue and each sought to erect a system of Indian alliances as a bulwark against the other.[123]

---

122. Even after paper began to circulate, commodities continued to be used in making debt payments. For example, an act for the relief of debtors, passed in 1720, provided: "That for all debts contracted for current money before the making of this Act, and not yet due, the debtors shall pay the same in merchantable rice, in good and merchantable casks, at forty shillings per hundred, besides ten shillings for each cask, or in merchantable pitch, in good and merchantable barrels, at eight shillings and nine pence per pound, according to the time the same shall become due, or sooner, if the debtor thinks fit so to do." Statutes at Large of South Carolina, III, 107.
Provision was made by an act of 1719, for the payment of a tax in rice. Ibid., IX, 773. "An Account of the Rise and Progress of the Paper Bills of Credit in South Carolina ...." (Hereinafter cited as "Account.") This is the report of the province to the Board of Trade in 1739. It is found in ibid., IX, 766-780.

123. See Verner W. Crane, The Southern Frontier, 1670-1732, 1928, chaps. i-iv.

An appreciation of these facts is essential to an understanding of South Carolina's currency history. Just as Massachusetts, similarly exposed to the French on the north, was the first colony to issue bills of credit when during King William's War she was forced to this expedient to meet the cost of the unsuccessful expedition against Quebec in 1690; so South Carolina was the second when during Queen Anne's War she emitted ₤4,000 in bills of credit in 1703 "to satisfy the debts" growing out of the unsuccessful expedition of that year against St. Augustine.[124] The bills bore twelve per cent interest, and taxes were levied to retire them. So great, however, were the exigencies of defense, that the funds raised by the taxes were appropriated to other uses. From then on until 1707 a succession of acts levying taxes to retire the bills was passed, but no sooner was each act passed than it was followed by another act continuing the bills and appropriating the funds to more pressing uses.[125] Whether any of the bills had been retired by 1707 is doubtful. In that year an issue of ₤8,000 in new bills was authorized.[126] These bills, which bore no interest, were to be exchanged for the old ones, and the surplus was to be paid out to the public debtors. The old bills

---

124. S. C. Statutes, II, 206-212 (#205, passed May 8, 1703). See Crane, chap. iv.
125. "Account," S. C. Statutes, IX, 766-767.
126. Ibid., II, 302-307 (#262, passed July 5, 1707).

had not been a legal tender, but had been receivable in payment of taxes. The new bills were made a legal tender in private transactions for sums up to forty shillings. Provision was made for retiring the new issue by taxes.

But the bills in circulation were destined to increase rather than diminish. The Carolina system of Indian alliances was being subjected to strain. Tribes formerly friendly were falling away. Punitive measures were resolved on, and early in 1708, bills to the amount of £3,000 were emitted to finance an expedition "for the attacking and suppressing of the deserted Savannas or their confederates."[127] This sum proved inadequate and two months later an additional £5,000 in bills were voted. Of the sum, £3,000 were for use against the "revolted Savannas," and £2,000 were printed in 20 and 40 shilling bills to be exchanged for the larger bills to earlier issues.[128] This issue brought the total amount of bills in circulation up to £14,000. Sterling exchange, which had been at 115 to 117 1/2 in 1700, had by now risen to 150.[129]

Although provision had been made to retire the new issues, the taxes levied for that purpose, as had become customary, were put to other uses, and the amount in

---

127. Ibid., 320-323 (#275, passed February 14, 1707/8).
128. Ibid., 324-327 (#277, passed April 24, 1708).
129. "Account," S. C. Statutes, IX, 780.

circulation continued at the same figure until in the year 1711 the occasion arose for two new issues. The first issue was for ₤3,000, of which ₤2,000 were used to pay the debts of the colony, and the remaining ₤1,000 were to be exchanged for old bills.[130] The second issue of ₤4,000, which became known as the "Tusquerora bills," was emitted to aid the neighbouring province of North Carolina in its war against the Tuscarora Indians.[131] As a result of the emissions of 1711, the amount of bills in circulation had risen to ₤20,000.

The fiscal situation had by this time become critical. It appeared to the legislature in 1712 that the "vast charges" of the late troubled years "were become at last so greatly burthensome and considerable, that there was no hopes or probability that the same could be discharged in any tolerable time," by the usual forms of taxation; and in consequence a novel expedient was resolved upon. The result was the first land bank in the continental colonies. There were ₤16,000 in old bills in circulation, exclusive of the Tuscarora bills. It was proposed to issue ₤52,000 in new bills. Of this sum, ₤16,000 should be used to retire the old bills; an additional ₤4,000 should be applied on the public debts;

---

130. Ibid., II, 352-354 (#297, passed March 1, 1710/11).
131. Ibid., II, 362 (Title only. Passed November 10, 1711); "Account," ibid., IX, 768-769.

and the remaining ₤32,000 should be put out on loan on landed security to individual borrowers. It is an indication of the frontier conditions that prevailed, that the annual interest charge provided was twelve per cent. The principal apparently was to be repaid in annual installments, and these sums, together with the interest payments, were to be retired from circulation.[132] The bills in circulation now rose to ₤56,000.

For three years the currency of the province remained on this footing. The bank act appears to have been efficiently administered, and perhaps ₤4,000 of the bills were retired annually.[133] In 1715, however, the long-faithful Yamasee, incited by the Creeks, fell suddenly upon the South Carolina Indian traders and the outlying plantations, and precipitated the most serious Indian war in the history of the province. The struggle lasted into the next year, when the Yamasee were forced to flee into Spanish territory. It was not until 1717, however, that an uncertain peace was restored with the Creeks.[134] The exertions of the province in breaking the great Indian conspiracy occasioned new emissions of bills of credit. The year 1715 saw the issuance of ₤30,000, to be closely followed the next year by issues

---

132. "Account," ibid., IX, 769-770. The act is in ibid., IX.
133. "Account," ibid., IX, 774.
134. Crane, chap. iv.

of Ł5,000 and Ł15,000, respectively.[135] These issues brought the number of bills in circulation at the end of 1716 up to Ł90,000, and by 1715 exchange had risen to 200.[136]

After the issues of 1716, there was another three year period in which there were no further emissions. Moreover, various taxes were levied looking forward to reducing the number of bills in circulation. One such act declared that "it is found by experience that the multiplicity of the bills of credit hath been the cause of the ruin of our trade and commerce, and hath been the great evil of this Province, and that it ought with all expedition to be remedied."[137] But as had happened so often in the past, events again intervened. Late in 1719 the people of the province threw off the government of the proprietors. These "confused times" were the occasion for two new issues, one in 1719 for Ł15,000, and another in 1720 for Ł10,000. These were the so called "rice bills" or "rice orders." To support their credit a tax in rice was levied, and the orders were redeemable in rice at the rate of 30*s.* per cwt. In the meantime

---

135. S. C. Statutes, II, 627-633 (#297, passed August 27, 1715); 634-641 (#356, passed March 24, 1715/16). The Ł15,000 Act is not in the Statutes. See "Account," ibid., IX, 773.
136. "Account," ibid., IX, 771.
137. Ibid., III, 35 (#387, tax act of December ?, 1717).

they were to pass current between man and man.[138] These issues brought the total circulation up to something slightly in excess of ₤100,000; and exchange was reported to stand at 500 in 1720.[139]

The new issues were accompanied by the usual tax acts, and attempts were made to retire some of the older bills. In 1723 it was estimated that there were ₤8,000 of the bank bills still outstanding, and ₤72,000 in other issues. It was proposed at this time to issue ₤120,000 in new bills, ₤80,000 for exchange, and ₤40,000 to be applied on the province debts. Such an act was passed in February, 1723, but with unusual celerity it was disallowed by the home authorities the following August.[140] In the meantime, however, the bills had been put in circulation. And the best that could be done was to retire ₤13,500 by 1727,[141] when further retirements were stopped, because the funds were needed to combat the old enemies of the province, the Indians, and the Spaniards at St. Augustine, to which were added on this occasion pirates off the coast.[142]

---

138. "Account," S. C. Statutes, IX, 773; ibid., III, 112-115 (#424, passed December 10, 1720). The act of 1719 is not printed.
139. "Account," ibid., IX, 780.
140. Ibid., p. 775; ibid., III, 188-193 (#472, passed February 23, 1722/23).
141. Under the provisions of "An Act for calling in and sinking the Paper Bills" (#483, passed February 15, 1723/24). S. C. Statutes, III, 219-221.
142. "Account," ibid., IX, 776.

A provisional royal governor, Francis Nicholson, had come out in 1721 and remained until 1725, when the government devolved upon the President of the Council, Arthur Middleton. Middleton headed the government until the arrival of a new royal governor in the person of Robert Johnson, who came over in 1730. During Middleton's time it appears there had been no taxes levied for the annual support of government, and as a result, debts to the amount of ₤104,775 had accumulated. When Johnson arrived, his instructions permitted him to allow the revenues accruing from former tax acts to the fund for sinking the outstanding bills of credit to be diverted for a period of seven years to the aid of "any poor Protestants that shall be desirous to settle in the Province," provided at the same time an act was passed to make secure the future payment of the quit rents. What actually took place was that in 1731 a quit rent act was passed, and ₤5,000 annually was appropriated from the sinking fund to aid the protestants, but by far the greater part of the revenues were applied toward the settlement of the debts hanging over from President Middleton's administration.[143] It should be noted, however, that in 1735 it was provided that all the money arising from the negro duty was to be applied to the aid

---

143. "Account," ibid., IX, 776-777.

of the Protestants, and a tax on slaves was levied to retire the public orders that remained outstanding.[144]

As to the bills of credit themselves, the ₤106,500 outstanding were ordered reprinted by an act passed on August 20, 1731.[145] No fund was established to retire the bills, and they were made a legal tender in all payments.[146] These bills, reprinted in 1748,[147] continued current throughout the colonial period. No additional legal tender paper currency was ever issued afterwards. It was the restraining hand of the British authorities, however, rather than any change of attitude on the part of the South Carolinians, that prevented further issues. In 1736, and again in 1746,[148] acts containing suspending clauses were passed for the emission of ₤210,000 in new bills, ₤100,000 to be exchanged for old bills, and ₤110,000 to be placed out on loan. Both of these acts, however, were disallowed by the Privy Council and never became effective.

While South Carolina was denied additional issues of legal tender bills after 1731, she evolved effective

---

144. *Ibid.*, III, 409-410 (#593, passed June 7, 1735).

145. *Ibid.*, pp. 305-307 (#534).

146. A tender of payment in these bills even though refused constituted a satisfaction of the debt. See Section iv of the act.

147. *S. C. Statutes*, III, 702-703 (#760, passed May 20, 1748).

148. *Ibid.*, pp. 423-430 (#597, passed May 29, 1736), pp. 671-677 (#738, passed June 17, 1746).

substitutes in the form of public orders, and, later, tax certificates. The only difference between the two appears to have been that the public orders had the longer currency. Both were issued in convenient denominations to the public creditors at the time taxes were laid to pay off the debts due. The orders or certificates, as the case might be, were receivable in the payment of taxes. While not a legal tender between man and man, custom nevertheless caused them to circulate much as the legal tender bills did.

While public orders had been issued earlier in the interims between various issues of bills of credit, they first came into prominence in 1731, when the sum of ₤104,775 was issued to pay the accumulated debts of President Middleton's administration.[149] These orders were declared current for the period of seven years, bore interest at the rate of five per cent, and were made receivable for payment of the negro and other duties, which were to provide funds for their redemption. Their period was afterwards extended. It appears that by the end of 1741, ₤81,844 of the orders had been sunk, and that by the end of 1749, only the remnant of ₤1,345 was still outstanding.[150]

---

149. Ibid., pp. 334-341 (#543, passed August 20, 1731).
150. Report of Committee of Conference on the Currency, 1749. South Carolina Council Journal, XVII, 766-

In 1736 in order to put the colony in a better "posture of defence," complete the fortifications at Charlestown, and aid the newly-founded colony of Georgia, then threatened by invasion, additional public orders to the amount of Ł35,000 were authorized.[151] They bore no interest, and were to be drawn in by a general tax levied annually over the next five years. The orders of 1731 had borne interest; as has just been seen, the new orders did not. There was doubtless a tendency to hold the old orders out of circulation for the sake of the interest. There was no such motive so far as the new ones were concerned. In 1730 exchange had been at 700; by 1736 it had risen to 740; and by 1739 it had moved up to from 800 to 820.[152] These figures probably give some indication of the effect of the public orders on the value of the currency.

In the year 1740 there were two further issues of orders, one for Ł25,000, and the other for Ł11,508.[153] These were grants in aid of a proposed expedition of Georgia against St. Augustine. In 1742 South Carolina again came to the aid of Georgia upon that colony's

---

770. MS, Historical Commission of South Carolina, Columbia, S. C.

151. S. C. Statutes, III, 461-464 (#619, passed March 5, 1735/36).

152. "Account," ibid., IX, 780; "Protest of Three Members of Council," May 26, 1736, in David Ramsay, History of South Carolina, 1785, II, 93.

153. S. C. Statutes, III, 546-553 (#666, passed April 5, 1740); pp. 577-579 (#676, passed September 19, 1740).

being invaded by a Spanish force, and, to finance the effort, public orders to the amount of ₤63,000 were issued.[154] The last issue of public orders during the period was in the year 1745. At that time it was felt that the fortifications of Charlestown were in need of improvement, and the sum of ₤20,000 in orders was issued for the purpose.[155]

The orders of the various issues were all with reasonable promptness drawn in by taxes, as may be seen by reference to the note below.[156] In 1749, we are told, the amount of paper currency outstanding was ₤133,045, being made up of the ₤106,500 legal tender bills reprinted in 1746, and ₤26,545 in public orders. Measured by the sterling exchange rate, the value of the currency had risen. Exchange in 1749 stood at 700 to

---

154. Ibid., pp. 595-597 (#695, passed July 11, 1742).
155. Ibid., pp. 653-656 (#729, passed May 25, 1745).
156.

South Carolina Public Orders

Year of issue	Amount of issue	Amount outstanding in 1749	Year in which redemption had been, or was to be, completed
1731	₤ 104,774	₤ 1,345	1749 or 1750
1736	35,000	-----	1742
1740	36,508	-----	1745
1742	63,000	25,200	1752
1745	20,000	Funds available for redemption	1749

Source: "Report of Committee of Conference on the Currency," 1749. S. C. Council Journal, MS, XVII, 766-770.

720, whereas in 1739 it had been at 800 to 820.[157]

The close of the period saw the fiscal affairs of the province in better order. The early frontier phase had passed. Demands for defense were no longer so great in proportion to the resources of the province. The home authorities had placed a restraining hand upon new issues of bills of credit, and the public orders, which had taken their place in financing extraordinary demands upon the government, were redeemed with reasonable dispatch. The province had, nevertheless, shown herself inclinable to increasing her paper money, especially in the case of the proposed emission of Ł110,000 to be placed out on loan, which was so ardently desired in 1736 and again in 1746. It should be remembered, however, that Ł110,000 in South Carolina money at that time was the equivalent of no more than Ł25,000 in Pennsylvania currency. Reduced to these figures, the sum does not appear so exorbitant. By the close of the period, however, the province was beginning to accumulate a stock of specie, and this fact no doubt tended to lessen the demand for a new paper issue.

The colony of Georgia did not issue bills of credit

---

157. "Report," 1749. *Ibid.*, XVII, 766-770.

before 1755. During the period under consideration, she was yet but a struggling infant. Settled in 1733, the colony could count 1,700 whites and 420 blacks by 1751.[158] The settlers received support from home, and in the early years the merchants that furnished them with supplies frequently drew bills of exchange upon the trustees in London. This did not prove satisfactory, and in 1735 the trustees resolved to send over their "sola bills."[159] These bills were in the nature of drafts upon the trustees payable in London in sterling, and were made out in the denomination of ₤1. Those that furnished supplies to the colony were paid in the bills, and before they were sent to London for collection, they frequently enjoyed a circulation. They were often at a discount, however, and do not seem to have provided a satisfactory currency.[160]

In 1735, the trustees sent over ₤1,000 in silver coins, and later some copper half-pence.[161]

By 1751 bills of credit had been in use in all the colonies save Virginia and Georgia for periods varying from eighteen to sixty-one years. During the time much

---

158. Greene and Harrington, American Population before 1790, p. 181.

159. William E. Heath, "The Early Colonial Money System of Georgia," Georgia Historical Quarterly, XIX (1935), pp. 150-151.

160. Ibid., passim.

161. Ibid., pp. 151, 155.

knowledge had been gained from experience, even if at times it had been dearly bought. Practically everywhere fiscal methods had improved.

The situation in South Carolina was in some respects similar to that in New England outside of Massachusetts. Her currency was greatly depreciated. And while the act of Parliament did not affect her, the royal instructions effectively prevented her from issuing further legal tender bills. Thenceforward, she had to resort to public orders and to tax certificates, which, although they passed current, were not a legal tender. There was one difference, however, between South Carolina and New England. Her issue of ₺106,500 in legal tender bills, outstanding since 1731, was never called in.

North Carolina still hankered for a paper currency and her future course was to be a troubled one.

The five Middle colonies, New York, New Jersey, Pennsylvania, Delaware, and Maryland, had all been more moderate and more successful in their use of bills of credit, and had come to look upon paper currency as a useful and necessary adjunct to their development and prosperity.

CHAPTER IV

EARLY ATTEMPTS AT IMPERIAL CONTROL OF COLONIAL CURRENCY: COIN

> The liberty taken in many of your Majesty's Plantations, to alter the rates of their coins as often as they think fit, does encourage an indirect practice of drawing the money from one Plantation to another, to the undermining of each other's trade; which cannot be otherwise remedied than by reducing of all foreign coins to the same rate in all your Majesty's Dominions in America.
>
> -- Representation of the Board of Trade to the Privy Council, 1703.

BY THE BEGINNING of the eighteenth century the efforts of several of the American colonies to attract coin away from their neighbors by passing acts enhancing its value had reached such proportions that the practice became the subject of imperial regulation of a general nature.[1] South Carolina[2] and Pennsylvania particularly had been complained of. It was the legislation of the latter colony, however, and the complaints that it aroused that brought the matter to a head. In March,

---

1. See the early pages of Curtis P. Nettels, *The Money Supply of the American Colonies before 1720*, 1934, chap. ix, for an account of the various colonial acts raising the value of coin before 1700. See also *supra*, Table I, p. 8, for the values of coin in the several colonies at this time.

2. William Popple to Mr. Thornburgh, Whitehall, July 22, 1701, *Calendar of State Papers, America and West Indies, 1701*, #660; Mr. Blathwayt to Mr. Popple, August 22, 1701, *ibid.*, #775.

1700, Robert Quary, judge of the vice-admiralty court and surveyor of the customs for Pennsylvania and New Jersey, wrote home from Philadelphia, urging that the devaluation of coin in that province had been prejudicial to the king's revenue. He reported that until about 1698 a piece of eight had passed in Pennsylvania for 6s., but that at that time it had been raised to 7s. 8d. Under the old valuation the merchants when paying duties had allowed twenty-five per cent toward making up the difference between the Pennsylvania currency and sterling. Under the raised valuation the merchants continued to pay but twenty-five per cent additional, so that the revenue was the loser.[3]

The attempt of Pennsylvania to raise the value of coin had repercussions in the neighboring colony of Maryland. On May 25, 1701, the governor of that colony, Nathaniel Blakiston, wrote home to the Board of Trade "that the last Assembly were ... very pressing for advancing the coyne" of the colony because, since it was valued below that of Virginia, Pennsylvania, and New York, it was being carried away to those places. The governor stated that he had informed the Assembly that he "could not meddle with the Coyne of the Province" until he had received permission from home, and that that

---

3. Robert Quary to the Commissioners of Customs, Philadelphia, March 6, 1700. *Ibid.,* 1700, #190, p. 109.

body had in turn requested him to acquaint the home authorities of the difficulties the province lay under and to ask permission to raise the value of their coins so that they might "be upon an equal foot at least with some of their neighbors."[4]

As a result of Governor Blakiston's letter, the Board of Trade entered upon an examination of the situation with respect to the value of coin in the colonies generally and considered the possibility of reducing them to a uniform footing by royal proclamation. The logical thing, perhaps, would have been to reduce the colonial values to parity with sterling. It appears that the Board of Trade considered valuation at this figure, even though it would have raised serious problems of deflation. It was, however, the legal rather than the economic aspects of the matter that caused them to decide upon a higher figure. In 1697 Massachusetts had rated the piece of eight, Mexico, Seville, and pillar, "of full seventeen penny weight" at six shillings, and the law, a perpetual one, had been confirmed by the crown.[5] The attorney general, Edward Northey, gave it as his opinion that since the law had received

---

4. Blakiston to Board of Trade, Maryland, May 25, 1701. Ibid., 1701, #477, p. 261.
5. Acts and Resolves of Massachusetts Bay, I, Laws of 1697, c. xvi, p. 296. Passed and published October 31, 1697.

the royal approbation it could not be altered by royal proclamation.[6] In consequence, unless Massachusetts could be prevailed upon to repeal the law -- and of this there was slight prospect -- the only course open was to adopt the valuation of the Massachusetts act.[7] Preliminary, however, to representing the necessity of a royal proclamation, the Board cleared the way by recommending the disallowance of an act passed in Pennsylvania, November 27, 1700, which rated the piece of eight of fifteen pennyweight at seven shillings, and allowed an advance of four pence for every pennyweight additional. This brought the value of the seventeen and one-half pennyweight piece up to seven shillings ten pence. The recommendation of the Board was complied with, and the act disallowed on July 30, 1703.[8] The way was now clear

---

6. Cal. State Papers, 1702-1703, #765, Attorney General to the Board of Trade, May 31, 1703.

7. The Massachusetts act valued the piece of eight of 17 dwt. at 6s. The proclamation, upon a report from the mint, valued the piece of eight of 17 1/2 dwt. at 6s. It appears that there was no intention in any way to nullify the Massachusetts act by the proclamation. Rather, the report from the mint indicated that the piece of eight, Seville, Mexico, or pillar, weighed 17 1/2 dwt., and this weight was adopted. See Representation of Board of Trade to Queen, November 23, 1703. Cal. State Papers, 1702-1703, #1299.
Nettels, p. 243, n. 25, discusses the conflict between the proclamation and the Massachusetts statute.

8. Cal. State Papers, 1702-1703, #866, #892; Penna. Statutes, II, c. lxxii, pp. 87-88; Acts of the Privy Council, Colonial, II, #905.
The attorney general gave his opinion "that H. M. may by her royall proclamation make foreign coynes currant money at such rates as she shall think fitt in any

for the proclamation. On November 23, the Board represented that the "liberty taken in many of your Majesty's Plantations, to alter the rates of their coins as often as they think fit, does encourage an indirect practice of drawing the money from one Plantation to another, to the undermining of each other's trade; which cannot be otherwise remedied than by reducing of all foreign coins to the same rate in all your Majesty's Dominions in America." To this end the Board proposed that pieces of eight of seventeen and one-half pennyweight be rated at six shillings, and other coins in proportion.[9] The Privy Council, viewing the representation favorably, referred it to the officers of the mint. Assays were made by the distinguished mathematician and philosopher, Isaac Newton, who was the master-worker of the mint, and a table of values was drawn up, which in due course was embodied in the proclamation of June 18, 1704.[10]

The values set out in the proclamation were to be

---

of her Plantations in America as well under Proprieties as under H. M. immediate Government, so far as doth not contradict any Law confirmed by the Crown..." Attorney General Edward Northey to Board of Trade, July 2, 1703. Cal. State Papers, 1702-1703, #866.

9. Cal. State Papers, 1702-1703, #1299.
10. Acts of the Privy Council, Colonial, II, #911; Cal. State Papers, 1704-1705, #310, #405; Board of Trade Journal, 1704-1708, pp. 1, 15, 16, 25-26. The proclamation is in "British Royal Proclamations relating to America, 1603-1783" (Clarence S. Brigham, ed.), in Transactions and Collections of the American Antiquarian Society, XII, 161-163.

The table of values follows:

effective January 1, 1705 "for the Discharge of any Contracts or Bargains to be made after" that date; and thenceforth to pass coins at any higher rate was to incur the royal displeasure. Four hundred copies of the proclamation were printed, and circular letters "to all her Majesty's Governours and proprietors in America" enclosing copies of the proclamation were sent off.[11] The proclamation was duly published in the colonies. Soon, however, the letters from the colonial governors report-

Piece	Weight		Value of Piece in Sterling		Highest Rate at which Piece is to pass in Plantations	
	dwt.	gr.	s.	d.	s.	d.
Sevill Pieces of Eight Old Plate	17	12	4	6	6	
Sevill Pieces of Eight New Plate	14		3	7 1/4	4	9 1/2
Mexico Pieces of Eight	17	12	4	6	6	
Pillar Pieces of Eight	17	12	4	6 3/4	6	
Peru Pieces of Eight	17	12	4	5	5	10 1/2
Cross Dollars	18		4	4 3/4	5	10 1/4
Ducatoons of Flanders	20	21	5	6	7	4
Ecu's of France or Silver Lewis	17	12	4	6	6	
Crusados of Portugal	11	4	2	10	3	9 1/4
Three Gilder Pieces of Holland	20	7	5	2 1/4	6	11
Old Rix Dollars of the Empire	18	10	4	6	6	

All Halves, Quarters and Lesser Pieces are to Pass in Proportion to the above Rates.
Acts and Resolves of Massachusetts Bay, VIII, 472.

11. Board of Trade Journal, 1704-1708/9, pp. 26, 27; Cal. State Papers, 1704-1705, #411, #424.

ing the reception it had received began to reveal the confused state of the colonial currency and the difficulties of bringing order out of chaos.

From Virginia, where the piece of eight had passed at five shillings, Governor Francis Nicholson reported that no alterations in the value of coin had been made, and that money still passed as it had been accustomed to. Moreover, he continued, it would be difficult to require the various coins to be passed by weight because there were "no Towns nor Goldsmiths in the Country where people might know the several species and have them weighed." The general supposition in Virginia, he reported, was that the proclamation "did not oblige people to take pieces of eight at 6s., but only that they [should] not exceed that rate" and was "chiefly designed agt. the Northern Provinces where they raise their money to what value they please." Since any raising of the rate at which coin passed in Virginia would be prejudicial to the royal revenue, Nicholson counselled that it would "be most for H. M. interests and service to take no further notice" of the matter.[12]

In Pennsylvania, whose conduct had been the immediate cause of the proclamation, Lieutenant Governor John Evans reported that, although the proclamation had

---

12. Governor Nicholson to Board of Trade, Virginia, Mar. 3, 1705. Cal. State Papers, 1704-1705, #924.

been published "with all due solemnity in Philadelphia and the other principall parts of [the] Government," it had not been effective in lowering the value of coin. So great was the scarcity of money, and so great would be the inconvenience of paying former debts in an appreciated currency, that the people of the colony "resolved by general Compact to receive all fformer dues in coine under the same denomination off value that it passed ffor [at] the time of the contract ... , and for new Bargains they [were] perticular in their agreement" as to the value at which coin should be received. With respect to the future, the Pennsylvanians showed an inclination to wait until New York's course of action became known.[13]

In New York the proclamation was published by the governor, Lord Cornbury, on February 5, 1705. The effect upon trade was paralyzing.[14] While the legal rate in Massachusetts was six shillings for the piece of eight of seventeen pennyweight, the current practice was to receive a piece of eight of only fifteen pennyweight at six shillings. It was the custom to clip all heavier pieces to this weight.[15] The merchants at Boston had

---

13. Lieutenant Governor Evans to Board of Trade, Philadelphia, February 13, 1705. Ibid., #864.
14. Lord Cornbury to Board of Trade, New York, February 19, 1705. N. Y. Col. Doc., IV, 1131.
15. Cornbury to Board of Trade, February 19, 1705. Ibid., 1131-1133; "Petition of the Merchants of the City

prepared to take advantage of New York's enforcing of the proclamation, and had let it be known that they would receive money at the old rate of six shillings for fifteen pennyweight pieces, and in some cases had even offered a premium. The result was that on the day the proclamation was published in New York, the postboy set out for Boston with as much money as he could carry, "and for four or five days all manner of Trade was stopped; [and] there was no Market, nor ... could [one] buy anything with ready money."[16] Indeed, so disastrous were the effects of the proclamation upon the trade of New York that sixty-eight merchants of the colony petitioned the governor to suspend the proclamation. The governor, upon taking the advice of the council, acceded to their request, and wrote a long letter home explaining his action and laying the plight of the colony before the Board of Trade. In the meantime, by direction of the governor, silver continued to be accepted in payment of "all ... Branches of the Revenue at the rates it formerly went," eight shillings the ounce of silver.[17]

The Board of Trade seemed convinced of the neces-

---

of New-York relating to Foreign Coin," February 19, 1705, ibid., 1133-1135; Joseph Dudley to Board of Trade, Boston, July 25, 1705, Cal. State Papers, 1704-1705, #1274.

16. Cornbury to Board of Trade, February 19, 1705. N. Y. Col. Doc., IV, 1131. See also Merchants' Petition, February 19, 1705. Ibid., 1135.

17. See note 16.

sity of Lord Cornbury's action in suspending the proclamation in New York, finding the governor "obliged thereunto by the necessity of the affairs and trade of [the] Colony, occasioned by the refractory humours and disobedient proceedings of the people of New England and [the] other Proprieties."[18]

The fate of the proclamation in Massachusetts has in a measure already been indicated. Governor Joseph Dudley, after publishing the proclamation, tried to get the legislature to pass a law to make it effective by placing a penalty on the offering of "clipt ... or other light money by tale." The legislature, however, balked at the mention of penalties, and even proposed to make the annual tax payable at the rate of eight shillings the ounce of silver, which was equivalent to rating a piece of eight of fifteen pennyweight at six shillings. The governor, in his turn, refused to assent to such an increase in the value of silver, and finally the old legal rate of six shillings for a piece of eight of seventeen pennyweight (equivalent to approximately seven shillings the ounce) was adhered to.[19] The governor's victory, however, was short-lived, for the next year (1706) the courts began to rate silver at eight shil-

---

18. Board of Trade to Lord Cornbury, July 18, 1705. N. Y. Col. Doc., IV, 1156-1157.
19. Governor Dudley to Board of Trade, Boston, July 25, 1705. Cal. State Papers, 1704-1705, #1279.

lings the ounce, which was the value at which the merchants were then accepting it for several years past.[20]

As the reports from the colonies accumulated, the Board of Trade realized that the purpose of the proclamation, the reducing of foreign coin to the same rate in all the colonies, was as far from realization as ever. The chief difficulty seemed to grow out of the willingness of individuals, particularly the merchants of New England, to accept silver at a higher rate than that provided in the proclamation. The Board, upon receipt of the letters from the governors of Pennsylvania, Virginia, and New York, wrote to the attorney general on July 4, 1705, seeking his opinion as to what might be done in the exercise of the prerogative "to enforce an exact obedience to [the] Proclamation ... in the charter Governments, or how ... the said Governments [might be obliged] to a due compliance..."[21] The attorney general did not reply immediately. The following October the agents for Barbados complained to the Board that the faithful observance of the proclamation in that island, while the other colonies maintained their higher rates, had been "to the unspeakable prejudice of Barbados" and

---

20. Nettels, Money Supply, p. 243, n. 25; p. 246.
21. W. Popple, jr., to Mr. Attorney-General, July 4, 1705. Cal. State Papers, 1704-1705, #1217. See also Board of Trade Journal, 1704-1708/9, pp. 150-151. (July 3 and 4, 1705.)

had "almost drained [the island of its] coin."[22] The
Board immediately renewed its request of the preceding
July to the attorney general concerning means of enforcing the royal proclamation. This time that official replied forthwith, and his opinion made evident the difficulties involved in attempting to enforce a uniform value for coins by royal proclamation. He gave it as his judgment that the proclamation "well established" the value of foreign coins in the colonies, and that they were made a legal tender at the rates therein set out. No one was obliged to take them at a higher rate, but if he did so voluntarily, it was no offence. If, however, the charter or proprietary governments made laws to give coins a currency at rates higher than those permitted by the proclamation, the attorney general was of the opinion that they were "guilty of a high misdemeanour, and [that] their Charters, or at least the power of making Laws, [might] be seized into His Majesty's hands by Quo Warranto" proceedings. "But," he continued, "the acts of particular persons ... will not prejudice the Charters or Corporations." The only way to make the proclamation effective, he concluded, was to secure the passage of an act of Parliament that would lay a penalty upon all persons that received coin at values other than

---

22. Agents of Barbados to Board of Trade, October 17, 1705. Cal. State Papers, 1704-1705, #1376.

those directed by the proclamation.[23]

Upon the receipt of the attorney general's opinion, the Board continued its inquiry into conditions in Barbados. The agents for the island and several merchants trading there were summoned, and, attending, gave it as their opinion that it was not the enforcing of the proclamation rates that had drained the island of its specie, but rather the fact that the balance of trade had lately turned against Barbados. It was their desire that, rather than relax the proclamation in Barbados, "her Majesty's letters might be writ to inforce the execution [of the proclamation] in all the Plantations."[24]

The Board apparently thought it well to broaden the inquiry and requested "some of the merchants trading to New Yorke, Virginia, Maryland, Pennsylvania, Jamaica, and the Leeward Islands" to attend.[25] Among those that attended were agents as well as merchants, and, in some

---

23. Board of Trade Journal, 1704-1708/9, pp. 170-171 (October 17, 1705). Attorney General to Board of Trade, October 19, 1705. Cal. State Papers, 1704-1705, #1382.

24. Board of Trade Journal, 1704-1708/9, October 24, 25, and 30, 1705.
Sir John Stanley, William Bridges, Colonel William Cleland, and Milishu Holder, agents for Barbados, attended.

25. Ibid., October 31 and November 6, 1705.
Colonel Blakiston, former governor of Maryland, and Mr. John Hyde, a merchant trading to Virginia, attended on behalf of Virginia and Maryland; Colonel Charles Lodwick and Mr. Congreve on behalf of New York; Mr. Johnson on behalf of Carolina; and Colonel Robert Quary, lately returned from Pennsylvania, was also in attendance.

cases at least, the two capacities were combined in one person. Upon being "acquainted with the difficulties some of the Plantations laboured under in relation to" the proclamation, "all agreed that it would be of ill consequence that the proclamation should be left in force in some of the Plantations and not in others, and were therefore of opinion that all the Plantations should [either] be bound or loose...."[26]

After hearing the opinion of the group, the Board "resolved to take [the] matter into further consideration" -- which it next did eighteen months later.[27] This delay is curious in view of the fact that during the period before the question again came up for determination, letters from the colonial governors indicated that the proclamation was as far from being complied with as ever, despite the adjuration of the Board to the governors to continue in their endeavors to have it accepted by the people.[28] During the period of delay the situation seems to have been most critical in Barbados. Whether because of the proclamation or because the balance of trade had turned against it, the island ap-

---

26. Ibid., November 6, 1705.
27. Ibid., May 16, 1707.
28. Dudley to Board of Trade, Boston, July 25, 1705, Cal. State Papers, 1704-1705, #1274; Evans to Board of Trade, Philadelphia, November 9, 1705, ibid., 1706-1708, #40; Board of Trade to Dudley, February 4, 1706, ibid., #85; Cornbury to Board of Trade, New York, August 10, 1706, ibid., #463.

pears to have been drained of its silver. To supply the resulting deficiency of currency, the Barbados assembly had erected what was probably the first colonial land bank. Although the Board of Trade moved the disallowance of the act as soon as it was received, and in so doing observed that "the proper method for supplying the deficiency of cash, is to promote the increase of it by incouraging a quicker importation of silver ...," it did nothing at the time to aid Barbados to achieve the desired end, either by relaxing the proclamation as to her, or providing for its effective enforcement elsewhere.[29] It was not until May 16, 1707, that the Board "took into consideration the several papers in the office relating to the coin in the plantations" and ordered a representation drawn thereon. On June 10, the representation was transmitted to the Queen. After citing the conditions that obtained in New York, New England, and Barbados, the Board represented "that an Act of Parliament be passed here, for the better enforcing your Majesty's said proclamation in the several Plantations, under such penalties as shal be thought reasonable and necessary ...; [and] that the ... Propriety and Charter Governments may

---

29. Board of Trade Journal, 1704-1708/9, September 17, 20, October 3, 8, 10, 15, 16, 17, 22, 25, 28, 30, 31, November 1; Cal. State Papers, 1706-1708, #529, #540, #542, #546 (Order of Disallowance, October 21, 1706); Acts of the Privy Council, Colonial, II, #1007.

be brought under the same dependence on your Majesty as those other Plantations now under your more immediate Government." "Till one or both of those provisions are made," the Board concluded, "we cannot but think that the putting your Majesty's ... proclamation in execution in some of the Plantations, whilst others (particularly the Propriety and Charter Governments) pay no regard thereto, may endanger their being entirely drain'd of the money necessary to carry on their trade."[30] Nearly six months passed without action by the Privy Council, and on October 24, the Board, in connection with the depressed condition of Barbados, where the assembly, it was reported, ardently desired an act to raise the value of coin, again urged an act of Parliament to enforce the proclamation.[31] In January 1708, the Privy Council referred the matter to the attorney and to the solicitor general; but before their opinions were received, a select committee of the House of Lords, presided over by Lord Halifax, intervened on January 10 with an order to the Board of Trade "to prepare a draught of an Act of Parliament for establishing the rate and value of the fforeign Coyns in the Plantations."[32] The Board im-

---

30. Board of Trade Journal, 1704-1708/9, May 16, June 6, 10, 1707.
31. Ibid., October 24, 1707; Cal. State Papers, 1706-1708, #1157, Board of Trade to Earl of Sunderland, October 24, 1707.
32. Board of Trade Journal, 1704-1708/9, January 12, 1707/8.

mediately prepared a draft on the lines suggested in the attorney general's letter of October 17, 1705.[33] When the Lord's committee received the draft, it called in "some of the merchants" trading to the various colonies. The merchants imparted considerable misinformation by stating that "all the plantations except the proprietors have complied with the Proclamation," and differed among themselves "concerning the rates they would have money go at ...."[34] They made certain suggestions, some submitted later in writing, which seem to have been incorporated in the bill.[35] Lord Halifax reported the bill to the House on February 27; on March 6 it was sent to the Commons and was assented to by that body with slight amendments on March 27; and the bill received the royal assent on April 1, 1708.[36]

The act[37] recited the proclamation at length and provided "that if any person within any of the ... colonies or plantations, as well those under proprietors and charters, as under her Majesty's immediate commission and government, shall after [May 1, 1709], for the dis-

---

33. Board of Trade Journal, 1704-1708/9, January 12, 13, 15, 19, 1708.
34. Manuscript of the House of Lords, VII (new series), 230.
35. Ibid., 230, 333-334.
36. Leo F. Stock, Proceedings and Debates of the British Parliaments respecting North America, III, 170-198, passim.
37. Danby Pickering, Statutes at Large, 6 Ann c. 30.

charge of any contracts or bargains to be thereafter made account, receive, take, or pay any of the several species of foreign silver coins mentioned in the before recited proclamation, at any greater or higher rate than at which the same is thereby regulated, settled, and allowed ..., every such person ... shall suffer six months imprisonment ...; any law, custom, or usage in any of the said colonies or plantations to the contrary hereof in any wise notwithstanding; and shall likewise forfeit the sum of ten pounds for every such offence; one moity thereof to her Majesty...; the other moity to such person or persons as shall sue for the same, to be recovered with full costs of suit, by action of debt, bill, plaint, or information, in any of her Majesty's courts of justice within any of the said plantations, or in any of the courts of justice in the charter or proprietary governments where such offence shall be committed."[38]

While the foregoing provision emphatically prohibited the passing of foreign silver at higher than the proclamation rates, a further section of the act, in order to provide expressly for colonies such as Virginia and Maryland, where silver passed at rates below those of the proclamation, provided that no person should be

---

38. It may be well to call attention to the fact that only foreign silver was affected by the proclamation and the act. The silver coin of Great Britain and all gold coins fell outside the scope of both instruments.

compelled to receive silver at proclamation rates.

The act further provided that in the future the rates at which foreign silver should pass might be altered by royal proclamation, or that colonial laws ascertaining such rates might be assented to, as might have been possible in the absence of the act.

When all the provisions of the act are taken into account, it would appear that all colonial laws placing values on foreign silver in excess of the proclamation rates that were in existence at the time of the passage of the parliamentary act were presumably nullified; but that if in the future a colonial governor should brave the royal displeasure and assent to an act fixing rates higher than those of the proclamation, the law, unless disallowed, would stand regardless of the parliamentary enactment.

On May 14, 1708, a circular letter was sent to all the colonial governors, enclosing a copy of the act and enjoining them that they take care that the act "be duly complyed with."[39] The act, however, seems to have been little more effectual in bringing uniformity into the currency of the colonies than had been the proclamation four years before.

Governor Dudley duly published the act in both his

---

39. Board of Trade Journal, 1704-1708/9, May 10, 14. 1708; Cal. State Papers, 1706-1708, #1477.

governments of Massachusetts and New Hampshire and wrote to the Board of Trade that there should "be nothing wanting on [his part] to Make H. M. subjects [sensible] of the ffavor done them" by the act, and of "the injury the Plantations have done themselves in raising the value of pieces of eight ...."[40] But Dudley's efforts to convince the people of the unwisdom of the practice were unavailing. Coin continued to pass in private transactions in Massachusetts and apparently also in New Hampshire at the old rate of eight shillings the ounce.[41] After the publishing of the act in 1708, however, the courts in giving judgments rated the piece of eight of 17 1/2 dwt. at 6s. and the treasury paid and received coin at that rate. This was the practice in both of the colonies under Dudley's jurisdiction at least as late as November, 1710.[42] But by this time inflation had taken a dif-

---

40. Dudley to B. T., Boston, March 1, 1709. Cal. State Papers, 1708-1709, #391.
41. Lt. Gov. John Usher of N. H. to B. T., July, 1709; ibid., 1708-1709, #663; same to same, Boston, February 8, 1710, ibid., 1710-1711, #113; Wart Winthrop to Samuel Reade, Boston, March 5, 1708, Mass. Hist. Soc., Collections (sixth series), V, 164-166.
42. Dudley to B. T., Boston, November 15, 1710. Cal. State Papers, 1710-1711, #491. The state of the enforcement of the act enforcing the proclamation led to a three-cornered correspondence between John Usher, who served as lieutenant governor for New Hampshire under Joseph Dudley, who was governor of both Massachusetts and New Hampshire, the Board of Trade, and Dudley. Usher intimated to the Board of Trade that silver still passed at the rate of 6s. for a 15 dwt. piece of eight in the two colonies. He admits the courts give judgment for a 17 1/2 dwt. piece, but such is the quality of his

ferent turn. So industriously had the silver of the province been gathered up and shipped to England during the last seven years, that little was to be had, and, as Dudley writes, "our Province chequer notes [Massachusetts bills of credit] are of that currency and honour, that wee buy all merchandize goods, ships, houses, estates of land, or whatever els with those bills preferable to money ...."[43] In 1712, "the bills by common consent and agreement" having "obtained a universal currency throughout the province in all private trade and dealings betwixt merchants and others," the assembly made them a legal tender.[44] From this time forward, silver became in the nature of a commodity whose value was determined jointly by its amount, by the amount of bills of credit in circulation, and by the demand for it to

---

literacy that one now, even as the Board of Trade then, has trouble in making out exactly what he means. The Board took Dudley to task for his failure to enforce the act. Dudley replied defending himself at some length. The Board expressed itself as satisfied with what he had to say. Usher to B. T., New Hampshire, July, 1709, ibid., 1708-09, #663; B. T. to Dudley, January 16, 1710, ibid., 1710-11, #34; B. T. to Usher, same date, ibid., #35; Usher to B. T., Boston, February 8, 1710, ibid., #113; same to same, Boston, July 3, 1710, ibid., #283; Dudley to B. T., Boston, November 15, 1710, ibid., #491; Dudley to Mr. Popple, same date, ibid., #492; B. T. to Dudley, January 29, 1711.

43. Dudley to B. T., November 15, 1710, Cal. State Papers, 1710-11, #491.

44. Acts and Resolves of Mass. Bay, I, 700-701 (Province Laws, 1712-13, c. 6; passed November 8, 1712). See also "Diary of Samuel Sewall," November 12, 1712. Mass. Hist. Soc., Collections (fifth series), II, 365-366.

pay balances abroad. The act of Parliament was never effective in preventing silver coin in Massachusetts and New Hampshire from passing in private transactions at rates higher than those established by the proclamation, and after bills of credit were made legal tender it had no effect in protecting long-term creditors against a depreciating currency.

The parliamentary act of 1708 probably had no effect whatsoever in Connecticut. In 1709 that colony began to issue bills of credit.[45] In May of the next year the assembly enacted that the taxes to retire the bills should "be paid either in bullion at the rate of eight shillings the ounce, troy, or in ... bills of publick credit ..., and in no other manner."[46] This act adopted the rate at which silver had for some time passed in the colony; but within four months it was amended and silver was made receivable in the treasury "as it shall generally pass in New England at the time of payment."[47] Whatever may have been the immediate effect of this amendment, the inclusion of a similar clause in future tax acts had the effect of placing higher and higher rates on coin as bills of credit in New England depreciated.[48]

---

45. *Public Records of the Colony of Connecticut,* 1706-1716, pp. 111-112.
46. *Ibid.,* p. 157.
47. *Ibid.,* p. 166.
48. *Ibid.,* passim. See Figure III, p. 29 above for the depreciation of silver in New England.

The reaction of Rhode Island to the legislation of Parliament was characteristic. Governor Samuel Cranston informed the Board of Trade that with the "approbation and advice" of the council he had caused the act of Parliament to be published, and protested that they would "not be wanting to see [it] duly Complyed with." Nevertheless, he appears to have taken away with his left hand what he gave with his right, for he continued: "Notwithstanding that, as we are linkt to the Province of Massachusetts (perticularly to the Towne of Boston) as to our traffick and dealing together, we cannot, without great inconveniency and prejudice differ from them in the valuation and rates of foreign coine. Therefore, if we should suspend that matter about the Coine, till we can see or understand what meth[ods] they will take in that Province, I hope H. M. and your Lordsh[ips will pardon] us. I do not give your Lordships this intimation by any order from [the colony], but as my owne sentiment."[49] It was not until a year had elapsed that the Board of Trade replied to Governor Cranston's letter and advised him on no "account to delay the execution ... of the law, but pay an exact and punctual obedience thereto."[50] The answer of the colony to this admonition of

---

49. Cranston to B. T., Newport, December 5, 1708. Cal. State Papers, 1708-09, #229.
50. B. T. to Cranston, January 16, 1710. Ibid., 1710-11, #39.

the Board of Trade may be found in the act of assembly of July 30, 1710, authorizing the issuance of the colony's first bills of credit. The act provided that each bill should "be in equal value to current silver money of New England."[51] In other words silver was to pass in Rhode Island at the value trade placed upon it, enactments of Parliament and admonitions of the Board of Trade to the contrary notwithstanding.

The parliamentary act had saved to the crown the power of assenting to colonial laws establishing the rates at which silver should pass within their borders. It was not intended, however, that this privilege should be used to defeat the main objective of the legislation, the establishing of a uniform rate at which foreign silver coin should pass in all the colonies. Nevertheless, no sooner had a copy of the act been received in New York than that colony attempted to crawl through the loophole and passed an act rating silver at eight shillings the ounce.[52] Lord Cornbury, just before he was superseded as governor, joined with the assembly and council in representing to the queen the necessity of the act. The chief fear seemed to be the ruinous effect the act was expected to have upon the colony's West

---

51. Records of the Colony of Rhode Island, IV, 96.
52. Colonial Laws of New York, I, 620-621 (c. 173; passed October 6, 1708).

154

Indian trade. All the colony's heavy money (unclipped pieces of eight), which furnished the "chief returns" to England, came from that source. The petitioners were of the opinion that, "if the money must pass here at the same rate it does at Jamaica and other Islands of the West Indies, ... it will not be worth the merchants' while to bring money, but [they] will rather bring the produce of those Islands in return for the produce of these parts, which they carry thither, and so leave this Province without money, for want whereof the merchants here will not be able to make such returns to Great Britain as they used to doe, and consequently this Province will not be able to take off by a great deal, so much of the manufactures of that your Majesty's Kingdom as it has hitherto done, to the great damage of this Province as well as the manufactures of Great Britain." The petition concluded by pointing out that the "rates contained in [the] Act [were] the same which ... money now goes at in the Provinces of Connecticut, Massachusetts Bay, New Hampshire, Rhode Island, and New Jersey, and has gone at the same rate in this Province upwards of 20 years past."[53]

The petition indicates the difficulty of establish-

---

53. Address of the Governor, Council and Assembly of New York to the Queen (October 18, 1708). Cal. State Papers, 1708-09, #157, i. See also Cornbury to B. T., same date, ibid., #157.

ing the value of coin in the colonies at rates that involved deflation over wide areas. Nevertheless, the Board of Trade was not impressed with New York's statement of the case and immediately recommended the disallowance of the act. The Board represented that "the intent of the [Act of Parliament of 1708] was that there should be but one and the same value of the species of foreign coins throughout all [her] Majesty's Plantations in America" and "that, should the New York Act be continued ..., it may reasonably be presumed the other Plantations will also pass laws of the like nature, and thereby raise the value of such coins as they shall think most to their particular advantage; which method," the Board concluded, "would entirely defeat the intent" of the parliamentary act.[54] The New York act was disallowed by the Privy Council on March 3, 1709.[55]

---

54. Representation of the Board of Trade to the Queen, February 22, 1709. *Ibid.*, #375; also in N. Y. Col. Doc., V, 67-68.
The representation further criticizes New York's position: "When your Majesty's royal proclamation for settling the rates of foreign coins was sent over to New York in 1704, the complaints then made by that Government were, that if the said Proclamation was duly put in execution at New York, that Province would suffer very much thereby, for that the neighboring Provinces of the Massachusetts Bay or Pennsylvania did not pay any obedience thereunto; and therefore the Lord Cornbury suspended the execution of the said Proclamation within his Government, but they did not then make any objection to the rates at which your Majesty was pleased to order the said coins to pass."

55. Cal. State Papers, 1708-09, #399.

Before news of the disallowance had reached New York, the government had changed, and the lieutenant governor, Richard Ingoldesby, had published the act of Parliament. He was, however, forced to write that the people paid no obedience to it and that the assembly took upon itself "thus far to make the Act of no significance that [it] will pass no Bill for money, but to be paid at the value it was before the Act took place."[56] When news of the disallowance of the New York act valuing silver at eight shillings the ounce reached the colony, the assembly resolved to accomplish by indirection what it had failed to accomplish by direct legislation, and promptly repealed its legislation forbidding the clipping of standard pieces of eight. "If they were to pass at 6$\underline{s}$. each, part of the silver might be cut from the heavy coins so that the 8$\underline{s}$. an ounce rate could be more easily maintained."[57]

Besides this conniving at the clipping of coin, the

---

56. Ingoldesby to B. T., New York, July 5, 1709. Ibid., #621. Ingoldesby writes further: "Mr. Cockerill, who pays the forces here, has paid them according to [the] Act [of Parliament] ever since May 1st [1709], and the Publick Officers conform to it, but nobody elce does that I hear of. I pray your Lordships' directions herein, whether I shall cause the Attorney General to preferr [an] information or indictment against one or two persons, and trye if that will bring the people to the necessary obedience, or what other measures I shall take." Ingoldesby, however, was removed and in consequence never had an opportunity to receive an answer to his inquiry.

57. Nettels, p. 246, n. 34; Colonial Laws of New York, I, 714 ($\underline{c}$. 217; passed October 30, 1710).

colony found another means of evading the act of Parliament. The debts of the colony were paid and taxes levied, not in pounds but in ounces of plate[58] or in "Lyon dollars," which were omitted from the list of coins included in the proclamation. The various sums due the creditors of the colony were converted into plate at the rate of eight shillings the ounce; and the particular number of ounces due each was stated in the appropriation act. This practice precluded the governor's paying out the plate at the proclamation rate of 6*s.* 10 1/2*d.* the ounce. The governor and council resisted the efforts of the assembly to circumvent the act of Parliament, but they were finally borne down.[59]

At this time (1709) New York began to issue bills of credit. These were also made the instrument for evading the parliamentary regulation. After a while they came to be issued "for the same Value, and equal to the current Coin passing in [the] Colony," and were made a tender in public payments and between man and man.[60] The issuing of bills of credit to pass at the rate of current coin, either together with or without the device of paying the colony's debts and levying taxes in ounces

---

58. Silver bullion or, in this case, pieces of eight taken by weight.
59. Nettels, p. 46, n. 34 and the references there cited.
60. Colonial Laws of New York, I, 815-826 (*c.* 280; passed September 14, 1714).

of plate rather than in monetary units, furnished the means of evading the parliamentary legislation throughout the years.[61]

"The resistance of New Jersey paralleled that of New York. An act of 1709 granted taxes in standard pieces of eight valued at 8s. an ounce. The Assembly, wrote [Lieutenant Governor] Ingoldesby, 'will pass no bill for money but to be paid in at the value it was before the ... Act [of Parliament] took place. In 1711 the province emitted bills of credit and made them equal to current coin: that is, 8s. in bills were worth an ounce of silver."[62]

The response of Pennsylvania to the legislation of Parliament was prompt and unique, and is to be found in an act of assembly passed April 30, 1709.[63] The act manifest an intent to comply with the proclamation rates while at the same time providing for an adjustment of the price level downward in proportion to the increased silver content of a six shilling piece of eight. All

---

61. Ibid., c. 292 (passed 1715); c. 347 (1717); II, c. 393 (1720); c. 396 (1720); c. 405 (1721); c. 421 (1722); c. 431 (1722); c. 437 (1723); c. 447 (1724); c. 450 (1724); c. 464 (1725); c. 470 (1726); c. 492 (1726); c. 509 (1728); c. 532 (1729); c. 551 (1730); c. 554 (1730); c. 591 (1732); c. 625 (1734); c. 631 (1735); c. 666 (1737), the loan office act; III, c. 676 (1739); c. 700 (1740); c. 745 (1743); c. 825 (1746); c. 832 (1746); c. 845 (1747).
62. Nettels, p. 246, n. 34. Ingoldesby's letter is in Cal. State Papers, 1708-09, #621.
63. Statutes of Pennsylvania, II, 244-297 (c. 166).

debts contracted prior to May 1, 1709, the date upon which the parliamentary act became effective, were to be paid in silver at 9__s__. 1__d__. the ounce, which was the rate at which the metal had passed in the province for some years. This provision did not violate any section of the parliamentary act. The unique feature of the act, however, was the provision that after May 1, 1709, when the value of a piece of eight was reduced from 8__s__. to 6__s__., the prices of all goods were to be "computed at three-fourths part of the sum and no more, which the seller would have taken for them according to the rates of the present currency, if no change had been made therein ...," and that "all officer's fees, salaries, and other perquisites, workmen's and labourer's wages and prices of commodities and manufactures that have for any number of years past been fixed and generally known" were to be settled at three-fourths their former amount when paid in pieces of eight at the proclamation valuation.

The act was in force for a period of five years, until in 1714 it was disallowed by the Privy Council.[64] The objection to the act grew out of the clause that attempted to reduce the price level by a quarter. It was feared that this would in respect to the other colonies

---

64. *Ibid.*

have the effect of raising coin in Pennsylvania to its old value.[65] The objection, however, appears ill-

---

[65]. The solicitor general, Robert Raymond, stated his objection as follows: "I can't but take notice of a clause therein, whereby 'tis enacted that the prices of goods, wares and merchandizes whatsoever, shall after May 1st, 1709, be computed at 3/4 of the sum and no more which the seller would have taken for them if no change had been made in the currency of their coins by H. M. Proclamation of June 18, 1704; and the British Act of 6th of her present Majesty ...; which clause may not only be the foundation of many disputes, but may possibly render H. M. Proclamation and the British Act which were intended to make the foreign coins go at the same rate in all H. M. Plantations ineffectual; because by lowering the price of goods by 3/4 in Pennsylvania, in consequence in respect to the other Plantations the coin there will be raised to the old value; and therefore whether this is a sufficient reason for repealing this act, I must submit to your Lordships [i.e., the Board of Trade]." Solicitor General to B. T., December 22, 1713. Cal. State Papers, 1712-14, #525. The Board of Trade concurred in the objection and recommended the repeal of the act. Board of Trade to Queen, January 15, 1714. Ibid., #553.

The problem raised is a complex one. The real objections to the acts of the various colonies raising the value of coin was that they led to progressive and ever widening inflation. If one colony's coin came to be rated at, say, a quarter more than the rate in another colony and the matter were allowed to rest there, after the effects of the change upon price levels had once worked themselves out, there could be no valid objection to such a state of affairs any more than to the fact that in a later era £1 = $4.86. One may well consult in this connection Nettels, p. 232-233, where he discusses the effects of raising of the rates at which coin passed in a colony. It is to be presumed that, since the Pennsylvania rate of 9s. 2d. the ounce had prevailed since 1700 at least, the effects of the change upon price levels had pretty well worked themselves out.

A fall in Pennsylvania prices was bound to follow the increasing of the silver content of the six shilling piece of eight. Pennsylvania with admirable forethought, one would think, attempted to accomplish this as quickly and equitably as possible. All this, however, appears to have been beyond the ken of the solicitor general, Robert Raymond. On the other hand, it

founded. Such an adjustment would in time come in any event. The law aimed at preventing the hardships that were bound to result from the fact that some prices would, if the matter was allowed to take its course, be adjusted more quickly than others.

Fortunately, the adjustment appears to have been accomplished during the five years throughout which the act was in force. The repeal of the act caused some complaints, and the assembly considered a new law; but the bill appears to have died in committee.[66] There is every reason to believe that the proclamation rates were approximated in Pennsylvania during the decade after the parliamentary act became effective.[67] During the de-

---

should perhaps be said in his behalf that he is one of the few lawyers in any age that ever objected to a legislative enactment on the grounds that it might "be the foundation of many disputes."

Essentially the same problem was later met in essentially the same way when Massachusetts returned to silver in 1751, and when bills of a new tenor succeeded bills of an old tenor as happened, for example, in North Carolina and Connecticut.

66. Penna. Votes, II, 1106, 1112, 1118, 1120, 1124.
67. The assembly in 1739 gave the following rates for silver and gold:

Years	Silver Rate/oz.		Gold Rate/oz.		
	s.	d.	£.	s.	d.
1700-1709	9	2	7		
1709-1720	6	10 1/2	5	10	
1720-1723	7	5 #	5	10	
1723-1726	8	3 z	6	6	6
1726-1730	8	1 z	6	3	9 z
1730-1738	8	9 z	6	9	3 z
1739	8	6 z	6	9	3 z
1749	8	6 zx	6	5	zx

pression period between 1720 and 1723 the price of silver appears to have been bid up as it was wanted for returns to England.[68]

    # Silver coin purchased with gold.
    z Silver or gold purchased with bills of credit. Ibid., 2523.
    x In 1749 a committee of the assembly reported that silver and gold had for several years passed current at the rates given above. Ibid., III, 3284.

There is also contemporary evidence to the effect that the proclamation rates were approximately observed from 1709 to 1720. See, for example, the passage from "the further sentiments of the Gentlemen, Merchants, etc. in Relation to a Paper Credit" (1723) on page 1490, ibid., II. In Votes and Proceedings, II, passim, there is evidence that the province used the new currency in keeping its accounts. There are also various petitions asking for the raising of the rates of coin. In 1716 the assembly resolved that it should be raised, but did nothing to make the resolve effective (p. 1164).

In 1721 a Philadelphia merchant wrote: "We generally account Par [of exchange with England] but 33 1/3 [advance] because it really is so in silver Money." James Logan to John Andrews, November 19, 1721; quoted in Lester, "Currency Issues in Pennsylvania," Journal Political Economy, XLVI (June, 1938), p. 331. This would be true only if the proclamation rate was observed.

Governor Keith wrote in 1723: "Pennsylvania is hitherto the only Colony which has strictly observed her late Majesty Queen Anne's Proclamation confirmed by Act of Parliament, for ascertaining the value of forreign coins in the Plantations ...." Keith to B. T., Phila., December 12, 1723. Cal. State Papers, 1722-23, #786. Although Keith was mistaken if he included Maryland and Virginia in the list of colonies that had failed to observe the proclamation rates, there is every indication that he stated with substantial accuracy the situation in Pennsylvania.

In the light of this and similar evidence Professor Nettel's statement referring to this period (p. 241, n. 35) that "in private transactions the piece of eight passed as if Parliament had not acted" appears ill-founded.

    68. Penna. Votes, III, 1828 (quoted, supra, pp. 75-76).

In Maryland, where the proclamation had been observed from the beginning, the assembly in December, 1708, adopted the proclamation rates "for the discharge of any Contracts or Bargaines made after" May 1, 1709. The rates were also to prevail "in payments of all Dutys and Impositions ... and all officers fees which by the Laws are rated in money." These rates prevailed until Maryland's introduction of paper currency in 1733.[69]

In Virginia "the uncertainty of the Coin, [had] for a long time been a matter of General Complaint, and the remedying of it," wrote Governor Spotswood in 1711, had "been attempted without success in former Assemblys, the great Difficulty being to settle a Currency without prejudicing her Maj'tie's Revenues."[70] This difficulty had

---

69. The following quotation from the act gives some indication of the situation in the province with respect to specie: "And in Reguard there is at Present litle other money in this province than the Dollars Commonly Called dog dollars and they being neer such weight and fineness as that they would by the forementioned proportion pass at foure Shillings and six pence. And the inhabitants of the province being not so well acquainted with other fforeigne Coynes nor at present Provided with weights and Scales, it is humbly pray'd that it may be Enacted

"And be it further enacted ... that the said Dog dollars be Current in all payments as aforesaid at four shillings and Six pence as Vsuall untill such time as her Majesty ... or the General Assembly of this province shall otherways ordain and Enact."

The "dog dollars" were the same as those elsewhere called "lion dollars." To some the figure impressed upon the coin appeared to be a dog, but to others perhaps more given to exaggeration, a lion. Hence the different names for the same coin in different colonies.

70. Spotswood to B. T., March 6, 1711. Virginia Hist. Soc., *Collections*, I, 54-55.

at last been got over, and the standard piece of eight had been rated at $3\frac{3}{4}$d. the pennyweight (equivalent to slightly less than 5s. 6d. the piece). The coins enumerated in the act were made a legal tender for all debts contracted thereafter. Her majesty's revenues, salaries payable out of them, and protested bills of exchange, however, were excepted from the act and remained payable in sterling money.[71]

Gold and English silver coins continued to pass at rates well below those in other colonies, which, as Governor Spotswood wrote, "lessened very much the current cash of the country by draining from hence all the gold and British silver coin." In 1714 an act was passed raising the rates of these coins. Gold was to pass at 5s. the pennyweight. Both gold and English silver coins were made a legal tender.[72]

The act, however, overvalued gold in relation to the value that had been placed on foreign silver coins in 1710, with the consequence that in later years silver was drawn out of the colony and replaced by the overvalued gold. To correct the situation the rates at which foreign silver coins should pass were raised in

---

71. Hening, III, 502-504 (9 Anne, c. 10). Assented to December 9, 1710. JHB, 1702-1712, p. 298.

72. Spotswood to B. T., January 27, 1715. Cal. State Papers, #188; Hening, IV, 51-53 (1 Geo. I, c. I). Assented to December 24, 1714. JHB, 1712-1726, p. 117.

1728. The standard piece of eight was rated at 4d. the pennyweight. This was equivalent to 5s. 10d. the piece, or still 2d. under the proclamation rate of 6s.[73] Here the matter rested until the introduction of bills of credit during the French and Indian War altered the picture.

North Carolina was yet upon a commodity currency basis and very little coin circulated in the colony. In 1712 she issued her first bills of credit. Successive issues soon depreciated in value. This, of course, had the effect of raising the rate at which such coin as found its way into the colony passed. An attempt in 1715 to attract "Lyon Dollars" to the colony by rating them generously in proportion to commodities and making them current in all payments failed to accomplish its purpose.[74]

South Carolina had been one of the colonies chiefly complained of in the years before the proclamation. In 1701 an act had rated 12dwt. pieces of eight, Mexico, Seville, and pillar, at 5s. The act, however, was for but two years duration. In 1703 and again in 1707 the act was revived and continued for a similar period in each case. Despite the act of Parliament of 1708, the

---

73. Lt. Gov. William Gooch to B. T., June 8(?), 1728, Cal. State Papers, 1728-29, #241; Hening, IV, 218-220 (1 Geo. II, c. 9); assented to March 30, 1728, JHB, 1727-1740, p. 52.

74. Supra, pp. 107-108.

province once again revived the act in 1709 and continued it for a period of two years. In 1711, however, it was allowed to lapse and was never thereafter revived.[75] After the introduction of paper currency, however, the act had little significance. As a committee of the assembly expressed it in 1739, after the introduction of bills of credit in the year 1703, gold and silver had "for the most part been dealt for as a merchandize, and not as a currency in payments, or a medium of trade." Consequently, as the bills of the province depreciated, the rates at which gold and silver passed rose.[76]

The proclamation of 1704 and the enforcing act of 1708 were largely, though not completely, ineffectual. They failed completely to place the currency of the colonies upon a uniform footing. Outside of a temporary en-

---

75. *Statutes at Large of S. C.*, II, #184, ratified March 1, 1701 (title only); the reviving acts follow: #209, May 8, 1703; #260, July 5, 1707; #283, May 7, 1709. The rates established by the act of 1701 are to be found in "An Account of the Rise and Progress of Paper bills of Credit in South Carolina." *Ibid.*, IX, 779.

76. *Ibid.*, 779-780.
The rates given for silver follow:

Year	Shillings/ounce
1700	7 1/2
1710	8
1720	27 1/2
1730	35 -- 37 1/2
1739	42 1/2 -- 45

forcement of the proclamation rates in the courts and in public payments in Massachusetts and New Hampshire, they were ignored from New Jersey northward. Pennsylvania observed the act of 1708 for over a decade and Maryland observed both the proclamation and the act until she issued bills of credit in 1733. In Virginia coin was rated below the proclamation figures by both the acts of 1710 and 1728, and it was not until the issuance of bills of credit in the 'fifties that coin passed at rates higher than those fixed by the proclamation. North Carolina nullified the proclamation with respect to what little coin found its way into the colony by her ever-depreciating issues of bills of credit. In South Carolina the paper issues had the same effect.

CHAPTER V

EARLY ATTEMPTS AT IMPERIAL CONTROL OF COLONIAL CURRENCY: BILLS OF CREDIT. THE CURRENCY ACT OF 1751.

The Circumstances of the sev^l Provinces being various & very different in [respect to bills of credit], each Province may require a distinct Consideration.

-- Representation of the Board of Trade to Parliament, 1741.

THE INTRODUCTION of bills of credit in the colonies during Queen Anne's War presented much the same problem as had the acts raising the rates at which coin had passed, but in a new form. Another phase of the problem, however, the effect of depreciating issues on creditors, was to occupy the center of the stage. England had had experience with a debased coinage; bills of credit, however, were something new. They bore some analogy to the credit instruments of individuals, which upon indorsement had at times enjoyed a limited circulation. The principles that applied to these came to be applied to the bills of credit of the colonies as the Board of Trade gropingly evolved a policy respecting them.

The bills of credit of Massachusetts did not begin to depreciate to a marked degree until after the close of Queen Anne's War. Those of South Carolina began to depreciate earlier, but the fact that the province was under proprietary rather than royal government delayed the raising of the question before the Board of Trade. In fact, the matter of bills of credit first received the attention of the Board as a result of the land bank established in Barbados by act of June 18, 1706.

The intent of the act[1] was declared to be "to remedy or supply the want of cash in the Island and help creditors to pay their debts." Inhabitants "having an Estate of Inheritance in Barbados" might borrow sums in bills equal to one-fourth the value of their estates. The loan was for one year, but was renewable from year to year for a period of five years. The interest rate was eight per cent. The bills were declared a legal tender in all public and private transactions.[2] The Board of Trade considered the act "of an unusual and extraordinary nature and importance" and gave it its immediate attention. The merchants trading to Barbados and representatives of the Royal African Company, both groups having interests in the island that might be affected by the act, were given an opportunity to be heard and present memorials to the Board.[3] Both groups ob-

---

1. Board of Trade to Queen, October 17, 1706. Cal. State Papers, 1706-08, #542.
2. Ibid.
3. Board of Trade Journal, 1704-1708/9, September

jected; and largely on the basis of the objections uncovered in their memorials,[4] the Board of Trade drew its representation to the Privy Council asking the disallowance of the act.[5] The objections of the Board were several: (1) "The proper method for supplying the deficiency of cash, [was] to promote the increase of it by encouraging the importation of silver, but to put a disuse upon money in common payments, and to render it less needful by setting up Bills of Credit, or anything else to serve instead of it, tends to slacken the industry of the merchants in procuring it. By which method tis justly to be feared that the Island at the expiration of the Act will labour under a greater scarcity of money than it did before." (2) As no provision was made "for turning [the] Bills into money when required," the bills would inevitably depreciate, and since they were a tender in payment of debts, this would impose "an intollerable hardship on creditors who [had] already lent their

---

17, 24, October 3, 8, 10, 15, 16, 17, 22, November 1, 7, 1706.

4. The Royal African Company thought that the bills "must inevitably" pass at a discount, and since they were a tender, "a very great loss" would result to the company and to all others "who shall be forced to take their present debts in paper." Cal. State Papers, 1706-08, #529.

The merchants trading to Barbados objected at length. Their chief objection was similar to that of the Royal African Company, but in addition the administrative features of the act came in, not altogether without justification, for their share of criticism. Ibid., #540.

5. Ibid., #542 (October 17, 1706).

monies under covenants and obligations of receiving the like sums in currant money." (3) Since the bills were receivable in public payments his majesty's revenue would be "greatly damnifyed." And (4) the bills would prove a "general obstruction" to the trade of the island. Numerous ancillary objections were also expressed, but the ones set out above will serve to indicate the attitude that the Board took when it first faced the problem of bills of credit. It was in all its particulars the attitude of the merchant-creditors with whom the Board had advised.

As a result of the Board's representation, the act was forthwith disallowed by the Privy Council.[6] Moreover, an instruction was sent to the governor of Barbados enjoining him to move the legislature to make provision for the creditors that had suffered by being forced to receive the bills of credit issued under the disallowed act.[7] And in order that like incidents might not happen in the future, a circular instruction was sent to the various royal governors requiring them to refuse their assent to all bills "of unusual and extraordinary nature and importance wherein," it read, "our prerogative or property of our subjects may be prejudiced," un-

---

6. *Acts of the Privy Council, Colonial*, II, #1007 (October 21, 1706).

7. Leonard W. Labaree, *Royal Instructions to British Colonial Governors*, I, #326.

less such bills had been approved in advance by the crown or contained a suspending clause.[8] The restraint imposed by the instruction was of such a general nature, however, that a royal governor pressed by a persistent assembly had little difficulty in convincing himself that the act in question did not fall within the restraint. In consequence, the instruction proved largely ineffectual.

In 1709, three New York acts[9] issuing bills on a different basis, the credit of the colony, came before the Board. The Board objected to the acts: (1) because the bills were issued equal to silver rated at eight shillings the ounce, which was contrary to the policy embodied in the proclamation of 1704 and enforcing act of 1708; and (2) because the bills of credit were made a legal tender, which, it felt, would result in losses to creditors.[10] On this point the Board used language practically identical with that used in its representation of three years before on the Barbados act. Since the bills had been used to support an expedition against Canada and were already in circulation, the Privy Council allowed the laws to stand despite the Board's recommendation that they be disallowed.

---

8. Ibid., #224.
9. Colonial Laws of New York, I, c. 186; c. 190; c. 191.
10. Cal. State Papers, 1708-1709, #879.

The Massachusetts law of 1712[11] making the bills of credit of that province a legal tender brought the situation in New England to the attention of the Board on complaints from the postmaster general and the treasury. It was feared that it would be detrimental to the royal revenue if the post office were forced to receive bills of credit in payment of postage.[12] Upon inquiry it was found that Massachusetts had of late issued bills without establishing a fund to retire them. This caused the Board to recommend that the governor "be directed for the future not to give his assent to any Act for making bills of credit current, unless the said Act do at the same time establish a sufficient fund for the payment and discharge of such bills."[13] As the years wore on, the principle here enunciated became of first importance in determining the Board's policy towards bills of credit. It was probably derived by analogy from private credit instruments, which, when the maker was known as one who paid them promptly at stated times, maintained their value. But as a sufficient principle for regulating paper issues, it was defective. While it may have aided in giving the bills a circulation and thus aided in preserving their credit, it achieved this

---

11. Acts and Resolves of Mass. Bay, I, 700-701 (Province Laws, 1712-13, c. 6; passed November 8, 1712).
12. Cal. State Papers, 1712-1714, #340; #378.
13. B. T. to Treasurer, June 26, 1713. Ibid., #378.

latter result chiefly because it limited the amount of bills in circulation at any one time by preventing successive issues from accumulating.[14] Insofar as it did this, well and good; but it was perfectly possible for the bills to depreciate if issued in sufficient quantities even though their retirement was provided for by a tax fund levied at the time of issue. This occurred, for example, during the French and Indian War.

As has been pointed out earlier,[15] the end of Queen Anne's War and the prospect of a contracting circulating medium in Massachusetts portended depression. The situation gave rise to a demand for a new issue of bills of credit to replace the province bills then being retired. Two methods of accomplishing this end were proposed: (1) an issue by a private bank; or (2) a similar issue by public authority. The latter prevailed when the Massachusetts assembly authorized the issuance of ₤50,000 by the province in 1714. The proponents of a private bank, however, carried the matter to England, where in 1715 they sought a royal charter for their

---

14. Let us recur to our formula $MV = PT$, supra, p. 59, n. 69.
   If the fact that the bills were issued on tax funds caused people to have greater confidence in them and in consequence more readily to accept them in trade, T was increased; if it kept the bills outstanding from accumulating, M was decreased. Both of these facts depressed P; or, conversely, prevented the bills from depreciating.

15. Supra, pp. 25-26.

scheme.[16] After hearing both supporters and opponents of the proposal,[17] the Board of Trade became convinced that there was "a great want of money in New England for carrying on their trade, and other necessary occasions." This want, the representation continued, had been "in some measure supplied from time to time by Acts of Assembly for issuing out Bills of Credit for considerable sums." The Board felt that until it had opportunity to hear from the province it could not determine "whether this method, or a private Bank as propos'd, [would] be of most service." But it did go on record as thinking "it absolutely necessary that something of this kind be set on foot as soon as possible, to furnish a sufficient medium for carrying on of trade in those parts, the want of which is found to be a great obstruction to Navigation and the improvement of Naval Stores."[18] This latter object was then a favorite project of the Board, and it seemed to view the proposal of the private land bank with some favor because its promoters "consented that one half of the net profits arising from the ... Bank, shou'd be appropriated to the public service for raising

---

16. Board of Trade Journal, 1714/5-1718, passim. See "land bank" under "New England" in index.
17. Ibid.; Cal. State Papers, 1714-15, #389, i., #458, i., #488 (where the scheme is outlined), #508 (pp. 224-225), #521, #543, #550, #552, #579, i.
18. B. T. to Mr. Secretary Stanhope, August 26, 1715. Ibid., #582.

of Naval Stores in New England."[19] Here one finds for the first time from the Board an intimation that in some circumstances bills of credit may serve a useful purpose in providing a medium of trade. This marks quite a departure from the position taken nine years earlier in the case of the Barbados land bank, where the proper method of relieving a want of money was held to be the encouraging of the importation of silver. The fact, pointed out over and over again to the Board in the course of its inquiry into the matter, that the silver of New England was constantly being drained off to England because of New England's unfavorable balance of trade had evidently made some impression. If New England were to retire her bills and accumulate a supply of silver to take their place, she would be forced to buy less English goods. These considerations brought the Board around to a more favorable view of bills of credit, at least in the circumstances.

The Board of Trade also bestowed its approval upon the issue of ₤16,607 in bills of credit provided by the New York act of 1717,[20] although the act came in for strong attack both from within the province and from the London merchants trading there.[21] Other aspects of the

---

19. Ibid.
20. Colonial Laws of New York, I, 938-991 (c.347).
21. Board of Trade Journal, 1714/15-1718, April April 22, May 2, 6, October 8, 1718; ibid., 1718-1722,

act besides the bills of credit features were under attack, but these latter aspects also came in for their full share of condemnation. On the other hand, the act was strongly supported by Governor Hunter and the New York Council.[22] The Board of Trade was wholly convinced by this defense and confuted the merchants on every point. In fact, "so far from agreeing with" them that the bills would "be to the prejudice of the trade of New York" the Board doubted "not, [that] if the credit of the bills [was] maintained according to the tenor of the Act, the trade of the Province [would] be greatly encouraged and facilitated thereby, as it appears to have been since the first bills were issued."[23] It should also be noted that the Board took this position despite the fact that the bills of credit authorized by the act of 1717 were not to be retired until the years 1734 to 1739, at which time the funds arising from the excise were to be used to draw them in. On the whole, the Board recommended the confirmation of the act but not without expressing the opinion that it should have contained a suspending clause, as had a similar act passed in New York in 1714. "In order to prevent the future in-

---

April 28, May 13, 15, 27, June 18, 19, 1719. Cal. State Papers, 1719-20, #157, #165, #166.
    22. Ibid., #218; also in New York Colonial Documents, V, 522-526.
    23. Ibid.

crease of paper credit and the anticipation of any fund upon which money may be raised to supply the emergencies of the Government," it seemed to the Board to be "absolutely necessary that the Governor should be enjoyned by H. M. command ... not to give his assent to any other bill of this nature, and to transmit to one of H. M. principal Secretaries of State and to the Board every six months accounts of the produce of the funds appropriated for sinking the bills of credit, and of the amount of the bills accordingly sunk ...."[24]

The matter dragged on until the next year, when the Privy Council approved the act but ordered instructions be sent to the various governors of the royal provinces requiring a suspending clause in such bills in the future, excepting only "Laws for Raising and Settling A Publick Revenue for defraying the Necessary Charges of the Government of the said Provinces Respectively, According to the Instructions Given to the Respective Governours of such Provinces."[25]

Instructions were accordingly drafted and sent; and during the remainder of the colonial period, with the exception of certain temporary local relaxations occasioned by circumstances of the times, the instruction remained

---

24. Ibid.
25. Order in Council, May 19, 1720. Acts of the Privy Council, Colonial, 1680-1720, #1293.

in force.[26] Nothing was done, however, with respect to the recommendations of the Board that the governor of New York be required to report every six months indicating the number of bills retired. While, as a matter of fact, the funds provided proved insufficient to the purpose of retiring the bills and at times such as did accrue were diverted to other purposes, actually the fact was not productive of any serious results.

By 1720 the policy of the Board of Trade towards bills of credit had assumed its more important outlines. Paper issues, both on tax funds to meet the expenses of government and on loan on landed security to supply a medium of trade, had met with the approval of the Board. The legal tender quality bestowed upon such bills had been tacitly acquiesced in. Provision, however, was always to be made at the time of issue for retiring the bills, and such provisions were ordinarily not to be broken through. Since a law authorizing bills could not be disallowed once the bills were in circulation without causing "confusion and disorder," the policy of requiring that such acts contain suspending clauses was adopted. In this manner, it was felt, large issues that might cause the bills of a colony to depreciate could best be prevented. This set of principles, could they be made

---

26. Labaree, *Royal* Instructions, I, #324, #325.

effective and should they be administered with judgment, was sufficient to prevent the abuse, yet permit the use, of a paper currency. The difficulties that developed arose largely from the fact that the instructions either were broken through or during time of war were relaxed; or that the supervisory powers of the Board were inadequate in the case of the proprietary and the charter colonies.

In fact, it was the course of events in South Carolina while that colony had been under proprietary rule that next brought the paper money question before the Board of Trade. As will be recalled, the exigencies of defense in that frontier province had occasioned numerous issues of paper money before the government of the province was provisionally taken over by the crown in 1721. The currency there had depreciated farther than anywhere else, having lost three-fourths of its value by 1720.[27] This occasioned complaint on the part of the London merchants trading to Carolina.[28] As a result, the South Carolina act of 1723, authorizing the issuance of ₤120,000 in new bills, ₤80,000 for exchange, and ₤40,000 to be applied on the province debts, as well as another act referred to therein, was disallowed, and the

---

27. See Figure III, supra, pp. 36-37.
28. Board of Trade Journal, 1722/3-1728, July 10, 25, 26, 1723; Cal. State Papers, 1722-23, #539.

governor was directed "not to give [his] consent on any pretence whatsoever, to any Act for encreasing of paper credit, or for altering or diverting the funds established by former Acts of Assembly ..., for the gradual payment of sinking of bills issued, before H. M. re-assumed the Government of the ... Province ...." Moreover, the governor was directed "to propose to the Assembly, to settle effectual funds for the speedy sinking and discharge of such additional bills of credit" as had been issued under the disallowed act.[29]

The effects of paper issues in South Carolina made the Board a bit chary concerning similar issues elsewhere; nevertheless, it allowed large issues in Massachusetts, Pennsylvania, Delaware, New Jersey, and Maryland during the next few years.[30] And in 1730 even South Carolina itself was authorized for seven years to divert to other purposes funds that would otherwise be used to retire outstanding bills;[31] and, "several persons, as well merchants as planters, having lately represented ... the absolute necessity that some paper money should be allowed to have a currency in [the] province

---

29. Supra, p. 121; Cal. State Papers, 1722-23, #710. See above, p. 121, for the results of this instruction.
30. Supra, pp. 80, 89, 96, 100; Board of Trade Journal, 1722/23-1728, April 26, 27, May 5, 1726; ibid., 1728/29-1734, March 8, 16, 1732, February 6, July 10, 18, 24, August 13, October 16, 17, 22, 28, 1735.
31. Labaree, Royal Instructions, I, #338.

under proper regulations, as well for carrying on the annual services of ... government there as for the daily circulation of trade among the inhabitants," the governor was empowered to give his "assent to an act or acts for the establishment of a new paper currency upon such a foot as may best answer the necessities of the province ...." But any such act was to contain a suspending clause.[32]

The South Carolina assembly, however, never succeeded in drafting an act that met with the approval of the home authorities, although in 1736 and again in 1746 it attempted to issue ₤110,000 in new bills to be placed out on loan.[33] On the other hand, the efforts of the Board of Trade to secure the adoption of an act to provide funds for the retiring of the ₤106,500 in bills outstanding after 1731 failed completely.[34]

In 1730 the situation in New England received attention. The governor of Massachusetts and New Hampshire was enjoined to take care that the bills of those provinces that were outstanding on particular funds "be called in and sunk according to the periods and provi-

---

32. Ibid., #339.
33. Supra, p. 123.
34. For a discussion of how South Carolina used public orders and tax certificates to meet the ordinary and extraordinary expenses of government after 1731, thus partially evading the restraints laid upon her from home, vide supra, pp. 123-127.

sions of the respective acts by which they were issued." Henceforth, such an instruction was in effect in these governments until 1757 and 1761 respectively.[35] In Massachusetts, which had by one subterfuge or another evaded the provision of the circular instruction of 1720 requiring a suspending clause in paper money acts, Governor Jonathan Belcher was restrained from giving his assent to any such acts that did not contain a suspending clause, unless the act provided "for the annual support and service" of the government. In such case the sum was limited to ₤30,000, and no larger sum than this was ever to be current at any one time. Similar instructions for New Hampshire placed the annual amount at ₤6,000. But the desire of Massachusetts at this time for paper issues was ardent, and Governor Belcher broke through his instructions. In 1737 he was taken to task for assenting to three acts that within the space of seven months authorized the reissuance of over ₤106,000 in bills that should have been retired, and was strictly enjoined and required upon pain of the highest royal displeasure and of being immediately recalled from his government to faithfully comply with his instructions in the future.[37]

---

35. Labaree, Royal Instructions, I, #327.
36. Ibid., #328.
37. Ibid., #329.

Despite the strengthening of the restraints applying to Massachusetts and New Hampshire during the 'thirties, the attitude of the Board of Trade towards bills of credit cannot be said to have been entirely unfavorable during the quarter century between 1715 and 1740. In fact, during this period the Board recommended the disallowance of paper acts in only two provinces, South Carolina and Barbados. It is true that it not infrequently wrote the colonial governor of the misgivings with which it recommended to the Privy Council the approval of some particular paper money act passed in his province, but even this was usually the result of promptings from some group of English merchants trading to America. In fact, on more than one occasion the Board recommended the allowance of an act over the strong and determined protest of such groups. On the whole, its attitude towards the paper currency issues of the colonies during this period may be said to have been reluctantly sympathetic and essentially reasonable. Within the principles it had evolved for itself by 1720, it was willing to consider any proposed issue on its merits; but it ordinarily wished to reserve to itself the decision as to the necessity of the issue. This was the reason that it sought to have suspending clauses included in all acts providing for extraordinary issues.

Certain factors, however, operated to change the

situation for the future. One was the fact that the Board of Trade lacked the power to curb the ever increasing paper issues of Rhode Island, which complicated the currency situation in New England; another was the inveterate opposition of the English merchants trading to America to a paper currency in the colonies; and a third, in large degree growing out of the first two, was the intervention of Parliament in currency matters.

From the time of the creation of the land bank in Barbados in 1706 on, one group or another of English merchants trading to America could usually be relied upon to oppose the approval of acts providing for sizeable issues of bills of credit in the colonies. On the whole, however, they seemed to be quicker to oppose new issues than they were to support plans for the extinguishment of the paper currency of a colony. This no doubt grew out of the fact that in the former case they consulted their interest as creditors; and in the latter, their interest as merchants anxious to increase trade. Sometimes, however, when the creditor-interest of the merchants outweighed their trade-interest, which was most apt to happen in the case of merchants trading to a province where depreciation had been rapid and severe, the merchants sought a reduction of the paper currency and a return to the proclamation standard. South Carolina furnishes an example of this. The situation there in 1729 called forth a memorial to the Board of Trade from the merchants trading to America. They expressed themselves as "fully convinced of the wisdom and good tendency" of the act of Parliament of 1708 enforcing the proclamation of 1704 respecting the value at which coin should pass in the colonies and were of the opinion that had it been "duly observed, and properly enforced" it "wou'd have prevented the misfortunes and injustices the good and well-meaning traders, widows and orphans [had] been subjected to, where paper money hath been introduced by designing men, to defraud their creditors." To remedy the injustice they prayed that the paper currencies of the colonies, particularly that of South Carolina, "be reduced and abolished and ... Proclamation payments restored in their full force and vertue ...."[38] The petition, however, fell upon unreceptive ears, for as has been indicated above, the needs of trade prevailed and additional paper issues were authorized in South Carolina the next year.[39] Nevertheless, it was indicative of what one might expect in the future.

A decade later, consideration before the Board of Trade of the South Carolina act of 1736 for reissuing her old bills and placing £110,000 of new currency out on

---

38. Cal. State Papers, 1728-1729, #867. Signed by John Lambert, Steph. Godin, John Hewlett, Jos. Wyeth and twenty-eight others.
39. Supra, pp. 181-182.

loan brought a proposal from Mr. Wood, the agent for the London and Bristol merchants, in June, 1738, "for remedying the present mischiefs and inconveniences attending the commerce of the Plantations, from the practice of issuing paper money and raising of the coin."[40] While Mr. Wood's scheme was under consideration, a proposal of Robert Dinwiddie, then collector of customs in Bermuda, was transmitted to the Board. He had in mind the introduction of "a new sort of British coin" into the colonies. The two schemes received some attention from the Board in November, 1738.[41] The next spring, Thomas Lowndes, who besides other interests in South Carolina had for some time served as the absentee provost marshall of the province, proposed to submit a scheme for remedying "the great evils attending" the paper currency of America.[42] A week later James Glen, the governor of South Carolina, who was then in London, attended a meeting of the Board and presented a proposal that had been handed him for a new paper currency in South Carolina.[43]

While this discussion of the paper currency of the American colonies was in progress, Parliament acted. On

---

40. *Board of Trade Journal,* 1734/5-1741, June 7, 15, 22, 1738.
41. Ibid., October 18, November 2, 1738.
42. Ibid., May 30, 1739.
43. Ibid., June 6, 1739.

June 13, each house adopted a resolution asking the crown to direct the several colonies to transmit accounts of their various paper issues since the year 1700, together with the rates at which gold and silver had passed during stated years since that time.[44] Who proposed the resolution does not appear. At the time the Rhode Island agent, Richard Partridge, wrote that he could give no reason for the action "unless it proceeded originally from the L.ds of Trade who are also Members of Parliamt."[45] This in the absence of direct evidence is perhaps as good a deduction as any other. Certain it is that the Board already had the matter under its consideration.

The passage of the parliamentary resolution was the signal for a grand inquest into the currency situation in the colonies. Copies of the addresses of the Lords and the Commons were forthwith sent over to the colonial governors.[46] The following December the Board of Trade again brought the subject up for consideration. On January 15, 1740, Thomas Lowndes, having first communicated his proposal with respect to the colonial currency

---

44. Journals of the House of Commons, XXIII, 378-379.
45. Gertrude S. Kimball (ed.), Correspondence of the Colonial Governors of Rhode Island, I, 126-127. Partridge to Gov. Wanton, London, February 2, 1740.
46. Board of Trade Journal, 1734/5-1741, July 4, 5, 1739.

to the merchants, transmitted it to the Board. Soon the colonial agents were summoned, and throughout the months of January, February, and March, as the answers to the parliamentary addresses began to be received, the matter received the sustained attention of the Board. In due course, it drafted a representation to Parliament, but for some reason decided not to present it and contented itself with merely transmitting to the two houses on March 27, the information that it had received from the colonies.[47]

Near the end of the session, the House of Commons gave the matter its attention and, after preagreement among those interested as to what should be attempted at that session, "very briskly came in to" some resolutions on the matter, "they being proposed and agreed on at a Committee of the whole House one day, then reported and concluded on the next." The Massachusetts agent, Christopher Kilby, managed to present a petition from that province and to get a hearing before the bar of the House, but, as the Rhode Island agent reported, "it did not seem to make Impression upon them so as to alter the Scheme of their Intentions." The House immediately reached its

---

47. Ibid., August 29, December 6, 1739; January 15, 17, 23, 31, February 12, 19, 27, March 5, 6, 7, 11, 12, 18, 19, 20, 25, 27, 1740. Partridge to Wanton, April 12, 1740. Kimball, op. cit., I, 147-148. The representation of March 27, transmitting the material is in N. J. Archives (1st series), VI, 78-81.

resolutions on the matter.[48] In describing the action of the House, Richard Partridge wrote at the time:

> ... it is observable that [the resolutions] were proposed and carryed through at the Instance of three of the Members principally who are of the side of the Minority of the House being Anti-Courtiers viz. S^r. Jno. Barnard[,] Saml. Sandys and All^r Hume Campbell Esq^{rs}. and it is believed that the Chief view of some of them in it, was more with a view to puzle and perplex the Ministry and Spirit up the Plantations against them than anything else .... [49]

Whatever the motive behind them, the purport of the resolutions was that the act of Parliament of 1708 respecting coin had "not been duly observed, as it ought to have been," and that many indirect practices had grown up and illegal currencies had been introduced "to the Prejudice of the Trade of his Majesty's Subjects." The House further was of opinion that the issuing of bills of credit in America and the making them a legal tender had "frustrated the good Intentions" of the act of 1708 and had "been a great Discouragement to the Commerce of [the] Kingdom."

To remedy the situation, the House resolved that his Majesty be graciously pleased: (1) to "require and command" the colonial governors to obey their instructions that the act of 1708 "be punctually and *bona fide,* observed"; (2) to settle the rates of gold coin by royal

---

48. Partridge to Wanton, May 2, 1740. Kimball, op. cit., I, 152-155; Journals of the House of Commons, XXIII, 526-529.

49. Partridge to Wanton, May 2, 1740, loc. cit.

proclamation; (3) to "require and command" the colonial governors to observe their instructions "not to give Assent to; or to pass, any Act, wherby Bills of Credit may be issued in lieu of Money," without the inclusion of a suspending clause; and (4) to direct the Board of Trade to prepare accounts of the currency of each of the colonies to be laid before the House at its next session, "together with their Opinion what will be the most easy and effectual manner of sinking and discharging all such Bills of Credit, with the least Prejudice to the Inhabitants of the said Colonies and Plantations, and Interruption of the Commerce of this Kingdom." It is interesting to note that a motion asking the crown to direct the Board of Trade to lay before the House "Copies of the severial Memorials, Representations, and other Papers" presented at various times "by the Merchants and Traders of London, Bristol, or Liverpool" relating to the acts raising coin, the paper money acts, etc. of the colonies since 1716 was voted down 71 to 69.[50]

In another resolution the House desired that the crown direct the Board of Trade "to prepare forthwith a complete Collection of all the Laws which have been made, and are now in force, in any of the British Colo-

---

50. *Journals of the House of Commons*, XXIII, 520-521, 526-529, 609-610. The resolutions bore the date of April 25, 1740.

nies in America ..., distinguishing which have, and which have not, had his Majesty's Royal Approbation, and the respective Times when such Approbation was given"; and that the same be printed.[51]

Instructions to the royal governors that their instructions enjoining the observance of the act of 1708 be observed were shortly ordered, drafted, and committed to the care of the several colonial agents to be transmitted "with all expedition" to the respective governors.[52] The charter and proprietary colonies also received their meed of attention; and instructions were sent to the governors of Maryland, Pennsylvania, Connecticut, and Rhode Island, enjoining the punctual observance of the act of 1708. At the same time the governor of Pennsylvania was instructed to assent to no act issuing bills of credit unless it contained a suspending clause.[53]

The Privy Council considered the matter of issuing a royal proclamation setting the rates at which gold coins should pass in the colonies, but after some correspondence with the treasury, let the matter drop.[54]

---

51. *Ibid.*
52. *Acts of the Privy Council, Colonial, 1720-1745*, #496; *Board of Trade Journal, 1734/5-1741*, May 14, July 9, August 1, 19, 1740; Labaree, *Royal Instructions*, I, #320.
53. *Acts of the Privy Council, Colonial, 1720-1745*, #496; *Board of Trade Journal, 1734/5-1741*, August 1, 1740; *Penna. Colonial Records*, IV, 470-472.
54. *Acts of the Privy Council, Colonial, 1720-1745*, #507.

The Board of Trade on its part went forward with its inquiries into ways and means of settling the paper currencies of America. Letters were written to the colonies asking for suggestions, and in October (1740) the agents were called before the Board and were questioned on the matter. But, since the agents "had received no instructions on that head from their constituents, they were not able to offer anything further, than what they had already offered in their former discourses on that subject." Nevertheless, numerous papers and schemes were submitted, then and later. Various London merchants were called in for their sentiments on the matter. And among them was Alderman William Baker, who throughout the decade of the 'forties was to prove the persistent foe of paper issues in America. To further complicate matters, the proposed Massachusetts land bank unpropitiously came before the Board for consideration at this time.

Late in January, 1741, the various papers on the currency received from the colonies since the last session of Parliament were transmitted to both Lords and Commons, and a representation was sent the latter house.[55]

The Board felt itself destitute of the proper in-

---

55. Board of Trade Journal, 1734/5-1741, January 21, 22, 29, 1741.

formation "to lay before [the] House such a Proposition for the sinking and discharging of the ... Bills of Credit [of the colonies], as may be in every respect an adequate Remedy for the Evil complained of, and," it added with considerable wisdom, "so much the rather because the Circumstances of the sev^l Provinces being various & very different in this Respect, each Province may require a distinct consideration." Despite the complexities of the situation the Board felt obliged to comply as best it could with the address of the House and made certain recommendations: (1) That his Majesty "may be graciously pleased to repeat his Orders to his Governors of the Plantations not to give their Assent for the future to any Bill ... for the issuing or reissuing of Paper money in their respective Governments of any Sort upon any Account, or for any Purpose whatsoever, unless the bill contained a suspending clause. The penalty for violating the instruction was to be dismissal from office under the highest displeasure of the king. (2) That the tax funds already established be duly applied to the retirement of the bills. (3) That when bills have been issued on loan to private persons, "such Persons be compelled to make Payment thereof, agreeable to the Securities given for that Purpose." And (4) "that in all Cases where Bills of Credit have been issued without proper Funds for the sinking of them, or where such Funds have been diverted or proved ineffectual, the Governors should be directed to recommend in his Majesty's Name to their Assemblies forthwith to provide sufficient Funds by Act of Assemblies for the gradual Discharge of such Bills."[56]

The Board, however, was not over-sanguine as to what its proposals would accomplish, for it concluded:

> We hope that these Propositions for reducing & discharging the Paper Currency in the Plantations may have a good Effect in those Governments which are held by immediate Commission under his Majesty, But We are very doubtfull whether they will produce the like Effect in the Charter Governments, who do apprehend themselves by their particular Charters, & Constitutions to be very little dependent upon the Crown, & for that Reason seldom pay that Obedience to his Majty's: Orders which might reasonably be expected from them. [57]

Here indeed was the nub of the matter. The session of Parliament ended with no action taken on the recommendation of the Board of Trade.

One matter relating to currency, however, did at this time receive attention from the Board, the Privy Council, and Parliament. That was the Massachusetts land bank. The governor of Massachusetts was instructed "to continue to discourage [it] by all legal means ... and likewise any other bank or project of the like nature that may be attempted to be set up ...."[58] Parlia-

---

56. Report of the B. T. to House of Commons, January 21, 1741. N. J. Archives (1st series), Vl, 122-125.
57. Ibid.
58. Board of Trade Journal, 1734/5-1741, November 11, 12, 1740; January 29, March 13, June 18, 1741; Acts of the Privy Council, Colonial, 1720-1745, #504.

ment, by extending the Bubble Act to the colonies, likewise discountenanced the scheme.[59]

The Board of Trade had appraised the situation correctly when it expressed doubts as to the willingness of the charter colonies to conform to the desires of the home government with respect to bills of credit. Both Rhode Island and Connecticut saw threats to their charter rights in the resolution of 1740. Connecticut, however, did not assume the truculent attitude that Rhode Island did. The Connecticut assembly sought to convince the Board of Trade that the colony had "not Granted Large and frequent Emissions of paper Currency"; that its issues had been small compared with those of "Some other Colonys"; and closed by assuring the Board "that we shall take Effectual care as much as in us Lyes, to pay all Due Regards to his Majestys intentions, and to the Sense of the house of commons on this occasion ...."[60] With Rhode Island, though, it was the old story. She could not live up to the parliamentary act of 1708 unless Massachusetts did.[61] And the colony's agent was notified that he was "strenuously to oppose any attempt that

---

59. *Statutes at Large,* XVII, 459-463 (24 Geo. II, c. 37).
60. Conn. Assembly to B. T., November, 1740. Conn. Hist. Soc., *Collections,* V, 308-312.
61. Governor Ward to Richard Partridge, Newport, November 20, 1740. Kimball, *op. cit.,* I, 186-187. *Ibid.,* 200-201.

[might] be made agst. [the colony's] striking off any more bills of Credit without the Royal Assent."⁶² If Rhode Island felt that she could not act except in conjunction with Massachusetts, there were those in Massachusetts that felt that nothing could be done until Rhode Island was restrained, and that an act of Parliament was the proper method of accomplishing the desired end. In 1739 Governor Jonathan Belcher of Massachusetts had written to the Board of Trade

> ... the little neighbouring Colony of Rhode Island [has by its] large emissions of ... bills [of credit "without any foundation to support their value"] greatly contributed to the sinking of all the bills of C^r issu'd in this Province. I would therefore humbly propose to your Lordships that a bill might be brought into the Parliament of Great Britain, with proper penalties, forbidding all the King's provinces & colonies in America from striking any more bills of credit than might be sufficient for defraying the charge of each government where they might be emitted, & that sufficient provision be made in the act whereby they are emitted for calling them in within the year in which they go out. This would naturally give them a value as they are passing. ⁶³

With respect to Massachusetts and New Hampshire, the Board of Trade in considering the instructions of the newly appointed governors of those colonies sought to leave out the article that had permitted Belcher, who had administered both governments, to assent annually to issues of £30,000 and £6,000, respectively, to meet the

---

62. Same to same, Newport, July 15, 1741. Ibid., pp. 200-201.
63. Belcher to B. T., October 24, 1739. Mass. Hist. Soc., Collections (sixth series), VII, 225-227.

expenses of government, provided no more than those amounts were in circulation at any one time. The proposal to omit the articles was in line with the Board's recommendation to Parliament that no such bill should in any circumstances be assented to unless it contained a suspending clause. The agents of the two provinces, however, were able to secure the retention of the clauses by the Privy Council, although a special injunction that these sums be not exceeded was included.[64]

No sooner had William Shirley, the newly appointed governor of Massachusetts, reached his government than the paper currency problem was forced on his attention. The assembly and council passed a bill for raising the sum of ₤36,000 in bills of credit. Shirley felt obliged to refuse his assent, but transmitted the bill to the Board of Trade in order that he might obtain the prior consent of the crown to its passage. The consideration of this request gave the opponents of a paper currency the opportunity to press their measures upon the Board. Alderman William (later Sir William) Baker and Captain John Thomlinson, merchants both, were the leaders. Thomlinson had for some years served as agent for the province of New Hampshire, and in this capacity he had frequently appeared before the Board. Baker's

---

[64]. _Acts of the Privy Council, Colonial_, 1720-1745, #515.

first appearance had been when he and Thomlinson in their capacity as merchants trading to New England had been summoned to appear before the Board in the spring of 1739 when the Massachusetts currency was under consideration. The next year both men had appeared before the Board in the company of others against the Massachusetts land bank and had again been heard when the Board had under consideration "that part of the addresses of the House of Commons, concerning the sinking and discharging of the Bills of Credit in America." Both were able men of wide interests. Thomlinson had made many trips to New England as a sea captain and has been characterized as "a gentleman of great penetration, industry, and address." Baker was just beginning his long career in relation to American affairs. In 1747 he was to be elected to Parliament from Plympton, which office he was to hold until 1768. During the course of his career he was to touch American affairs at many points. In later years he became a trusted adviser of Newcastle, who in 1762 referred to him as "a strong thinker and often a very free speaker."[65]

Thomlinson had earlier presented the Board with an

---

65. Board of Trade Journal, 1734/5-1741, March 21, 23, 1739, November 11, December 2, 1740; Jeremy Belknap, History of New Hampshire (1831 ed.), p. 229; L. B. Namier, Structure of Politics at the Accession of George III, 1, 71n.; Namier, England in the Age of the American Revolution, see index under "Baker."

ingenious proposal for gradually reducing to proclamation rates the bills of credit then circulating in New England at rates equivalent to silver at 28s. the ounce.[66] His summons to appear before the Board along with Baker and others when the Board was considering the proposed Massachusetts bill for the emission of Ŀ36,000 apparently renewed his interest in the currency problem. On February 12, 1742, he "communicated to the Board a paper, entitled: Heads of an Act of Parliament to regulate the British American currencies, together with the reasons, and illustrations relating to the proposed Act." At the same time he delivered a "letter from several merchants at Boston, dated the 19th August, 1741, to the merchants in London, trading to New England, relating to the progress of paper currencies ... in those parts, particularly two neighboring publick combinations in the charter Governments of Rhode Island and Connecticut ...." together with certain supporting documents.[67]

After the Board had wound up its consideration of the Massachusetts application by recommending that permission be refused Governor Shirley to pass the proposed Ŀ36,000 act,[68] it gave attention to Thomlinson's pro-

---

66. October 29, 1740. N. J. Archives (1st series), VI, 111-116.
67. Board of Trade Journal, 1741/2-1749, February 12, 1742.
68. Ibid., March 2, 1742. Acts of the Privy Council, Colonial, 1720-1745, #530.

posal for a parliamentary act restraining paper issues in the colonies. Thomlinson, Baker, and some of the merchants discussed the proposal with the Board. From the fact that Baker and Thomlinson soon brought in an outline of "Heads for a Bill for the regulating the future payments of debts in America and for ascertaining the value of those heretofore contracted, but now undischarged," we may infer that the chief interest of the merchants in paper currency regulation at the time was the protection of their interest as creditors. The matter, however, languished and it was not until two years later that the project for parliamentary regulation was revived.[69]

William Shirley, who upon his going over to Massachusetts as governor had given the matter of the currency diligent attention, wrote a long letter on the matter to the Board late in 1743. It was read by the Board on February 23, 1744. Among other things, Shirley discussed his attempts to discourage the circulation of the bills of Rhode Island and Connecticut within the borders of Massachusetts. He had had some success in checking the currency of the bills in the country districts, he wrote, "but not in Boston, where their currency [was] countenanced and forced by some merchants and traders,

---

69. Board of Trade Journal, 1741/2-1749, March 11, 16, April 30, 1742; March 22, 1744.

who [had] a particular interest in doing it." Although he promised a further effort to combat this "mischievous currency" of the bills of the neighboring colonies when the General Court next met, he did not "think it possible to be effected without the aid of Parliament, by limiting the governments of Rhode Island and Connecticut as to their emissions."[70]

With Governor Shirley thus preparing the way by suggesting the same action that his predecessor, Belcher, had suggested before him, it is small wonder that, when Alderman Baker and Charles Townshend appeared before the Board of Trade to have some discourse "concerning an application proposed by them to be made to Parliament for remedying the ill-consequences arising from the emission of paper money in ... America," they were favorably received. Baker had some further discourse with the Board on April 3 and the matter was sufficiently matured that the merchants presented a petition to Parliament on April 18. The petitioners pointed out that despite the addresses of the House of Commons in 1741, "large Emissions of Bills of Credit have lately been made, and, as the Petitioners are informed, more are intended, whereby all Estates in those Provinces, where such Bills ... obtain

---

70. Shirley to B. T., December 23, 1743, John G. Palfrey, History of New England (1859 ed.), V, 106n.; Board of Trade Journal, February 23, 1744.

Currency, will be depreciated, and the Petitioners, among others greatly injured." In view of these facts, the petitioners apprehended that "the Mischief cannot be remedied, and the like prevented for the future, without the Interposition of the British Legislature."[71]

Upon consideration of the petition, leave was given to bring in a bill, and Sir John Barnard, Colonel Martin Bladen, a member of the Board of Trade, and Francis Fane, the Board's legal adviser, were to "prepare, and bring in, the same." Such a bill was presented to the House on May 4, and ordered to be printed. Nothing further, however, was done at the time, as Parliament was prorogued a week later; but action was expected when Parliament reconvened in November.[72] The printing of the bill, however, gave the colonial agents and others an opportunity to find out what was up. Copies were obtained and transmitted to America.

The bill embodied the principles of currency regulation transmitted by the Board of Trade to Parliament in 1741, together with certain additions aimed at correcting the defects that had been found in them. These were two: (1) that the royal governors frequently broke through their instructions and assented to paper money

---

71. *Ibid.*, March 22, April 3, 1744; *Journals of the House of Commons*, XXIV, April 18, 1744.
72. *Ibid.*, May 4, 1744. Partridge to Governor Ward, May 8, 1744, Kimball, op. cit., I, 254-256.

bills; and (2) that there was practically no check upon the charter colonies of Connecticut and Rhode Island. With respect to the first difficulty, Governor Lewis Morris of New Jersey stated the matter sententiously in discussing the proposed act with the assembly of that province. If a governor broke through his instructions and assented to a paper money bill that did not contain a suspending clause, and the currency authorized by the act was immediately placed in circulation, it was, as he observed, "not very practicable to repeal it." Nor had inducements been wanting to encourage governors to break through their instructions. "Assemblies," he continued, "have not been so unacquainted with the weak side of humane Nature, as not to do what they should not do, by denying to support the Government, or by giving large sums [to their governors] as a Reward for Imaginary Services; And Governors, who are made of the same Materials that other men are, have not been unsusceptible to Impressions made that way, and thought it more eligible to run the Hazard of breaking their Instructions than of starving by a close adherence to them."[73] As to the second difficulty, the effect of the paper issues of Connecticut and Rhode Island upon the currency situation in New England, particularly the unrestrained outpourings of the

---

73. Governor Lewis to Assembly, May 2, 1745. <u>N. J. Archives</u> (1st series), XV, 426.

latter colony, is by this time too familiar to need further comment.

To remedy the situation the bill introduced in Parliament provided: (1) that it should not be lawful for any governor to assent to a bill to emit bills of credit or to lengthen the periods of those already outstanding; (2) that all bills of credit then subsisting should be retired according to the tenor of the acts emitting them; (3) that the crown might, however, by appropriate instructions impower the colonial governors to assent to acts issuing such sums in bills of credit as were deemed requisite for the current services of the year, provided at the same time a fund was established to retire them within a reasonable time; (4) that the crown might likewise impower the governors to assent to acts issuing bills of credit for securing such sums of money as might be borrowed or taken up upon any sudden or extraordinary emergency of government, for the immediate support and defense thereof, provided at the time due care was taken to ascertain the value of the principal sum borrowed and to provide a sufficient fund for sinking and discharging both principal and interest; (5) "that no Bills made Since, or which shall be made by virtue of his Majesty's Instructions, shall be deemed or taken as a legal Tender for the Payment of any Private Debt"; and (6) that bills already outstanding on loan should be retired according to the tenor of their acts, that borrowers should be forced by all legal means to repay the sums borrowed by them, and in case of any loss or deficiency that the colony should make provision for it.[74] It was the remaining provision of the proposed act, however, that was novel, and that called forth the opposition of the colonies. It read:

> ... whereas some of his Majesty's ... Colonies or Plantations, particularly those under Proprietors and Charters, have not paid a due regard and Obedience to his Majesty's Royal Orders and Instructions, from time to time issued for the better Government thereof, but have assumed to themselves, an Exemption from and power of dispensing with or not obeying the same, under pretence of such Charters, or of his Majesty's Royal Grants to such Proprietors respectively. Wherefore for the better enforcing the due Execution of the Royal Orders and Instructions throughout all the British Colonies and Plantations in America, Be it enacted ..., That all Governors Councills and Assemblies, and every of them, and all Lieutenant Governors and other person or persons presiding as Governor within any of the said Colonies or Plantations, as well ... those under Charters and Proprietors as under his Majesty's immediate Commission and Government do, and they and every of them be hereby enjoyned and required to pay strict Obedience to such Orders or Instructions as Shall from time to time be transmitted to them or any of them, by his Majesty or his Successors, or by or under his or their Authority, And that all and every Acts, Orders, Votes or Resolutions, which shall or may hereafter be passed or made within any of the said Colonies or Plantations, contrary to such Orders or Instructions, shall be, and are hereby declared to be ------ any Law, Custom, or Usage to the contrary in anywise not [with]standing.[75]

It was conjectured that the blank was to be filled in

---

74. Taken from Governor Lewis's summary of the act. Ibid.

75. Quoted in an address of the N. J. Assembly to Governor Morris, April 18, 1745. *Ibid.*, pp. 412-413.

with the phrase "null and void" at least.

Here indeed was revolutionary doctrine, well calculated to set the colonists by the ears. Richard Partridge, the Rhode Island agent, long since cautioned to be on the alert to sniff out such heretical threats to Rhode Island liberties, had within four days secured a copy of the proposed bill and transmitted it to Governor William Greene. Since Parliament was to break up within the week, Partridge thought that nothing further was likely to be done with respect to the bill "till the Parliam^t. meets again in Nov^r.," when it was expected that the promoters of the bill would "Vigorously push for the getting it pass'd." By then he hoped for instructions from the colony and, since it was "now considerable time since" he had "received any thing from Rhode Island," he added the further hope that the instructions might be accompanied by "Suitable Remittances, for," as he expressed it, "its a pitty the cause sho^d. be starved."[76] Partridge's letter did not reach Rhode Island until October, too late to permit of his being sent instructions before Parliament met. The assembly did, however, get off a letter of instructions to him on November 3. It had, moreover, resolved that the cause should not be starved, and notified him that it

---

76. Partridge to Greene, London, May 8, 1744. Kimball, op. cit., I, 254-256.

had ordered ⅬL550 sterling to be remitted to him forthwith. Ironically enough, it had struck off "upon the large plate, made for the last bank" the sum of Ⅼ900 in new tenor bills of credit to raise the money. Partridge was instructed to procure the best counsel possible to oppose the bill, and he was notified that it was "expected that no Expence care or Pains [should] be wanting in opposing any Attempt made against [the] Charter" of the colony. "No Government," the assembly continued, "that is incorporated by a Charter and the Inhabitants have been born and lived and flourished under those Priviledges wou'd be so supine as to suffer them to be taken away without defending them."[77]

As for Connecticut, that colony was strangely lethargic in the face of the threat to her charter privileges. In March, 1745, the colony's agent, Eliakim Palmer, wrote that he had had no letters from the colony since November, 1743. He informed the Connecticut governor that the bill respecting paper money in America had been dropped for that session of Parliament, and expressed the hope that he might "have Instructions from the Colony on that head before the next."[78]

The proprietors of Pennsylvania forwarded Governor

---

[77]. General Assembly to Partridge, November 3, 1744. Ibid., 284-287. R. I. Colonial Records, V, 97.
[78]. Palmer to Governor Jonathan Law, March 25, 1745. Conn. Hist. Soc., Collections, XI, 269.

George Thomas of that province a copy of the bill that had been introduced in Parliament, together with the observation, that "the Gentlemen who brought it in, being of great Figure and Weight in the House, it is concluded that it will be well supported." Governor Thomas immediately (October 17, 1744) laid the bill before the assembly with the following recommendation and statement:

> As the interest of this Province may be greatly affected by this Bill, I think it highly adviseable that you immediately prepare a Set of Instruction[s], and transmit them by the first Opportunity, for obviating any Objections that may be raised against the Paper Currency here. Mr. Partridge [the Pennsylvania agent], as agent for Rhode-Island, has already engaged Mr. [Fernando John] Paris in behalf of the Colony. 79

The assembly forthwith gave the matter attention. They pounced upon the clause of the proposed act "intended to give the Force of Law to all such Instructions as the Crown shall from Time to Time send to the Plantation Governments" and resolved, that the bill, "if passed into a Law, appears to the House destructive to all of their Liberties, and likely to be attended with the most dangerous Consequences to all the King's subjects in America." Instructions were drafted and sent to the agent along with a sum of money "for defraying the Expences which shall arise on the Opposition directed to be given [the] Bill." [80]

---

79. Thomas to Assembly, October 17, 1744. Penna. Votes, IV, 3020. Also in Penna. Col. Rec., IV, 750.
80. Penna. Votes, IV, 3020-3021.

Pennsylvania's action set the pattern for New Jersey's. Governor Lewis Morris reported the matter to the Board of Trade in January, 1745, as follows:

> One Partridge, a Quaker, [Richard Partridge, also agent for Rhode Island and Pennsylvania,] who acts as agent of this Province (but is rather the agent of the Assembly, who he corresponds with and takes his directions from them,) sent to our Assembly a coppy of a bill to prevent the issuing of paper bills of Credit in the British Collonies, &c intended to be brought into Parliament desiring the directions of the house how to proceed concerning it.
> What directions he has from the House of Assembly I know not, but he has no directions from the Government concerning it.
> The Assembly ... after having as they say Considered the Bill, were unanimously of the Opinion, that if the said bill (or any bill of that tendency) should pass into a Law, it would not only be an Encroachment upon the fundamentall Constitution of this Collony and the Concessions made to the first settlers thereof by his Majesties Royall Ancestors, but allso destructive of the liberties and properties of his Majestie's subjects now inhabiting the same.
> This Opinion or Vote I have been told (but how truly I know not,) has been Coppied from the votes of the Pensilvania Assembly, and our Assembly in this Case have been but their Apes.

The New Jersey assembly doubtless was inspired by the action of Pennsylvania, although they embellished the resolution of the Pennsylvania body in their own way. Their objection to the bill was essentially the same as that of Pennsylvania. "What is represented as the most dangerous part of the bill and gives most uneasyness," Morris continued, "is the last Clause 'for the better Enforcing the due Execution of Royal orders and Instructions.' This they Endeavour to perswade the people is to govern by Instructions and not by Laws.

They deem instructions to a Governour to be directions to him w'ch he may follow or not, as he sees fit; & which they can (by taking propper measures) tempt or Compell him to break, -- Governours not being allwaies proof against their Efforts; But that what shall be done in this case shall be void, or penall to the doers, or perhaps both, is what they cannot easily beare & I hope not easily avoid."[81]

Governor Morris could not on this occasion refrain from indulging his penchant for disputing with the assembly. The assembly took the view that the bill before Parliament proposed to give all instructions the force of law; Morris sought to convince them that only those relating to paper currency bills were included. The assembly seems to have been correct in its view, and Governor Morris probably succeeded only in leaving the matter worse than he found it.[82] In the light of the resolution that the assembly adopted, it is only reasonable to assume that they did not neglect to give their agent instructions to oppose the bill. Governor Morris, on his part, sought to counteract any instructions the assembly might have sent Partridge. On January 31, 1745, he wrote to the agent concerning the bill pending in Parliament:

---

81. Morris to B. T., Kingsbury, January 28, 1745. N. J. Hist. Soc., Collections, IV, 220-221.

82. N. J. Archives (1st series), XV, 410-437.

Tho the Assembly, or you, might think it inconvenient or of dangerous consequence that governors should be injoined and required to pay strict obedience to such orders and instructions as shall be transmitted to them by his majestie, or his successors, &c and every act &c made contrary to such orders and instructions to be declared -- (void I will suppose at least,) yet I cannot see with what face any of the king's governours or councills could appeare against an act made to oblige them to pay an obedience to their master's orders, (whatever those under charters may think themselves at liberty to do,) which made it improper to give you as their agent any orders or directions concerning it: & I would desire you to observe that the orders of [the assembly] are not the orders of the government here, whose agent you are. [And that] you as agent are not to esteem [the orders of the assembly as] orders of the government nor to make use of them as such whatever they be. And I add that it would not be amiss both for you and friends in England, to write to your friends here, to diswade them if possible from entering into and persisting in such measures as must one day make them obnoxious to government at home. 83

The assembly spoke of "encroachment upon the fundamentall constitution" of the colony and of the destruction of "the liberties and properties" of subjects; the governor, only of "obedience to their master's orders." The two views were at opposite poles. The proposal to give the royal instructions the force of law raised the central problem of reconciling colonial self-rule with intercolonial and empire interest. It was not apt to be solved, however, as long as imperial representatives thought only in terms of colonial "obedience to their master's orders."

Before the New York assembly concluded its sitting

---

83. N. J. Hist. Soc., Collections, IV, 229-230.

in September, 1744, an account of the introduction in Parliament of the "Bill to prevent the issuing of Paper Bills of Credit in the <u>British</u> Colonies and Plantations in America, to be legal Tenders in Payment of Money" came to the attention of the assembly. No copy of the bill had been transmitted, and since from the title it appeared that it was apt to contain little objectionable to New York, consideration of the matter was deferred until the next session of the assembly in March, 1745. The New Yorkers little suspected that the bill contained more than the title indicated, but when the votes of the assemblies of Pennsylvania and New Jersey were made public in New York, indicating "what dreadful Apprehensions" those provinces had of the bill, every endeavour was made to procure a copy of the proposed act. In late December or early January, a copy was obtained. A reading of the bill convinced the New Yorkers of the threat that it contained. As the session of Parliament would be over before the assembly would meet, "a Meeting of most of the Members of the Council, and of the Assembly that were in Town, as likewise of a great Number of Merchants, and others," was held. They considered the bill and found no objections "to that Part which relate[d] to Bills of Credit, saving some small Explanations about the respective Periods for sinking of them." But as to the parts that gave the royal instructions the force of law, they conceived that if passed into a law they would "in Effect, subject all the British Colonies and Plantations in America, (and of Consequence all the People in them) to the absolute Will of the Crown, and those acting by its Authority"; and "they resolved unanimously, to have Sollicitations made, that those Clauses do not remain a Part of it."

For this purpose several persons voluntarily advanced sufficient money to purchase a bill of exchange for £150 sterling, and managers were appointed to transmit the money together with the proper instructions to England. Messrs. Samuel and William Baker were chosen to conduct the opposition to the bill, with instructions to "retain and imploy a good Sollicitour and able Council, in order to make the said Sollicitation in the strongest and most effectual Manner." As irony would have it, this was the same William Baker that of all others had been most responsible for the introduction of the bill in Parliament.

When the New York assembly met in March, the speaker reported the action that had been taken together with various documents to the house, which upon examination heartily approved the action taken and made provision that those that had advanced the money for the cause should be reimbursed from the public treasury.[84]

---

84. New York Assembly Journal, II, 47-50; March 13, 15, 1745. Also N. Y. Col. Doc., VI, 639, 643.

Meanwhile on the other side of the water, Alderman Baker had been busy in the cause of currency restraint. In mid-summer, 1744, he had communicated to the Board of Trade a copy of an act passed in Rhode Island the preceding February for issuing ₤40,000, new tenor, to be let out on loan, together with copies of protests against the act made in the House of Deputies and the House of Magistrates of the colony at the time of its passing.[85] He was evidently bent upon keeping the fires of resentment to the paper issues of the colonies burning brightly so that he could go forward with his measure when Parliament opened in the fall.

In fact, no sooner had Parliament reconvened than Baker was again before the Board, this time accompanied by his solicitor, Mr. Hammersly, desiring that they might have access to certain papers in the possession of the Board relating to the paper currency of America, and more particularly to that of Massachusetts, Connecticut, and Rhode Island. His request was promptly granted. But when two weeks later, Richard Partridge's solicitor, Ferdinand John Paris, who evidently had gotten wind of what was up, appealed to the Board for the same permission, "he was acquainted, that it being a matter of great importance, the Board would consider thereof, and

---

85. Board of Trade Journal, 1741/2-1749, July 12, 1744.

he should have an answer in a few days." It was not, however, until six weeks later that he was given access to the same papers that Mr. Hammersly had had.[86]

On two occasions in February, Alderman Baker again attended the Board and discussed the bill it was intended to bring up in Parliament.[87] It might be noted that Baker could not as yet have received word of New York's action in appointing him to oppose the bill.

Meanwhile, the Rhode Island agent kept an anxious watch on developments in Parliament, expecting that the bill would be brought up at any time and taking steps to oppose it.[88] But his fears were needless; the bill did not come up. Whether Alderman Baker, having received his appointment as New York's agent to oppose the bill, had succeeded in that capacity in convincing himself in his capacity of merchant-creditor that it would be unwise to proceed with it; or whether, as seems more likely, it was because the House of Commons, as Richard Partridge reported,[89] had "their hands full of business ... of more Moment, particularily that of the Miscarriage of the Sea Engagem^t with the French and Spaniards" the

---

86. Ibid., December 4, 19, 1744; February 5, 1745.
87. Ibid., February 19, 21, 1745.
88. Partridge to Deputy Governor Joseph Whipple, December 15, 1744, Kimball, op. cit., I, 294; Partridge to Governor Greene, December 27, 1744, ibid., 295-297.
89. Partridge to Greene, March 25, 1745. Ibid., 311.

year before; the fact is that the threat to colonial liberties passed for the time being. It was, however, to rise again. But the colonies had been aroused, and forewarned was in this case forearmed.

Indeed, the war with the French that had broken out in 1744 and was to last until 1748, was to occasion modifications in the policy of the British authorities with respect to paper currency, as well as to delay further efforts at reform. The exigencies of the struggle with the French upon the New England border had caused the Massachusetts governor, William Shirley, to request a change in his instructions so that he would no longer be bound not to assent to issues in excess of £30,000 in any one year, which sum was quite inadequate to carry on the war.[90] A new instruction was forthcoming, and on September 9, 1744, Shirley was empowered "in cases of emergencies to give [his] consent to such acts as may be necessary for the supply of the treasury of [the] province with bills of public credit during the continuance of the present war, provided the money thereby raised be appropriated to the necessary support and defense of [the] said province only." This opened the way for Massachusetts' "great inflation."[91]

---

90. The other part of the instruction, that no more than £30,000 should be outstanding at any one time, seems never to have been taken seriously either by the governor or by the home authorities.
91. *Board of Trade Journal*, 1741/2-1749, August

Although temporarily stopped by the necessities of the war in their efforts to secure currency reform by act of Parliament, the London merchants overlooked no opportunity to accomplish their desired ends. When Parliament agreed upon the sum of £235,000, sterling, as the amount to be granted to the New England colonies to reimburse them for the expenses occasioned by the expedition against Louisburg in the spring of 1745, the merchants determined that so favorable an opportunity to substitute a species currency for the paper of New England should not be neglected.[92] In January, 1747, they petitioned the Treasury, urging "that as the sums granted by Parliam^t are sufficient for a Medium of Exchange throughout New England," they "be remitted in a Coin or in such other Specie as may have Established Value fix'd upon it as a Standard for Estimating of private Debts." The occasion of the grant, the merchants contended, was "the most favorable if not the only Conjuncture that has ever Occur'd" for re-establishing a sound currency in

---

28, 1744; March 28, April 9, 1745; Acts of the Privy Council, Colonial, 1720-1745, #600; Labaree, Royal Instructions, I, #332; supra, pp. 33-34.

92. The sums appropriated for the various New England colonies follow:

Massachusetts	£183,649
New Hampshire	16,356
Connecticut	28,864
Rhode Island	6,333

Statutes at Large, XIX, 228-240 (21 Geo. II, c. XXIII).

New England. To this end, they urged that the money granted by Parliament be withheld "until some Effectual Measures are taken by the several Governm^{ts} there for Establishing [an] Equitable Rule for Discharging their Bills of Credit & for Putting a Period to the pres^t Paper Currency or in Case of their Neglect or Refusal not until the whole can be Regulated by the Parliament of this Kingdom." And, as one might expect, Alderman William Baker's name appeared among those of the twenty-five signers of the petition.[93]

The colonies opposed the merchants' proposal strenuously, and at last prevailed. The money was paid unconditionally. Massachusetts, however, used her portion to return to a silver basis; and other of the colonies used their shares of the grant to draw in such of their bills of credit as the sums received made possible.[94]

Although the merchants failed to gain their point before the treasury, they were ever on the alert to oppose the approval of acts providing for paper issues not directly connected with the wartime emergency. Led by Alderman Baker and James Crokatt, they appeared in force against the South Carolina act of 1746 for issuing £210,000, £110,000 of which was to be placed out on loan, the remaining sum to replace the worn bills of an earlier

---

93. Conn. Hist. Soc., Collections, XV, 183-186.
94. See chapter vi, infra.

issue. The act contained a suspending clause and came before the Board early in 1748. The matter hung fire for years, but the merchants were finally triumphant, and the act was disallowed in 1754.[95]

In the case of the New Jersey act of 1748 authorizing the issuance of ₤40,000 on loan, an act which likewise contained a suspending clause, the opposition came from another quarter. Ferdinand John Paris, representing "himself and others, creditors of the publick of the said province," appeared against the act when the colony's agent, Richard Partridge, sought to have it confirmed. Paris was spirited to oppose the measure by Robert Hunter Morris, who was then in London. Morris sought to secure the disallowance of the measure in retaliation for the refusal of the New Jersey Assembly to allow the claims of his father, Lewis Morris, the late governor of the province. In this effort he was successful, and the law was disallowed in November, 1749.[96]

In January, 1749, the Board of Trade was in process of once again giving attention to the South Carolina act

---

95. *Board of Trade Journal*, 1741/2-1749, February 9, 11, 19, 26, March 1, April 22, 1748; January 23, 25, 31, December 8, 1749; November 2, 1750; June 6, November 8, 1753; et passim. *Acts of the Privy Council, Colonial*, 1745-1756, #213.

96. Donald L. Kemmerer, *Path to Freedom, The Struggle for Self-Government in Colonial New Jersey, 1703-1776*, p. 213. *Board of Trade Journal*, 1741/2-1749, October 20, November 11, 15, 1748; July 18, 19, 1749. *Acts of the Privy Council, Colonial*, 1745-1766, #32.

of 1746, and it also had before it the matter of Massachusetts' reported action with respect to retiring her bills of credit. A consideration of these matters appears to have suggested to the Board that, now that the war was over, the time was not unpropitious for reviving its old project of regulating the paper currency of the colonies generally. It called in its old advisers in the matter, Alderman Baker and Captain Thomlinson, and throughout late January and early February spent three days in considering the draft of a bill that had been introduced in Parliament in 1744.[97]

By February 16, the matter had been sufficiently matured to permit the raising of the question in Parliament. Leave was given to bring in a bill, and Horatio Walpole, Sr., the old foe of a paper currency Alderman Baker, now a member of Parliament, and the following members of the Board of Trade, Lord Dupplin, Baptist Leveson Gower, Francis Fane, John Pitt, Thomas Robinson and James Grenville, were named "to prepare, and bring in, the same." The bill was presented to the House on March 3, and ordered to be printed.[98]

The bill as brought in was essentially the same as the one introduced in 1744, although there were certain

---

97. Board of Trade Journal, 1741/2-1749, January 23, 24, 27, 31, February 2, 9, 1749.
98. House of Commons Journals, XXV, 746, 766.

additions and some clarifications. Paper money bills assented to by any governor contrary to his instructions were declared "null and void, and of no Force or Effect whatsoever." Moreover, every colonial governor was given a negative on the acts of the assembly of his province and was to be bound, apparently in all matters, not just paper currency matters alone, by instructions from the crown. This provision would extend the power to govern by royal instruction to the proprietary and more particularly the charter colonies. The clause of the former bill denying the legal tender quality to bills of credit in the future was also strengthened. All outstanding bills of credit, as in the bill proposed in 1744, were to be called in and sunk at the end of their respective periods; and it was further declared, "That after the Arrival of the Period for sinking the Bills, all Creditors, not withstanding the Tender, and actual Receipt of them, shall, and may sue for, and recover the Value of their Debts in Money in any of his Majesty's Courts of Record, as fully as if no such Paper Bills of Credit had been at any Time tendered and accepted."[99]

The colonial agents had long anticipated the revival of the Board's project to regulate the paper currency of America and were prepared to oppose the move. Now as

---

99. *Independent Advertiser*, Boston, May 1, 1749, wherein the bill is abstracted.

before, it was the provision in the bill that extended royal instructions to the proprietary and charter colonies and gave those with respect to paper currency the force of law to which the colonies chiefly objected. The Rhode Island agent, Richard Partridge, had long been on the lookout for the renewal of this threat to the charter liberties of that colony. Eliakim Palmer, the Connecticut agent, was on this occasion likewise ready to oppose the measure. Within two weeks after the bill had been introduced, Partridge and Palmer presented petitions against it to the House of Commons. They pled their charter rights and asked to be heard by counsel before the House before such a bill should be enacted. This request they were granted.[100]

Partridge, who was agent for Pennsylvania as well as Rhode Island, originally thought to present one petition for both his governments; but Thomas Penn, one of the Pennsylvania proprietors, had him put in a separate petition for Pennsylvania. Penn thought that of all the colonies, Pennsylvania "had the best Case much, and therefore should hurt [them] Selves to joyn any other Colony." The petition was received and permission to be heard by counsel granted. Penn also succeeded in having the House order an account of the exports and im-

---

100. *House of Commons Journals*, XXV, 791-794 (*Mercurii, 15° die Martii, 1749*).

ports of Pennsylvania to and from Great Britain for the years 1722 to 1747 in order to show the great increase of trade between that province and the mother country since Pennsylvania first issued paper currency in 1723.[101]

The London merchants trading to Pennsylvania, in contrast to the merchants trading to the other parts of America, could always be relied upon to say a good word for the paper currency of the province. Penn prepared to take advantage of this fact and drafted a petition for them to sign on behalf of his province. The petition having been signed "by a large number" of the merchants was presented "by one of the Merchants for the City as a merchantile Matter" on March 22. The merchants, so the petition read, did not conceive that the paper bills of Pennsylvania had "been injurious to any Person whatsoever" and were "apprehensive" lest the passage of the bill into law "would lessen the Trade & Exports of this Kingdom, and affect the general Credit of the ... Province."[102]

On April 7, William Bollan in a lengthy petition on behalf of Massachusetts pled the charter rights of that

---

101. Ibid., 793; Thomas Penn to Governor James Hamilton, London, March 17, 1749, Penn Letter Book, MS, II, 268, in Historical Society of Pennsylvania; same to same, London, June 6, 1749, ibid., 268-270.
102. Penn to Hamilton, March 17, 1749, loc. cit.; House of Commons Journals, XXV, 806-807.

province. This represented a reversal of Massachusetts policy. At the time she had made provision to retire her bills of credit she instructed her agents "to make a proper Application" for an act to put a period to the whole paper currency of New England. She had even sought the services of Eliakim Palmer, the Connecticut agent, to aid in the affair, but with a sensitiveness of conscience not always present in the colonial agents of this period, he had decided he could not serve two masters, and had declined the appointment. When the currency bill, however, sought also to make the royal instructions more binding, Massachusetts had to choose, and elected to defend her charter rights.[103]

On the day after the Massachusetts petition was presented, Robert Charles presented a petition for New York. New York's strategy was similar to that of Pennsylvania. Charles urged on behalf of his colony that he did not "apprehend that any Complaints are made by the British merchants trading thither." And to "effectually evince the upright Intention of the ... Colony, with respect to their Paper Currency" he noticed two acts lately passed there and now awaiting the royal approbation:

---

103. Ibid., 814-815; Gov. Shirley to Duke of Bedford, Boston, January 31, 1749, Charles H. Lincoln (ed.), Correspondence of William Shirley, I, 465; Palmer to Gov. Law, London, April 15, 1749, Conn. Hist. Soc., Collections, XV, 298.

"the one for appointing Commissioners to state the Public Accounts, the other for the more effectual Cancelling the Bills of Credit of [the] Colony." On the same day, Peregrine Furye, the South Carolina agent, also presented a petition. He urged the necessity of paper as a medium of exchange in South Carolina and asked that his colony might be excepted from the paper money provisions of the bill. And as to "such Parts of the ... Bill as relate to the enforcing all Royal Orders and Instructions throughout the British American Colonies ..., without restraining them even to Paper Currencies, which appear to be the primary object of [the] Bill," he expressed the hope, "that a Bill which may so materially affect the Constitution of the British subjects in America," may not pass into law. Bollan, Charles, and Furye were all given opportunity to be heard by counsel at the appropriate time.[104]

By successive postponments, consideration of the bill was put off until May 1. In the meantime, however, the representatives of the colonies were busy opposing the measure out of doors. All the colonial agents already mentioned appear to have been active. James Abercromby seems also to have busied himself on behalf of South Carolina; and Thomas Penn, with whom Lord Baltimore

---

104. House of Commons Journals, XXV, 818, 819.

joined, was unremitting in his opposition to the measure.[105]

On June 6, Penn wrote to Governor Hamilton:

> Since I wrote you last I have been almost wholly imployed in Opposing the Paper Money Bill wch was strongly Supported by the Board of Trade[,] Mr. [Horatio] Walpol [Sr.] & [Alderman] Baker .... I ... drew up a Short state of our Money to wch was Subjoined some Observations on that part of the Bill which enforces the King's instructions or those from any Acting under his Authority ... I delivered it in to Mr. [Henry] Pelham [the chancellor of the exchequer] & many leading Members on whom it had a very good Effect, and induced several to Alter their opinions of this matter ... We ... represented so Strongly against the Orders & Instructions, especially Lord Baltimore who desired to Joyn me in this and my Self, that the bringers in of the Bill, agreed before the [counsel] were heard to Strike out all the Clauses relating to it, and only went on the first part of the Bill generally intending to prevent all future Money from being a legal tender[.] [T]his I conceive would render it of little Use, and drew up something on that head which I Gave to a few leading Members of the Committee who were afterwards of the Opinion that some must be allowed a legal Tender.... [106]

Penn also waited on Sir John Barnard, whose opinion on financial matters was of great weight in the House, and "who," as Penn writes, "was some Years ago as great an Enemy of these Currencys [as any of the members now opposing them] tho' he did not attend the House Committee on this business," and convinced him that the Pennsylvania currency was "so Necessary that he promised

---

105. House of Commons Journals, XXV, 823, 830, 844, 852 (April 11, 13, 21, 1749); S. C. Council Journal, MS, XXIV (1749), 760-764 (this letter is in all probability Abercromby's); XXV (1749), 171.
106. Thomas Penn to Governor James Hamilton, London, June 6, 1749, Penn Letter Book, MS, II, 268-270.

[Penn] to attend it in Case they persisted in their design totally to Abolish it ...."[107] Barnard, it will be recalled, was one of the committee that brought in the currency bill in 1744.

The Connecticut agent, Eliakim Palmer, also claimed credit for the suppression of the clauses relating to the royal instructions. No doubt many contributed to that result, but in all probability the pleas of the two proprietors, Thomas Penn and Lord Baltimore, availed most because the currency of Pennsylvania and Maryland had not been complained of, while that of the charter colonies of Connecticut and Rhode Island, particularly that of the latter, was the chief matter of complaint.[108]

The effort of the friends of the colonies was not confined to winning support for their views from members of Parliament and those in official positions. The London merchants were not neglected. Those trading to Pennsylvania and to New York were well disposed; the former, as has already been pointed out, went so far as to petition Parliament and ask to be heard on the matter. Only three of the merchants trading to South Carolina, however, could be induced to concert measures with those trading to Pennsylvania and to New York. The London mer-

---

107. Ibid.
108. Palmer to Law, April 15, 1749, Conn. Hist. Soc., Collections, XV, 297.

chant trading to South Carolina, James Crokatt, who by one of those perverse coincidences not altogether unknown in such matters was soon to be appointed the South Carolina agent in the room of Peregrine Furye, was exceedingly active in his support of the bill. He even proposed to raise a subscription among the merchants to combat the activities of the agents; but the merchants trading to Pennsylvania, who met at the same coffee house used by Crokatt's group, succeeded in having the proposal rejected.[109]

On May 1 and 2, the opponents of the bill appeared in force, well fortified with arguments against it. All those that had presented petitions were heard by counsel. This number included not only the colonial agents, but, it will be recalled, also the London merchants trading to Pennsylvania. They also presented as witnesses Mr. Barclay, Mr. Hyam, and Mr. White, "who," Thomas Penn wrote, "fully proved all we had asserted to the Satisfaction of the House ...."[110]

After the grand hearing of May 1 and 2, the House gave the matter some further attention, but "finding," as Penn wrote, "that there was not such an Information

---

109. James Abercromby (?) to Governor James Glen of South Carolina, S. C. Council Journal, MS, XVII, 760-764 (December 13, 1749), South Carolina Historical Commission, Columbia, S. C.

110. *House of Commons Journals,* XXV, 850-854; Penn to Hamilton, June 6, 1749, *loc. cit.*

before them as was necessary to enable them to consider, as they ought to do, a matter of so great Importance, at last" voted an address to the king asking that an account of the paper currency in each of the colonies be obtained and laid before the House at the next session.[111]

Penn, naturally enough, was pleased to be able to report concerning Pennsylvania: "Our Management with regard to our Paper Money was much commended on all Sides & it was generally thought necessary to have some tho to the last my Lord Halifax [the president of the Board of Trade] & some others thought there was Gold and Silver enough for England & the Colonys also. This must be," Penn continued, "by Changing of the Ballance of Trade in favour of the Colonys & can be done no other way by them as I have hinted in my written paper than by discouraging the Uses of English Manufactures & wearing our own which I think sho^d. be more attended to."[112] The development of American manufactures was of course contrary to established mercantilist doctrine.

Although the representatives of the colonies had succeeded in having the most dangerous part of the proposed parliamentary legislation quashed, with respect to the regulation of paper currency itself, further action

---

111. Ibid.; House of Commons Journals, XXV, 857, 863-64, 868-871, 875-877, 881-882, 888 (May 5, 10, 22, 25, 30, June 13, 1749).

112. Penn to Hamilton, June 6, 1749, loc. cit.

seemed probable once the necessary information had been gathered. Lord Halifax at the head of the Board of Trade, as has been seen, was still unconverted to the views of the colonists. Indeed, Thomas Penn had promised him and some of the leading members of the House of Commons that Pennsylvania would issue no more bills until the currency had been regulated by Parliament. In fact, "the Modern Doctrine" was felt by some to be "destruction to all Paper Currency whatever."[113]

The assemblies of at least Connecticut, Rhode Island, Pennsylvania, and South Carolina signified their approval of the opposition offered by the agents on their behalf and for the future gave instructions to continue the fight.[114] The effort at currency regulation, however, was not renewed at the next session, and there is some reason to believe it might have languished indefinitely had not events in Rhode Island brought new complaints. This time the protests originated in the colony, rather than in the councils of the London merchants or within the chambers of the Board of Trade at Whitehall.

---

113. Penn to Hamilton, July 31, 1749, Penn Letter Book, MS, II, 270; Abercromby (?) to Glen, loc. cit.
114. Public Records of Conn., IX, 452-453; Records of the Colony of Rhode Island, V, 271 (Governor Greene to Partridge, Newport, June 18, 1749); Penna. Votes, IV, 3377-3285; S. C. Commons House Journal, MS, XXV, 168-172.

The occasion for the protests was the fact that the Rhode Island assembly in the late summer of 1750 had under consideration an act providing for the issuance of ₤50,000, new tenor -- the equivalent of ₤400,000, old tenor -- to be placed out on loan. Both Edward Scott and Patrick Grant wrote letters in September to the London merchant, Alexander Grant, Esq., reviewing the state of Rhode Island's paper currency and opposing a new issue; and on November 13, Captain John Thomlinson delivered the letters, or copies of them, to the Board of Trade, where they were read.[115] Even before Scott and Grant wrote, a group of seventy-two Rhode Islanders, among whom Grant's name appears, had petitioned the king

> ... that the legislature or the authority of this government, may be prevented and effectually restrained from making or emitting any more bills of public credit upon loan, without Your Majesty's royal permission, and be commanded to stop and recall their intended emission of August last, from circulating or being offered or taken in payment of debt, or from passing any acts whereby any extant bills of public credit may be either debased in value or postponed in their periods of being drawn in .... [116]

The petition was referred to the Board of Trade by the Lords of the Treasury on January 14, 1751. The Board gave the matter immediate attention, thought it well to broaden the inquiry, and called for copies of the currency reports that had been transmitted to the

---

115. *Board of Trade Journal*, 1749/50-1753, November 13, 1750.
116. Petition to the king, Newport, R. I., September 4, 1750, R. I. Col. Rec., V, 311-313.

Duke of Bedford in response to the address of the House of Commons in 1749. On February 6 the Board sent a representation to the Treasury and on the 14th received a reply "desiring the Board would consider what application would be proper to be made to Parliament" in the matter. Coincident with the arrival of this request from the Lords of the Treasury came Horatio Sharpe, the solicitor for Rhode Island petitioners. Sharpe "was called in and it was recommended to him that a petition sould be presented to Parliament in behalf of the inhabitants of Rhode Island with the assurance that the Board would countenance such an application."[117]

Here already was a formidable array of opponents of paper currency -- the Rhode Island petitioners, the Treasury, and the Board of Trade. Yet another ally was to be enlisted -- the merchants of London trading to Rhode Island. On February 26, the London merchants presented a petition to the House of Commons on behalf of themselves and the Rhode Island petitioners, adopting the prayer of the latter group practically verbatim. The petition was referred to a select committee among whose members may be found the names of Sir John Barnard, Alderman William Baker, various members of the Board of Trade, and other old time opponents of a paper currency

---

117. Board of Trade Journal, 1749/50-1753, January 14, 16, February 5, 6, 12, 16, 1751.

in America. As if these were not enough, there were also added "all the members who serve for the cities of London and Bristol, and the Town of Liverpool, and all the Merchants of the House."[118]

Richard Partridge, the Rhode Island agent, did not realize the formidable forces that had gathered when he the next day noted the introduction of the petition, but observed that "as Matters are Circumstanced I doubt the Petitioners will carry their point." Nevertheless, he prepared to oppose the bill, as he had standing instructions to that effect.[119]

The committee set about informing itself on the currency situation in Rhode Island. William Bollan, the Massachusetts agent, and Barlow Trecothick and Alexander Grant, who were concerned in trade with Rhode Island, testified to the depreciation of the bills of the colony in between 1742 and 1749. Silver had risen during this time from 28s. the ounce to 60s. or thereabouts, denoting a depreciation of over fifty per cent in the value of bills. The various papers relating to the situation were called for, and after a full inquiry, certain things began to emerge. One was the fact that "the Bills of Credit issued in One [New England] Government have a

---

118. House of Commons Journals, XXVI, 62-66.
119. Partridge to Roger Wolcott, London, February 27, 1751, Conn. Hist. Soc., Collections, XVI, 35.

promiscuous currency in the other Three Governments."
This not unnaturally led the committee to conclude that
since "Experience has shewn it to be impracticable to
prevent the Introduction of Bills of Credit issued in
One Government, into the other Three, without an Act of
Parliament of Great Britain," a bill should be brought
in applying to the whole of New England. Among those
appointed to draft the bill was Alderman Baker.[120]

Partridge, now representing Connecticut as well as
Rhode Island, hastened to lodge petitions urging the
charter rights of his colonies and was later heard by
counsel. William Bollan, the Massachusetts agent, who
had earlier testified on behalf of the Rhode Island petitioners, now that Massachusetts had been included in
the bill also presented a petition in which he pled the
charter privileges of his province and its recent conversion to sound money doctrine as evidenced by its return to silver. But the efforts of the agents availed
naught. Both the logic of the situation and the strength
of those combined against them conspired to bear them
down.

One is unable to follow the legislative history of
the bill in detail. It appears, however, that the old
scheme to subject the charter colonies to royal instruc-

---

120. House of Commons Journals, XXVI, 117-122 (March 12, 1751).

tion had been revived. There was brisk debate, and we know that the bill was considerably altered by amendments, -- "the Sting being taken out," as the Rhode Island agent later wrote. The embattled New Englanders received aid from one other colony, that of New York. The agent of that colony, Robert Charles, petitioned and was heard against the bill. Nevertheless, "the Ministry were determined to carry it through," so determined in fact that the chancellor of the exchequer, Henry Pelham, "attended the Whole time [the bill was under consideration by the Committee of the Whole] & spoke several times in Support of the Bill." Sir Peter Warren, says Partridge, "was very much the New England Peoples Friend in the House ...." But Sir Peter was not a host in himself, and Partridge, bowing to the inevitable, resolved to withdraw his petition on behalf of Rhode Island and save costs. He was wise. The amended bill passed the Commons; the Lords agreed to it without change; and on June 25, 1751, it received the royal assent. An era in the paper currency of New England had ended.[121]

The currency act of 1751[122] embodied old principles

---

121. House of Commons Journals, XXVI, April 1, 2, 17, 22, 25, 29, May 2, 9, 15, 20, 22, 23, 31, June 4, 7, 10, 18, 25, 1751; Partridge to Wolcott, April 11, 26, Conn. Hist. Soc., Collections, XVI, 48-49, 54, 68-69, 82-83; Partridge to Greene, May 5, 1751, Kimball, op. cit., II, 130-133.

122. Statutes at Large, XX, 306-309 (24 Geo. II, c. 53).

of paper currency regulation, some of which can be traced back to the Board of Trade's first encounters with bills of credit in the colonies. The immediate ancestor, however, was the bill introduced into Parliament in 1744 and in slightly different form again in 1749. The act of 1751 opened by declaring that the act of Parliament of 1708 for ascertaining the rates at which foreign coins should pass in the colonies had "been entirely frustrated" as a result of the depreciating paper issues of New England, together with the fact that they had been declared a legal tender, "by means whereof," the act stated, "all debts of late years have been paid and satisfied with a much less value than was contracted for,[123] which hath been a great discouragement and prejudice to ... trade and commerce ...."

To correct the evils complained of, the act provided: (1) That after September 29, 1751, it should not be lawful for the governor, council, or assembly of Rhode Island, Connecticut, Massachusetts Bay, or New Hampshire to assent to any bill, &x. for making any further bills of credit or for extending the periods of those already outstanding. Any acts assented to in vio

---

123. This is not entirely so. In Massachusetts by laws of 1742 and 1747 an endeavor was made to require the payment of obligations in bills in amount equal to the silver value of the debt when contracted. The endeavor, however, was not entirely successful. Vide infra, pp. 246-248.

238

lation of this prohibition were "declared to be null and void, and of no force or effect whatsoever." (2) That all outstanding bills of credit be retired at the end of their present periods. (3) That the colonies might, nevertheless, pass acts for issuing "such reasonable sums" in bills of credit as should "be requisite for the current services of the year"; provided at the time of issue tax funds were established sufficient to retire the bills within two years. (4) That acts might be passed issuing such sums in bills of credit as should "be necessary or expedient upon sudden and extraordinary emergencies of government, in case of war or invasion"; provided, such acts ascertained "the real value of the principal sum" authorized and the interest (if any) to be paid thereon, and established a tax fund to retire the bills and pay the interest within five years. (5) That all bills of credit subsisting on loan should be called in and sunk at the end of their respective periods. (6) That all persons who had borrowed such bills be "compelled, by all due and legal means, to satisfy and discharge the sums by them borrowed," and, in case of a deficiency, the colony raise the sum necessary to complete the retiring of the bills by an equitable tax. (7) That no bills of credit issued after September 29, 1751, should be a legal tender in private transactions. (8) That nothing in the act should be construed "to make any of the bills now subsisting" a legal tender. (9) That if after September 29, 1751, any governor should assent to any bill &c. for issuing bills of credit, extending their periods, &c. prohibited by the act, such act, &c. should "be *ipso facto* null and void and such governor ... [should] be immediately dismissed from his government, and for ever after rendered incapable of any publick office or place of trust."

The act sought to retain bills of credit as an instrument of governmental finance, but at the same time, by denying them the legal tender quality, sought to protect creditors against a depreciating currency. The bills of credit of New England continued to serve as a medium of trade despite the fact that they were no longer a legal tender. While long-term creditors were protected by the act, those through whose hands depreciating bills of credit were continually passing were not. But this is the history of a later period.

Throughout the first-half century of attempts at imperial regulation of the colonial currency one may observe the play of various forces, now conflicting, now complementary, -- the interests of trade, the demand for debtor relief, the demand for creditor protection, the needs of governmental finance. The first attempt at regulation, the proclamation of 1704, sought primarily to prevent the confusion to trade that resulted from the progressive raising of the value of coin over ever widening areas, and only incidentally sought creditor protection. The same may be said of the act of 1708 enforcing the proclamation. The first encounter with bills of credit in the case of the Barbados issue of 1706 raised two problems: those of debtor relief and creditor protection. Although there are occasions when debtor relief is as legitimate as is ever creditor protection, the situation in Barbados was such that the merchant creditors were able to make out the better case, so that at the very outset the Board of Trade developed a creditor-protection bias. In fact, never once did it recognize that issues of bills of credit might be legitimate debtor-relief measures, as for example, were those in Pennsylvania in 1723. At best it only saw in them measures that might facilitate trade.

Very early the Board recognized bills of credit as useful instruments of government finance, and almost equally early it recognized that they were in some sections necessary as a medium of trade so long as the balance of trade was such as to drain off the silver of the section to pay balances in England. Were those sections denied a reasonable amount of paper currency to serve the needs of trade, they would have to accumulate silver or gold. This would of necessity lead to a curtailment in the importation of British manufactures and give impetus to the movement to establish and foster colonial industries. This ran counter to well-established mercantilist principles, and in consequence was something to be avoided.

The problem of those responsible for formulating and applying an imperial policy with respect to colonial bills of credit was that of harmonizing the various interests involved. The effects of unbridled emissions of bills of credit by one colony were frequently intercolonial and even empire-wide in their extent. This called for a remedy coextensive with the mischief done. In the absence of any effective means of intercolonial cooperation, it was only logical that the imperial authorities should attempt the remedy. By 1720 the Board of Trade had evolved a set of principles roughly adequate to the task, could they be but promptly and wisely applied, and could some way be found of extending effective imperial control to the charter colonies. For two decades the Board of Trade, perhaps in a rather halting manner, tried to harmonize the various interests involved; and the situation got out of hand conspicuously only where the imperial authorities lacked the power to exercise a restraining influence, that is, in the charter colonies, of which Rhode Island was the offender.

After 1739 the influence of the British merchants waxed and in consequence protection of the creditor interest became the dominant objective of imperial policy. In order to achieve this objective completely it was necessary to extend imperial control more effectively to the charter colonies. These considerations led to the attempts at parliamentary legislation during the decade of the 'forties, which were interrupted only by the exigencies of King George's War. The use of bills of credit as an instrument of wartime finance, however, accentuated the problem; and as a result the opponents of a paper currency gained strength after the war. But they met with determined opposition on the part of the colonies, particularly with respect to that part of their program that called for the tightening of imperial control through extending and strengthening the royal instructions. In the end, only New England, which as far as its currency was concerned was a unit, and which of late had been the chief source of complaint, was restrained by parliamentary action. None the less, the other colonies were expected henceforth to be circumspect in their paper issues. And the imperial authorities, through the instrumentality of the suspending clause, were always to be given the opportunity of judging of the necessity of any extraordinary issue. Such a policy called for prompt and wise action, with an even-handed weighing of all the factors involved. But the eight years of alternating disputes and procrastination that preceded the final decision on the South Carolina act of 1746 did not augur well for either the smooth or effective working of this policy. Indeed, paper currency throughout America was on the defensive; and at least one, who was at once merchant and colonial agent, thought it doubtful if any colonial paper currency act would ever again receive the royal approbation.[124]

---

124. James Crokatt, London merchant and agent for South Carolina. S. C. Commons House Journal, MS, XXVI (1750-1751), pp. 62-63, Crokatt to S. C. Com. of Corresp., London, May 11, 1750.

CHAPTER VI

MASSACHUSETTS RETURNS TO SILVER; THE CURRENCY OF NEW ENGLAND, 1751-1764

> Then good OLD TENOR, fare thee well,
>   Since thou art dead and gone;
> We mourn thy fate, e'en while we tell
>   The good things thou hast done.
> Since the bright beams of yonder sun,
>   Did on New-England shine,
> In all the land, there ne'er was known
>   A death so mourn'd as thine.
>
> -- From <u>A Mournful Lamentation for the sad and deplorable Death of Mr. OLD TENOR, a Native of New-England, who expired on the 31st Day of March, 1750.</u>

> From an aversion to a silver currency, the body of the people changed in a few months, and took an aversion to paper, though it had silver as a fund to secure the value of it.
>
> -- Thomas Hutchinson on the return of Massachusetts to a silver currency.

> The late Act for the Regulation of our Currency has occasion'd many Reflections and Altercations, and each Party have represented the Act, and its Consequences, in different Lights, according to the different Views, Interests, Circumstances, Prejudices, and Party of the Relator or Writer, which you know is not a very uncommon Case.
>
> -- <u>A Gentleman in Boston to his Friend in New-York,</u> October 1, 1750.

THE province of Massachusetts had, as it were, anticipated the passage of the Currency Act of 1751 by already making provision for a return to a silver currency. The great effort of the Third Intercolonial War was the expedition against the French fortress at Louisburg on Cape Breton Island, which took place in the early spring of the year 1745. Success attended the colonial venture, and in May the stronghold capitulated. Massachusetts had been the leader in the matter, and though all the New England colonies had participated in financing the expedition, it was Massachusetts that had borne the major share of the cost. This expense she met by an outpouring of bills of credit.[1] Depreciation set in at once. It was obvious that the demands of the war were greater than could be met by the resources of the province. It is not remarkable, therefore, that as early as July, 1745, a petition to the king was prepared, asking reimbursement for the expenditures incurred as a result of the Cape Breton expedition. The matter was entrusted to the young lawyer, William Bollan, who was at the time just embarking for England. In London he was joined by Christopher Kilby in presenting the petition. Of the two, however, it was Bollan, who by his "address, assiduity and fidelity" was responsible for obtaining full reimbursement.[2] But only after a considerable lapse of time, for it was not until May 13, 1748, that Parliament

---

1. Supra, pp. 33-34.
2. Thomas Hutchinson, The History of the Colony and Province of Massachusetts-Bay (Mayo ed., 1936), II, 334.

appropriated ₤183,650 sterling for the purpose.[3]

In the meantime, the continuation of the war had occasioned additional issues of bills of credit, with that medium ever depreciating in value. A law passed in 1742 at the instance of Governor William Shirley, soon after his coming over as governor, had attempted to give some protection to creditors against a depreciating currency by requiring that debts contracted thereafter be paid in silver at the rate of 6s. 8d. the ounce or, this wanting, in such an amount in bills of credit as was the equivalent of the silver value of the debt.[4] But the plan broke down in administration. The councilor that in each district fixed the depreciation, says Hutchinson, "never had firmness enough in any instance to make full allowance, but when silver and exchange had rose 20 per cent. or more, an addition was made of 4 or

---

3. 21 George II, c. 23, Statutes at Large, XIX, 228-240; Commons Journal, XXV, 658.
4. Acts and Resolves of Mass. Bay, II, 1083-1085 (Province Laws, 1741-42, c. 12, passed January 15, 1742). The act provided (Sec. 4), "That, if the bills ordered to be emitted this present year, or other bills hereafter to be emitted, shall be depreciated, or commonly pass at any lower rate than they are set at by this act, or by the act by which such other bills shall be emitted, that then, and in such case, the justices of the respective courts shall give judgment, for so much in silver, as the true debt appears to be, and in want thereof, for so much in ... province bills, with the addition of so much more as will make amends for the depreciating said bills from their present stated value [6s. 8d. per ounce], or the value at which such other bills shall be stated."

5 only," the "popular cry" being against a full allowance.[5] Further, as the value of the bills was determined only every six months at the oftenest, the act did not, in Hutchinson's words, "prevent the loss from depreciation of the bills in those persons hands through which they were continually passing."[6]

Nor did the price of silver and exchange, even if the full rate of depreciation of the bills measured by these prices had been allowed, serve as a fair index of depreciation; for, as has been pointed out earlier, an increase of the adverse balance of trade of a colony would under these circumstances tend to raise the price of silver measured in bills of credit, as the merchants that had to make remittances home bid one against the other for it. Moreover, these changes were often sudden and violent. These facts were recognized by the assembly in 1747, when it provided that in determining the value of the bills of credit of the province "regard [should] be had not only to [the price] of silver and bills of exchange, but to the prices of provisions and other necessaries of life ...." But even this broadening of the base to be included in the index of depreciation met the objections to the plan only partially. There is no reason to believe that the law was any better

---

5. Hutchinson, History, II, 307.
6. Ibid.

administered after its amendment than before. In fact, the mechanics of arriving at a valuation of the bills of credit were undoubtedly made more difficult.[7] That the whole experiment was far from successful is evidenced by the fact that even Governor Shirley, who valued himself on the scheme, was forced to admit that it had been "in a great measure eluded." Nevertheless, he thought it had "had so much Effect as to make Debtors sometimes sick of the Depreciations of the Bills (which were very sudden and irregular) and on that account less adverse to putting an end to 'em."[8]

---

7. Acts and Resolves of Mass. Bay, III, 373-375. 1747-48, c. 12, passed September 12, 1747. The value of bills of credit, the act asserted, "cannot be truly estimated by the prices of any one or two particular commodities or merchandizes, such as bills of exchange and silver now are ..., ... the prices of which bills ... have been found liable to be very suddenly and immoderately increased by a few persons for the sake of serving their own particular trade or interest, whereby the bills of credit have often been, to the great greivances of debtors, much depreciated with respect to bills of exchange and silver, tho', at the same time, they have kept their value with respect to all other commodities and merchandizes in this province: now," the act continued, "for preventing any further inconvenience which may arise to the debtor from estimating the value of bills of credit by comparing them with the prices of bills of exchange, and silver alone, --
Be it enacted ...
That when any valuation shall be made of the bills of publick credit on this province, ... regard shall be had not only to silver and bills of exchange, but to the prices of provisions and other necessaries of life, and to the difference that may arise from the plenty or scarcity of them, or other circumstances which may casually occasion the rise or fall of them, at the respective seasons wherein such valuation shall be made ....
8. William Shirley to Duke of Bedford, Boston,

In any event, the continued depreciation of the currency and the defects of the remedies applied by the acts of 1742 and 1747 confirmed the able Speaker of the Massachusetts House, Thomas Hutchinson, in his opposition to a paper currency. When news of the grant that Parliament had made to reimburse the province reached Boston, he, as he writes in his History, "imagined this to be a most favorable opporutnity for abolishing bills of credit, the source of so much iniquity and for establishing a stable currency of silver and gold for the future." Hutchinson estimated that in 1749 there would be about ₤2,200,000, old tenor value, outstanding in bills of credit. It required eleven or twelve pounds in the bills to equal one pound in sterling at the rate of exchange then prevailing. Hutchinson estimated that the ₤180,000 sterling granted by parliament would redeem ₤1,980,000 at eleven Massachusetts currency for one sterling. This would leave ₤220,000 outstanding in bills to be retired by a tax. Further, he proposed that after the bills had been retired, "silver of sterling alloy at 6s. 8d. the ounce," or Spanish "milled dollars [pieces of eight] at 6s. each should be the lawful money of the province"; and "no person should receive or pay within the province bills of credit of any of the other

---

January 31, 1748. Charles H. Lincoln (ed.), Correspondence of William Shirley, II, 466-467.

governments of New England."[9]

Hutchinson laid his proposal before the governor, who thought it "founded in justice and tending to promote the real interest of the province." But as "he knew the attachment of the people to paper money, [he] supposed it impracticable." Hutchinson, nevertheless, laid the "proposal before the house, where it was received with a smile and generally thought to be an Utopian project." More out of deference to the speaker than for other reason, the proposal was referred to a committee, which for much the same reason desired the speaker "to bring in a bill for the consideration of the house." This Hutchinson did, but when the proceedings "came to be known abroad, exceptions were taken and a clamour raised from every quarter," since "the major part of the people, in number, were no sufferers by a depreciating currency, [because] the number of debtors is always more than the number of creditors ..."[10]

On the other hand, "those who were for a fixed currency were divided." Some wished merely to retire the "superfluous" bills by redeeming them for bills of exchange; others favored a gradual retiring of the bills lest, it was said, "<u>a fatal shock</u>" be given to trade. "The last," says Hutchinson, "was the objection of many

---

9. Hutchinson, <u>History</u>, II, 334-335.
10. <u>Ibid., p. 335.</u>

men of good sense." Dr. William Douglass, "who had wrote well upon the paper currency and had been the oracle of the anti-paper party was among them and ... discovered as much rancor against the author and promoters of this new project as he had done against the fraudulent contrivers of paper money emissions."[11]

Although silver was currently valued in bills at 60s. the ounce, some were for redeeming them at 30s. the ounce, the figure that had prevailed before the issues of the late war had been placed in circulation. Hutchinson opposed this because it would have provided an enrichment for the present holders of the bills without indemnifying those that had suffered as a result of the depreciation. A compromise, however, was agreed upon and provision was made for redeeming the bills at the rate 50s. the ounce of silver; rather than at 55s. as was at first proposed.[12]

Despite the fact that "some of the directors and principal promoters of the land bank scheme,[13] [who were] at this time members of the general court, unexpectedly" supported Hutchinson's proposal, the advocates of the measure failed to carry the house. But the struggle was not yet lost. On the morning of the day

---

11. Ibid.
12. Ibid., pp. 335-336.
13. John Choate and Robert Hale.

following the rejection of the proposal, two members of the house, "zealous adherents" to the country or paper money party, "and who had been strong opposers of the bill," came early to the house to inform the speaker that, could the proposal be brought before the house again, they were ready to support it. Though they were not satisfied with several parts of the bill, they had become alarmed over some of the schemes of those that were for a gradual reduction of the bills and were ready to support it as the lesser of two evils. These two members moved and seconded a reconsideration, and the matter was again got before the house. This time it was carried. Both the council and the governor concurred, and the bill became law, January 26, 1749.[14]

The act, which had been passed by so narrow a margin, authorized the provincial treasurer to draw in the outstanding bills of credit during the year following March 31, 1750. In exchange for the bills, he was to pay out silver at the rate of one piece of eight for every 45s. in old tenor and for every 11s. 3d. in new or middle tenor. To supplement the parliamentary grant a tax of ₤75,000, new tenor, was levied to bring in funds sufficient to retire all the outstanding bills of

---

14. Ibid., pp. 336-337; Acts and Resolves of Mass. Bay, III, 44. The two country members were Joseph Livermore, representative of Weston, and Samuel Witt, representative of Marsborough.

credit. For the future, the colony was to be on a silver basis. All debts due after March 31, 1750, were to be deemed "payable in coin'd silver only," at rates for the various tenors in which the debts might be discharged equivalent to those at which the bills of such tenor might be exchanged for silver at the treasury. New contracts entered into after March 31, 1750, were understood "to be in silver, at six shillings and eight-pence per ounce" and all pieces of eight of full weight were to be taken at 6s., which, it will be remembered, was the value established by the Proclamation of Queen Anne.[15]

As there was a large circulation of the notes of the neighboring New England colonies in Massachusetts despite earlier attempts to exclude them, these colonies had been asked to join Massachusetts in retiring her bills of credit. Perhaps in order to bring pressure to bear upon them to follow Massachusetts' example or, it may be, for fear that they would not, the law prohibited the circulation of their bills within the borders of Massachusetts. Anyone passing or receiving such bills was made liable to a forfeit of fifty pounds. Officers of the government and "taverners, inholders, [and] retailers" were required to take oaths not to receive the

---

15. Acts and Resolves of Mass. Bay, III, 430-441 (Province Laws, 1748-49, c. 15).

bills. Moreover, Massachusetts bills in the hands of the inhabitants of Connecticut, New Hampshire, and Rhode Island were not to be redeemed in silver, but in such bills of their respective governments as might be in the hands of the inhabitants of Massachusetts.[16]

Despite these provisions of the act, those of sober judgment in Massachusetts, considering in the light of past experience the difficulties of preventing the circulation of the bills of the neighboring colonies, were doubtful as to its effectiveness. Governor Shirley expressed this opinion when he wrote to the Duke of Bedford, that he hoped the provisions of the act would "preserve a medium of Silver within this Province, 'till a final Period [could] be put to the whole paper Currency in New England by an Act of Parliament ...."[17]

Immediately after its passage, the act was transmitted to the provincial agent, William Bollan, who pressed for its immediate confirmation. This was secured on June 28, 1749. Two weeks earlier, on June 16, the parliamentary grant had been paid over to Bollan and Sir Peter Warren, who had been authorized to receive it on behalf of the province. Bollan and Warren proceeded to buy silver as they had been instructed. From the

---

16. Ibid.
17. Shirley to Duke of Bedford, Jan. 31, 1748/9, Correspondence of William Shirley, I, 464-465.

Bank of England and upon the market they purchased 650,000 ounces of Spanish silver at a net cost of ₤173,129, 5s. 11¾d. sterling. They also purchased nine tons of copper half-pence and two-farthing pieces at a cost of ₤2,111, 4s. 8d. sterling. The total cost of the money was therefore ₤175,240, 10s. 7¾d. The remainder of the parliamentary grant of ₤183,649, 2s. 7 1/2d. was consumed by expenses. The money was sacked and boxed and shipped to New England on H.M.S. Mermaid, Captain Montague, arriving at Boston on September 18, 1749.[18]

Although there had been great opposition on the part of many people, and although this was a day in which political convictions frequently found expression in mob violence, the passage of the act occasioned no immediate unrest. But as the period for drawing in the paper approached, "discontent appeared more visible, and upon the arrival of the money there were some beginnings of tumults, and the authors and promoters of the measure were threathened."[19] "The paper," it was said, "was not worth hoarding, but silver and gold would all fall to the share of men of wealth, and would either be exported or

---

18. Andrew McF. Davis, Currency and Banking in Massachusetts Bay, I, chap. xII; Acts and Resolves of Mass. Bay, III, 454-462; Boston Weekly News-Letter, September 21, 1749. Davis in the chapter cited gives a full and detailed account of the procuring of the silver, together with a detailed statement of the kind and denomination of the coin.

19. Hutchinson, History, II, 337.

hoarded up, and no part of it would go to the labourer, or the lower class of people, who might take their pay in goods, or go without." But as the bills were drawn in and replaced by silver, experience soon demonstrated "that it was as easy for a frugal industrious person to obtain silver, as it had been to obtain paper." Although there had earlier been some riots in Boston, as well as the nearby towns, "the prejudice against silver] in the town of Boston," writes Hutchinson, was now "so much abated, that when a large number of people from Abing-[t]on, and other towns near to it, came to Boston, expecting to be joined by the like people there, they were hooted at, and insulted by the boys and servants, and obliged to return home disappointed."[20] Nevertheless, the tumults were sufficient to cause the passage of a riot act in February, 1751.[21]

Meanwhile, the assembly had concerned itself with the various problems occasioned by the policy adopted by the drawing in act. One of the first problems that arose was that of providing small change. It was resolved to issue small bills to the amount of ₤3,000 "lawful money" to be secured by an equal amount of silver in Spanish milled dollars in the hands of the treasurer.

---

20. Ibid., III, 6.
21. Ibid., II, 337; III, 7. Acts and Resolves of Mass. Bay, III, 544-546 (Province Laws, 1750-51, c. 17; passed and published, February 14, 1751).

Provision was made for redeeming the bills in silver when they were presented in sums "equal to One, Two, or any other number of Dollars."[22]

As only Spanish silver had been rated by the drawing in act, it was thought necessary to rate English silver coins, the various gold coins in circulation, and English half-pence and farthings in proportion to the rates already placed on Spanish silver. This was accomplished by act of March 31, 1750.[23]

---

22. Ibid., XIV, 358-359 (Resolves, 1749-1750, c. 237, 238; both passed January 27, 1750).
The small bills were of the following denominations:

Dollars (Spanish) equal to	Pence (lawful money of Massachusetts)
1/4	18
1/8	9
1/12	6
1/16	4 1/2
1/24	3
1/72	1

"In such a Proportion of each denomination as the Committee [empowered to issue and sign the bills] think best; [provided] that the whole Sum amount to, and do not exceed Three Thousand Pounds lawful Money."

23. Ibid., III, 494-495 (Province Laws, 1749-50, c. 19; passed March 31; published April 7, 1750).
The rates applicable for contracts entered unto on and after March 31, 1750, follow:

Piece	Value		
	£	s.	d.
Guinea	1	8	
English crown		6	8
Half-crown		3	4
English shilling		1	4
English six-pence			8

(Continued, notes, next page.)

The coins listed give some idea of the diverse nature of the specie in circulation in the colony.

When the time arrived for calling in the bills of credit, the assembly appointed a committee to sit each day of the week except Saturday and Sunday to receive and tally such bills as were presented for exchange. When this had been done it issued its order upon the treasurer for the silver equivalent of the bills. Each day the committee burned the bills that it had received. The treasurer was to pay out Spanish silver and copper half-pence and farthings or the small bills that had been authorized in fixed proportion to all who presented orders, to the end that the various denominations of coin and small bills might be evenly diffused throughout the province.[24]

The committee was charged to take particular pains to see that no silver was paid out in exchange for Massachusetts bills presented by, or on behalf of, the inhabi-

Piece	Value		
	£	s.	d.
"Double Johannes or gold coin of Portugal"	4	16	
Single Johannes	2	8	
Moidore	1	16	
"Pistole of full weight"	1	2	

"Three English farthings for one penny; and English halfpence ... in proportion."
24. Ibid., XIV, 369-370 (Resolves, 1749-1750, c. 265; passed March 31, 1750).

tants of the other New England colonies. Massachusetts
inhabitants possessed of the bills of the neighboring
governments might leave them with the committee, in
which case they were used to redeem Massachusetts bills
in the hands of those outside the colony. The Massachusetts bills or their silver equivalent arising from such
exchanges were at the end of every two months paid out
to the Massachusetts inhabitants that had deposited
bills of Connecticut, New Hampshire, or Rhode Island.[25]

The redemption of the bills went forward, but before the period provided for completing their retirement
had expired, the treasury had run out of silver. When
March 30, 1751, the last day for the redemption of the
bills, arrived, many appear to have been still unredeemed
By resolution of the assembly, the committee in charge
of drawing in the bills was authorized to continue its
sittings and the issuance of its certificates until the
third of June next.[26] The assembly at that time had
under consideration a bill for meeting the problem presented by the lack of silver in the treasury, which
seems to have been occasioned by the fact that "many of
the constables and collectors of the towns ... [had]
neglected or delayed to pay in the sums committed to
them to collect," and also to the fact that some of the

---

25. Ibid.
26. Ibid., 502 (Resolves, 1750-51, c. 240).

silver received by the parliamentary grant had been used to meet the expenses of government. ₤17,834, old tenor appear to have been used for this latter purpose.[27]
The bill became law on April 26, and made provision for redeeming in silver one-eighth of the sum called for by each of the committee's certificates. Payment of the other seven-eighths was promised by December 31, 1751, with the addition of a one per cent premium and interest at six per cent. As the taxes came in, and the treasurer accumulated as much as ₤3,000 lawful money, he was to advertise the fact in the newspapers and redeem the full amount of the outstanding certificates in the order of their priority. In the meantime, the certificates were made receivable for the province taxes.[28] When June 4 arrived, the sittings of the committee were once more extended, but this time until June 12 only.[29]

---

27. Report of committee on Treasurer's Accounts for the year May 27, 1752 to February 8, 1753, ibid., 723-724 (Resolves, 1752-53, c. 240).

28. Ibid., III, 554-556 (Province Laws, 1750-51, c. 24; passed April 26, 1751). In its original form the bill (passed by the house on April 16) had made the certificates legal tender in all transactions. The council and governor opposed this feature as being contrary to the intent of the original drawing-in act and rejected the bill. In its final form, as indicated in the text above, the certificates were made legal tender for payment of taxes only.
See ibid., XIV, 531 (Resolves, 1750-51, c. 307, passed April 27, 1751), for resolve construing the above act.

29. Ibid., XIV (Resolves, 1751-52, c. 4; passed June 4, 1751).

By this time, as is indicated by a report of the
committee charged with drawing in the bills, dated June
3, 1751, bills to the amount £1,792,236 5s. 1d., reduced
to old tenor terms, had been drawn in.[30] This would appear to leave the amount of £131,996 3s. 9d. in old tenor
values still outstanding.[31] But as we have seen, the
certificates of the committee charged with exchanging
the bills of credit had not all been redeemed. The
parliamentary grant seems to have been sufficient to
redeem only £1,663,519 12s. 11d. old tenor.[32]

The state of the records makes it impossible to
follow in detail the final extinguishment of the bills.
After the committee for exchanging them ceased to sit on
June 12, 1751, the remnant of the bills outstanding was
from time to time made receivable in payment of taxes,
and various treasurer's reports indicate that moderate
sums were from time to time so received. The matter was
finally wound up as a result of an act passed January
25, 1754, whereby the treasurer was authorized to borrow
£5,000 lawful money to redeem the bills remaining in the
hands of the people. The sum authorized by the act was
sufficient to draw in £37,500 of the bills in old tenor

---

30. Joseph B. Felt, Massachusetts Currency, p. 131.
31. Ibid., p. 136.
32. Committee on the Treasurer's Accounts, May 27, 1752, to February 8, 1753, Acts and Resolves of Mass. Bay, XV, 723-724 (Resolves, 1752-53, c. 240).

terms; and later reports of bills burned make it appear that the sum provided was more than adequate for the purpose. The final period of redemption ended June 1, 1754, and it was made an offense subject to a penalty of ten pounds to "receive or pay away" any of the bills after that date.[33] The drawing in of the bills, which was in process during a period of over four years, seems to all intents and purposes to have been completed by the final redemption date established by the act. Massachusetts was now on a specie standard.

It will be recalled that many of the opponents of the act for drawing in the bills of credit feared a "shock to trade" if the paper currency of the province should be terminated. Thomas Hutchinson, who may rightfully be credited with being the father of the measure,[34] stated, when writing his History, that "the apprehension

---

33. Ibid., III, 717-719 (Province Laws, 1753-54, c. 26, passed Jan. 5; published January 26, 1754). The treasurer's advertisement dated January 29 pursuant to the above act appears in the Boston Weekly News-Letter, January 31, February 7 and 14, 1754.

34. Governor William Shirley to Duke of Bedford, Boston, January 31, 1748/9, Shirley, Correspondence, I, 467. From Hutchinson's statement (History, II, 335) we learn that he, after having drafted his proposal, presented it to Shirley, who, although approving it "as founded in justice and tending to promote the real interest of the province," yet because of "the attachment of the people to paper money ... supposed it impracticable." Shirley, who was not averse to taking credit to himself when writing to his superiors at home, was constrained to acknowledge that the passage of the act owed itself to Hutchinson's efforts, even though he implied that he himself had more to do with formulating

of a shock to trade proved groundless; the bills being dispersed through every part of the province, the silver took place instead of them, a good currency was insensibly substituted in the room of a bad one, and every branch of business was carried on to greater advantage than before."[35] As a summary statement applying to the general effects of the act, one can have little quarrel with this judgment, even though it is from the pen of one who took much pride in the fact that he was the author of the scheme. Unfortunately, the figures of trade with England during this period are not available for Massachusetts alone; but the figures for New England, most of whose trade was carried on through Boston, indicate that both imports from and exports to the mother country increased rather than diminished during the years when

---

the proposal than appears to have been the case. In the letter cited above he writes that he is persuaded that the bill would not have passed the house of representatives "had not their present Speaker Mr. Hutchinson, in concert with whom alone [the] Act was originally Plann'd, and all measures previously settled, by his extraordinary Abilities and uncommon Influences with the Members, manag'd and conducted it through the Opposition and Difficulties it long labour'd under in passing the House; being almost the whole Business of five Weeks there ...."

35. Hutchinson, History, II, 337. Hutchinson states further that "the other governments, especially Connecticut and Rhode Island, who refused upon being invited to conform their currency to the Massachusetts, felt a shock in their trade which they have not yet [c. 1766] recovered. The latter had been the importers, for the Massachusets, of West India goods for many years, which ceased at once."

the Massachusetts bills of credit were being retired.[36]

While Hutchinson's statement may be accepted as an adequate summary of the general effects of the act, a more detailed view of the economic effects of the passage of the act and of the retirement of the bills during the six months after redemption began is possible and perhaps desirable. In the first place, it should be observed that it is not easy to isolate the effects of the drawing in of the Massachusetts bills. The fact that the war with the French was over and the ever increasing issues in bills of credit occasioned by that struggle had ceased would in itself have been sufficient to cause complaints of a scarcity of money and of a decay of trade. Such certainly had been the experience of the province in the years following Queen Anne's War.[37] Moreover, the prohibition of the circulation within the borders of Massachusetts of the bills of Connecticut,

---

36. Emory R. Johnson, et al., History of Domestic and Foreign Commerce of the United States, I, 120-121.

Year	Exports £(stlg.)	New England Imports £(stlg.)	Year	Exports £(stlg.)	Imports £(stlg.)
1748	29,784	197,682	1752	74,313	273,340
1749	39,999	238,413	1753	83,395	345,523
1750	48,455	343,659	1754	66,538	329,433
1751	63,287	305,974			

The drawing-in act was passed in January, 1749; redemption began March 31, 1750; by June 3, 1751, approximately nine-tenths of the bills had been retired.

37. Supra, pp. 25-26.

New Hampshire, and Rhode Island might be expected to have its effect. It was estimated at the time that the bills of these colonies circulating in Massachusetts were equal in amount to one-quarter of the Massachusetts bills extant. Of course some of the Massachusetts bills were in circulation in the neighboring colonies, so that what took place was the drawing home of these Massachusetts bills in exchange for a like sum of bills of the neighboring colonies circulating in Massachusetts.[38]

---

38. One who was possessed of bills of the neighboring colonies and who because of his business activities had occasion to make purchases or pay debts in the other New England colonies could use his bills for that purpose. But all who found themselves possessed of such bills when their currency in Massachusetts terminated were not so fortunately circumstanced. A practice arose, however, that in many cases solved the problem. An inhabitant of Massachusetts owing another, who perhaps had use for bills outside the colony, made payment by sending his bills to some one in a neighboring colony, who held them subject to his order. He then made payment of his obligation to his fellow inhabitant of Massachusetts by the tender of an order on the holder of the bills in the neighboring colony. The bills were accepted by the creditor, usually "at a reasonable Discount."

This practice gave rise to a lively discussion in the newspapers. The opponent of the practice urged that the order to the holder of the bills outside the province, since it was a negotiable credit instrument involving slight risk, would itself obtain a currency in Massachusetts; and in effect, while the bills of the other colonies would cease to circulate, a credit instrument based upon them would take their place. In this way the banishment of the bills would be completely illusory. The fears of the writer were probably needless. Nevertheless, the controversy is indicative of the infinite variety of problems, the solution of which was necessary in effecting the return to a silver medium.

To the Author of the Letter in the Boston-Gazette of the 4th Instant, Boston Weekly News-Letter, September 6, 1750; To the Author of the Letter in the

But that there was a net diminution in the circulating media of Massachusetts as a result of the prohibition of the further circulation within her borders of the bills of the neighboring colonies appears undeniable.[39]

With these facts in mind, we may trace the course and effects of redemption. During the last years of the inflation there appears to have been what would in modern terminology be called a flight from currency into goods. As a contemporary writer described it:

> ... a general notion prevail'd, for some Time, before the [act for drawing in the Massachusetts bills was passed in January, 1749,] that our money was good for nothing, and indeed many judicious People, seeing our Bills depreciate so fast, and to such a Degree, thought their Money the worst Estate they had. Those that esteem'd it as good for nothing, thought themselves well off if they could get something for it; Those that thought it good for something, readily parted with it for those Things that they thought better. This occasion'd a quick Circulation; hence Money seem'd to be extraordinary plenty.[40]

When depreciation was stopped by the passage of the act for drawing in the bills of credit, the flight from the currency came to an end. In fact, Massachusetts bills, which made up three-quarters of those in circulation, appear to have been hoarded; and for some months before

---

Weekly News-Letter of the 6th Inst., ibid., September 20, 1750.

39. This appears true despite the fact that the circulation of the bills of the other New England colonies was probably never entirely suppressed.

40. Extract of a Letter from a Gentleman in Boston to his Friend in New-York, dated October 1, 1750. Boston Weekly News-Letter, December 20, 1750.

redemption began, there were "hardly any of them to be seen passing," and none circulated but the bills of Connecticut, New Hampshire, and Rhode Island, which although they appeared plentiful at the time, amounted to no more than a quarter part of the sum outstanding in Massachusetts bills.[41]

The hoarding of the Massachusetts bills and later of the silver for which they were exchanged; the suppression of the circulation of the bills of the neighboring provinces; and the fact that some of the silver was immediately shipped off to London, New York, and Pennsylvania to pay adverse balances,[42] all occasioned complaints of a scarcity of money and a decay of trade. "One gentleman, writing from Boston in June [1750], declared that 'Trade is quite dead' and that 'the Town is as dull and still as on Sunday.'" "All countenances are dull"; he continued, "we curse one another; especially those are cursed that were for the Act."[43] A little later another Bostonian bewailed the plight of that port. "You can't possibly imagine," he wrote, "what an alteration there is in our affairs for want of a medium there being scarce any money of any sort to be seen ex-

---

41. Ibid.
42. Ibid.
43. Lawrence H. Gipson, *British Empire before the American Revolution*, III, 14, quoting a writer from Boston, whose letter appeared in the *Pennsylvania Journal*, June 7, 1750.

cept a few coppers, and they seem to diminish; all trade seems to be stagnated." But in one respect the situation showed change. The Sunday stillness, so lately reported to be enveloping the town, must certainly have been broken by the fact that as now reported "little else goes on but drinking."[44]

But such complaints, while indicative of the feelings of some of the inhabitants of Boston, are not to be taken too literally. It seems probable that the Boston writer first quoted accurately summed up the situation when on October 1 he wrote: "The late Act for the Regulation of our Currency has occasion'd many Reflections and Altercations ..., and each Party have represented the Act, and its Consequences, in different Lights, according to the different Views, Interests, Circumstances, Prejudices, and Party of the Relator or Writer, which," he added, "is a not very uncommon Case." He then gave his own judgment in the following words: "That we have neither Paper nor Silver among us, is not in fact true; we have among us Silver enough for a Medium."[45]

The export of silver to pay balances in London, New York, and Pennsylvania seems to have been but a

---

44. Letter from Boston, *Pennsylvania Journal*, August 2, 1750. Quoted in Gipson, op. cit., p. 14, note.
45. A Gentleman in Boston to his friend in New-York, ... October 1, 1750. *Boston Weekly News-Letter*, December 20, 1750.

temporary phenomenon. Perhaps a quarter part of the silver first paid out after March 31, 1750, in exchange for bills was sent out of the colony; but before October the outflow to England had ceased. For some time prior to that month bills of exchange had been plentiful and were to be had at five per cent less than silver. Their use also made possible the saving of the freight and insurance charges that had to be met when specie was shipped.[46]

Certainly by the end of the year whatever shock to trade may have resulted from the return to a silver currency had dissipated itself. With increased prosperity the feeling against a silver currency died away. In fact, Hutchinson reports that "from an aversion to a silver currency, the body of the people changed in a few months, and took an aversion to paper, though it had silver as a fund to secure the value of it";[47] and that

---

46. Ibid. "The popular Cry is, that [the silver dollars] are all exported as fast as they are taken out; but by all that I can learn, the Truth is, there has not been near a Quarter of them exported, and that was when the Treasury was first opened, for lately there has been none sent to England, Bills of Exchange being so plenty, and to be had at so reasonable a Rate, that the Merchants who have occasion to make Remittances, I am told, can purchase them at 5 perCent. cheaper than Dollars, besides the saving Freight and Insurance. We have a good deal of Money imported from Hallifax, and many Bills of Exchange, and are like to have, as long as that new Settlement remains unable to supply itself with such Things as they want from us, and can't well do without."

47. History, III, 7.

he, as the author of the act, "was as much prais'd for his _firm,_ as he had before been abused for his _obstinate, perseverance_" in securing its adoption.[48]

The paper currency that Hutchinson referred to was the ₤3,000 in small bills authorized by the assembly.[49] "The whole sum was prepared," he writes, "but a small part only was issued, and scarcely any person would receive them in payment, choosing rather a base coin imported from Spain, called pistorines, at 20 per cent more than their intrinsick value."[50]

For a number of years prior to the return to silver it had been the practice to allow the taxes on estates and polls to be paid in bills of credit, specie, or various commodities produced in the province. The province treasurer and the eldest councilor in each of the counties formed a committee to establish the rates

---

48. Peter Orlando Hutchinson (ed.), _Diary and Letters of Thomas Hutchinson,_ I, 54.
49. Supra, p. 256.
50. Hutchinson, _History,_ III, 7. The failure of the small bills to circulate is indicated by the reports of the general assembly committees concerned with the oversight of the treasury and by various orders of the assembly. _Acts and Resolves of Mass. Bay,_ XIV, XV, _passim._ An order to the treasurer, April 26, 1751, recites:

"Whereas there is a Number of Pistareens & other small Pieces of Silver of a baser Kind in the Hands of the Treasurer.

"_Ordered,_ that he use his best discretion in converting the same into Spanish mill'd Dollars for the best Advantage of the Province." _Ibid.,_ XIV, 529 (Resolves, 1750-51, _c._ 301).

at which the commodities would be received at the treasury. The practice was continued during the years over which the bills of credit were drawn in. The last act allowing such payment appears to have been passed in 1755.[51] After that time payments in specie prevailed.

It is obvious that the policy adopted in 1749 when provision was made for drawing in the bills of credit of the province included a resolve not to have recourse to their use in the future as an instrument of governmental finance. Since the method in use in the province for nearly two generations had been to meet the usual as well as the extraordinary expenditures of government by the issuance of bills of credit in anticipation of taxes, some alternative had now to be found. The possibility of levying and collecting taxes in advance of ex-

---

51. Ibid., III, IV, the several tax acts, passim. The act of 1755 (III, 859, Province Laws, 1755-56, c. 2) reads:
"... the inhabitants of the province have liberty, if they see fit, to pay the several sums for which they may be respectively assessed, ... in good merchantable hemp, or in good merchantable, Isle-of-Sable codfish, or in good refined bar-iron, or in bloomery-iron, or in hollow iron-ware, or in good Indian corn, or in good winter rye, or in good winter wheat, or in good barley, or in good barrel pork, or in barrel beef, or in duck and canvas, or in long whalebone, or in merchantable cordage, or in good train oyl, or in good beeswax, or in good bayberry-wax, or in tryed tallow, or in good pease, or in good sheepswoll, or in good tanned sole-leather" rated as indicated in the text above.

This list, which had appeared in successive tax acts for a number of years, serves pretty well as a census of the products of the province.

penditures had two disadvantages. In the first place, in advancing the date of the tax levies it hastened an evil always to be deferred. But more important was the fact that it was frequently impossible to estimate in advance the funds needed. This was pre-eminently true during time of war. Confronted by these formidable obstacles to gathering in tax funds in advance of expenditures, the assembly had recourse to borrowing. The experience of the people with government promises, however, had been such, that, as Hutchinson writes, "few people, at first, inclined to lend to the province, though they were assured of payment in a short time with interest. The Treasurer, therefore, was ordered to make payment to the creditors of government in promissory notes, payable to the bearer in silver in two or three years, with lawful interest. This," he continues, "was really better than any private security; but the people, who had seen so much of the bad effects of their former paper money, from its depreciation, could not consider this without danger, and the notes were sold for silver at discount, which continued until it was found that the promise made by government was punctually performed. From that time, the publick security was preferred to private, and the treasurer's notes more sought for than those of any other person whomsoever. This," he proudly concludes, "was the era of publick credit in Massachusetts

Bay."[52]

This statement accurately sums up the history of the period. Between 1750 and 1764 there were some fifty odd acts authorizing the treasurer to issue his certificates. These were issued either to those who would lend or to the public creditors. They bore interest at six per cent, and no certificate was issued for a sum less than six pounds. Insofar as they were paid out to the public creditors rather than given to voluntary lenders, they bore a striking similarity to the early bills of credit, which were issued in much the same manner, bore interest, and were not a legal tender. The chief difference is not in the form, but in the persistent determination of the legislature during this period to redeem them punctually and not lapse into the old practice of extending their periods and allowing the number outstanding to accumulate.

When the treasurer's certificates, or notes as they

---

52. Hutchinson, History, III, 7. The province also attempted to borrow in England. Early in 1755 the assembly authorized William Bollan, the province agent in London, to borrow in Great Britain for the use of the province "the sum of ₤23,000 sterling, in Spanish Mill'd dollars, at the lowest interest that can be obtained, for the space of six years." The silver so raised was to be shipped to Massachusetts. In all probability the effort to float the loan failed, for there is no evidence in the treasurer's reports that the money was ever received into the treasury. Acts and Resolves of Mass. Bay, III, 813 (Province Laws, 1754-1755, c. 33). Small sums may have occasionally been borrowed later, but they were negligible at most.

came to be called, were once endorsed, they became "negotiable without further writing." During the time of the war, notes were issued in small sums to pay the soldiers. These notes enjoyed a circulation and consequently exerted an influence on prices. Except for these small notes, however, the notes "were not generally circulated." In 1764 Governor Francis Bernard reported:

> At present [the notes] are allmost wholly in large Sums & kept up as Securities: and as they're more Valuable than cash, & the rule is in issuing new Notes to prefer the Creditors upon former Notes, Treasurers Notes are hard to be got & are not at all circulated. So that the present Currency is wholly Specie, & neither wants nor receives any assistance from Treasurers Notes. 53

Reference to Figure VIII will enable one to follow conveniently the annual issues and retirements of these notes, together with the amount outstanding near the end of each year. The issues before the beginning of

---

53. Governor Francis Bernard to Board of Trade, Boston, August 1, 1764. C. O. 323/19 (Library of Congress Transcripts). Harrison Gray, the province treasurer, in 1762 petitioned the assembly for compensation for "his extraordinary Services in issuing his Notes for ₤210,596.19.10 in paying off 6,000 Soldiers who served under General Amherst." Acts and Resolves of Mass. Bay, XVII, 179 (March 5, 1763). The Boston merchant, John Rowe, in 1759, in commissioning James Otis to collect a debt for him wrote: "Treasury notes will do as well as money." Rowe to James Otis, Boston, October 1, 1759, Anne R. Cunningham [ed.], Letters and Diary of John Rowe, p. 339. Merchants from time to time advertised that they would sell their goods for Treasurer's notes, which would be received at full value. Boston News-Letter, January 29, February 5, 1761. In the same paper on June 3, 1762, "A Convenient Dwelling-House" was advertised to be sold "for Cash or Treasurers notes."

TABLE IX

MASSACHUSETTS TREASURER'S CERTIFICATES

(End of year figures)

Year	Amount Issued £	Amount Cancelled £	Amount Outstanding £	
1750	27,400		27,400	
1751	30,845	16,746	41,499	
1752		22,382	19,117	
1753		7,248x	11,869	
1754	18,414	6,108	24,175	
1755	99,000	13,976	109,199	
1756	146,000	24,141	231,058	
1757	137,500	108,711	259,847	
1758	238,000	101,395	396,452	Superseded
1759	226,466	44,882	578,036	
1760	242,714	118,919	701,831	APPENDIX
1761	79,100	188,372	592,759	Table IX (Revised)
1762	77,951	160,350	510,360	
1763	83,650	174,000	420,010	
1764	138,000	181,654	376,356	
1765	197,000	87,775	485,581	
1766	157,000	247,029	395,552	
1767	125,850		521,402	
1768	100,000	203,123	418,279	
1769	164,150		582,429	
1770		129,468	452,961	
1771		102,543	350,418	
1772			350,418	
1773	13,000		363,418	
1774	14,550	37,078	340,890	

x Burning of March 21, 1754.

Source: List of issues, Report to Board of Trade, 1764, C. O. 323/19, L. C. P.; issuing acts in Massachusetts Acts and Resolves; burnings in ibid.

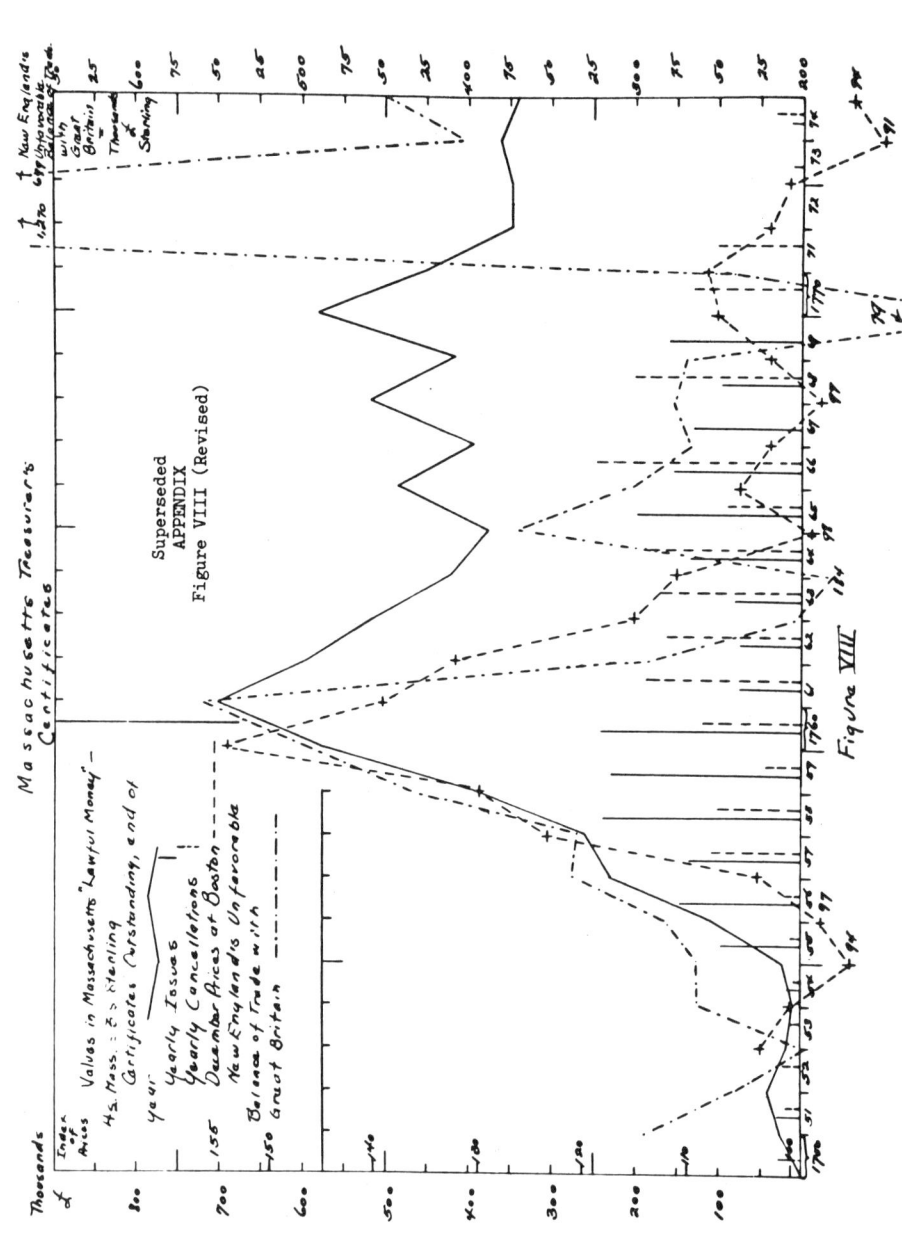

Figure VIII

the French and Indian War were relatively small. At the end of 1754 there were outstanding no more than ₤24,000 of the notes. In 1755 began the wartime issues, and the sum outstanding at the end of each year underwent a steady increase until by the close of 1760 there were some ₤702,000 in the hands of the creditors of the province. Beginning with the next year, however, retirements exceeded issues, and by the end of 1764 the amount outstanding had been reduced to about ₤376,000.

The amount of these securities outstanding in the peak year of 1760 represents a sum two and one-half times that of the greatest sum outstanding in bills of credit at the close of King George's War.[54] The bills of credit depreciated by about half, measured in silver, during that war. The treasurer's notes during the French and Indian War retained their silver value. But it should not be inferred from this fact that the currency of this latter period did not depreciate. Measured by what indices of prices are available, the value of the Massachusetts currency fell by about forty per cent between 1755 and 1760.[55] By 1764, however, the price

---

54. The sum outstanding in 1748, computed in old tenor terms, amounted to something near ₤2,100,000. The sum outstanding in 1760 was expressed in "lawful money," and amounted to ₤702,000. This sum should be multiplied by 7 1/2 to convert it into old tenor. This gives ₤5,265,000, which is almost exactly 2 1/2 times the former sum.

55. A. H. Cole, <u>Wholesale Commodity Prices in the United States, 1700-1861</u>, I, 7, 118.

level had fallen, and money had regained its value.[56]

The treasurer's notes undoubtedly played a part in these price fluctuations. It will be noted in Figure VIII that during the war period, with but one notable exception, a rise or fall during any year in the amount of treasurer's notes outstanding was accompanied respectively by a rise or fall in prices. The fall in prices was of greater magnitude in proportion to the diminution of treasurer's notes than had been the case with respect to the rise. This is probably partially explained by the fact that during the later years of the struggle more and more of the notes were gathered in by investors and held out of circulation for the sake of the interest. The fact that the notes bore interest, which caused them thus to be withdrawn from circulation and held as investments, probably did more to prevent a further depreciation of the currency and to restore its value after the war than did the fact that the notes had not been made a legal tender. This fact is of significance when one comes to appraise the restraints laid upon the colonies by the British government. It will be recalled that the Currency Act of 1751 denied the legal tender quality to all bills of credit issued in New England after that year. In fact, only modest issues to meet the current

---

56. *Ibid.*

expenses of government were contemplated except in cases of war or invasion. In both cases the bills were to be adequately secured by taxes levied at the time of issue. Ordinarily they were to be retired within two years, although the time was extended to five years in the case of wartime issues. The merits of these provisions were two: in the first place, by denying the bills the legal tender quality it was made impossible to force payment of an obligation upon a creditor in depreciated bills; and, secondly, by requiring that the bills be retired within two or five years some limit was imposed upon the amounts that would be circulating at any one time. And it was, other things being equal, the amount of bills in circulation that determined their value. The provisions of the act, however, fell far short of providing a complete remedy. The ordinary course of things during a war was for expenditures to increase from year to year until, in the case of the colonies, victory had been achieved. This being so, it was possible for vast sums to become outstanding within the five year limitation. And even though long-term creditors might be protected by the fact that the bills were not a legal tender, the full force of whatever depreciation might result was none the less borne by those "in whose hands the bills were constantly dying." The payment of interest by Massachusetts provided an added safeguard. It induced the holding of the bills (treasurer's notes) as securities, and to the extent that this was accomplished as effectively withdrew them from circulation and curbed their tendency to depreciate as if they had been retired by tax funds.

But when all this is said, it should not be forgotten that creditors suffered by the price rise occasioned by the French and Indian War just as creditors before had suffered by the depreciation of the bills of credit during King George's War. The fall of prices between 1760 and 1764 likewise worked a hardship on those that had contracted long-term debts during the period of high prices. In the earlier war the depreciation of the bills of credit had served as a tax. In the later war, the taxes were of a different kind. In either case the cost of the war was paid. The usual supposition is that the latter method of paying the cost of a war is more equitable than the former. This is, to a degree, doubtless true; but the differences in effect between the two methods often turn out upon examination to be not so great as is usually thought. [56] Certainly to paint the

---

56. Theoretically the matter looks something like this. If we assume: (1) that debts are payable in bills of credit in such amounts as are equivalent to the silver value of the obligation when contracted; and (2) that one person holds his money about the same length of time as any other; then the loss in value occasioned by the depreciation of the currency is little different in its effects than would be a modern sales tax raising a revenue

experience of King George's War in the somber hues of unrelieved calamity, while using only the bright colors of a new day in picturing "the era of publick credit" that followed, is to evince a lack of that sensitiveness to similarities of effect resulting from different instruments that is often of the very essence of economic and historical analysis.

As earlier a parliamentary grant arising out of the Cape Breton expedition had made it possible for Massachusetts to retire her bills of credit and return to a silver currency, so during the French and Indian War successive parliamentary grants in large measure enabled her to retire her treasurer's certificates and to remain on a specie standard. The various grants in which Massa-

---

sufficient to command the same amount of goods and services. These conditions, insofar as the acts of 1742 and 1747 providing for the payment of debts in bills in sums equal in value to the silver value of the obligation when contracted were effective, prevailed in Massachusetts during the period of her "great inflation."

I do not mean to suggest that our assumptions were fully met in Massachusetts during this period, or that even if they had been there are not objections to a depreciating currency. I merely wish to point out that under the conditions that obtained during King George's War, the differences in the effects of financing the war by the issuance of depreciating bills of credit over financing it by borrowing and issuing treasurer's certificates to creditors, as was the case during the French and Indian War, were not so great as is commonly assumed. We have become so used to seeing the word "fraudulent" or its equivalent coupled to paper issues by writers on the subject, and so used to seeing the word "sound" applied to the now more orthodox methods, that we have been blinded to the fact that upon a closer examination the two methods may turn out to be quite similar in their effects.

chusetts shared are set out in the note below,[57] and the share of Massachusetts in each, together with how and when it was received in the province, may be followed in Table X.

---

57. Parliamentary grants in which Massachusetts shared:

Year	Act	Amount ₤ Sterling	Reference: Statutes at Large
1756	29 Geo. II, c. 29	115,000	XXI, 465
1758	31 Geo. II, c. 33	27,380	XXII, 364
1759	32 Geo. II, c. 36	200,000	XXII, 534
1760	33 Geo. II, c. 18	200,000	XXIII, 34-35
1761	1 Geo. III, c. 19	200,000	XXIII, 302
1762	2 Geo. III, c. 34	133,333	XXIV, 197
1763	3 Geo. III, c. 17	133,333	XXIV, 33

TABLE X

Parliamentary Grants

Year	Share of Massachusetts £'s Sterling	Amt. Recd. in Province Lawful money	How Received
1756	£54,000	£68,744	Silver - £40,000
1757	---	---	Proceeds, bills of exchange - £28,744
1758	27,380	---	
1759	60,000#	35,000#	Gold
1760	60,634	80,000#	Gold
1761	57,602	81,600	Proceeds, bills of exchange drawn on agent.
1762	42,774	75,900	do.
1763	45,419	47,600	do.
1764	---	54,765	do.
1765	---	1,862 20,741	From treasurer of Penna. Proceeds of bills of exchange drawn on agent.
1766	---	(-1,753)	Subtract from 1766; protested bills redeemed.
----	5,191x	---	
1769	---	884	Proceeds of bills of exchange drawn on agent

| Total | £353,000 | £465,343 | |

\# Approximate.
x To be distributed between and added to grants of 1761 and 1762.

References: Worthington C. Ford (ed.), "Jaspar Mauduit," Massachusetts Historical Society, Collections, vol. 74, pp. 8n., 14n., 93, 126, 154, 155, 157; Reports of Committee on Treasurer's Accounts, Acts and Resolves of Mass. Bay, XVI, 107; XVII, 248, 416, 559; XVIII, 18-19, 134, 255-256, 472;

The rôle of the parliamentary grants in supplying funds that could be used to meet the expenses of the war or to retire the treasurer's certificates is an obvious one. Perhaps, however, something should be said as to how they aided Massachusetts in her effort to maintain a specie standard. The fact that the balance of her trade with England was unfavorable drained away specie to the mother country. Only if the balance could be improved or her trade with the West Indies and Southern Europe could be made to provide bills of exchange or specie to meet it could specie sufficient to meet the demands for a medium of trade be retained in Massachusetts. The trade carried on with the French and Spanish colonies during the war, despite the fact that it was a trade with the enemy, probably increased, and with it the supply of specie.[58] But the increase in the adverse balance with Britain was probably even greater. The figures are not available for Massachusetts alone, but changes in her balance with Great Britain are probably proportional to changes for New England as a whole. In

---

acts authorizing the drawing of bills of exchange on the London agent, ibid., IV, 458-459, 662-663, 719-721, 805-806; resolves relative to same, XVII, 47; XVIII, 218; George L. Beer, British Colonial Policy, 1754-1765, 1907, p. 54n.

58. Beer, chap. vi. Cf. later complaints quite general throughout the northern colonies of the stoppage of the inflow of silver from the foreign islands as a result of the peace. See, for example, the complaint cited below, chap. vii, note 34.

1754 the adverse balance of New England with the mother country amounted to £263,000 sterling. With the beginning of the war it rose steadily until in 1760 it had reached the sum of £562,000. It then declined until it was no more than £184,000 for the year 1763.[59] These changes may be conveniently followed on Figure VIII.

It will be recalled that the silver from the Cape Breton grant had no sooner begun to be paid out in exchange for bills of credit than some of it had been exported "to London, New-York, and Pennsylvania." Although this outflow soon ceased, there were renewed demands for silver to ship off as time went on and the balance with England grew more adverse. Such being the case, the successive parliamentary grants ameliorated the situation, either by providing specie, or by making possible the drawing of bills of exchange against the grant after it had been paid into the agent's hands in London.

---

59. Computed from figures in Johnson et al., Domestic and Foreign Commerce of U. S., I, 120-121.
New England's unfavorable balance of trade with Great Britain (excess of exports to over imports from Britain).

(£'s Sterling)

Year	Amount	Year	Amount
1750	295,204	1758	435,490
1751	242,687	1759	501,082
1752	199,027	1760	561,845
1753	262,128	1761	298,000
1754	262,895	1762	205,652
1755	282,263	1763	184,039
1756	337,012	1764	371,608
1757	335,848		

Massachusetts was granted £54,000 sterling in 1756. It was converted into specie, and by August had been transported to New York on a government vessel. The vessel, however, was ordered to sail directly to Halifax, and the captain was forced to leave the money in New York.[60] "As the Exigencies of Government [made] it necessary that the Money should be forthwith received into the Treasury," it was suggested that Governor Shirley, who had early that year from the moneys in his possession lent the province the equivalent of £30,000 sterling,[61] be asked to accept repayment in New York from the funds lodged there. The remainder of the grant, amounting, after the always present fees and charges had been deducted, to £21,558 sterling was to be transported to Boston as expeditiously as possible. The firm of Charles Alpthorp and Son, with whom the money had been deposited, engaged to pay the sum "in Boston, in lawful money, at 33 1/3 per cent advance [over sterling], as fast as they [could] raise it; and to compleat the whole in three months at furthest."[62] How the payment was made does not appear. It could have been accomplished either by bills of exchange or by shipment of specie; but it was doubtless Alpthorp's purpose to transfer the funds by the former method if possible. The

---

60. Acts and Resolves of Mass. Bay, XV, 584.
61. Ibid., III, 893-897 (Province Laws, 1755-56, c. 27; passed February 28, 1756).
62. Ibid., XV, 588.

£30,000 sterling (equivalent to £40,000 Massachusetts money) supplied earlier by Shirley had been in specie, doubtless sent over in that form from England to be used to meet the military expenses of the war. The grant was received then, part in specie, and part in all probability in the proceeds of bills of exchange.

In January, 1759, the province agent was instructed to transmit the grant of £27,380 sterling of the year 1758 "in Johanna's of full weight" if they could be procured, "otherwise in other [P]ortugal or Spanish Gold."[63] This he doubtless did, probably sending over the money within the year. It probably amounted to near £35,000 lawful money.[64]

Massachusetts' share of the grant of 1759 was shipped over in gold in October, 1760. It amounted to something in the neighborhood of £80,000 lawful money.[65] This was the last of the grants to be sent over in specie. The Massachusetts assembly would gladly have continued the practice, but it became difficult for the agent to secure specie at a price that would not entail a seven per

---

63. Ibid., XIV, 268-269 (Resolves, 1758-59, c. 150; passed January 20, 1759).
64. Only a summary statement of the treasurer's accounts for the years 1759-60 and 1760-61 is printed in the Acts and Resolves. This makes it impossible to ascertain from that source when the payment was received or precisely how much it amounted to.
65. Jaspar Mauduit, p. 8, note, quoting from letters of the province agent, William Bollan, dated August 8, October 8, 1760.

cent loss to the province.[66] At this point Governor Bernard was successful in convincing the assembly that it was "just the same thing, whether you bring a certain quantity of specie into the Province, or prevent the like quantity from going out of it."[67] This latter could be accomplished by selling bills of exchange payable in London out of the proceeds of the grant. This practice was adopted,[68] and from 1761 on the parliamentary grants were all transferred by this method. The audits of the treasurer's accounts show that from May, 1761, to May, 1766, ₤280,000 lawful money were received into the treasury from this source.[69]

Over a ten year period, the grants amounted to nearly ₤353,000 sterling. This sum either provided the

---

66. Ibid., pp. 14-15, note, relying on letters of Bollan.
67. Felt, pp. 144-145.
68. Acts and Resolves of Mass. Bay, IV, 458-459 (Province Laws, 1761-62, c. 3; passed June 17, 1761); 581-582 (1762-63, c. 10; passed June 12, 1762); 719-721 (1764-65, c. 4; passed June 14, 1764); 805-806 (1765-66, c. 4; passed June 21, 1765); XVII, 47 (Resolves, 1761-62, c. 107; passed July 11, 1761); XVIII, 218 (1766-67, c. 225, passed March 20, 1767).
69. See Table X. There seems to have been a lively demand for the bills. For example on June 17, 1762, the province treasurer advertised that he would sell bills of exchange upon the province agent to the amount of ₤45,000 sterling at 138 to 100. A subscription list was opened. The offering was so oversubscribed that each subscriber obtained only ₤350 in bills for each ₤1000 subscribed. Boston News-Letter and New-England Chronicle, June 17, July 22, 1762. The keen demand for the bills is further evidence of the aid derived by the province from the parliamentary grants in maintaining a specie standard.

province with, or made possible the retention within the province of, an amount of specie almost twice as large as the Cape Breton grant, which had made possible the return to a metallic currency. Thus viewed, the contribution of the parliamentary grants to the successful functioning of Massachusetts' specie standard during these troubled years was not inconsiderable.

The bringing over of the grants of 1758 and 1759 in gold created a problem, however. It was stated early in 1762 that as a result of these importations of gold, that metal had "become by far the greatest part of the medium of trade" within the province.[70] This would indicate that much of the province's silver had been shipped off during the preceding years. Gold coins had been rated in 1750,[71] but they had not been made a legal tender. Small wonder then, that when they became the most important element in the province's medium of trade, a demand should arise to confer this quality upon them. This was proposed in the house in November, 1761, where it was successfully carried. The proposal, however, met with the determined opposition of Thomas Hutchinson, who was then a member of the council; and it was negatived by that body.[72] Hutchinson feared

---

70. Acts and Resolves of Mass. Bay, IV, 490 (Province Laws, 1761-62, c. 22; passed January 31, 1762).
71. Ibid., III, 494-495 (Province Laws, 1749-1750, c. 19).
72. Felt, pp. 146-147.

that the measure would drive away the silver of the province and eventually depreciate the currency.[73] The vote in the council rejecting the measure had been so close that Hutchinson was afraid the proposal might be carried the next session. The thought filled him with anxiety, for he wrote, "If it succeed, I look upon it to be the first step of our return to Egypt."[74]

As Hutchinson had feared, the proposal was enacted into law at the next session, early in 1762. The various gold coins and the English silver coins rated by the act of 1750 were declared "a legal tender in all payments, publick and private." At the same time a minimum weight for each of the coins was specified.[75]

Formerly, the treasurer's certificates had promised redemption in silver. Henceforth, they were to provide for redemption in either silver or gold at the rates that had been established by law for the several varie-

---

73. As quoted in ibid., p. 147.
74. Ibid.
75. Acts and Resolves of Mass. Bay, IV, 515-516 (Province Laws, 1761-62, c. 28; passed February 8, 1762).
     Minimum weights for coins rated by the act of 1750. (Vide supra, p. 257, note 23.)

	dwt.	gr.
Johannes	18	10
Half-Johannes	9	5
Moidore	6	22 1/4
Guinea	5	9

"... and such of the coins which shall fall short of the respective weights aforesaid shall, nevertheless, be accounted a tender, with an allowance for such deficiency at the rate of gold at twopence halfpenny per grain."

ties of coin in circulation within the province. The treasurer was authorized to give out certificates in the new form in exchange for the old to all that might wish them.[76]

Happily, Hutchinson's forebodings that this introduction of a form of bimetallism would, by overvaluing gold, drive silver from the province, and that this would in turn lead to legislation raising the value of gold coin still further,[77] proved without foundation. The new plan seems to have functioned quite as satisfactorily as the old.

During the whole period Massachusetts kept up her determination to exclude the bills of Connecticut, New Hampshire, and Rhode Island from circulating within her borders.[78] The bills of New Hampshire and Rhode Island

---

76. Ibid., IV, 490-491 (Province Laws, 1761-62, c. 22; passed January 31, 1762); pp. 515-516 (c. 28, passed February 8, 1762); pp. 516-518 (c. 29, passed February 10, 1762). The advertisement of the province treasurer notifying holders of the certificates that they may exchange them appears in Boston News-Letter and New-England Chronicle, June 17, June 24, and July 1, 1762. The treasurer's reports indicate that a total of ₤195,051 in certificates were exchanged. Acts and Resolves, XVII, 248, 416.
77. Felt, p. 147, quoting Hutchinson.
78. Acts and Resolves of Mass. Bay, III, 714-716 (Province Laws, 1753-54, c. 23; passed December 27, 1753); pp. 1044-1046 (1756-57, c. 34; passed March 31, 1757); IV, 220-221, 1758-59, c. 36; passed April 24, 1759); p. 513 (1761-62, c. 26; passed January 30, 1762).

continued to depreciate during this time, while those of Connecticut were after some years placed upon a secure foundation. Massachusetts must have had considerable success in excluding the bills of New Hampshire and Rhode Island; but during the latter part of the period at least the bills of Connecticut appear to have been received in business transactions within the province despite the penalties of the law. Indeed, the Boston merchant John Gould, Jr., openly advertised in the Boston News-Letter in 1761 that he would "receive Connecticut Lawful Money" in payment for goods he lists for sale.[79]

During the period between the close of King George's War and the close of the French and Indian War, Massachusetts had accomplished a successful revolution in her currency and financial methods. She had availed herself of the fortunate circumstance of the large Cape Breton grant to place her currency upon a silver basis; she had financed her considerable contribution to the French and Indian War by taxing, borrowing where she could, and issuing treasurer's notes to the public creditors when circumstances forced her to; but in every case she redeemed her securities promptly in silver or gold.

---

79. Issue of March 12, 1761.

Moreover, these things were accomplished despite the fact that the contribution of Massachusetts to the war was greater in proportion to her resources than that of any other colony. Altogether, it was an enviable record. On the other hand, in comparing the record of the province with those of the other colonies during the period, it should be remembered that she received at the close of King George's War a parliamentary grant large enough to enable her to retire her paper currency. And after all, the providing of a medium to take the place of the paper was the great hurdle to be got over. Moreover, the commercial position of Massachusetts, permitting her, as it did, to engage in the profitable trade with the West Indies during the war, together with the large parliamentary grants that she received, greatly aided her in preserving a metallic medium during these strife-filled years.

The currency problems of New Hampshire at the close of King George's War were similar to those that had confronted Massachusetts. During the war New Hampshire had more than trebled her currency outstanding. At the close of 1751, there were in circulation £113,865 in new tenor bills, together with a negligible sum in old tenor.[80] The bills of New Hampshire had in general

---

80. Charles J. Bullock, *Essays on the Monetary History of the United States,* p. 245. The sum in new

terms undergone a common depreciation with those of Massachusetts and the other New England colonies; silver had risen from about 8s. to 15s. the ounce, new tenor, since 1744. New Hampshire had declined to act on Governor Shirley's suggestion that the New England colonies attempt to work out some scheme for retiring their bills of credit and putting their currency on a more satisfactory basis. But if after the close of hostilities no attempt was made to retire the bills outstanding, no more were issued for the time being, if for no other reason than that all legislative business had come to a stop because the governor refused to approve the assembly's choice of a speaker until that body admitted representatives from certain towns.[81] In the autumn of 1752 the quarrel was at last composed, and the legislature turned its attention to the public business that had accumulated during the four years of legislative deadlock.

---

tenor outstanding was equivalent to £455,424 old tenor. To this should be added something like £5,481 old tenor to give the total outstanding, or £460,905 old tenor. It seems advisable henceforth to use new tenor terms.

81. Dr. William Douglass, Summary, II, 37-38, 193n.; Documents and Records relating to the Province of New-Hampshire, VI, 69-126 (hereinafter cited as N. H. Prov. Papers). Dr. Douglass, atrabilious as always, writing at this time remarks: "New Hampshire ... have had no legislative capacity for some time, and [are] consequently incapable of augmenting their paper currency, much to the detriment of their governor, who by consenting to such emissions, might have obtained an addition to his salary."

It was during the legislative hiatus that Parliament had acted with respect to the paper currency of New England, and the New Hampshire assembly found itself faced with the problem of retiring its outstanding bills according to their periods, and at the same time meeting the exigencies of governmental finance without its customary instrument of legal tender paper currency. So impelling were the circumstances, that in October, 1752, the assembly authorized a scheme for investing the province money lately received from certain parliamentary grants and now in the hands of the province agent in London so that it might produce an annual sum to be applied to retiring the province bill otherwise unprovided for, and in May, 1753, reemitted ₤12,500 of the new tenor bills that were in the treasury. These actions together with the reasons for them were explained in a memorial to the king in July, 1753. The memorialists urged that it had been the emergency of the late war that had caused them to break through their "Determination & Resolution to have no more Paper Bills on the credit of the Province Extant than what was allowed by your Majesty's Immediate Instructions," i.e., ₤6,000. Provision for calling in all the war issues save the last had been made at the time of the emissions by levying taxes sufficient for the purpose.

The retirement of the issue of ₤6,000 new tenor in 1746 for the purpose of promoting "the intended Expedition against Canada" had been unprovided for insofar as taxes levied for the purpose were concerned. The act had, however, provided that in case the expenditure should be repaid by a parliamentary grant, "then the money so repaid should be put into the Treasury as a Fund for the immediate calling in and sinking [the] said Bills by exchange with the Possessors thereof or otherways as the General Assembly should order, and in case the sum so repaid should fall short of the sum expended" the difference "should be levyed by a Tax on the Polls & Estate of the Inhabitants ... in such way and manner as the Genl Assembly should determine at their next session after that matter could be ascertained." These are the only provisions of the act that may be interpreted as fixing a period for the retiring of the bills; strictly interpreted, however, they may be considered as having substantially that effect. What the assembly now proposed was that the province's share of the Cape Breton grant and of the grant to make reimbursement for expenses incurred in preparing for the intended expedition against Canada in 1746 should be left in the hands of the province agent in London and invested by him in the national stock, and that the annual interest arising therefrom should be used to retire the province bills otherwise unprovided for. In addition the money so arising was to be supplemented by a tax. This scheme would in effect constitute a postponing of the periods for retiring the bills and in consequence might be considered a violation of the Currency Act of 1751. It was also stated that provision had been made to retire the £12,500 reemitted in 1753 by a tax that called in the sum in five annual installments beginning in December of that year. The necessity for these measures was represented as arising from the fact that the province was "now Burthened with an annual Tax of £3,800 new Ten^r, besides what" must be raised "for the necessary support of the Governm^t in those years, which amounts to double the sum ever rais'd in this Province in any one former year and which by no means (as we can see) can be raised if our Paper Bills should be immediately called in and sunk, we having neither silver or gold passing amongst us."[82]

The memorial was sent to the province agent, Captain John Thomlinson, apparently with instructions to use it as his best judgment suggested. And that it turned out, was to suppress it. In October, 1753, he

---

82. Address of Council and Assembly of N. H. to the King, July 26, 1753, N. H. Papers, VI, 223-226. See also, ibid., p. 143 (House Journal, Oct. 7, 1752); p. 144, Com. of Correspondence to John Thomlinson, Portsmouth, N. H., Nov. 18, 1752.

wrote:

>As to the Memorial you have sent me ...[,] my present opinion is, That the presenting a memorial to his Majesty is improper at all times, But this memorial would be particularly improper, as it prays for leave to place your money in the Funds, which is already done in effect, and ... you have nothing to fear on that account, if you remain quiet on that head, and can in all other money affairs conform to the late Act of Parliament ..., as you must do, by all means, and if the ₤12,500 New Tenor you in May last pass'd an Act for, is contrary to the said Act of Parliament, are you to tell his Majesty that you have done it, when it is not in his Majesty's power to Excusing your Breach of an act of Parliament, or Grant an Instruction to his Governor to act contrary thereto? Therefore to present this Memorial to his Majesty (supposing it was decent at any time to Memorial the King) would (in my opinion) be involving you in such difficultys as not easily to be got over, and raise all your Enemys in judgment against you. Therefore I shall keep it by me in private; however I am glad to have such a clear State of the affairs of the Province in my possession, as it may be of great use to me if I should be call'd upon for any thing you have done amiss. 83

Thomlinson as agent for the province had received the sum of ₤16,356 sterling as New Hampshire's portion of the Cape Breton grant, and a sufficient sum from the grant of the next year for providing reimbursement for the intended expedition against Canada, that he was able to report in 1751 that he had nearly ₤30,000 sterling in his hands at the disposal of the province. 84

---

83. John Thomlinson to N. H. Com. of Correspondence, East Barnet, October 9, 1753, ibid., pp. 227-228.
84. The sum received from the Cape Breton grant was ₤16,355 13s. 4d. (21 Geo. II, c. 33 (1748)) and that from the grant to reimburse the province for the intended expedition against Canada (23 Geo. II, c. 21 (1750)) ₤21,446 10s. 10 1/2d. N. H. Prov. Papers, XVIII, 381-384, contains the treasury warrants for the two grants. Canada grant dated October 25, 1750; Cape Breton grant,

Thomlinson, who in his capacity as a merchant, it will be recalled, was an old opponent of a paper currency, had upon receiving the grants advised the province that the most agreeable thing that they could do, and indeed what it was expected in England that they would do, was to use the sum to retire their outstanding bills of credit.[85] Upon receiving the order of the province to invest the money, he wrote, "I am sorry to find the Province Money is like to continue in my hands, when it ought to be applied in one Shape or other, as I formerly wrote you, for the benefit of the Creditors of the Province ...."[86] Nevertheless, Thomlinson did his best to invest the money, although he encountered dif-

---

December 19, 1750. The province agent honored certain charges against the Canada grant. After these and the fees and expenses connected with the receipt of the grants had been met, there remained just short of £30,000 sterling. Thomlinson to Theodore Atkinson, London, March, 1750/51, ibid., pp. 370-372; same to same, East Barnet, July 19, 1751, ibid., pp. 385-388.

85. Thomlinson to Atkinson, London, March 4, 1750/1, ibid., p. 371.

86. Same to same, London, March 2, 1752/3, ibid., p. 402. Thomlinson had written to Theodore Atkinson, the provincial secretary, July 19, 1751:

I shou'd think [the House of Representatives] woul'd chuse a committee to be join'd to a Committee of his Majesty's Councill, & call in, and sink the Paper Money and give the Possessors thereof Bills of Exch^a for the Respective Sums so bro't in by them, at the rate of Exchange as the Massachusetts have done [He was wrong about Massachusetts.], and advise me properly of such Sums drawn on me, & they shall be paid punctually, or if they think proper to order me to try Silver, & send it over, I shall readily do it: but the former Method will be saving Freight, Insurance, and other charges -- " N. H. Prov. Papers, XVIII, 386.

ficulties in making advantageous purchases of the public stock.[87] In the years to come, the interest money was applied to the purpose of retiring the province bills or to meeting the extraordinary expenses occasioned by the French and Indian War.

Had the £30,000 sterling in the agent's hands been invested in silver and brought to the province, it would have been sufficient to redeem about £85,000 new tenor of the province bills at the rate of depreciation then prevailing. This would have left about £29,000 outstanding. In the light of the Massachusetts experience, it appears that a return to a specie currency would have been possible at this time, given sufficient determination on the part of the government. Nevertheless, conditions were not so favorable in New Hampshire as in Massachusetts, and the program proposed by the assembly, while probably outside the letter of the act of Parliament of 1751, was in accord with its spirit. Moreover, the action of the province in presenting the whole matter to the crown in its memorial was certainly straightforward, at least up until the point where the perhaps more realistic Thomlinson suppressed the document. All in all, it appears that the assembly was with reasonable good faith trying to work its way out of

---

87. Thomlinson to Com. of Correspondence, Oct. 9, 1753, *ibid.*, VI, 226-227.

what it felt was a difficult situation.

Nor were things to brighten in the future. No sooner had the province laid its plans for the gradual calling in of its currency, than the French and Indian War broke out. During the year 1754 the province retired ₤14,132, leaving the sum of ₤99,531 new tenor in circulation.[88] The expense of sending commissioners to the conference with the Iroquois at Albany and a little later that of ransoming "a number of persons now in Captivity among the French and Indians" occasioned the drawing of bills of exchange on the interest money in Thomlinson's hands in London. But the assembly demonstrated its good faith in both instances by levying a tax to retire a sum in bills of credit equivalent to the amount diverted from the interest fund.[89]

All the difficulties of the province, however, did not come from the trouble with the French and Indians. Part of it was inherent in the frontier economy that prevailed. In 1754 to make it easier for the people to pay their taxes, such payments were made receivable in rated commodities.[90] This, of course, coming as it

---

88. Bullock, p. 247.
89. N. H. Prov. Papers, VI, 285, 334.
90. Ibid., p. 274 (April 19, 1754). This was the revival of an old practice; and once revived, it was continued for a number of years. Ibid., 387, 516, 591, 669-670, 712, 751, 870; VII, 39, 80, 107 (as cited in Bullock, p. 247, n. 5).

did just before new issues of bills of credit, by lessening their use, lessened their value. But it is perhaps too much to have asked the members of the New Hampshire assembly to have foreseen the future.

When in 1755 the French and Indian War began in earnest, the province had recourse to bills of credit issued under the clause of the Currency Act of 1751 authorizing such issues in "sudden and extraordinary emergencies of government." The issues during the first three years of the war together with the depreciation they underwent may be followed in Table XI.

TABLE XI

NEW HAMPSHIRE NEW TENOR BILLS OF CREDIT

Date of emitting act	Sum emitted	Value in silver at time of emission: s./Spanish dollar	Value in silver when called in: s./Spanish dollar	Date called in	Fund provided to sink bills
1755 Apr. 11	30,000	15/	30/	₤6,000 annually Dec. 31, 1755, to Dec. 31, 1760	Tax on polls & estates
1755 Sept. 5	15,000	15/	30/	₤15,000 Dec. 31, 1760	do.
1756 Apr. 14	30,000	18/	30/	₤10,000 Dec. 25, 1759 ₤20,000 Dec. 25, 1761	do., "deducting the King's Bounty."
1756 Apr. 14	5,750	18/	30/	₤5,750 Dec. 31, 1761	Tax on polls & estates
1757 Feb. 25	20,000	25/	30/	₤10,000 Dec. 25, 1761 ₤10,000 Dec. 25, 1762	do., "deducting the King's Bounty."

Report of George Jaffrey, New Hampshire treasurer, to Board of Trade, September 22, 1764. C. O. 323/19, Library of Congress photostats. Bullock, p. 251, indicates an issue of ₤20,500 during the year 1758. The printed records give no information concerning the nature of this act (N. H. Prov. Papers, VI, 663, 665). It is merely entitled an "Act for supplying the Treasury with [₤20,500]." It may have provided for a reissue of bills of credit in the treasury, or it may have been merely a tax act. The omission of any mention of this sum in the Report of 1764 probably indicates that it was not a new issue.

By 1758 the bills had lost half their value. Since demands for funds showed no signs of abating, and since the British government had now embarked upon a policy of making grants to the colonies to reimburse them at least in part for their expenditures, the province began the emission of bills redeemable in sterling funds. Henceforward, these were the only form of bills emitted. The various issues may be followed in Table XII. Some of the later issues bore interest, and all the emissions were reported to have preserved their value.[91]

It is impossible to follow the retirements in detail for the years of the war. In 1764 the treasurer reported as to the emissions of 1755 through 1757, which were secured by tax funds levied at the time of the various issues, that

> The Sums of these Several Emissions, agreeable to the Periods prefixed in the Acts, were brought into the Treasury by Taxes; but as there was other Money Current of Different Value & of Different Denominations, to ease the Individuals who paid the Taxes, they had Liberty to pay their Taxes in any of the Bills then Current & those Different Bills to lay in the Treasury to redeem the Residue of those funds. So that in Effect, the Emissions above mentioned by this Deposit are brought into the Treasury & burn't.

Of the £67,000 issued in sterling bills from 1758 to 1762, £39,825 17s. 10d. were reported to have been retired by June 23, 1764.[92] Moreover, the interest

---

91. Bullock, pp. 252-253; Report to B. T., September 22, 1764, loc. cit.
92. Ibid.

TABLE XII

NEW HAMPSHIRE STERLING BILLS

Date of emitting act	Sum emitted £	Time when issued	Time provided for sinking	Amount to be sunk £	Funds for sinking
1758 Mar. 24	9,000	Jan. 1, 1759	Dec. 31, 1759	9,000	"The King's Bounty & Bills of Exch^a. on London."
1759 Mar. 7	5,000	Apr. 2, 1759	Dec. 25, 1762	1,000	do. & tax on polls & estates
	1,000	Nov. 1, 1759	[sic]		
	7,000	Jan. 1, 1760	Jan. 1, 1763	7,000	
	£13,000				
1760 Feb. 12	8,000	Mar. 1, 1760	Dec. 25, 1764	8,000	
	7,000	Jan. 1, 1761	Dec. 25, 1765	7,000	do.
	£15,000				
1761 Apr. 20	12,000	May 1, 1761	Dec. 25, 1765	12,000	
	8,000	Jan. 1, 1762	Dec. 25, 1766	8,000	do.
	£20,000				
1762 Mar. 22	10,000	Jan. 1, 1763	Dec. 25, 1767	10,000	do.
Total	£67,000	Amount sunk as of June 23, 1764		£39,825/17/10	

"The Drawing of Bills of Exchange on the Agent at London for the King's Bounty [i.e., the various parliamentary grants] and the Burthen of other Taxes, on the People of the Province, occasioned some Alteration in the Taxes prescribed in the Acts of the General Assembly by which the above Bills of Credit were created & issued and to be called in & Sunk." Report of B. T., Sept. 22, 1764, loc. cit. (Continued, notes, next page.)

bearing bills of the later issues seem to have been held out of circulation, as was usually the case with such issues.⁹³

From the data presented it is apparent that during the later years of the war the currency of New Hampshire was made up of diverse elements; new tenor bills, sterling bills, and rated commodities. Moreover, increasing amounts in gold and silver seem to have found their way into the province during the period. The province's share of the grant of 1756 was £8,000 sterling. This was converted in Spanish silver and Portuguese gold and shipped to America along with the Massachusetts funds arising from the same grant. The money was left with Sir Charles Hardy, the governor of New York. From this point, New Hampshire handled the matter as had Massachusetts. Governor Shirley was repaid the sum of £3,000 sterling that the province had borrowed from him; and the New York merchants, Charles Alpthorp & Son, engaged to pay the remaining sum of £4,639 9s. 7d. "in Boston

---

Bullock in his list of issues of sterling bills, p. 253 n. 4, has no account of the £9,000 issue of 1758. The act of 1762 authorized the issuance of £20,000, "Ten thousand pounds for sinking Canada & Louisburgh money & ten thousand pounds ... to be Improved as the General Assembly may order ...." N. H. Prov. Papers, VI, 844. The latter £10,000 were issued to meet the charges of the province. Ibid., 869. It appears doubtful, however, if the £10,000 authorized for exchanging the bills indicated above were ever issued.

93. Bullock, p. 253; N. H. Prov. Papers, VII, 65.

in Spanish milled dollars on Demand."[94] Thereafter references to gold and silver circulating in the colony are more frequent. The later grants seem to have been transferred by means of bills of exchange drawn upon the agent in London.[95]

Of the period under review, Belknap in his History of New Hampshire says: "At length sterling money became the standard of all contracts; and though the paper continued passing as a currency, its value was regulated by the price of silver, and the course of exchange."[96] By 1764 whatever sentiment there had been for paper money as such had died out. In this year a committee of both houses of the legislature, weary of the burden of the war, expressed the opinion that "an other Emission of paper currency would ... be fruitless & attended with mischievous consequences well known to every considering person the least acquainted with the circumstances of the Province."[97] In the light of the later record of

---

94. "Account of Gold and Silver Purchased for New Hampshire, 1756," London, April 3, 1756, N. H. Prov. Papers, XVIII, 443-444. John Thomlinson, John Handbury, and Barlow Trecothick handled the transaction. They purchased ₤2,123 8s. 9d. worth of Spanish silver, ₤5,509 16s. of Portuguese gold, and ₤6 4s. 10d. of miscellaneous coin making ₤7,639 9s. 7d. sterling in all. Charges and commissions consumed nearly all of the remainder of the grant of ₤8,000. Concerning the handling of the money on this side of the water, see ibid., VI, 578-579, 587-589.
 95. Ibid., VI, VII, XVIII, passim.
 96. Jeremy Belknap, History of New Hampshire (1813 ed.), II, 237.
 97. N. H. Prov. Papers, VII, 30 (January 28, 1764).

the province, this seems more than an excuse for evading a requisition of the crown and represents rather a genuine desire to abolish a paper currency. This the province was able to accomplish in 1771.

Connecticut also inherited the currency problems that were New England's common legacy from King George's War. At the close of the conflict she immediately took steps to rehabilitate her currency. It is true that the Connecticut program was at its inception neither so comprehensive nor so well thought out as was that of Massachusetts. But by the middle of the decade following the war, she had in her own way worked out a set of measures that embraced practically all of the points of the Massachusetts program. In view of these accomplishments, one is forced to the conclusion that Connecticut has suffered needlessly in comparison with Massachusetts, and largely, one suspects, because she had no masterly publicist such as Thomas Hutchinson to call attention to her good deeds.

Early in 1748, when Massachusetts was considering the matter of reforming her currency, Governor Shirley wrote to Jonathan Law, the governor of Connecticut, conveying Massachusetts' proposal of commissioners from the various New England colonies to discuss joint action in the matter of currency reform and suggesting a plan for Connecticut's return to specie. The plan involved borrowing silver in England to redeem the bills of credit of the colony.[98] Moreover, there were promptings relayed from England that the best way to prevent the attempts of the English merchants to force the withholding of the Cape Breton grant until the currency of New England was settled was to apply "the Money granted to redeem and finish [New England's] fatal Paper Currency."[99] Shirley's scheme, however, did not recommend itself to Governor Law, partly because of the difficulties involved in repaying the silver with interest after twelve years, but also because it seemed to him, as he stated it, "well calculated to defeat all the views we have had for setting up a Difference in our trade from them and making a Distinction between there Bills and ours ...."[100] What Law appears to have had in mind was a plan of developing trade directly with the outside world and thereby making Connecticut less dependent on the Boston merchants.[101]

The upshot of the matter was that Law in his speech

---

98. Shirley to Law, Boston, February 29, 1747/8, Conn. Hist. Soc., Collections, XV, 219-220; Law to Shirley, March 19, 1747/48, ibid., pp. 230-231; Law to Committee of War, Milford, March 20, 1747/48, ibid., pp. 231-232.
99. Josiah Willard to Law, Boston, March 5, 1747/48, ibid., 223-224.
100. Law to Committee of War, March 20, 1747/8, loc. cit.
101. In this connection see the letter of certain Norwich merchants to Law, February 16, 1747/8, Conn. Hist. Soc., Collections, XV, 212-214; also Law's speech to the assembly, May, 1748, ibid., XVI, 472-473.

to the assembly the following May discountenanced Shirley's proposal and suggested applying the colony's share of the anticipated Cape Breton and Canada expedition grants to the redemption of the outstanding bills of credit.[102] The May session ended with nothing done, but in October the assembly authorized the Governor to instruct the colonial agent, Eliakim Palmer, that if the colony's share of the Cape Breton grant were "paid to him without any restrictions as to the application of it," he should deposit it in some English bank were it would draw interest, and notify them immediately, "it being [their] design to draw [the money] again out of the bank with all possible speed, to appropriate it, so far as it [would] go, to draw in and discharge [the] bills of credit" of the colony.[103]

The following May the governor urged the setting up of a committee to receive and destroy all the bills of credit that should be brought into the treasury as a result of the parliamentary grants, as this would, he thought, set the colony "in a better light & be freer from Exception, than only a Good intention, which may be Suspected will never be put into Execution."[104]

---

102. Law's speech to assembly, May, 1748, ibid.
103. *Public Records of the Colony of Connecticut*, IX, 410-412 (Assembly Journal).
104. Law to assembly, May, 1749, Conn. Hist. Soc., *Collections*, XVI, 490-491.

The reply of the assembly to this suggestion took the form of "An Act to call in, exchange and discharge, the Bills of Credit which have been issued by this Colony and are still outstanding."[105] The act as amended the following October[106] appointed two committees to handle the business of retiring the bills. The governor was authorized to draw bills of exchange on the funds arising from the Cape Breton and Canada expedition grants in the hands of the agent in London. The committee was to sell "the bills of exchange so drawn, and receive therefor one half the value thereof in bills of public credit of [the] Colony and the other half in coined silver sterling alloy ...." The funds thus arising were to be paid over to the treasurer, where the silver was to be used to redeem an equivalent amount of the bills of credit of the colony. The second committee provided for by the act was to burn all bills of credit received into the treasury as a result of the foregoing operations. The advantage of requiring half the value of the bills of exchange to be paid in silver lay in the fact that it made possible the accumulation of a fund for the redemption of bills of credit in the hands of those that might have no occasion to purchase bills of exchange. To supplement the funds raised by the sale

---

105. Conn. Pub. Rec., IX, 447-449.
106. Ibid., 474-475.

of bills of exchange, three taxes of £9,000 new tenor each were laid on polls and estates for the years 1751, 1752, and 1753. In this way, it was thought to sink the entire amount of bills of credit outstanding.

At the same time the calling-in act was adopted, an act was passed fixing certain fees. It is interesting to note that the fees were expressed in proclamation money.[107]

The program embodied in the acts of 1749 was not destined to be carried out without change. In May, 1750, it underwent amendment.[108] The committee charged with the sale of bills of exchange was authorized to sell bills to the amount of £10,000 sterling on credit to "the now inhabitants of [the] colony." Security was to be taken and the bills were to be paid for on or before May 1, 1754, one-half in silver or gold, the other half in bills of credit. The purchasers of the bills were in the meantime to pay interest at the rate of three per cent. The effect of this amendment is obvious. It deferred by four years the calling in of the bills of credit that were redeemed out of the funds provided by the sale of the bills of exchange.

The data available do not permit of following in detail the drawing in of Connecticut's bills of credit.

---

107. Ibid., pp. 449-452.
108. Ibid., pp. 510-511.

On September 6, 1751 there were £340,218 18_s._ 7_d._ in old tenor terms reported to be outstanding on the credit of the colony.[109] Four years later, in November, 1755, Governor Thomas Fitch of Connecticut wrote to Governor Benning Wentworth of New Hampshire, that Connecticut had "made ample provision to draw in and sink the small remainder of the out standing Bills of Credit" of the colony.[110] The colony's share of Cape Breton grant, amounting to £28,863 19_s._ 1_d._ sterling, should, after making allowance for deduction, have provided funds sufficient to redeem approximately £300,000 old tenor of the colony's bills.[111]

The rate at which the bills of credit were redeemed seems to have varied. Taxes were made payable in bills at the rate of 14_s._ 7_d._ new tenor or 51_s._ old tenor for 6_s._ lawful money.[112] This would be at the rate of 8_s._ 6_d._ old tenor for 1_s._ lawful (or proclamation) money. On the other hand, in October 1754 the assembly in converting old tenor into lawful money used the ratio of 8_s._ 10_d._ to 1_s._[113] The Massachusetts redemption figure

---

109. Report of Com. of Audit, Conn. Hist. Soc., Collections, XVI, 101-102.
110. Fitch to Wentworth, Norwalk, November 12, 1755, ibid., XVII, 177-178.
111. See Roger Wolcott to Dr. Benjamin Avery, Windsor, February 7, 1753, ibid., XVI, 237-238.
112. Conn. Pub. Rec., X, 157 (May, 1753); 318 (October, 1754).
113. Computed from data in ibid., p. 319.
  Henry Bronson's statement, "A Historical Ac-

was 7s. 6d. for 1s.

Beginning on November 1, 1756, the accounts of the colony were kept in terms of lawful money, and during the year before that time merchants and others adopted the same practice.[114] Since the bills of credit that had been issued on loan had virtually all been retired

---

count of Connecticut Currency ...," p. 75 (in New Haven Hist. Soc., Papers, Vol. I), that Connecticut "paid about one-ninth, and repudiated the remainder" is completely inaccurate. This could only have been so if Connecticut's bills had all been issued equivalent to silver at proclamation rates and had been redeemed at the old tenor figure of 8s. 10d. to 1s. This was far from the case. All the issues of the late war had been new tenor issues, of which 1s. N. T. equaled 3 1/2s. O. T. They were received in taxes at 14s. 7d. for 6s. lawful money (equivalent to approximately 2s. 5d. for 1s.). Over 99% of Connecticut's currency reported outstanding in 1749 was new tenor (Law to Bedford, October, 1750, Conn. Hist. Soc., Collections, XV, 435). It appears, then, that instead of redeeming her currency at but one-ninth of its original value (measured in silver), the colony redeemed it at just over two-fifths of its value. This is but another instance of how the depreciation of the colonial currency has been unthinkingly misrepresented. It has been quite customary to talk as though all the currency outstanding at a given time had been issued at proclamation rates and had undergone whatever depreciation old tenor bills had since the first issue of paper currency. This practice, of course, makes the picture appear much worse than it really was, because the great bulk of the currency outstanding at any one time had been issued when silver in old tenor terms had already risen. The gauge of the depreciation of any given issue is the amount silver had risen in value since its issue.
    Moreover, the error does not always stop here. It is sometimes assumed that the first issues of bills of credit were equivalent to sterling. This blunder makes the situation appear that much worse. In no case were bills emitted at sterling rates (except in the case of the sterling bills of New Hampshire in the 1750's, and those of Georgia in the '50's and '60's.).
    114. Conn. Pub. Rec., X, 424; Bronson, p. 74.

by the year 1752,[115] the colony was now on a specie standard. Silver at proclamation rates and gold at its market value passed current, and contracts were made and discharged in coin.[116]

Another problem that required solution before the currency of Connecticut could be stabilized was that arising from the circulation within her borders of the bills of the neighboring colonies of New Hampshire and Rhode Island. The retiring of the Massachusetts bills had, of course, solved the problem with respect to them. As might be suspected, the bills of Rhode Island constituted the greatest problem and occasioned the greatest complaint. The mischief resulting from the circulation of the Rhode Island bills was called to the attention of the assembly in 1748 by a group of Norwich merchants. No action, however, was taken at the time. The prospect of the colony's being flooded with Rhode Island bills as a result of the action of that colony in setting up her ninth land bank in 1751 called forth further complaints, this time from the New Haven county and the Hartford county merchants. They urged the depreciating effect of the Rhode Island bills upon the Connecticut currency and that the circulation of the Rhode Island bills within the colony of Connecticut gave Rhode Island

---

115. Ibid., p. 75n.
116. Ibid., pp. 82-83.

the power to levy tribute on the people of Connecticut.
Measures to stabilize the Connecticut currency and to
prohibit the circulation of the Rhode Island bills were
prayed for.[117]   It was not until the following May,

---

117. The Norwich petitioners, February 16, 1747/8, observed: "The Rhode Islanders have the Last Fall Sapped our Interest by buying up wth Their pernicious bills our best provisions ...[,] and are now out buying up our Cows & best Stock[,] what They can with Those same pernicious bills." Conn. Hist. Soc., Collections, XV, 214.
 A later meeting of the Norwich merchants to consider the currency problem of Connecticut is discussed in "Extract of a Letter from a Merchant in Town to his Friend in the Country," December 24, 1750, Boston Weekly News-Letter, January 3, 1751.
 The New Haven county merchants, New Haven, May 6, 1751, in their memorial to the assembly urged: "... as y^r Hon^{rs} have of late years Constantly Resolved against Emitting any New bills of Credit of your own, that So the mischiefs Arising from a Sinking Medium among us might be prevented, Y^r Mem^{ts} humbly hope & pray that your Hon^{rs} would not Suffer the Same mischiefs to be brought upon us by our neighbours, y^r Hon^{rs} Cannot be insensible that the colony of Rhode Island by their present Large unequal proportion of outstanding bills are Enabled Annually to buy off A great part of the produce of this Colony the Labour of an Industrious people, to the no Small Detriment of the Inhabitants of this colony, and as ... Rhode Island have Lately Ordered to be Struck A Large Quantity of New bills of publick Credit, Y^r Mem^{ts} must think, ... that Should the Said bills be Allowed by Y^r Hon^{rs} to pass in payments in this colony, they would Soon Sap the foundation of trade & Commerce among us & introduce the greatest disorder, confusion & injustice; [and because it seems impracticable to attempt to circulate the Rhode Island bills at a discount the memorialists pray that the assembly will] by Statute with Severe penalties forbid the taking or passing any of Said bills in payment in this Colony ...." Ibid., XVI, 61-62.
 The Hartford county merchants' memorial, May, 1751, contains an almost classic passage: "And as the Medium of Trade is that whereby our dealings are valued and weighed we cannot but think it ought to be Esteem'd of as Sacred a Nature as any weights & Measures and in order to maintaine Justice must be kept as Stable[;]

however, that the assembly took action. It then prohibited the circulation within the colony of Rhode Island bills emitted since December 25, 1750, with the exception that they might be paid to satisfy contracts in writing specifying payment in such bills. The act carried no penalty.[118] It was, of course, aimed at excluding the bills of Rhode Island's latest land bank. The colony was not yet ready to abolish the circulation of the old Rhode Island issues that had long been current in Connecticut. Three years later, however, the assembly took another step forward and by statute excluded all bills of both Rhode Island and New Hampshire that had been issued since December 5, 1749, from being

---

for as a False weight and a false Ballance is an abomination to the Lord, we apprehend a False and unstable Medium is equally so[;] it occasions as much iniquity and is at least as Injurious." The assembly was urged "to provide that the Medium of Trade may be render'd Stable for time to come and that the Just Value of our now Outstanding Debts may be Secured to us ...." <u>Ibid.</u>, p. 63.

  In their reasons offered in support of their memorial, this same group paid their respects to Rhode Island: "Within about 18 months last past the Inhabitants of this Govern^t have Rec^d by a modest Computation 200,000 R: Island and N: Hampshire C^r mostly R: I. for which we have given our Provisions &c and which the purchasers were necessitated to buy & had this Falacious C^r been denyd would have p^d Silver (N: York at the Same time Supplyd the same purchasers with Such Commodities not so good in Quality for Silver) & even this sum wth w^t is due to the colony in St^r money would have been a handsom Silver Medium for a beginning but giving these Bills a C^r has left them in our hands instead of the Silver [and if we so continue it will lead to our ruin, &c.]." <u>Ibid.</u>, p. 65.

118. <u>Conn. Pub. Rec.</u>, X, 105 (May, 1752).

uttered or received within Connecticut after December 1, 1755. The statute further provided that after November 1, 1756, all bills whatsoever of the two governments should be excluded from Connecticut. The first section of the act carried a penalty of from ₤5 to ₤20 lawful money for each offence.[119]

Shortly after the passage of this act, the governor was instructed by the assembly to write to the governors of Rhode Island and New Hampshire, and inform them of the bills of their respective colonies circulating in Connecticut and of the action taken to exclude their circulation in the future. He was further to request information concerning what measures, if any, had been taken to call in the bills of those governments and suggest that if none had been taken justice required it.[120] By slow steps, Connecticut had at last gone the whole way. So long as the Rhode Island and New Hampshire bills were permitted to circulate within the colony, it was quite hopeless to attempt to stabilize the currency. As the act of 1755 expressed it, it was manifest that the bills of credit of Rhode Island and New Hampshire passing in Connecticut "not only long have been and

---

119. Ibid., pp. 406-407; see also pp. 423-424.
120. Ibid., 423-424; Governor Thomas Fitch's letter to Governor Benning Wentworth of New Hampshire, dated Norwalk, November 10, 1755, is in Conn. Hist. Soc., Collections, XVII, 177-178.

still continually are sinking in value, but by obtaining a customary valuation compared with the bills of [Connecticut] have a dangerous tendency to depreciate them also ...." The extent to which this was true may be seen from the fact that the Spanish milled dollar, which was worth about 52 1/2_s._, old tenor, in New England in 1749, had risen to 64_s._ at New Haven by February, 1752, and by the end of 1755, to 80_s._ These changes may be conveniently followed by reference to Figure IX, or in the note below.[121]

The French and Indian War broke out just as Connecticut was in the final stages of her effort to effect the reform of her currency. Moreover, her wartime finance had to be carried on within the confines of the Currency Act of 1751. Connecticut, although she opposed the act and sought to be left out of it at the time of its passage, seems never to have had any other thought than to conform her currency practices to it. When the statute was first received in the colony, the assembly

---

121.
Price of Dollars at New Haven
(old tenor terms)

1752	Feb. 21	64_s._	1754	70_s._
	Nov.	65		72
1753	Mar.	65	1755	70
	Aug.	65		72
1754		66		80
		68		

Ezra Stiles, _Itineraries,_ p. 8.

had ordered it printed for distribution to the towns. In 1755, when problems of war finance began to perplex the colony, the act was ordered read at the town meetings, no doubt to call again to the attention of the people the restrictions under which the colony was required to proceed.[123]

Connecticut adopted much the same measures to finance her contributions to the war as did Massachusetts. She borrowed where she could and under the force of necessity issued to the public creditors nonlegal tender bills of credit bearing five per cent interest. The first issue of bills of credit was in January, 1755, and the sum emitted, ₤7,500 lawful (proclamation) money. The following March, the further sum of ₤12,500 lawful money was emitted, and at the same time an ingenious scheme was adopted for combining the calling in of the colony's old bills of credit and its borrowing operations. Bills of credit might be exchanged for orders on the treasury payable in silver or gold with lawful interest, one-third in May, 1756, another third in May, 1757, and the final third in May, 1758. The bills so exchanged for orders were to be burnt at

---

122. Eighty copies were ordered printed "and dispersed to the several towns ..., for the information of all persons concerned ...." *Ibid.*, p. 65 (October, 1751).

123. *Ibid.*, p. 351 (March, 1755).

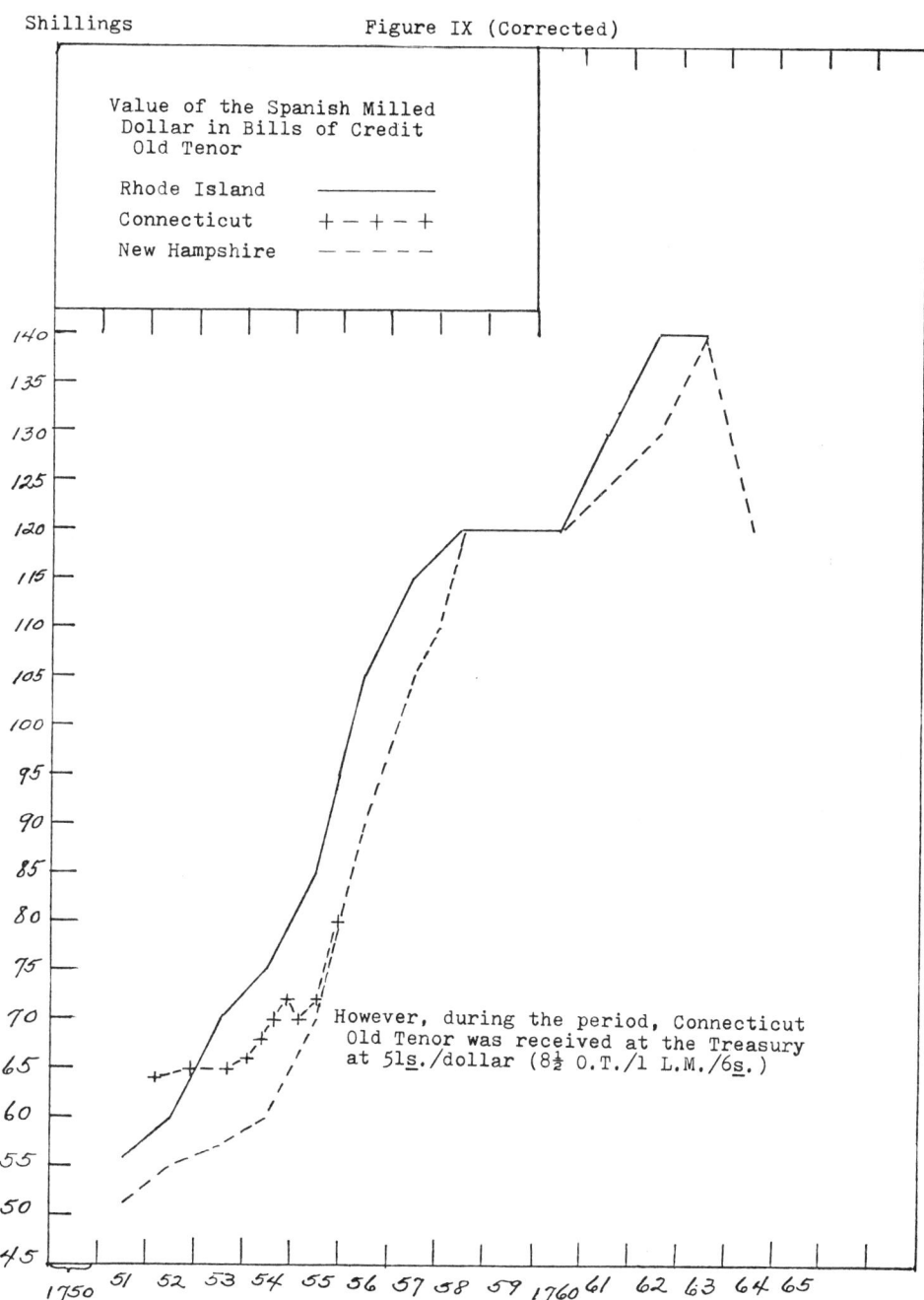

Figure IX (Corrected)

References:

    Rhode Island. List of values contained in act of 1763. R. I. Col. Rec., VI, 361.

    Connecticut. Value of the dollar at New Haven. Ezra Stiles, Itineraries, P. 8.

    New Hampshire. Value of the dollar in New Hampshire. Jeremy Belknap, History of New Hampshire (1813 ed.), III, 168; (Reprint, 1970), II, 168.

the treasury, and an equivalent sum of the silver and gold that had been accumulated for the purpose of retiring the old bills by selling bills of exchange upon the Cape Breton and Canada expedition grants was to be liberated for the use of the colony in meeting its war expenditures.[124] Old tenor bills were to be received at the rate of 58*s.* 8*d.* the ounce of silver and new tenor bills in proportion. This rate values the Connecticut currency considerably higher than the figure Ezra Stiles gives as the current value of bills in Connecticut at this time, which is equivalent to about 80*s.* the ounce.

The bills of credit authorized by these and later acts were secured by a tax sufficient to provide funds to call them in within the five year period required by the act of Parliament.[125] The bills were issued in denominations ranging from nine pence to forty shillings. The sums issued during the course of the war, together with the taxes levied to retire them, as well as the time of payment, are set out in Table XIII. The total sum issued from 1755 to 1764 amounted to ₤259,000 lawful money.

---

124. Ibid., p. 338-339. In 1758, the treasurer was authorized to borrow ₤25,000 lawful money at 6% interest. The bills of credit bore only 5% interest. Ibid., XI, 100-103.

125. See the references to the various acts following Table XIII.

The early acts authorized the treasurer to pay out the bills of credit "according to the value of such bills at the time of putting off the same." This would appear to manifest a fear that the bills would depreciate. Such, however, does not seem to have been the case. The report to the Board of Trade in 1764 indicates that they were equal to proclamation money when issued and states that their value "remained invariable[,] permanent[,] and stable."[126] The later emitting acts, seemingly in recognition of the fact that the bills had maintained their value, omit this clause and direct the treasurer to pay out the "bills of credit with the interest computed thereon." Since the bills were dated the day of the session of the assembly, this would appear to mean that whatever interest had accrued before they were paid out was to be computed and added to the value of the bills.

---

126. Loc. cit., Professor Gipson's statement, based on a note "drawn from some forgotten source," that during this period the bills depreciated to the extent that it took 7s. to equal 3s. sterling, whereas they were issued at 6s. to 4 1/2s. sterling, seems erroneous. This denotes a 37% depreciation in their value, which is not only at variance with the statements in the Report of 1764, which, it may be said, Professor Gipson earlier quotes, but is also contrary to the experience of Massachusetts with similar bills. Lawrence H. Gipson, "Connecticut Taxation," pp. 21, 24, in Connecticut Tercentenary Publications. Further evidence that the bills maintained their value is found in the fact that in 1761 they were received in Massachusetts on a par with the currency of that province. Vide supra, p. 290.

TABLE XIII

CONNECTICUT
Lawful money bills of credit bearing 5% interest

Date of issue	Sum emitted £	When payable	Funds appropriated x	When payable into the treasury for discharging the bills
1755				
Jan.	7,500	Jan. 1755	Tax 2d./£	Aug. 1757
Mar.	12,500^z	May. 1759	" 3 1/2 "	Dec. 1758
Aug.	30,000	Aug. 1760	" 3 "	Aug. 1759
			" 4 "	Apr. 1760
Oct.	12,000	Apr. 1760	" 3 "	Aug. 1759
	£62,000			
1758				
Mar.	30,000	May 1762	" 3 "	Dec. 1761
1759				
Feb.	20,000	May 1763	" 5 "	Dec. 1762
Mar.	40,000	Mar. 1764	" 10 "	Dec. 1763
May	10,000	May 1763	" 2 1/4 "	Dec. 1762
	£70,000			
1760				
Mar.	70,000	Mar. 1765	" 6 "	Dec. 1761
			" 9 "	Dec. 1764
1761				
Mar.	45,000	Mar. 1766	" 5 "	Dec. 1763
			" 7 "	Dec. 1765
1762				
Mar.	65,000	Mar. 1767	" 6 "	Dec. 1764
			" 8 "	Dec. 1765
1763				
May	10,000	May 1765	" 2 "	Dec. 1764
1764				
Mar.	7,000	Mar. 1768	" 1 1/2 "	Dec. 1767
Total	£359,000			

x "A tax of one penny on the pound raised about five Thousand Pounds." The taxes were assessed "on the Polls and other Rateable Estates consisting of Houses, Lands

Connecticut, Massachusetts, and New Hampshire received aid in retiring their bills of credit and in maintaining a circulation of specie in the colony from the parliamentary grants to reimburse the colonies for aid in carrying on the war. Connecticut's share of the first grant, that to recompense the colonies for their expenditures in 1755, was ₤26,000 sterling, of which ₤24,828 10s. 1d. was brought over in Spanish silver and Portuguese gold. After Governor Shirley had been repaid the sum of ₤10,000 sterling that had been borrowed from him, the balance of ₤14,828 10s. 1d. sterling, equivalent to approximately ₤19,772 lawful money, was delivered into the colony by the merchants, Charles Alpthorp and Son, in the fall of 1756.[127] Early in 1759, the sum of ₤9,158 in lawful money, half of the grant made in 1757, was imported in gold and silver,[128] and

---

Cattle and other Personal Estate, a List whereof is annually taken in the respective Towns ...." Report to Board of Trade, 1764. C. O. 323/19, L. C. photostats; also printed in Conn. Pub. Rec., XII, 339.

z This emission does not appear in the report of 1764, but the act authorizing it is to be found in ibid., X, 341. A reference in a later act makes it appear that the bills were emitted as authorized.

The emitting laws are at the following references respectively: Ibid., X, 328-331, 341, 401-404, 418-420; XI, 100-103, 214-215, 235-236, 254-255, 351-352, 482-484, 615-618; XII, 134-135, 233-234.

127. Gipson, "Connecticut Taxation," pp. 29-30; Conn. Pub. Rec., X, 546-547.

128. Gipson, op. cit., p. 30; Conn. Pub. Rec., XI, 237, 262; Thomas Fitch to Joseph Talcott, Norwalk, January 22, 1759, Conn. Hist. Soc., Collections, XVIII, 3. In this letter the amount of the shipment is given

in October, 1759, the colony's new agent, Jared Ingersoll, was authorized to send over in specie the sum of ₤15,000 sterling (equal to ₤20,000 lawful money) from the current parliamentary grant.[129] Henceforward, the share of Connecticut in the various parliamentary grants was transferred to the colony by means of bills of exchange drawn upon the agent in London. "From March 15, 1759, to July 28, 1765, bills of exchange amounting to ₤172,467 10s. 8d. sterling were drawn by Governor Fitch against the Connecticut funds on deposit in London."[130]

---

as 14,000 oz. of silver and 503 oz. 3 dwt. 12 gr. gold.
129. Ibid., 345.
130. Gipson, op. cit., p. 31; Conn. Hist. Soc., Collections, XVIII, 353.
The sums authorized to be drawn in bills of exchange follow:

Date		Amount	Services
1758, May		One-half of the sum granted for the services rendered in 1756.	
		₤ sterling	
1759, Oct.		22,000	(services of 1758)
1760, Oct.		17,000	(services of 1759)
1761, Mar.		17,000 x	(services of 1759)
1761, May		6,500	(services of 1759)
1762, May		35,000	(services of 1760)
1762, Oct.		9,309 18s.	(services of 1760)
1763, May		The sum granted for the services rendered in 1761.	
1766, May		₤8,500 "of the money ... now in the hands of Mr. Agent Jackson."	

x At this time the drawing of ₤34,000 in bills of exchange was authorized. The sum, however, included the ₤17,000 authorized in October, 1760.
Conn. Pub. Rec., XI, 129, 346, 437, 490-491, 502; XII, 61, 78, 135-136, 467. The list given in Gipson, op. cit., p. 30, is incomplete.

The contribution of the parliamentary grants to the maintenance of a circulating specie in the colony may be appreciated when one learns that even with the aid offered by the grants, the colony was said to be "very dreined of money" in the spring of 1762.[131]

The several sums received from the parliamentary grants were applied in mitigation of taxes to the retirement of the bills of credit issued to finance the war. In 1764 all the emissions "antecedent to that of March 1762," with the exception of "some small Sums" of the emission of 1761, were reported to have been "called in, sunk and discharged." These later emissions were not yet due. This would leave outstanding something over ₤85,000 lawful money out of a total issue of ₤359,000.[132]

In view of the record, one cannot deny that Connecticut, despite her slow and halting start, successfully rehabilitated her currency during the decade of the 1750's and managed well her finances during the French and Indian War.[133]

---

131. Conn. Pub. Rec., XI, 617.
132. Report to B. T., 1764, C. O. 323/19, L. C. photostats; Conn. Pub. Rec., XII, 339.
133. Since there is no price index available for Connecticut, one cannot trace the effects of her wartime finance measures upon her price level. Probably the effects were not unsimilar to those in Massachusetts. It is also probable that the Connecticut bills of credit issued during the war, since they bore interest, were in considerable amounts held out of circulation as investments. Direct evidence on this point is lacking. We know that they did circulate in trade even though they

The currency of Rhode Island from the close of King George's War until the close of the French and Indian War was in a state of confusion. Yet toward the end of the period there were unmistakable evidences that Rhode Island was at last tiring of her long dalliance with a depreciating paper currency. And strange as it may seem, when in 1763 Rhode Island undertook to reform her currency, the act that she adopted showed a greater regard for the interests of existing creditors than did any similar act ever adopted in the American colonies. But this came only as the result of much sad experience.

It was the unregenerate attitude of the colony, manifest in the establishment of her ninth land bank in 1751, it will be recalled, that led to the laying of the parliamentary restraint upon New England in 1751. The immediate effect of the curb upon Rhode Island was slight. Her new land bank was already in operation and her bills outstanding on taxes had some years to run. There were outstanding in 1748 of the latter bills £135,336 in old tenor terms. Of bills on loan, calculated on the assumption that they were retired accord-

---

were not a legal tender, and the extent to which they were held as investments can only be conjectured on the basis of what happened to similar issues in such colonies as Massachusetts, New Hampshire, Rhode Island, and Maryland, where the common tendency was to withhold the bills from circulation.

ing to the provisions of the several loan acts, there should have been £480,000 old tenor outstanding in the same year. This appears to tally well with the amount actually in circulation, which appears to have been near £485,434.[134] The only retirement in the next few years of bills out on tax funds was the sum of £24,280 old tenor retired in 1751 out of funds provided by the selling of bills of exchange upon the colony's share of the Cape Breton grant. Only a fraction of the grant, however, was improved to this purpose.[135] The retirements of the bills out on loan were allowed to fall behind schedule during the years after the close of King George's War. When one adds to this the emission of the equivalent of £200,000 old tenor in 1751, it is easily seen that the prospects were that the colony's currency situation would be worse before it would be better.

The outbreak of the French and Indian War occasioned an issue of £240,000 old tenor on tax funds in 1755.[136] The purpose was to finance the colony's

---

134. Computed from report of committee of audit, August 19, 1749, R. I. Col. Rec., V, 273.
135. Report of Com. of Audit, August 13, 1762, ibid., VI, 329. Rhode Island's share of the grant was £6,332 12s. 10d. sterling (21 Geo. II, c. 33). This was the equivalent of roughly ten times that sum in Rhode Island old tenor. It is evident, then, that substantially less than half of the grant was applied to retiring the colony's bills.
136. At this time the colony reverted to an old

share in the expedition against Crown Point. The bills bore no interest and were to circulate for two years; tax funds to retire them were provided, and the great majority of them were sunk within the period. Pursuant to the Currency Act of 1751, the bills were not made a legal tender between man and man.

In 1756, when a second expedition against Crown Point had to be financed, the colony emitted ₤14,000 in bills of credit "equal in value to the lawful money of the Province of Massachusetts Bay and of the colony of Connecticut." The bills bore no interest, and were to be retired out of tax funds within two years. This issue marks Rhode Island's first step on the way to currency reform. It was also the last of the war issues that did not bear interest. Beginning the next year, the practice of Massachusetts and Connecticut was adopted, and later issues were for lawful money and bore interest at five per cent. They were made redeemable out of tax funds or the parliamentary grants within the five year period called for by the Currency Act of 1751. In all, ₤94,909 were issued on this basis between 1756 and 1762. The issues of the period 1750-1764, together with the sums outstanding at various times, insofar as the partial data available make

---

tenor issue. Preceding issues had been of a new tenor, although accounted in old tenor terms.

possible the presentation of the picture, may be followed in Table XIV, and in graphic form in Figure X.

It should also be said on behalf of Rhode Island, that she attempted to "hire" money at six per cent interest for the purpose of carrying on the war. While she succeeded to some extent in raising funds by this method, it proved impossible to raise by such means any large proportion of the sums needed to finance the war.[137]

Rhode Island participated in both the Cape Breton and Canada Expedition grants of King George's War, her share in the latter being £7,507 4*s.* 3 1/2*d.* sterling.[138] The colony likewise appears to have shared in all but one of the grants made by Parliament during the French and Indian War, being omitted from the grant of 1758. The partial data available as to the extent

---

137. The report of 1764 stated: "Besides the bills emitted ..., this colony is largely in debt for money hired of private persons, during the course of the war...." Ibid., p. 410.
    See act of October, 1758, as an example of those authorizing the treasurer to borrow. Ibid., p. 170.
138. Kimball, op. cit., II, 77, 103, 115.

TABLE XIV

Part A

RHODE ISLAND ISSUES OF BILLS OF CREDIT, 1751-1764

Year	Loan	Crown Point Old Tenor	Lawful Money	
			Ŀ L. M. 1:18	Ŀ O. T. 1/3
1751	200,000			
1755		240,000		
1756 Feb.			8,000	146,667
1756 Aug.			6,000	110,000
1758 May			10,000	183,334
1758 Oct.			10,909	199,997
1759 Mar.			12,000	220,000
1759 Apr.			4,000	73,333
1759 June			4,000	73,333
1760 Mar.			16,000	293,333
1760 May			11,000	201,667
1762 Mar.			5,000	91,667
1762 Apr.			2,000	36,667
1762 May			2,000	36,667
1762 Sept.			4,000	73,333
Total	Ŀ200,000	Ŀ240,000	Ŀ94,909	Ŀ1,739,998

of her participation is set out in the note below.
While the money received from the several grants eased the burden of the colony, it did not play the significant role in the colony's currency system that similar grants did in Massachusetts and Connecticut.

During the period the value of the colony's old tenor currency continually declined. The value of the Spanish milled dollar rose from 56<u>s</u>. in 1751 to 85<u>s</u>. in 1755, and 120s. in 1758. These changes may be followed in detail in Figure IX, or in the note below.[140] The

---

[139]. PARTICIPATION OF RHODE ISLAND IN THE PARLIAMENTARY GRANTS:

Year	Sum Granted ₤ stlg.	Sum Received ₤ stlg.	Ref.: Kimball, <u>op. cit.</u>
1756	7,000	6,684 12 3	II, note, p. 186, p. 200
1758	none		
1759	8,798	?	II, 297
1760	9,328	?	II, 320
1761	?	8,861 12	II, 332
1762	6,082	6,082 6	II, 354, 356
1763	?	?	

In 1764 Rhode Island received ₤1,910 3s. sterling from Pennsylvania, being Rhode Island's share of <u>one</u> of the grants overpaid to Pennsylvania. <u>Penna. Votes,</u> VII, 5651.

[140]. Value of the Spanish milled dollar in Rhode Island bills of credit, old tenor terms.

Year	Shillings	Year	Shillings
1751	56	1758	120
1752	60	1759	120
1753	70	1760	120
1754	75	1761	130
1755	85	1762	140
1756	105	1763	140
1757	115		

Source: The depreciation scale set out in the act of 1763. <u>R. I. Col. Rec.,</u> VI, 361.

state of affairs that resulted is indicated by a letter writer in the Newport Mercury in March, 1762, who writes:

> The General Assembly having paid little or no Regard to the Old-Tenor Bills, they have, since their first Emission, depreciated in their value in Proportion, as 23 1/4 is to 1; and as all our Dealings are kept in that Denomination, the Lawful Bills, so called, by being Connected with them, in the Proportion of 1 to 18 1/3, when they first come out, pass at 27 1/4 per Cent. discount with Silver: But as these Bills have, with great punctuality, been sunk and paid off, they in a short Time disappear, and are laid up soon after their Emission, till the Time of their Redemption, by which a Profit of more than Ten per Cent. per Annum will arise upon them; so that they cannot properly be called a Currency. 141

The writer closed by proposing a plan to reconstitute the currency. There was other discussion of the currency in the newspapers at this time.[142] But no action resulted until the next year, when the assembly meeting in June adopted an act placing the colony on a lawful money basis after January 1, 1764.[143] In 1751 the colony had made provision to enforce thereafter the payment of debts in bills of credit in sums equal to the silver value of the debt as declared in the enact-

---

141. Newport Mercury, March 16, 1762. The Report of 1764 to B. T. says of the lawful money interest-bearing bills: "The whole of the bills emitted on this plan, have at all times fully kept their value; their only defect seemingly to be, that they carry too high an interest, which occasions their being hoarded, and thereby not answering the end of a medium." R. I. Col. Rec., VI, 409.

142. The writer quoted above refers to a discussion in the Newport Mercury of February 23, 1762. Unfortunately a copy of this issue is not available.

143. R. I. Col. Rec., VI, 358-364.

ment; and the courts were instructed to render judgments accordingly.[144] The later history of the colony, however, makes it appear that the act was not enforced. It was to retrieve the situation created by the depreciation of the currency during the last decade and to make provision for the time not far distant when the bills of credit would be called in at the end of their periods that the act of 1763 was passed. It was enacted "that lawful money of this colony is, and shall hereafter be, silver and gold coins; and that nothing else shall be taken and understood to be lawful money ...." Henceforward, all debts were to be understood to be contracted in lawful money, unless the contrary appeared. Book accounts might ordinarily be discharged in silver, gold, or "in bills heretofore emitted by this colony, called lawful money." The Spanish dollar was rated at the proclamation rate of 6$\underline{s}$. and other coins in proportion. Anyone that paid such coins at a higher rate was made subject to a penalty of £6 lawful money. Old debts were made payable in lawful money or bills of credit[145] equivalent to the nominal value of the debts

---

144. Ibid., pp. 335-336 (act of 1751); 343 (interpreting resolution of 1752).
145. One provision of the act (ibid., VI, 362) reads: "... all securities made, or to be made, before the said 1st day of January, for the payment of bills of credit called lawful money bills, may, and shall be discharged in such bills according to their nominal values; and ... all securities that are made for the

when they first became due and bore six per cent interest until paid. This was the unique provision of the act. It protected creditors against the depreciation of the Rhode Island currency between the time a debt became due and the time its collection could be enforced. No protection was granted against depreciation during the period a debt ran, but even so, the partial protection granted showed a greater concern for the interest of creditors than was ever evinced in any of the other colonies in similar circumstances.[146]

Rhode Island had at last reached the turning of the road. The last of the land bank issues was to reach the end of its period in 1766. In 1764 there were out-

---

payment of bills of credit of the old tenor, or for the bills called lawful money may be paid and discharged in the bills specified in such securities, and <u>that such bills shall be a legal tender</u> for any such debt...." (Italics not in original.) The provision that the lawful money bills should be a legal tender was in direct violation of the Act of Parliament of 1751.

146. A book account was assumed to have become due at the time of the last entry.

Although one of the protests lodged against the bill at the time of its passage reads, "That if it be reasonable that any depreciation be allowed, it ought to take place at the date of the contract, and not at the time of payment," the case is not altogether one-sided. It may be argued that when a creditor lent money or extended credit, he was presumed to know the tendency of the Rhode Island currency to depreciate, and to take measures to protect himself (e.g., charge a higher rate of interest, or higher prices for goods sold on credit). He could not so well foresee the period of time it would take to force payment of a debt after it became due, and in that case could not so well protect himself.

The scale of depreciation established by the act is given in note 127, above.

standing but ₤40,000 of the lawful money bills issued to finance the war, two-thirds of which were to be retired within the next year. And by 1767 the remaining lawful money bills, together with the last of the old tenor bills, would come "to a final end."[147] Rhode Island was in the process of returning to a specie of standard, -- but not with entire confidence: "In a colony, where the constant demand for remittances to the mother country, makes it impossible for silver and gold to continue," the report of the assembly to the Board of Trade in 1764 concluded, "what will be the medium and instrument of commerce, when paper bills are at an end, we know not."[148]

In New England the clocks had not all struck at once, but by 1764 the hands of them all had come full round. The day of colonial New England's experiment with a legal tender paper currency was approaching its close. No longer did the prevailing sentiment in any of the New England colonies favor a paper currency. All the colonies had in greater or lesser degree returned to more orthodox measures of finance. Massachusetts between 1750 and 1754 and Connecticut by 1756 had returned to a specie standard; Rhode Island was to

---

147. Report to B. T., October 30, 1764. *R. I. Col. Rec.*, VI, 409.
148. Ibid., p. 410.

effect her return to specie between 1763 and 1767 or shortly thereafter; and New Hampshire was to do likewise by 1771. A cycle had ended in New England. But in the colonies to the southward it still had its course to run.

CHAPTER VII

THE CURRENCY OF NEW YORK, PENNSYLVANIA, DELAWARE, AND NEW JERSEY, 1750-1764

Paper Money, [our] only means of an immediate Exertion.

-- John Watts, New York merchant, to General Robert Monckton, April 14, 1764.

IN 1742 the Lords Commissioners for Trade and Plantations had written to Lewis Morris, his majesty's governor for the province of New Jersey, charging him to "take effectual Care for the punctual Sinking the outstanding Bills" of credit of the province and the "preventing their increase[,] that in time and end may be put to a Currency which has been attended with so many Inconveniencies."[1] Throughout the 'forties the Board sought parliamentary aid to achieve this end throughout the colonies generally. But when Parliament was finally prevailed upon to act, it imposed restraints only upon New England. Nevertheless, the Board of Trade under Lord Halifax sought to take advantage of the fact that "the sense of Parliament" with respect to paper currency in America had now, as it viewed it, been determined, and strove by means of the royal in-

---

1. N. J. Archives (1st series), XV, 241, letter dated August 3, 1742.

structions and the royal disallowance to impose upon colonies elsewhere the same restraints that Parliament had laid upon New England. And in doing so, it sought to bolster its authority by appealing to "the sense of Parliament," although it might have been replied, that since the colonies to the southward of New England had not been included in the restraints of the Currency Act of 1751, it was not unreasonable to assume that the sense of Parliament as to them was that they should not be so restrained.

The conflict that resulted is well illustrated by events in the Middle colonies. In New York, however, it did not arise immediately. At the close of 1747, that colony had just under ₤190,000 in bills of credit in circulation, and as the emitting acts had made provision for only a gradual retirement, there were yet ₤126,000 in circulation at the close of 1754.[2] The prospect of a war with the French, however, raised the paper money problem anew. In May, 1754, Lieutenant Governor James De Lancey, who was then administering the government of the province, and who was apparently well aware of the prevailing feeling concerning the debts of the late war and the matter of raising funds for an impending one, wrote to the Board of Trade in

---

2. See Table XVI and Figure XI, below.

anticipation of the probable outcome of the conference to be held the next month with the Iroquois at Albany:

> As one of the points in view at the meeting of the Commiss^{rs} at Albany, is to concert measures for building Forts in advanced places on the frontiers, to cover these Colonies, and in case of War to annoy the French; I would propose to your Lord^{sps}, that I might have his Maj^{ty}'s leave to pass a Bill for emitting ₤20,000 in Bills of Credit, to be put out at interest for the space of ten years at six per cent, and then to be paid into the Treasury and sunk; the whole of the Interest to be applyed in building and supporting the Fortifications on the Frontiers and to no other use. This fund would produce ₤1,200 per annum; and as the assembly are averse to Taxes at this time, those of the last war not being yet at an end, it seems to me this measure is most likely to go down with them, and I can not think it will have a bad effect on the credit of our paper currency, for, from the best information I could obtain, we have about ₤115,000 [3] paper currency, and we now sink annually by the funds appropriated to that purpose ₤9,500. [4]

As matters were pressing and as the proposal touched a point upon which the Board of Trade was unusually sensitive, that body got off a reply with unwonted haste. On July 5, 1754, it wrote to De Lancey:

> The proposition you mention in your letter of 21 of May of being permitted to pass an Act for issuing ₤20,000 in Bills of Credit requires a very serious consideration[.] [W]e are inclined to believe from the Nature of paper currency in General, that a moderate quantity issued upon proper security and having a proper fund for its redemption within a reasonable time may operate to the advantage of a Colony and may also be the least burthensome method of levying money for the supply and support of Government[;] but then we are clearly of opinion that the making such paper-money a

---

3. De Lancey's information was not of the best. There were ₤132,532 in circulation at the time according to computations from various accounts.
4. De Lancey to B. T., May 21, 1754, <u>N. Y. Col. Doc.</u>, VI, 840.

legal tender in all payments is unnecessary, improper and inconsistent with the sence of Parliament here, and therefore if you shou'd meet with such difficulty in raising money for the supply and support of Government in the present emergency in the usual way as might induce you to fall upon this method we think that the bills ought by no means to be declared to be a legal tender and that the interest arising from the loan of the bills should during their continuance be appropriated and applied to the services of Government in the manner prescribed in His Majesty's Instruction [i.e., made subject to disposal by warrant of the governor and council] and provided also that you do not give your assent to any Act of this sort without a clause being inserted therein suspending its execution until His Majesty's pleasure be known. 5

Here one finds a good statement of the Board's thinking during this period on the matter of a paper currency.

Lieutenant Governor De Lancey had his first brush with the assembly over the paper money question in November, 1754. He pressed for an appropriation for the defense of the province and hinted at the possibility of raising funds by the emission of bills upon loan. Any such act should, he pointed out, contain a suspending clause; the bills of credit authorized should not be made a legal tender between man and man; and "the interest arising from the loan of the bills, should, during their continuance, be appropriated and applied to the services of government, in the manner prescribed by his Majesty's instructions."[6]

---

5. Ibid., p. 848. The letter was signed by Dunk Halifax, James Oswald, and Andrew Stone.
6. State of New York, Messages from the Governors, I (Colonial Period), 558; New York Assembly Journal, II, 409-410, November 21, 1754.

The reply of the assembly was immediate and emphatic, and left their position nowise in doubt.

> We are truly sensible, Sir, [they wrote] of the ruinous Conditions of our Fortifications and the Necessity not only of repairing them, but of erecting others for our greater Security and Preservation; but no Man in the Province knows better than your Honour, that we have not yet recovered the Waste and Desolation we sustained during the late French War, nor have we yet paid the Debt we then Contracted, our northern Settlements having not yet paid what was laid upon them. These Circumstances, Sir, render it impracticable for us, to raise such further Sums, as appear now necessary, in any other Manner than by a Paper Emission. But to emit Bills of Credit without making them a lawful Tender, we are confident, will be absolutely useless and without Effect, for we are fully persuaded, that no Man in the Province will be willing to accept of that for Money, which he knows that another may refuse to receive as Money from him, and if a Law, even under this Restriction, must have its Execution suspended till his Majesty's Pleasure can be known, this his Majesty's loyal Colony may fall a Prey to some ambitious avaricious Enemy, before any Return can be made.[7]

De Lancey returned to the fray the next day, urging the needs of defense, and stating the customary arguments of the Board of Trade against a paper currency. Nor did he fail to point out how the London merchants had suffered from a depreciating currency.[8] The assembly, however, was unmoved and passed a set of resolutions adhering to its position already expressed.[9] The issue was clearly joined: the interests of the London mer-

---

7. *Ibid.*, pp. 411-412 (November 27, 1754); extracted in *Messages from the Governors*, I, 559-560.
8. *N. Y. Assembly Journal*, II, 420-421 (November 28, 1754); *Messages from the Governors*, I, 560-561.
9. *N. Y. Assembly Journal*, II, 421 (November 28, 1754).

chants on one hand; the needs of colonial defense on the other. And who is to say that the arguments of the assembly were not compelling?[10]

The session ended in a deadlock, and no funds were provided for the defense of the colony. The situation being what it was, one can understand why De Lancey after reporting to the Board of Trade the assembly's refusal to provide funds in accordance with the royal instructions should conclude: "so that I am My Lords in the greatest perplexity imaginable not knowing how to act in this critical situation of affairs."[11]

In the meantime, his majesty's secretary of state,

---

10. Of course if the bills circulated freely without being declared a legal tender, they were de facto a legal tender even though they were not so de jure. The moment they ceased to so circulate and anyone refused them, at that moment they in effect became a legal tender for one man and not for another, i.e., for those that had received them, but not for those that now refused them. This would work a hardship on those that found themselves possessed of them. The object of denying the bills of credit the legal tender quality was primarily to protect long-term debtors. In the case of debts due in sterling, the practice in New York was to give judgments in bills of credit in sums sufficient to purchase the sterling amount of the debts. This being so, the London merchants as long-term creditors were not in need of protection in that colony. Cf. John Watts to Moses Franks, December 22, 1765, "Letter Book of John Watts" in N. Y. Hist. Soc., Collections, LXI, 406. Watts writes of the New York currency after the wartime experience. "For it neither depreciated, nor if it did, could One English Creditor be affected by it, because the Debtor is obligd to make good to him the Value of a pound Stirling, whatever be the Exchange or denomination of our paper Currancy ...."

11. De Lancey to B. T., December 15, 1754, N. Y. Col. Doc., VI, 928.

Sir Thomas Robinson, had on October 26, written to the governors in America, enjoining each of them *inter alia* to use his "utmost endeavours to induce the assembly of [his] province, to raise forthwith as large a sum as can be afforded, as their contribution to [a] common fund, to be employed, provisionally, for the General service of North America" for defense against the French.[12] The receipt of this letter caused De Lancey to call the assembly to meet in February, 1755; and he promised to "endeavour to prevail upon them to put the Country in posture of defence; but," he continued in his letter of January 31, 1755, to the Board of Trade, "as these services cannot be carried on without a paper emission, I shall be under a necessity to give into it, tho' I shall insist that the funds for sinking the Bills be sufficient to do it in five years, agreable to the act made for restraining the New England Colonies."[13]

By this time it was obvious that no issue of bills upon loan would in anywise answer the needs of the province. The assembly, however, on February 19, 1755, provided for the emission of Ł45,000 in bills of credit on tax funds. The five year limitation in the Currency Act of 1751 was approximated, taxes payable in each of

---

12. Robinson to De Lancey, October 26, 1754, *ibid.*, p. 916.
13. *Ibid.*, p. 937.

the years from 1756 to 1760 were levied to retire the bills, and their currency was to terminate in November, 1761. At every other point, however, the governor gave way. The act contained no suspending clause, and the bills were made a legal tender in all private transactions as well as at the treasury.[14] De Lancey excused himself to the Board of Trade for having consented to the bill by saying:

> I hope the necessity of securing the Province and of obtaining money for the King's Troops under the command of General Braddock in pursuance of His Maj^{ty}'s pleasure signified to me by Sir Thomas Robinson's letter, will plead for my excuse in breaking through my Instructions by giving my assent to a Law for a paper Emission without a suspending Clause; I could not get money in any other way, as your Lord^{sps} may be convinced of from what passed between me and the Assembly on this subject last fall; I have done the best I could, I had the advice of his Maj^{ty}'s Council for this measure, I had no view of advantage to myself, but the General one, of providing for His Maj^{tys} service and the preservation of a Country which is evidently of more concern to His Maj^{ty}'s Empire in America than any on the Continent. These were the only consideration which influenced my conduct; the goodness of the Fund and the short period in which the Bills are sunk will, I am convinced[,] keep them up to the credit at which they are admitted.[15]

Truly the position of the royal governor, placed as he was between the upper and the nether millstones -- between royal instructions often issued in the interest of some particular group in the mother country, and the

---

14. *Colonial Laws of New York,* III, 1038-1050 (c. 970).

15. De Lancey to B. T., March 18, 1755, *N. Y. Col. Doc.,* VI, 941.

exigencies of defense and the colonial interest as expressed in the colonial assemblies -- was not an enviable one.

The provisions of the act of February 17, 1755, set the pattern for later issues, with the exception that as the expenses of the war mounted, the period of the bills was extended, in some cases to as long as ten years. De Lancey approved one further issue, that of ₤10,000 the following May,[16] when he was succeeded by the new governor, Sir Charles Hardy, who assumed the administration of the government in September.

Governor Hardy came with a new instruction respecting bills of credit. In order to make provision for raising funds in the present emergency, the old requirement that all acts for issuing bills of credit should contain a suspending clause was abolished, and the governor was empowered to assent to such acts "upon sudden and extraordinary emergencies of government in case of war or invasion," but "upon no other occasion whatever." Moreover, funds were to be provided by the issuing act for calling in the bills within five years, and the bills so emitted were not to be declared a legal tender in any private transaction. The instruction was based on certain of the provisions contained

---

16. Col. Laws of N. Y., III, 1078-1093 (c. 977); passed May 3, 1755.

in the Currency Act of 1751.[17] The instruction was at once a loosening and a tightening of the restraint imposed upon the province. Henceforth the governor was permitted during times of emergency caused by war or invasion to assent to paper money acts that did not contain a suspending clause; but at all other times he could assent to none at all, whether or not they contained a suspending clause. While this was not of immediate importance, in time it posed a serious problem.

Governor Hardy and those that succeeded him in the administration of the affairs of the province were no more able to enforce a compliance with their instructions than De Lancey had been. The suspending clause difficulty was now removed, but there was still the matter of the five year period and that of the bills being denied the legal tender quality in private transactions. The assembly refused to grant funds in accordance with these restrictions, and as grants of funds were indispensable, the governors were forced to give way. At first the Board of Trade viewed the breaking through of the instruction with "some concern," but hoped that the "necessity of the service" would justify the governor's giving way.[18] Later the Board, although

---

17. Representation of B. T. to Lords Justices, April 22, 1755, N. Y. Col. Doc., VII, 79.
18. B. T. to Hardy, April 13, 1756, ibid.

still viewing this and similar actions of the assembly with "great concern," expressed the logic of the situation when it said: "We shall not in the present exigency of the Times, take upon us to advise the repeal of [the acts], as they appear to be so essential to the good of His Maj^{ty}'s service."[19]

The emissions of the war period may be followed in Tables XV and XVI, and in graphic form in Figure XI. The total issues of the war amounted to ₤535,000 New York currency, equivalent at the time of issue to some ₤309,000 sterling.[20] In fact, so necessary was the instrument of paper currency to the conduct of the war, that in 1759 at the request of the British commander in chief in America, Sir Jeffrey Amherst, the assembly struck the sum of ₤150,000 in bills of credit to be issued in the form of a loan to the British commander. The sum was to be repaid the next year by bills of exchange drawn upon the paymaster general in England.[21]

The period of the ₤40,000 put out on loan under authorization of the act of 1737 had been prolonged by

---

19. Same to same, March 10, 1757, ibid., p. 221. See also Hardy's letters to B. T.: February 23, 1756, ibid., p. 37; August 2, 1756, ibid., p. 121; December 2, 1756, ibid., p. 210.
20. Report to B. T., July 20, 1762. C. O. 323/19, L. C. photostats.
21. Amherst to De Lancey, Camp at Lake George, July 8, 1759, N. Y. Col. Doc., VII, 399-400; Col. Laws of N. Y., IV, 350-355 (c. 1087); passed July 3, 1759.

an act passed in 1743.[22] In 1750 the loans stood payable in equal installments in the years 1754 to 1757. At that time the period was extended for three years and the appropriation of the interest money to the uses of government was extended for a similar period until April, 1757.[23] The loans fell due during the period of the French and Indian War, and as the revenue from the loan money was sorely needed, the life of the loan bills was extended from year to year, the last continuing act being passed in 1763.[24] By this last enactment it was provided that the loans should be called in, one-fourth in each of the years, 1765, 1766, 1767, and 1768. The interest money stood appropriated until April, 1765.

The assembly was on the alert to see that the outstanding bills of credit were retired according to their periods and on two occasions, in 1758 and again in 1762, took the treasurer to task for his failure to retire the bills promptly.[25] In fact, the assembly gave

---

22. Supra, p. 71.
23. Colonial Laws of N. Y., III, 784-787 (c. 897); passed November 24, 1750.
24. Ibid., IV, 156-159 (c. 1036), passed December 1, 1756; 199-202 (c. 1055), passed December 24, 1757; 301-304 (c. 1074), passed December 16, 1758; 385-387 (c. 1102), passed December 24, 1759; 491-494 (c. 1133), passed November 8, 1760; 554-556 (c. 1158), passed December 11, 1762; 708-710 (c. 1214), passed December 13, 1763.
25. N. Y. Assembly Journal, II; see under these these years, passim.

TABLE XV

NEW YORK WAR ISSUES

Date of emitting act	Sum emitted ₤	Bills current until	Fund retiring (as provided by emitting act)	Reference: Colonial Laws of New York
1755				
Feb. 19	45,000	Nov. 1761	Tax on real and personal estates	III, 1038-1050 (c. 970)
May 3	10,000	Nov. 1762	do.	III, 1078-1093 (c. 977)
Sept. 11	8,000	Nov. 1761	do.	III, 1131-1139 (c. 988)
	₤63,000			
1756				
Apr. 1	10,000	Nov. 1766	do.	IV, 43-59 (c. 1008)
Apr. 1	52,000	Nov. 1768	do.	IV, 60-76 (c. 1009)
	₤62,000			
1758				
Mar. 24	100,000	Nov. 1768	do.	IV, 215-235 (c. 1059)
1759				
Mar. 7	100,000	Nov. 1768	do.	IV, 317-337 (c. 1082)
July 3	150,000	July 1759	Loan to Gen. Amherst. To be retired of funds from bills of exch. on paymaster.	IV, 350-355 (c. 1087)
	₤250,000			
1760				
Mar. 22	60,000	Nov. 1768	Tax on real and personal estates	IV, 398-418 (c. 1112)
Total	₤535,000	Value in sterling when emitted ₤308,717 Value in sterling, July, 1764 ₤297,136		

Reference: Report to B. T., July 20, 1764, C. O. 323/19, L. C. P.

TABLE XVI

NEW YORK BILLS OF CREDIT

Year	Emitted ₤	Cancelled ₤	Outstanding ₤
1747 N[x]	28,000		189,495
1748 J		4,119	185,375
1748 N		13,374	172,001
1749 J		4,981	167,020
1749 N		4,003	163,016
1750 J		7,078	155,938
1750 N		2,000	153,938
1751 J		2,496	151,442
1751 N		3,227	148,214
1752 J		3,603	144,611
1752 N		3,651	140,960
1753 J		4,400	136,560
1753 N		4,028	132,531
1754 J		4,050	128,481
1754 N		2,400	126,081
1755 J	55,000	6,003	175,078
1755 N	8,000	4,001	179,076
1756 J	62,000	5,211	235,865
1756 N		5,092	230,773
1757 J		6,387	224,386
1757 N		5,105	219,281
1758 J	100,000	6,338	312,943
1758 N		5,745	307,198
1759 J	100,000	18,002	389,196
1759 N	150,000	58,010	481,186
1760 J	60,000	51,832	489,355
1760 N		78,968	410,387
1761 J		24,618	385,768
1761 N		19,610	366,158
1762 J		23,062	343,096
1762 N		12,289	330,807
1763 J		20,444	310,363
1763 N		23,200	287,163
1764 J		19,384	267,779
1764 N		23,895	243,885
1765 J		54,281	189,604
1765 N		23,102	166,502

(continued)

TABLE XVI

(continued)

Year	Emitted £	Cancelled £	Outstanding £
1766 J		20,000	146,502
1766 N		15,000	131,502
1767 J		12,000	119,502
1767 N		9,703	109,799
1768 J		15,744	94,055
1768 N		6,707	87,348
1769 J		1,610	85,738
1769 N		2,879	82,858
1770 J & N		1,267	81,591
1771 J & N	120,000	3,020	198,571
1772 J & N		4,131	194,440
1773 J & N		4,040	190,400
1774 J & N		2,686	187,714

x   J, June; N, November.

For source and method, see p. 72, note 14.

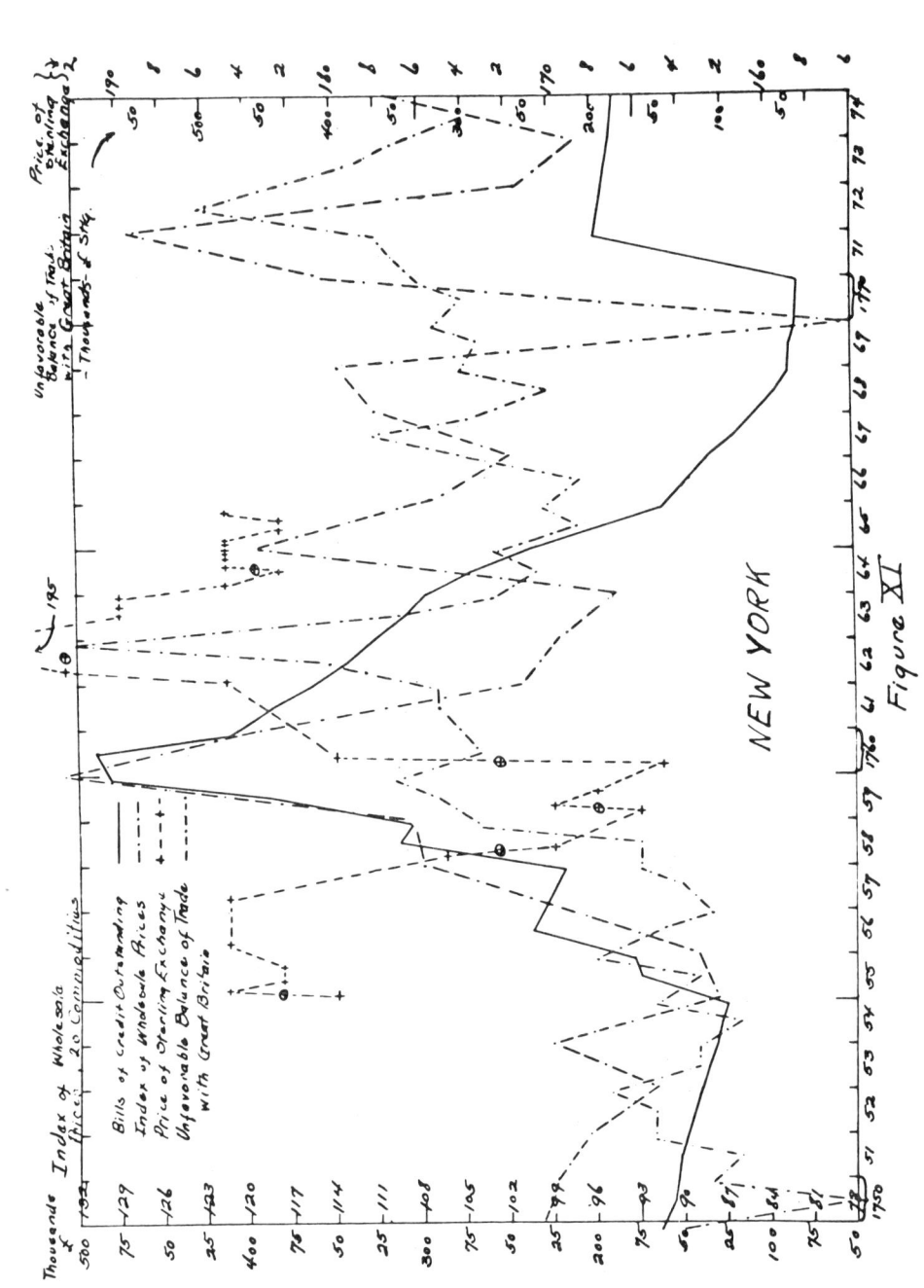

Figure XI — NEW YORK

every evidence of wishing to hasten the retirement of the bills even in advance of their periods. When in September, 1756, Governor Hardy announced that he had received the colony's share of the first parliamentary grant, amounting to ₤14,323 15s. 3d. sterling (equivalent to ₤24,982 8s. 2 1/2d. New York currency), the assembly resolved with respect to its disposal that "at present no Method appears to us, more consistent with the Intent of [Parliament in making the grant to reimburse the colonies for the services of 1755], than the Cancelling those Paper Emissions which were Struck for those very Services...."[26] The increasing needs of the war, however, caused the assembly to appropriate the money to the further prosecution of the struggle.[27] Throughout the continuance of the war, the several parliamentary grants were applied by the colony to finance her martial efforts. At the conclusion of hostilities, however, the sums that remained from the grants were applied in abatement of taxes to retire the outstanding bills of credit.[28]

As had been the case in New England, the parlia-

---

26. Ibid., p. 503 (September 29, 1756).
27. N. Y. Col. Laws, IV, 163 (c. 1039, passed February 26, 1757); 247 (c. 1063, passed June 3, 1758).
28. Ibid., 801-804 (c. 1249, passed October 20, 1764). In all, some ₤59,250 New York currency was appropriated to that purpose. This is not included in the ₤195,000 mentioned below.

mentary grants proved of great aid to New York, both in financing her contribution to the war and in meeting demands for payments to the mother country. By the end of 1764, the colony had received approximately ₤195,000 New York currency from this source. The various grants may be seen in Table XVII. The first grant of ₤14,323 15s. 3d. sterling (equivalent to ₤24,982 8s. 2 1/2d. New York currency) was brought over in 1757 in specie. The ₤36,666 16s. 5 1/2d. New York currency realized from the grant of 1759 and the ₤2,977 7s. 8d. sterling granted the colony in 1760 as reimbursement for services of the year 1756 was received in the colonial treasury in 1761 part in specie and part in the proceeds of bills of exchange sold on the money in the hands of the agents in London. After this year no specie was imported and all grants were transferred by drawing bills of exchange on the agents in London.[29]

Valuable as the parliamentary grants were in providing specie and exchange, they were in New York's case small in comparison to the sums of specie brought into the colony's and the bills of exchange sold there as a result of the fact that large numbers of his Majesty's forces were located in the colony. The money to pay and provision the troops was provided in two ways:

---

29. Robert Charles and Sir William Baker served as the agents of the colony in receiving the money.

TABLE XVII

NEW YORK PARLIAMENTARY GRANTS

(Received by end of 1764)

Year of Grant	Act	Received £ stlg.	Received £ N. Y. currency	Service of Year
1756	29 Geo. II, c. 29	14,324	24,982	
1759	32 Geo. II, c. 36	23,070)	)	1758
		)	36,667	
1760	33 Geo. II, c. 18	2,977)		1756
1760	do.	?	45,000[a]	1759
1761	1 Geo. III, c. 34	?	46,875	1760
1762	2 Geo. III, c. 34	20,027 4,368[b]	36,549 5,263	1761
1763	3 Geo. III, c. 17	?		1762
		Total	£195,334	

[a] The sum authorized to be drawn, Act of April 14, 1761, CLNY, IV, c. 1145.
[b] Owing from Pennsylvania (not all received by end of 1764), Penna. Votes, VII, 5651.

Source: N. Y. Assembly Journal, II, 545, 679-680, 712, 725, 754-755.

specie was imported; and bills of exchange were drawn on the paymaster general in England. The whole sum of the money raised to pay the troops and much of that spent for "extraordinaries" within the colony, whether arising from importing specie or selling bills of exchange, was a net addition to the fund of specie and exchange in the colony available to pay balances abroad. In the case of provisions the matter is not so simple. If the provisions were purchased in the colony with funds from England it might at first appear that this would constitute a net addition to the colony's fund of specie or exchange. But if the provisions would otherwise have been exported, as was in considerable measure the case, the specie or exchange that the colony gained by their purchase from English funds was cancelled out by the loss of specie or exchange that would have resulted from their exportation. Many of the provisions provided, however, were imported from England and Ireland.

One cannot from the sources available reach any precise estimate of the funds that flowed into New York from these operations. But on any estimate they were considerable. Some indications of the sums involved for all America may be obtained from the declared accounts of the money contractors. From 1754 to 1756, the sum handled was Ł473,191 7s. 4d. sterling, and from 1756 to the end of the war, £3,563,642 6$\underline{s}$. 4 1/2$\underline{d}$. Furthermore, these sums did "not include the pay of officers, either regimental or staff, or the stoppages made in England, or the cost of provisions, or the ordnance charges."[30] There were sizeable importations of specie into New York, both from England and from the other colonies. These latter importations arose from the fact the bills of exchange drawn on the paymaster in England were sold in four centers, Boston, New York, Philadelphia, and Maryland and Virginia.[31] Much of the specie raised in these other centers was transported to New York. The effect of all this was well set forth by Benjamin Franklin, who was in New York in the year 1756 and from his observations wrote: "This only I can plainly see, that New York is growing immensely rich, by Money brought in from all Quarters for the Pay and Subsistence of the Troops."[32] Of course, the drawing of specie to New York from the other colonies had repercussions elsewhere. The effect was most severe in Virginia, where because it drained the colony of its

---

30. Stanley Pargellis, <u>Lord Loudoun in North America</u>, p. 290, n. 15.

31. "Memorial and State of the Exchange with the British Colonies in North America" (1754?), in Stanley Pargellis (ed.), <u>Military Affairs in North America, 1748-1765</u>, pp. 41-43.

32. B. F. to William Parsons, New York, June 28, 1756, Albert H. Smyth (ed.), <u>Writings of Benjamin Franklin</u>, III, 336.

silver it was one of the factors that occasioned recourse to paper currency in that colony.[33]

The rôle of the West Indian trade in supplying specie and exchange during the war is difficult to appraise with any certainty. It seems, however, that trade with the Spanish islands during the later years of the war constituted a not unimportant source of specie.[34]

Of the many forces at play during the period, now one, now another, seems to have exerted the dominant influence upon prices and exchange rates. Reference to the changes in the amount of bills of credit outstanding, the changes in the unfavorableness of the balance of trade with England, and the fluctuations of wholesale prices and of the price of sterling exchange indicated in Figure XI will aid one in untangling this complex matter. From the beginning of 1755 until the end of 1759 the trend of bills of credit outstanding was sharply upward. The bills outstanding then decreased rapidly until the end of 1768. The rise in the amount of paper currency outstanding in the years 1755 to 1759

---

33. Robert Dinwiddie to Henry Fox, May 24, 1756, R. A. Brock (ed.), "Official Records of Robert Dinwiddie," in Virginia Hist. Soc., Collections (new series), IV, 415.

34. To the Merchants and Manufacturers of Great-Britain; The Memorial of the Merchants and Traders of the City of Philadelphia [1765], speaks of "the advantageous Trade, which the Colonies had with the foreign Islands, during the last War, and the great Importation of Specie arising therefrom ...."

was paralleled quite closely by increases in the unfavorableness of the balance of trade with England. Wholesale prices, however, showed only a moderate upward trend during the period, and exchange fell sharply between early 1757 and the spring of 1760. The rise of wholesale prices was damped during this period largely because of falling exchange rates, and the falling exchange rates, in the face of rising amounts of paper currency in circulation and an increased adverse balance of trade with England, can be accounted for only by the fact that the importation of specie and the selling of bills of exchange on England to meet the expenses occasioned by the troops stationed in New York increased the supply of these articles relatively to the increased demand for them for remittances. The decreased expenditures after 1759, however, occasioned a reversal of the trends. Although the amount of bills of credit in circulation decreased rapidly and the adverse balance with England for the time fell off, both exchange and wholesale prices rose precipitately, reaching their peak at the end of 1762. Both then fell sharply to mid-1764, after which during the next two years they leveled off.

By the end of 1763, things wore a different cast than they had during the flush days of the war when the colony was "growing immensely rich, by Money brought in from all Quarters." The tide had turned. On December 2, 1763, the New York merchant John Watts wrote to a business associate: "Exchange on London [at] 90 per Ct: [advance;] the Trade has swept off all Gold & Silver for remittances, & even given 2 1/2 per Ct: Advance, so that we have nothing remaining but Paper Currency."[35] The fact that New York entered the period of currency restraint and trade regulation that followed the war with her specie exhausted and her paper medium contracting rapidly, affected in no small degree her relations with the mother country during the critical years to come.

If in New York the conflict engendered by the restraints imposed upon paper currency by the authorities in England did not develop until the outbreak of the French and Indian War, it was otherwise in Pennsylvania. The only issue of bills of credit in Pennsylvania during King George's War had been that of £5,000 in 1746, the full amount of which was still in circulation in 1749. In addition there were the £80,000 that had subsisted on loan since 1739. The total sum of £85,000 in circulation at the end of the year 1749 amounted, after allowances for the difference in value of the two

---

35. To Gedney Clarke, "Letter Book of John Watts, 1762-1765," New York Historical Society, Collections, LXI, 204-205.

currencies, to about half that in circulation in New York.

Beginning with 1750, the ₤5,000 issue of 1746 was to be retired at the rate of ₤500 a year. The ₤80,000 on loan, however, was to circulate until 1756, after which it was to be retired in equal annual installments over a period of six years. During King George's War the amount of specie in the province had increased until in 1749 there was more in circulation than at any previous time in the history of the province. There were at this time perhaps three or four pounds circulating in specie for every pound in paper. But this supply of specie, which had been brought into the province as a result of the war, could not be expected to remain in normal times when the balance of trade with England was so unfavorable. In fact, the outflow seems already to have begun, for in July, 1749, the province secretary, Richard Peters, wrote to the proprietor, Thomas Penn, in England and reported that "Vast Sums of money in heavy Pistoles have been carried to Virginia for their Bills of Exchange & it is said a large Sum in pieces of Eight is remitted by this Ship."[36]

---

36. Peters to T. Penn, Philadelphia, July 5, 1749, Penn Official Correspondence, MSS, IV, 225. Historical Society of Pennsylvania.

Despite the fact that there was an unprecedented amount of specie in circulation in the province, or perhaps to make preparations as against that day when it should depart, the assembly in February, 1749, proposed the emission of the sum of ₤20,000 to be placed on loan.[37] The governor, James Hamilton, delayed action on the bill, ostensibly that he might have "some Time" the better "to form a right Judgment."[38] In the meantime, however, news was received of the bill to regulate paper currency in America then under consideration in Parliament. When the assembly reconvened in August, the governor adroitly made use of this fact to dissuade that body from further attempts at increasing the paper circulation of the colony. And Richard Peters wrote home to Thomas Penn that he supposed the bill for an addition of ₤20,000 to the currency of the province "thrown into a sound napp by the noise made about Paper Money in England," and that it would "not awake except the Application to Parliament end in favour of this sort of Currency."[39]

Thomas Penn, who of the two proprietors was the one that actively concerned himself with the government of the province, was not opposed to a paper currency as

---

37. Penna. Votes, IV, 3242, et seq.
38. Ibid., p. 3249.
39. Philadelphia, August 7, 1749, Penn Official Correspondence, MSS, IV, 232-233.

such. On the contrary, as has been seen, he was extremely active in opposing the efforts of the London merchants and the Board of Trade to induce Parliament to restrain the colonies in this particular.[40] None the less, he felt it expedient to promise Lord Halifax of the Board of Trade and several of the important members of Parliament that his province would pass no further paper currency acts until such time as Parliament had acted; and he so informed his governor.[41]

It was not until 1752, the year after Parliament had legislated with respect to New England, that the currency question again became pressing. On January 20, 1752, Richard Peters wrote to Thomas Penn:

> ... there are several Petitions for a Paper Money Act, [and] the speaker [Isaac Norris] declares loudly for an Addition to the Currency & ... on this account the next Session [of the assembly] which begins the first Monday in the next month is likely to be a little troublesome.[42]

---

40. On October 9, 1749, Penn wrote from London to Governor Hamilton:
"I do not wonder at the [Pennsylvania] peoples being very uneasy when they consider the Consequences [of the bill so lately before Parliament]. [E]very one is sensible that in two or three Years almost the whole of the Gold and Silver that during the War was brought into the Colonys will be shipped hither, and wee shall have little but paper left, so that I think it absolutely necessary to continue the strongest opposition to any such Bills, and shal expect yours and the Assemblys observations on what has been done, and Instructions for our future conduct."
Penn Letter Book, MS, II, 290. Historical Society of Pennsylvania.

41. T. Penn to Hamilton, July 31, 1749, Penn Letter Book, MS, II, 270; T. Penn to Richard Peters, August 2, 1749, ibid., 275.

42. Penn Official Correspondence, MSS, V, 213.

As Peters had foreseen, the paper currency question was raised in the assembly and a bill was brought in to re-emit the present currency of the province for a period of ten years and to strike the further sum of ₤40,000 to be placed on loan for a period of sixteen years.[43] Governor Hamilton refused his assent to the act on the pretext that he did not think it advisable at that time, when the late regulation imposed on New England was so "fresh in the Memory" of the Board of Trade, to pass an act increasing the paper currency of the province.[44]

The reason offered by the governor for refusing his assent was but a subterfuge. The real reason was of another sort, as becomes clear from a letter that Hamilton wrote to Thomas Penn at the end of the session. Hamilton thus explained his withholding his assent:

> You had mentioned to me in a paragraph of your letters of 29' of July 1751, that you did not intend for the future to pass any paper-money or Excise Law but on Condition, that the produce should be either appropriated in the Bill, or be left to the Governor and assembly jointly to do it. [The practice for sometime hitherto had been to place the funds at the disposal of a committee of the assembly.] As this came not to me by way of Instruction, but rather as I may call it, in the way of Conversation, in reasoning upon that Subject, I was not sure, that it was your deliberate Opinion, from which you would not recede. However, as it was in some sort, a signification of your pleasure,

---

43. James Hamilton to Thomas Penn, Philadelphia, March(?), 1752, ibid., p. 227; Penna. Votes, IV, 3483-3500, passim.
44. Ibid., 3500-3501.

I determined to pay the same regard to it, as if it had been an Instruction. Then the question was, whether I should propose such a Clause by way of Amendment, or give the Bill the go-by upon other Reasons, till I could be certainly informed from yourself, that you had well weighed the Matter, and were resolved to insist upon such an appropriating Clause in all future Bills for raising of Money. 45

Hamilton chose the latter course because he felt that to propose such an amendment "would raise a great ferment among the people, and be considered ... as a violent attack upon their liberties and priviledges." If after he had raised the question, he should be obliged for any reason to give up the point, it would, he felt, "only serve to show the Weakness of the Government, and render [him] extreamly odious, as having very bad designs upon the People's Liberties."[46]

The response of the assembly to the governor's first refusal of his assent was to reduce the proposed addition to the currency to ₤20,000. When on the receipt of the amended bill the governor sent the assembly "a more peremptory" message of refusal, that body "immediately concluded to adjourn to the 10' of August ...."[47]

Hamilton earnestly besought Penn to consider well whether it would be wise to engage in a contest with the assembly on the point of the appropriating clause, and

---

45. Penn Official Correspondence, MSS, V, 227.
46. Ibid.
47. Ibid. See also Penna. Votes, IV, 3501-3505.

with great prescience outlined the course of events should such a dispute be embarked upon.

As the Cry of paper Money is once raised, [he continued in his letter to Penn,] it cannot now be still'd again. There is not the least Doubt, but a Bill will be offer'd at least once every year till it be obtaind; and therefore [the] appropriating Clause, becomes a Matter of great Moment to You, and well deserves your most serious Consideration. In my humble opinion, it should never be proposed unless You are determined at all Events inviolably to adhere to it. It is certain that at first, the Assembly will bounce violently and be very angry, and the Province will be thrown into a Flame on that Account; & probably You will have but little Money paid into your Receivers Hands [i.e., the receivers of the quit rents] during the Contest. Added to all this, (and it ought to be well weigh'd) the Assembly, by the great funds they have in their Hands of at least Ł6,000 a year, will be able to accumulate a Vast sum of Money befor the present acts expire [i.e., the loan office act and the excise act, which in themselves had for years produced a revenue sufficient to meet the expenses of the province], with which to carry on any Contest, or to gratify their adherents, for without Doubt, the sluices of their liberality will be stopp'd to all others. On the other Hand, when the Re-Emitting and Excise Acts expire, which will be in about four years and an half, and the Money begins to sink; It seems to me, they will be under a necessity of Complying, rather than want a Medium of Commerce, but that is a long time to carry on a Contest. And untill they do comply, Every Officer of the Government, who relies on the publick for any thing, is held in Bondage, the whole dependence of the Province is drawn upon them; Men of Fortune, from whom One would expect better things, gradualy slide into their dirty ways of thinking; and by Those means The Government, upon any Contention, is left without either weight or Adherents. 48

Thomas Penn consulted with his brother Richard, and the two proprietors fully determined "never to consent to any Law for emitting or re[-e]mitting Paper

---

48. Hamilton to T. Penn, Penn Official Correspondence, MSS, V, 227.

Money without" a clause placing the interest money at the disposal of the governor and assembly jointly. They also took the same position concerning the excise law. "I assure you," Thomas Penn wrote to Governor Hamilton, "I shall hold out a much longer time than four years, if it shall be necessary[,] rather than not remedy this great Evil." Hamilton was sent an instruction with respect to a paper money bill, although no formal instruction was thought necessary in the case of the excise. He was, however, to delay the issue on the paper money bill as long as possible and not reveal his instructions except as a last resort.[49]

Penn counselled delay for two reasons: first, that the wrath of the assembly might if possible be prevented from descending upon the proprietary party until such time as that body should find itself without a revenue because the loan office and excise acts had expired; and second, because Penn feared that it would be impossible so soon after the Currency Act of 1751 to secure the royal approval of a paper money act over the opposition of Lord Halifax at home. As soon as Penn had received Hamilton's report of the assembly's proposing a paper money bill, he had sought out Lord

---

49. Thomas Penn to Hamilton, London, June 5, 1752, Penn Letter Book, MS, III, 162; same to same, London, July 13, 1752, ibid., 144.

Halifax and discussed the matter with him:

> ... I found him [Penn wrote] much concerned that Pennsylvania which had acted the best part hitherto in this Case, should [have proposed a new emission] so soon after the Parliament had passed a Law to prevent the issuing any more in the four Eastern Governments, and in the course of [the discussion he] expressed a great dislike to it in general [and does not] desire any addition[.] [H]e said we ought to be extremely careful how we act in this matter else [the] Act [of Parliament] will certainly be extended. I compared our Currency with that of Rhode Island, our People and Trade with theirs, and he was sensible there was a great disproportion in the Quantity of Currency in our favour; but much desir'd that if it should be found necessary to encrease the Quantity, that it should be only a small addition and that the Bill should not be passed for at least a year, and at the same time that a representation should be sent with it, setting forth the encrease of the Trade of Pennsylvania, and, of its Inhabitants. We then spoke of the Sum, when I proposed Twenty thousand Pounds, for I found more would not be allowed, and I myself you may be assured did not desire to make the Quantity too great .... He also said a great deal of the mischief that attended the Assembly's having the Power of disposing of the Interest Money, and if any more is issued in the King's Colonys, will give the same Instructions I have sent you. 50

Penn wanted to keep the way open at home for the confirmation of a Pennsylvania paper money act because he believed that an additional sum of paper money would be necessary to move the trade of the province when once its specie had been shipped off, but also because the eagerness of the people for a loan office was to be the lever by which the control of provincial expenditures was to be pried out of the grasp of the assembly. The stage was set for a struggle that was to grow increasing-

---

50. T. Penn to Hamilton, July 13, 1752, loc. cit.

ly acrimonious as it merged itself with disputes over wartime finance and the taxation of the proprietary estates later in the decade.

The assembly was yet in the dark as to the real reason for the governor's refusal of their paper money bill. In rejecting the assembly's amended bill in March, 1752, the governor had given it as his opinion that the province was "not in immediate Want of Money as a Medium of Commerce."[51] Before the assembly adjourned until the following August, it appointed a committee "to enquire into the State of our Paper Currency, our foreign and domestic Trade; and the Number of People within this Province," and to report at the next session.[52] Among the six members of the committee was Benjamin Franklin, and his hand is clearly seen in the report that the committee submitted when the assembly reconvened. This and supplementary reports issued as the contest developed constitute perhaps the best exposition and defense of the use of paper currency to promote the public weal that is to be found in colonial annals. The report argued the increase of population and trade, both foreign and domestic, of the province since the introduction of paper currency and, implicitly at least, the need for a proportionate

---

51. Penna. Votes, IV, 3504. March 10, 1752.
52. Ibid., p. 3507.

increase in the currency to circulate it.[53] Furthermore, the committee urged, "the manner of issuing this Medium contributed no less to those happy Effects than the Medium itself." The placing of the money on loan in sums from ₤12 1/2 to ₤100 to one person, "for a long Term, on easy Interest, and payable in yearly Quotas; ... put it in the Power of many to purchase Lands, and make Plantations ... and thereby to acquire Estates to themselves, and to support and bring up Families .... This easy Means of acquiring landed Estates, has, we suppose, been one principal Encouragement to the great Removal hither, of People from Ireland and Germany, where they were only, and could scarce ever expect to be other than Tenants. And the happy Contrivance in our Money Laws, by which the yearly Quotas are, as fast as paid in, re-emitted to other Borrowers, made the same Quantity of Currency serviceable in their Turns to a much greater Number of People; thereby lessening the Necessity and Demand for striking great additional Sums, which, if carried to Excess, might depreciate the Value of the Currency." "This easy Method of obtaining Money for the Purchase and Improvement of Lands," had not "kept Pace, as it ought to have done, with the growing

---

53. This was explicitly stated in a later report (February 6, 1754): "Your Committee ... apprehend the Occasions for a Medium of Trade must have increased equally with ... Trade ...." Ibid., V, 3628.

Numbers of People" so that there was a waiting list of 1000 "Appliers" at the loan office, "and within these Ten Years, a vast Multitude of our Inhabitants have, to procure Settlements, wandered away to other Places."[54] There was no wish to add to the currency other than a moderate sum. In fact, at no time in the whole history of colonial Pennsylvania did such a desire exist.

With this statement of the case, the assembly let the matter rest at its August session, but again sent up its bill in January, 1753. The governor again rejected the bill on the plea that the time was yet "very unseasonable" for an application to the crown for an addition to the currency of the province.[55] The assembly adjourned until May, at which time, after receiving a petition from "a considerable Number of the Inhabitants of the County of Lancaster" urging the scarcity of currency, it replied to the governor's objections, and again sent up its bill.[56] No answer being immediately forthcoming from the governor, the assembly adjourned until August.

In the meantime, Governor Hamilton, finding himself deserted by the men of fortune and influence upon whom he and Penn had relied for support, wrote to Penn

---

54. Ibid., IV, 3515-3520.
55. Ibid., p. 3551.
56. Ibid., pp. 3554-3561.

apprising him of the state of affairs and suggesting that it might be well to reconsider the matter of insisting upon the instructions. Richard Peters had written about the same time and had apparently suggested a way out of the dilemma. Allow the governor to assent to a paper money bill containing an appropriating clause in the usual form, but insist upon a suspending clause, taking refuge behind the royal instruction sent over in 1740 as a result of the address of the House of Commons of that year that no paper currency acts should be assented to unless they contained such a clause. Then "by previous management" Penn was to contrive to have the law disallowed at home because it did not contain an appropriating clause of the kind the proprietors desired.[57]

---

57. Hamilton to T. Penn, February 9, 1753, Penn Official Correspondence, MSS, VI, 9-11; R. Peters to T. Penn, April 18, 1753, ibid., 41-43; T. Penn to Hamilton, April 2, 1753, Penn Letter Book, MS, III, 222-223; same to same, August 12, 1753, ibid., 237.

Hamilton's letter urging a reconsideration of the matter of insisting on the proprietary instructions had been counteracted by a letter that Richard Peters wrote Thomas Penn on March 21, 1753:

"... It is notorious that the Paper money Petitions were forced and I really believe the sensible part of the Province think a Bill of this Sort premature and at this time peculiarly unreasonable. But what then? -- Now it is begun. You may be assured one will be presented every year, and as the necessity will be more apparent the nearer the time approaches for the sinking of the present Currency which commences in the Year 1756. The Clamours will encrease. A ReEmission will be unavoidable and an Addition likewise, if Gold & Silver dont continue with us. Behold a fair Opportunity

With something like this in mind, Penn forwarded a dispensing instruction enabling Governor Hamilton to assent to a paper currency bill with an appropriating clause in the usual form, provided it contained a suspending clause. While Penn gave Hamilton this option, he was apparently still willing to join the issue with the assembly on the original instruction.[58] Governor Hamilton, when the assembly reconvened in August, 1753, returned the paper currency bill presented him the preceding May, and indicated his willingness to assent to the bill if some few amendments, to which he presumed the assembly could "have no Objection," were included.[59] The assembly willingly concurred in certain of the amendments; but concerning the governor's proposal of a suspending clause, it unanimously resolved, "That the House cannot agree to this amendment, because we apprehend the Clause destructive of the liberties derived to us by the Royal and Provincial Charters, as well as injurious to the Proprietaries Rights, and without any Precedent in the Laws of this Province."[60] The governor then produced the royal in-

---

for the Proprietaries to put the disposal of the publick money on such an Issue as may give Authority to the Government and Stability to the Constitution."
    58. T. Penn to Hamilton, April 2, 1753, ibid., 222-223. Same to Same, August 12, 1753, ibid., p. 237.
    59. Penna. Votes, IV, 3572-3573 (August 29, 1753).
    60. Ibid., pp. 3574, 3579.

struction sent over in 1740.[61]

The assembly entered into a minute examination of the governor's new contention, reiterated its previous resolution on the suspending clause, and took the position that whatever may have been the validity of the royal instruction originally, it could no longer be considered binding, since Parliament had entered into a full determination of the question of paper currency in America, and had left Pennsylvania outside of the scope of parliamentary regulation. Moreover, the assembly began to suspect that this sudden regard on the part of the governor for the royal instruction of 1740 was not the real reason for his actions, and were confirmed in their suspicions of several years standing that the governor was bound by proprietary instructions.[62]

In the meantime, on the other side of the water, Thomas Penn consulted with his brother Richard, and resolved to present the question of whether the royal instruction was binding on Pennsylvania to the attorney general, Sir Dudley Ryder, for his opinion. This was

---

61. Ibid., pp. 3575-3577.
62. Ibid., pp. 3578-3603, passim; Hamilton to T. Penn, September 8, 1753, Penn Official Correspondence, MSS, VI, 99. Thomas Penn in commenting on the assembly's denial of the applicability of the royal instruction wrote: "I know enough of the indecent behavior of an American Politician to judge how they break any order from the Crown." Penn to Peters, November 16, 1753, Penn Letter Book, MS, III, 274-276.

done and that eminent lawyer, who was soon to become chief justice of England, expressed the opinion that it was "by no Means safe, or advisable, or consistent with his Duty, [for the governor] to pass such Bills, without a suspending Clause."[63] Despite Ryder's opinion, it is by no means clear that the royal instruction was binding on Pennsylvania. Lord Halifax, with whom Thomas Penn discussed the matter, considered it still in force. But, Penn adds,

... whether it is or is not proper to be sent to Charter Governments, to ours in particular, [Halifax thought] should be examined, and [he] thought it proper for us to take advice of Council, which we shall do; I have been informed that the Lords of Trade did about a year since send this question to the Attorney and Sollicitor General, to which they have not received any answer, and it is supposed they will not give one, as they cannot such an one as will be agreable.[64]

Penn seems to have been inclined to agree with the assembly that an instruction requiring a suspending clause in a provincial enactment was "injurious to the Proprietaries Rights," for he repeatedly offered to aid the agent of the assembly, Robert Charles, in any effort that Charles might make to secure the exemption of the province from the instruction.[65]

When the new assembly met in October, 1753, the

---

63. Penna. Votes, V, 3780.
64. T. Penn to Hamilton, January 29, 1754, Penn Letter Book, MS, III, 285-287.
65. T. Penn to Richard Peters, November 16, 1753, ibid., pp. 274-276; T. Penn to Hamilton, January 29, 1754, loc. cit.

governor was so worn and ill that he was unable to transact any business, and the assembly adjourned until the following February. No sooner, however, had it met after adjournment than it again embarked upon a discussion of its proposed paper currency measure and sent up a bill to re-emit the ₤80,000 outstanding on loan and to place in circulation ₤40,000 additional.[66] By this time the incursions of the French in the Ohio valley had obtruded themselves upon the assembly. The governor transmitted to the assembly the orders from home respecting the raising of funds for the defense of the province and returned the paper currency bill with a suspending clause amendment. Then followed a lengthy exchange of arguments relative to the royal instruction of 1740.

The matter of providing funds for defense was not lost sight of, however, and after some consideration and a short adjournment it was proposed in May to emit ₤30,000 in bills of credit, ₤10,000 for the king's use, the remaining ₤20,000 to be exchanged for the torn and ragged bills then in circulation. The ₤10,000 issued for the king's use were to be retired from the proceeds of the excise, which was extended for a period of ten years. The governor, considering the emergency, was

---

66. Penna. Votes, V, 3627 ff.

willing to assent to the bill without a suspending clause, provided the period of extension of the excise were reduced to four years. The governor was still in pursuit of the grand design of his constituents -- to terminate the revenues of the assembly so that it could be forced to assent to the proprietors' demands. The assembly, however, would not recede from its position. A little later on it increased the amount granted to the king's use to Ł15,000 on the same terms. But Hamilton again refused his assent, and the assembly adjourned until fall.[67]

Governor Hamilton had long since grown weary of the contest with the assembly, as his letters to Thomas Penn abundantly illustrate, and for some time he had desired to be relieved of his duties.[68] When the new assembly convened in October, Hamilton's successor, Governor Robert Hunter Morris, had arrived. He brought with him instructions from the Penns and a copy of Sir Dudley Ryder's opinion concerning the duty of the governor to enforce the royal instruction of 1740. Upon the assembly's sending up a bill to strike Ł40,000 in bills of credit, Ł20,000 of which were for the king's use and were to be retired from the excise over a period of

---

67. Ibid., pp. 3691-3739.
68. Hamilton to T. Penn, September 8, 1753, Penn Official Correspondence, MSS, VI, 99; same to same, November 26, 1753, ibid., 137-139.

twelve years, and the remainder for exchange, the contest began anew. Governor Morris cited the royal instruction and produced a copy of Ryder's opinion that it should be obeyed. Nevertheless, he was willing to assent to the assembly's bill should the bills of credit issued for the king's use be retired within five years.[69]

---

69. How the affair was handled by the proprietary officials is described by Richard Peters in his letter to Thomas Penn, December 16, 1754:

"[The assembly offered Governor Morris] the old Excise Bill for Ten Years to end in 1766, granting £20,000 instead of £15,000 to the King's Use.

"Much time has been employed by the Governor and myself in the Consideration of your Instructions, and Mr. Hamilton and Mr. [William] Allen [the chief justice] were taken into the Consultation, (who continue to act a very friendly Part to the Proprietaries and their Governor, and are willing to do all in their Power for the regaining a just authority.)

"The Questions before Us were: What would be the likeliest Method to obtain a Grant of Money, the publick Safety, which ought ever to have the Preference, requiring this. Whether this Grant was likeliest to be obtained by amending the Bill agreable to the Royal and Proprietary Instructions, or by either and which.

"On canvassing the Matter it was clearly seen, that if the Proprietary and Royal Instructions were both made use of, the Assembly would give no Money. They would cry out here were new Attempts, and say more to the Proprietaries than they had said to the Kings, nay perhaps drop the last, and adhere to the Bill against the other, and then it was thought the Proprietaries would run a greater Risque of Censure at home, for their insisting at this Time on a particular Matter respecting themselves which they might have done at any time for these Twenty years without Inconvenience to the King's Business, and it might endanger the carrying of their Point against the Assembly. Should the Governor take no Notice of the King's Instruction, this would have no better Effect, the Assembly would most certainly refuse all Money on this Lay. Should he wa[i]ve at this Time the Proprietary Instruction, and only insist on the Kings, the Assembly would be gravelled, it was thought, in the most sensible Manner, and be put under

But the assembly was no more amenable to this suggestion from Morris than it had been to a similar one from Hamilton. Furthermore, it gave voice to its suspicion that the real reason for Morris's action was that he was bound by proprietary instructions.[70]

The dispute dragged on until January, 1755, when the assembly, after sending what was to prove a fruitless representation to the king, adjourned until May.[71]

---

the Necessity of appropriating whatever they should raise to the King's Use without leaving any Remainder for their own Disposal, in which case, the Governor could assent to the Bill without a Breach of either of the Instructions, or the least Damage to your particular Cause, nay this would be much aided, as the assembly when this Excise was gone would be obliged to sue for more Paper Money for Current Services, and then the Bill might be amended on your own Instruction, and the Debate go home this Sessions and receive the Royal Determination.

"So many Reasons favour this last Opinion, that it at length prevailed, and the Governor has accordingly this Day drawn up a Message on the Plan of the Royal Instruction, and it will be delivered to morrow morning."

In the light of this letter, it seems apparent that despite the protestations of regard for "the publick Safety" with which the passage opens, the friends of the proprietors cared more for gaining for the proprietors a voice in the control of expenditures.

Penn Official Correspondence, MSS, VI, 245.

70. Penna. Votes, V, 3791.

71. This representation, in which the assembly voiced the suspicion that the governor was prevented by proprietary instructions from assenting to their bill for Ł20,000 for the king's use, was referred to the Board of Trade. That body held a hearing, at which the Penns and the province agents were heard by counsel. The next day Thomas Penn of his own volition appeared before the Board and substantiated the statement of his counsel the day before that he had not given any such instruction as the assembly complained of. Moreover, he stated "that he was ready to communicate to his

The urgency of defense needs, however, caused Morris to call it together again in March. The assembly again raised the amount it was willing to appropriate to the King's use, this time to ₤25,000, which was to be retired from the excise over a ten year period. Of the sum, ₤5,000 was to be given to General Braddock, the remainder, as well as any extra produce of the excise during the period, was to be controlled by a committee of the assembly. Governor Morris refused his assent.[72]

The assembly by its own resolution now issued for the king's use ₤15,000 in provincial orders, payable after twelve months from the interest money accruing at the loan office, and carrying five per cent interest

---

Majesty's ministers any or all of his instructions." And he further assured "the Board that so far from having given any such instruction, he had particularly recommended to his ... Governor to concur with the Assembly in any proper measure for the good of his Majesty's service at this conjuncture." The members of the Board "expressed themselves well satisfied with these assurances" and indicated "that they were not desirous of seeing any of [Penn's] instructions."
    While Penn may not have departed from the strict letter of the truth, he was far from frank. One, however, could scarcely expect him to confess to even a sympathetic Board of Trade the scheme he was embarked upon to bring the assembly around to his terms. That his majesty's service suffered thereby, there is no gainsaying.
    The Board absolved Penn, and the Privy Council was satisfied with the Board's judgment.
        Ibid., p. 3851; Board of Trade Journal, 1754-1758, April 29, May 6, 7, 28, 30, 1755; Acts of the Privy Council, Colonial, 1745-1766, #269; Root, op. cit., pp. 203-204.
    72. Penna. Votes, V, 3791-3874, passim.

until paid.[73]

Spring wore into summer, General Braddock marched over the mountains and was defeated. In the meantime, the dispute between the assembly and the governor had continued. News of the defeat brought an immediate proposal from the assembly to issue ₤50,000 bills of credit for the king's use. These sums were to be retired "by a Tax of <u>Twelve-pence per pound</u> and <u>Twenty Shillings per</u> Head, yearly for two Years, on all Estates, Real and Personal, and Taxables, within [the] Province." Here was raised a new question, the taxing of the proprietor's estates along with those of the inhabitants of the province. As Governor Morris was under instructions not to assent to any such law, he refused to pass the bill.[74]

The view has sometimes been taken, that the assembly, made up in large part of Quakers, was in objecting to the governor's amendments to its appropriating acts doing no more than finding pretexts for not giving any-

---

73. <u>Ibid.</u>, p. 3877. Thomas Penn disapproved of this action by the assembly. On July 3, 1755, he wrote to Richard Hockley, the receiver of the quit rents in the province: "I desire you will not take any Paper Currency on our account that is not issued by the authority of a Law. You judge rightly that the Assembly and their Abettors do not want Proprietors or Governor, but to establish a Republick if it was in their Power." Penn Letter Book, MS, IV, 121-123.

74. <u>Penna. Votes</u>, V, 3878-4008, <u>passim</u>.

thing to finance a war.[75] Such a view is hard to substantiate. There was nothing unique in the action of the Pennsylvania assembly. Much the same struggle took place elsewhere, particularly in New York and New Jersey. There neither the royal governors nor the crown proved so obdurate as did the proprietors and the governors in Pennsylvania. In the latter province the proprietors, actively aided and abetted by the proprietary officials on this side of the water, chief among whom was the provincial secretary, Richard Peters, were engaged in a well-laid plot to turn the hands of the clock backward and wrest from the representatives of the people the control over their finances. Both the proprietors and the assembly used the weapons at their command. It was the proprietors, however, that were proposing innovations, and, by any democratic standard, innovations of a retrograde nature. The assembly, as events progressed, constantly increased the sum that it endeavored to appropriate. Although it could not have been fully informed of the proprietary plot against the growth of representative government in the province, it did not intend to surrender its privileges even in the face of the emergency.

When the news reached England that Governor Morris

---

75. Winfred T. Root, _Relations of Pennsylvania with the British Government, 1696-1765,_ pp. 204-205.

had refused his assent to the ₤50,000 voted by the assembly for the king's use, it caused unfavorable comment among those in authority. Thomas Penn thereupon concluded "that the times are critical, and everybody's eyes are on us," and proposed that the proprietors should make a "free gift" to the public in the sum of ₤5,000 to be paid out of the <u>arrears</u> of the quit rents. It was hoped that the assembly would then exempt the estates of the proprietors from their tax bill. In such case Governor Morris was authorized to assent to the bill without scrupling on the matter of appropriating any surplus that might arise from the tax.[76]

News of the grant was sufficient to secure exemption of the proprietors' estates from taxation, although, contrary to Thomas Penn's instructions to Governor Morris, the assembly inserted a clause in the bill that the exemption was "in consideration of [the proprietors'] free gift of ₤5,000." The sum granted to the king's use was ₤65,000, of which ₤55,000 was to be provided by striking bills of credit.[77]

During the next year, the matter of taxing the

---

76. T. Penn to Morris, October 4, 1755, Penn Letter Book, IV, 161; Richard and Thomas Penn to Morris, October 5, 1755, Penn Official Correspondence, MS, VII, 121.

77. <u>Penna. Votes</u>, V, 4150-4164; T. Penn to Morris, October 4, 1755, <u>loc. cit.</u>; <u>Penna. Statutes at Large</u>, V, 201-212 (<u>c</u>. 406), passed November 27, 1755.

proprietors' estates again proved troublesome. Before any determination of the dispute had been reached, Governor Morris was succeeded by William Denny, who arrived in August. One of the first things that the assembly did after Governor Denny's arrival was to ask for his restraining instructions, which he obligingly laid before them. As, among other things, he was restrained from assenting to any act taxing the estates of the proprietors generally, and as the needs of defense were urgent, a compromise was reached in the granting of supplies to the crown for the year 1756. In September the sum of ₤30,000 was granted in bills of credit to be retired over a period of ten years from the revenue from the excise, which was extended for that period. The assembly, however, did not neglect at the same time to enter into a minute examination of the proprietors' instructions to their governor. And it is difficult to deny that, in its larger aspects, they had the better of the argument.[78]

---

78. Penna. Votes, V, 4240-4345, passim; Penna Statutes, V, 243-262 (c. 412), passed September 21, 1756.
A full examination of the merits of the dispute over the taxation of the proprietary estates would require a chapter in itself. A few of the points at issue may, however, be noted. The proprietors suggested that their "free gift" of ₤5,000 in 1755 "was about twenty times more than the Tax upon all our Estates there, if truly and proportionally rated, according to all other Estates in the ... Province," and that the desire of the assembly was to make them pay an unfair share of the tax by, among other things, pro-

Again in 1758 the dispute over the taxation of the proprietary lands flared up. Pressed by the necessities

---

viding for assessment by officials in the choice of whom they had no voice. Their instruction was a lengthy one (Penna. Votes, V, 4300-4306) and was aimed at many things besides protection of the proprietors. All taxes were to be levied for a single year only, and the tax acts were to exempt "all unoccupied and unimproved Lands whatsoever, and also all [proprietary] Quitrents ...." (p. 4305). The proprietors were willing, however, "to bear of just Proportion ... in any necessary Tax for the Defence of the ... Province which shall be equally laid upon the Lands of the Inhabitants and also upon any of our Manors or Lands, which are actually let out on Leases ..., provided [such] Tax ... shall be payable by the Tenants and Occupiers, who shall deduct the same out of the Rents payable by them to us." (p. 4306)

The reply of the assembly committee (pp. 4335-4345) pointed out that for many years the revenue of the province had consisted solely of the returns from the excise and the interest money accruing at the loan office, from both of which "taxes" by their very nature the proprietors had been exempt. None the less, funds so raised had been used to provide expensive presents for the Indians in order that the peace might be kept and the country thereby defended. The taxing of proprietary lands, it was pointed out, was not unusual, being used "both in New Jersey and Maryland; and located unimproved Lands have formerly been taxed in this Province." Then, in anticipation of Henry George, the committee continued: "Had such [unimproved lands] been taxed every where from the first Settlement of America, we conceive it would have tended to the Encrease of the Inhabitants, and the greater Strength of the Colonies; for then such immense Quantities of Land would not have been monopolized and lain dormant, but People would more easily have obtained Settlements, and been seated closer together" (p. 4338).

The committee denied that in either intent or effect the proprietary lands had been overtaxed in their recent bill, and concluded that the estimate of their value by the Penns was much too modest (pp. 4338-4340): "And yet this their enormous Estate is, by their Instructions," the report continued, "to be exempted, while all their Fellow-Subjects groan under the Weight of Taxes for its Defence! it being first attacked in the present War, and Part of it on the Ohio, the Prize contended for by the Enemy. -- For though they, towards

of defense, the assembly gave way, and in April voted £100,000 in bills of credit to be retired by a tax similar to one laid the year before from which the proprietary estates were exempted.[79] The next year,

---

the End of this Instruction pretend to be 'most ready and willing to bear a just Proportion along with their Tenants in any necessary Tax for the Defence of the Province,' yet this appears clearly to be a mere Pretence, since they absolutely except their Quitrents, and their located unimproved Lands, their Fines, and the Purchase-Monies they have at Interest; that is, in a Manner their whole Estate, as your Committee know of little they have left to be taxed, but a Ferry-house or two, a Kitchen, and a Dog Kennel" (p. 4340).

As to the proprietors' contention that unimproved lands "yield no annual Profit," the committee pointed out that in a growing plantation, they yearly increased in value; and that, as a matter of fact, such land in "the Conestogoe Manor" had in thirty years increased 800 per cent in value (p. 4340).

With regard to the quit rents, which the proprietors had urged were exempt from taxation in his majesty's provinces, the committee replied that there they were "applied to public Purposes, generally for the Service of the Colony that raises them" (p. 4342).

In the light of this exchange of arguments, one can readily realize why the representatives of the people of the province should reach the conclusion that the proprietors were reluctant to bear their fair share of the expense of protecting the province. The proprietors apparently thought of their privileges as never changing, and they failed to realize that they were survivors of an order that was passing. They completely lacked the larger wisdom that is capable of cooperating with inevitable change. Nor is it necessary for one to uphold the assembly at every point to reach this judgment. In such disputes one usually finds a certain amount of obdurancy and unreasonableness on each side. After making full allowance for the manifestations of these qualities by the assembly, the judgment remains the same.

One may consult Root, Relations of Pennsylvania, pp. 208-216, for a discussion of this dispute.

79. Penna. Votes, VI, passim, especially 4794-4797; Penna. Statutes, V, 337-352 (c. 431), passed April 22, 1758.

however, it was the governor's turn to yield. After receiving an urgent letter from General Amherst, who had failed in his earlier efforts to prevail with the assembly, Governor Denny assented to an act for emitting ₤100,000 in bills of credit for the use of the crown. The proprietary estates were not exempted from the tax levied to retire the bills. Furthermore, the act made provision for collecting the proprietors' share of former taxes after first crediting the ₤5,000 gift of 1755. As soon as Governor Denny affixed his signature to the bill, the speaker handed him an order on the loan office "for the Sum of <u>One Thousand Pounds</u>, for his Support, which his Honour ... received very kindly, and was pleased to return his Thanks to the House for the same."[80]

The following June, Colonel John Hunter, the representative of the crown, desired to borrow ₤50,000 from the province until such time as funds could be drawn from England. The province was in no position to extend such a loan without an emission of bills of credit. The assembly not only resolved to issue the sum of ₤36,650 for the purpose, but improved the opportunity by re-emitting its bills outstanding on loan, which

---

80. <u>Penna. Votes</u>, VI, passim, especially 4984-4985; <u>Penna. Statutes</u>, V, 427-443 (<u>c</u>. 444), passed April 22, 1758.

were by this time in the process of being retired. The circulation of the loan bills was extended for a period of sixteen years (i.e., until 1778). The remainder of the sum to be lent Colonel Hunter was to be in the form of old loan bills that had been repaid to the loan office, but not yet destroyed. Only ₤1,650 of the ₤80,000 on loan had at this time been destroyed. This sum was to be replaced from the new issue. The loan was to be repaid within a year from the proceeds of bills of exchange drawn on the money contractors in London, and bills of credit to the sum of ₤35,000 were to be retired. Governor Denny assented to the measure.[81]

The ₤1,000 tendered Governor Denny with such indecent haste after he had approved the bill providing for the taxation of the proprietary estates was construed by the Penns as a bribe, and Denny was shortly removed. Moreover, the proprietors set about to secure the disallowance of both the ₤100,000 act and the reemitting act. Benjamin Franklin, who had gone over early in 1757 "to solicit the Removal of [the province's] Grievances, occasioned by Proprietary Instructions, &c.," with whom was joined Robert Charles, endeavoured to secure the approval of the laws. A full hearing was

---

81. Penna. Votes, VI, passim, especially 5020; Penna. Statutes, V, 427-443 (c. 444), passed June 20, 1759. See also supplementary act of September 29, 1759, ibid., pp. 456-460 (c. 448).

held before the Board of Trade, at which both parties were represented by legal talent of the highest order. The day went against the assembly, and the Board recommended the repeal of both acts. By this time the proprietors had consented to the taxation of their quit rents as well as their improved lands out on lease, but they were still opposed to the taxation of their unimproved lands. In this and all their other objections they were upheld by the Board, and notwithstanding the fact that the bills of credit authorized by the act were already in circulation, the Board recommended the disallowance of the ₤100,000 act with the observation it was "fully of the opinion that this act is one of the most proper objects for the exercise of His Majesty's power of repeal, which has been at any time referred to our consideration."[82]

The re-emitting act fared no better at the hands of the Board. That body, in a somewhat inconsistent representation, while acknowledging the benefits that had been derived from the Pennsylvania loan office, concluded that the re-emitting act was premature even though the bills had for three years been in the process of retirement, and that the sixteen year period

---

82. Penna. Votes, VI, 4504, 4506; representation to the Privy Council, June 24, 1760, in Penna. Statutes, V, 679-734; Root, op. cit., pp. 208-216.

of re-emission was too long. Serious objections were made to the fact that the bills were declared a legal tender, especially in the payment of the quit rents, which by their contracts called for payment in sterling money.[83]

The agents, not content to give up the contest, carried the matter to the Privy Council. While they were defeated there on the matter of the re-emitting act, a compromise was effected concerning the ₤100,000 act. It was allowed to stand after the agents had entered into an agreement pledging the assembly to amend the law so as to remove the objections of the Board of Trade. This pledge, however, the assembly refused to honor.[84]

Before the decision by the Privy Council on the ₤100,000 act of 1759, the assembly had voted a similar sum on the same terms in 1760.[85] After this emission, there were no further issues of bills of credit until the defense needs occasioned by Pontiac's Conspiracy

---

83. Representation of B. T., loc. cit. The meaning of the provision declaring the bills a legal tender in payment of quit rents was that they constituted a legal tender at the rate of ₤133 1/3 Pennsylvania currency to ₤100 sterling. At an earlier time the proprietors had agreed so to receive them for a limited period and for a consideration.

84. Acts of the Privy Council, Colonial, 1745-1766, 415; Penna. Votes, VI, 5180 ff.; Root, op. cit., p. 215.

85. Penna. Statutes, VI, 7-22 (c. 453), passed April 12, 1760.

obliged the assembly in 1764 to vote ₤55,000 in bills of credit to be retired by a tax that excepted the proprietors' "waste and unlocated land."[86]

Thus ended a period during which disputes over paper currency had "disturbed the tranquility of the province and embarrassed the public proceedings." Nor was the agitation to subside in the years to follow. The refusal first of the proprietors and later of the crown to sanction the continuation of the loan office was particularly unfortunate, both from the standpoint of the welfare of the province itself and from that of its later influence upon the relations of the province with the mother country.[87]

---

86. *Ibid.*, pp. 344-367 (*c.* 513), passed May 30, 1764.

87. Whatever may be thought of Thomas Penn's ideas on proprietary rule, it cannot be denied that he had an exceptional understanding of paper money. He, for instance, never succumbed to the favorite fallacy of the Board of Trade that it was the declaring of the bills of credit a legal tender that constituted "all the fraud and abuse" attendant upon their use. (Representation of 1764, N. J. Archives (1st series), IX, 413.) And on all occasions he was ready to raise his voice in defense of the province's right to confer the legal tender quality upon them. The Board of Trade took great stock in issuing bills on fixed funds and retiring them at the end of short and certain periods. This idea has merit in connection with wartime emissions, where it is necessary to prevent the accumulation and consequent depreciation of the issues. The great merit of bills of credit in wartime was that they constituted, in an era when there were no banks and when it was impossible to borrow the sums needed, a colony's "only means of an immediate exertion." In using bills of credit as an instrument of war finance it was necessary that retirement should be begun as early as possible

So far, the political rather than the economic aspects of paper currency in Pennsylvania have received

and in as large sums as possible in order to prevent later issues from too greatly increasing the sum of bills in circulation. The Board of Trade's ideas that such bills should be issued on fixed funds and retired at the end of short and certain periods contributed to this result. But neither this or any other way of managing such wartime issues would prevent entirely a disturbance to prices and, to a lesser degree, exchange rates.

If the Board of Trade's ideas had merit with respect to wartime issues, they were almost completely devoid of it when it came to loan office issues emitted to supply the want of a circulating medium. Here the desideratum was a supply of currency that expanded proportionately as the needs of the trade grew. This could best be accomplished by a sum of bills issued on loan, and as the loans were paid off, relent and continued in circulation. Then from time to time as the needs of trade grew, there should be a moderate infusion of new issues into the bills in circulation. The Board of Trade's ideas, if applied here, constituted a disturbing element, causing alternate inflation and deflation. The men of Pennsylvania realized this, and if left to their own devices there is every indication, that, wartime emergencies excepted, they would have regulated their paper currency in accordance with the needs of trade.

Thomas Penn understood all this. In fact, it is to him that we are owing for the most explicit contemporary statement on the matter that has come to notice. There exists in Thomas Penn's hand in the Penn Official Correspondence, MSS (Vol. V, p. 201), an undated draft of arguments favoring a paper currency, wherein appears this statement: "It is objected that [paper currency] should not be issued on any foundation, but a fund by which it shall be exchanged for money in a short time, and sunk exactly as is provided in the Act for raising it and that it should not be a Tender. If it is so issued it cannot be a standing Medium of Trade, but must vary much in its quantity Current, as the whole is issued out at once, and perhaps the end of two years not one shilling left, so that this method of issuing it cannot answer the purpose of a medium of Trade." (This was the method contemplated in ordinary times by the Currency Act of 1751.)

It is to be regretted that one who understood

chief attention. It is difficult to determine how rapidly the specie introduced into the province during King George's War was shipped off. Although by 1753 complaints of the scarcity of currency were being received by the assembly, Richard Hockley, the receiver of the quit rents, reported in February of that year that "full four fifths" of the money received by him was gold and silver, chiefly the latter.[88] This would indicate that there were in circulation in the province besides the ₤80,000 of paper, some ₤300,000 in specie. Beginning with this year, however, wholesale prices began to fall and exchange rates to rise. These movements continued until the year 1756, when they were arrested; during the next year, a reversal of the trends took place. In 1755 had begun the issuance of wartime bills of credit. The wartime issues may be followed in Table XVIII, and the sums outstanding on the various funds in Table XIX.[89] The changes in the

---

so well the uses and management of a paper currency, should have contributed so much to preventing his province from availing itself of its benefits.

88. Hockley to T. Penn, Philadelphia, February 24, 1753, Penn Official Correspondence, MSS, VI, 17.

89. I had made these computations before I saw Mr. Richard A. Lester's article "Currency Issues to Overcome Depression in Pennsylvania, 1723 and 1729" (Journal of Political Economy, XLVI, 324-375 [June], 1938). In comparing my figures with those given by Mr. Lester (Table 4, p. 353) I found wide divergences in the sums outstanding from the middle 'fifties on. Examination revealed that Mr. Lester had overlooked some of the cancellations, which took place at both the loan

TABLE XVIII

PENNSYLVANIA WAR ISSUES OF BILLS OF CREDIT

Year	Issue £	Fund	To be Retired
1755 Apr. 2	15,000[x]	"Provincial Notes" on loan bills	Payable after one year
1755 Nov. 27	55,000	6d./£ "clear Yearly value of real and personal estates" and 10s. "on single Freemen not worth £30"	4 years, 1756-1759, inc.
1756 Sept. 21	30,000	Excise, 4d. gal. "on Wine, Rum, Brandy and other Spirits"	10 years, Oct. 1756-Oct. 1766
1757 Mar. 23	45,000)	1s./£ "clear Yearly value of real and personal estates" and 10s. "on single Freemen not worth £30"	4 years, to March 1761
1757 June 17	55,000)		
1758 Apr. 22	100,000	18d.) as above 20s.)	3 years, Oct. 1760-Mar. 1764
1759 Apr. 17	100,000	18d. as above 20s. "on single Freemen not otherwise rated £15"	3 years, Oct. 1764-Mar. 1767
1759 June 20	35,000[z]	Loan to Col. John Hunter, agent for the crown's money contractors	By bills of exchange drawn on cont. in England
1760 Apr. 12	100,000	Same as issue of April 17, 1759	3 years, Oct. 1767-Mar. 1770

(continued)

TABLE XVIII

(continued)

Year	Issue £	Fund	To be Retired
1764 May 30	55,000	18d. as above 15s. "on single Freemen over and above the Tax for their property"	2 years, Oct. 1770-Mar. 1772

Total £590,000

Total exclusive of "Provincial Notes" and loan to Col. Hunter	£540,000
Value in sterling when issued	£334,171
Value in sterling July 20, 1764	£313,043

----

    x "Made payable to the Bearer after Twelve Months, with Interest at Five per Cent per Annum, until paid." Penna. Votes, V, 3877.

    z Issuing act later disallowed by the crown. An additional £1,650 were also printed to replace loan bills burned.

    Source: Report to Board of Trade, 1764. C. O. 323/19, L. C. P.

TABLE XIX

PENNSYLVANIA PAPER CURRENCY OUTSTANDING

(in September of each year)

Year	On Loan £	Provincial Notes (of 1755) £	On Taxes £	Total £
1750	80,000		4,500	84,500
1751	80,000		4,000	84,000
1752	80,000		3,500	83,500
1753	80,000		2,500	82,500
1754	80,000		1,500	81,500
1755	80,000		1,000	81,000
1756	80,000	11,510	56,000	147,510
1757	80,000	8,915	173,551	262,466
1758	78,350	7,545	243,879	329,774
1759	78,350	7,205	348,007	433,562
1760	78,350	6,905	400,944	486,199
1761	59,846	6,505	371,753	438,104
1762	44,356	4,525	300,172	349,053
1763	22,108	3,795	260,409	286,312
1764	19,434	120	308,504	328,058
1765	17,541	65	284,794	302,400
1766	17,541	65	261,130	278,736
1767	16,066	65	247,729	263,860
1768	15,200	10	219,240	234,450
1769	10,402	5	220,089	230,496
1770	8,346	5	196,117	204,468
1771	2,929	5	181,560	184,494
1772	2,053	5	172,585	174,643
1773	1,519	5	152,637	154,151
1774	96,146	5	124,322	220,473
1775	149,902	5	166,693	316,600
1776	149,508	5	339,913	489,426

Source: See note, next page.

NOTE to TABLE XIX

References:

    Issues on loan: Penna. Statutes, IV, c. 363; Penna. Votes, VIII, 7106-07; 7265-66.

    Burnings of loan issues: Votes, VII, 6217, 6223-28, 6246, 6428, 6564; VIII, 6711, 6888, 7016, 7138-39, 7293, 7584.

    Issues of Provincial Notes: Votes, V, 3877; Phillips, Historical Sketches, I, 40.

    Burnings of Provincial Notes: Votes, VII, 6235, 6428.

    Issues on taxes: Statutes, Acts of June 24, 1746; Nov. 27, 1755; Sept. 21, 1756; Mar. 23, 1757; June 17, 1757; Apr. 22, 1758; Apr. 17, 1759 (Phillips, I, 43). Statutes, Apr. 12, 1760. Phillips, I, 44. Statutes, Mar. 9, 1771; Mar. 12, 1772; June 26, 1773; Mar. 18, 1775; Sept. 30, 1775; Resolutions of Nov. 8, 1775; Nov. 18, 1775, Apr. 6, 1776 (also Votes, VIII, 7509-13).

    Burnings on taxes:

Year	Penna. Votes	Year	Penna. Votes
1750-		1766	VII, 5929
1755	VII, 6234	1767	VII, 6053
1757	VI, 4658-59; VII, 6236	1768	VII, 6266
1758	VI, 4861-62; VII, 6236	1769	VII, 6428
1759	VI, 5047; VII, 6237	1770	VII, 6564
1760	VI, 5147, 5150; VII, 6237	1771	VIII, 6711
1761	VI, 5273; VII, 6238	1772	VIII, 6888-89
1762	VI, 5364-65; VII, 6238	1773	VIII, 7016
1763	VI, 5468-69; VII, 6239	1774	VIII, 7138-39
1764	VII, 5647-54, 6239	1775	VIII, 7293-94
1765	VII, 5781-87	1776	VIII, 7584

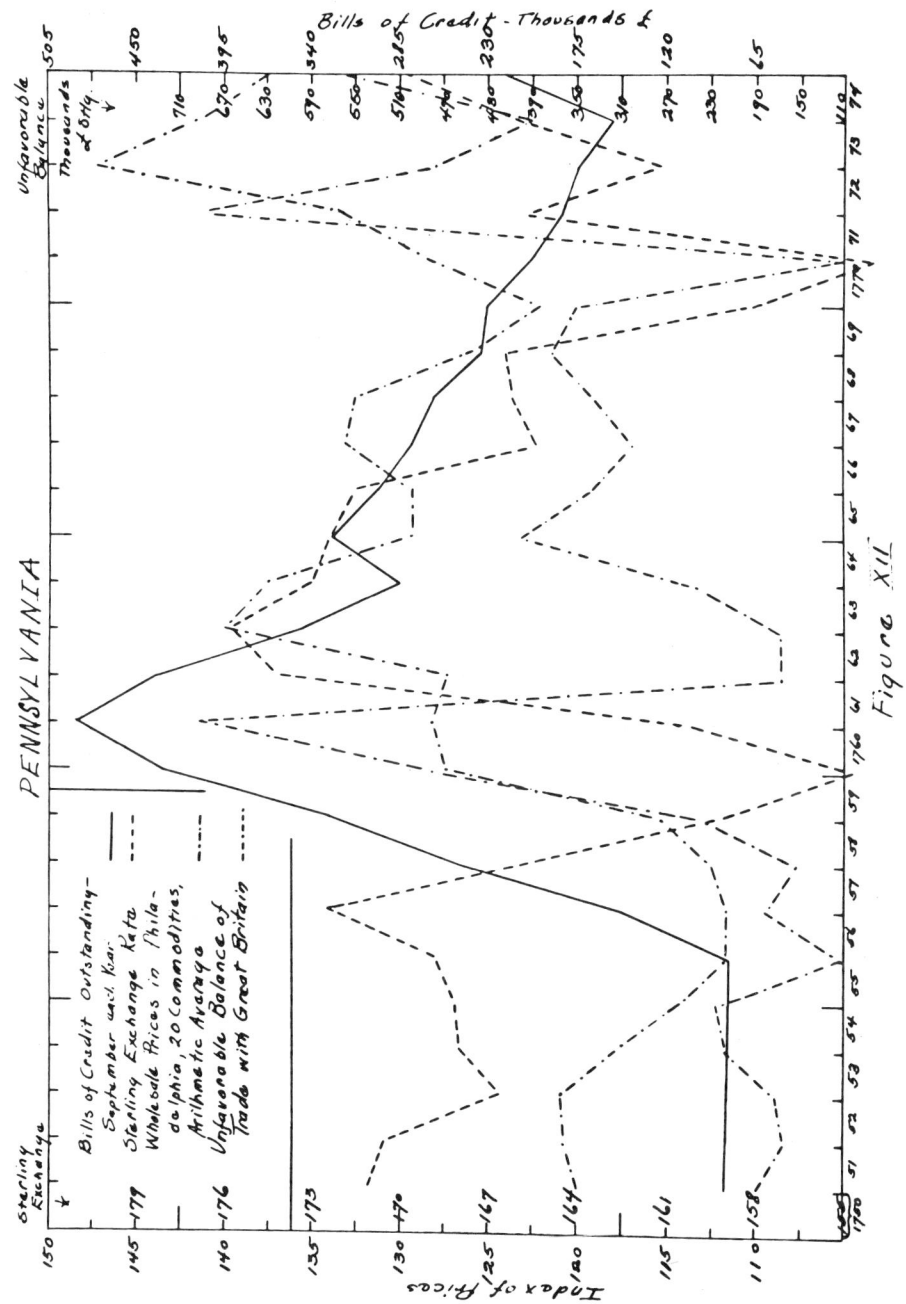

Figure XII

amount of bills of credit outstanding from year to year, together with the fluctuations in the wholesale price index and in the price of exchange, may be seen in Figure XII. One finds the same forces at play in Pennsylvania as were found operating in New York. The influx of specie into the province and the selling of bills of exchange on London to transfer funds for the support of the troops in Pennsylvania not only depressed the rate of exchange in the early years of the war, but, for reasons discussed in connection with New York, retarded the rise of prices. The specie imported did not tarry long and even much of the stock originally there was soon carried off. A committee of the assembly in February, 1757, observed as follows: "There was current in this Province [c. 1750] at least <u>Four Hundred Thousand Pounds</u> of Gold and Silver, most of which, with what has been yearly imported, is since drawn out of the Province for Payment of the Army at <u>New-York</u> and <u>Halifax,</u> and for Payment of our Debts to the Merchants in

---

office and the treasury and are so reported that it is difficult to be sure that one has them all. Consequently his figures progressively exaggerate the amount of bills outstanding as the years go by. For the year 1770, for example, his figures indicate ₤343,503 outstanding, while the figure reached when one takes into account the cancellations that Mr. Lester has overlooked, is ₤204,486, the former figure being sixty-eight per cent greater than the latter. If one is interested, by referring to the references given by Mr. Lester below his table and to those given in connection with the Table XIX, above, a check of the two computations can be made.

England; so that a Piece of Gold is now rarely received in Payment."⁹⁰ The drawing off of specie to New York and Halifax was of course accomplished by selling sterling bills of exchange in Pennsylvania, and carrying away the specie received in return. This went on as long as the war lasted. The years 1758 and 1759 witnessed great increases in the provinces imports from Great Britain. When a year or two later these were paid for, this, added to the fact that the specie of the province had dwindled and the drawing of bills on England was decreasing, caused exchange to rise abruptly. The greatest amount of bills of credit were in circulation at the end of 1760, when there were some ₤486,000 extant. While this is six times the amount of paper currency in circulation at the beginning of the decade, it must be remembered that adding the specie then circulating to the paper, the total amount of money in the province in 1750 was about the same as the paper in circulation in 1760. Since a considerable amount of the specie had in the meantime been carried off, there probably was, at a guess, not more than a half more money, paper and specie together, in circulation in 1760 than in 1750. During these ten years both the population and trade of the province had grown.

---

90. Penna. Votes, VI, 4522.

The average annual value of the trade with Great Britain for the three years centered around 1760 shows a 109 per cent increase over the similar figure for the three years centered around 1750.

During the period a rise in wholesale prices sometimes preceded, sometimes followed, the rise in exchange rates. After 1762 the trend of both was downward until 1769. In these fluctuations of wholesale prices and exchange rates, the paper currency issues had their influence. But as has been indicated, there were other factors at work, which were at times the dominant influence. In fact, prices rose by only 26 per cent from their 1755 low to their 1762 peak, which is but a moderate rise for a war of the magnitude of the one in which the colonies were engaged. And that such a rise of prices was not the peculiar evil of legal tender bills of credit is indicated by the fact that the price rise in Pennsylvania was, if the respective price indexes be comparable, less than half that that took place in Massachusetts during the war. Massachusetts, it will be remembered was on a specie standard.[91] Perhaps war itself should shoulder some of the blame that has been

---

91. In fairness to Massachusetts it should be stated that her contribution to the war was greater than that of Pennsylvania. On the other hand, her reimbursement by Parliament was also greater. For a further discussion of this point see what was said, supra, pp. 278-279.

customarily heaped on paper currency.

Pennsylvania received aid from the parliamentary grants in the way that has already been discussed in connection with other of the colonies. She participated in but three of the grants, those provided by the acts of 1759, 1760, and 1761. In all, these sums when transferred to the province by means of drawing bills of exchange on London amounted to ₤127,131 Pennsylvania currency. This represented an over payment, however, and the sum of ₤17,049 Pennsylvania currency was paid over to Massachusetts, New Hampshire, Rhode Island, New York, New Jersey, and Virginia. This left the net sum accruing to Pennsylvania at ₤110,083 Pennsylvania currency. Part of the bills of exchange to transfer the money were drawn in the fall of 1761, and the remainder probably in 1762. The grants are detailed in Table XX.

During the period under review, Pennsylvania's currency history was largely determined by the hazards of proprietary scheming and restraint and of wartime necessity. The period ended with the province's conspicuously successful forty-year experiment with a loan office terminated as a result of the opposition of proprietors and crown, and prevented from being revived by the interposition of Parliament.[92] With the retirement of her

---

92. That is, by the Currency Act of 1764. See chap. viii, below.

TABLE XX

PENNSYLVANIA PARLIAMENTARY GRANTS

Year	Granted £ stlg.	Rec'd £ stlg.	Rec'd in Province £ Pa. cur.	Exchange	Rec'd in Province	Ref.: Penna. Votes
1759	25,000[x]	25,000	42,500	170	Oct. 12-Nov. 25, 1761	VI, 5365 VII, 6198
1760	23,500[x]	23,300	39,610	172 1/2	Probably rec'd in 1752 and maybe 1763	VII, 6198
1761	24,500[x]	28,563	49,271	172 1/2	do.	do.
		£76,863	£131,381		(Refund (of over-	
		-2,500	-4,250	170 -	(draft on (London	do.
		£74,363	£127,131		(agents	
		-10,266	-17,049	-	(Sums re-(funded (to other	VII, 5651 VII,
Net sums		£64,097	£110,082		(colonies	5785

x Penna. Votes, VII, 5915.

wartime issues in the years that followed, a currency stringency developed. As in New York, this fact was to condition her relations with the mother country.

Delaware had re-emitted her ₤20,000 loan issue in 1746 for a period of twelve years. With the exception of a ₤3,000 exchange issue in 1753, there were no further issues of bills of credit in the colony until the French and Indian War broke out. Between the outbreak of the war and early in the year 1759, however, the assembly passed five acts granting a total of ₤16,200 to the king's use and authorizing the striking of an equivalent sum in bills of credit to be retired from the excise or by taxes on the real estate of the colony.[93]

But the most important issue of the period was yet to come. The currency of the loan issue of 1746 had expired in 1758. On May 7, 1759, the colony emitted ₤20,000 to be placed on loan and an additional ₤7,000 for the support of the war -- a total of ₤27,000, the largest single issue in the history of the colony up to that time. It was now thirty-six years since the colony's first loan issue, and since that time with the exception of the last year a sum in bills had always been outstanding on that basis. "By experience," the preamble

---

93. Richard S. Rodney, Colonial Finances in Delaware, pp. 27-28. The sums were ₤1,000, ₤2,000, ₤4,000, ₤8,000, and ₤1,200. Ibid., p. 67, note 27.

of the act of 1759 recites, the people of Delaware had found such an issue "to be very useful for carrying on the trade and commerce" of the colony, as well as returning a revenue in the form of the interest money for the support of government. The revival of the loan issue at that time proved fortunate, for unlike most of the colonies, Delaware retired her war issues by 1764. Consequently, had it not been for the loan bills, the colony would have found itself devoid of a paper circulating medium with the coming of the peace.[94]

The last of the wartime issues was that of 1760, which amounted to £4,000. Both this issue and the £7,000 granted the king the year before were to be retired during the five years beginning in 1763 by taxes on real estate. Delaware's participation in the parliamentary grants, however, eased the burden and made it possible to dispense with the taxes during the latter part of the five-year period. The colony's share of the grant of 1758 was £3,044 sterling, equivalent to £5,250 18s. Delaware currency. She likewise received £3,745 17s. sterling from the grants of 1759 and 1760, amounting to £6,459 18s. 9d. Delaware currency. The grants were applied towards the retiring of the wartime issues.[95]

---

94. Ibid., pp. 30-31.
95. Ibid., pp. 35-40. Whether Delaware shared in other of the parliamentary grants does not appear.

By 1760, at least, the currency of the colony had undergone a slight depreciation, if we may judge from the exchange rate. The currency equivalent of the sterling grants indicates an exchange rate of 172 in 1760-61, against one of 159 in 1749, or a rise of six per cent. But all such efforts to measure the depreciation of a currency by such modest fluctuations in the exchange rate as this are hazardous, for much more severe fluctuations frequently arose from causes entirely unrelated to paper issues.

Delaware ended the period as she had begun it. By 1764 her war issues appear, substantially at least, to have been retired, and she found herself again relying on her loan issue to supply a circulating medium.

New Jersey entered the decade of the 'fifties with her currency contracting. The ₤60,000 that she had had out on loan as a result of the acts of 1730 and 1733 had for some years been in the process of retirement. The efforts of the province to secure the royal approval for an act passed in 1748 for emitting ₤40,000 on loan had failed. The issues of the late war had been moderate. The result was that in 1749 there were but ₤37,800 in bills of credit of the province outstanding. And, through the retirement of the loan bills, these were to diminish until there were only ₤20,000 in circulation in 1753, ₤4,588 of the loan issues, and

₤15,302 of the war bills.[96]

Despite the fact that the currency of the province was rapidly contracting and the province's long-time source of revenue, the loan interest, was drying up, the years from 1749 to 1753 were marked by an absence of paper money agitation. This was due perhaps to the fact that the assembly was discouraged by the refusal of the crown to approve its loan office act of 1748 and that Robert Hunter Morris, who through his counsel Ferdinand John Paris had been largely responsible for defeating the assembly's attempts to have the law confirmed, could be counted on to oppose any further loan office projects.[97]

In 1753, however, a new loan office project was put on foot. This time it was proposed to emit ₤60,000.

---

96. See notes to Table XXI; Donald L. Kemmerer, *Path to Freedom, The Struggle for Self-Government in Colonial New Jersey, 1703-1776*, p. 238. Kemmerer in chap. xiii, "Financing the King's War," and chap. xiv, "Francis Bernard, Model Governor, Is Promoted," discusses the currency of New Jersey during this period.
The issues of the late war, amounting to ₤17,850, were to have been retired by March 25, 1753, from the interest money accruing at the loan office and from the parliamentary grants in which New Jersey hoped to share. No interest money was available, however. New Jersey's share of the grant to reimburse the colonies for the intended expedition against Canada had been ₤2,231 sterling, equivalent to ₤3,794 New Jersey currency. The agent, Richard Partridge, had held back ₤1,246 of this to pay his expenses. The remaining ₤2,548 were used to reduce the war issues outstanding to ₤15,302. *Ibid.*, p. 238, n. 5.

97. Vide *supra,* p. 220 ; Kemmerer, *op. cit.*, pp. 237-238.

A petition to the king was drafted praying that the governor might be permitted to give his assent to the loan office bill. The assembly urged that the currency of its loan bills was at an end and that as soon as the few remaining in circulation were retired "an end [would] be put to a Currency which [had] constantly maintained its Credit & been of great Service to the Publick." The assembly pointed out the debts of the province from the late war; the distress of the many needy people that had petitioned for relief; and the fact that if the province were allowed a paper currency, the people could then "the better spare that little foreign Specie of which they [were] possessed" to pay their debts to the British merchants and to purchase "such other of the British Merchandize which they may hereafter need."[98]

The presentation of the petition was entrusted to the province agent, Richard Partridge. As was customary,

---

98. *N. J. Archives* (1st series), VIII (pt. 1), 183-186. To characterize this petition, as Kemmerer does, as "a hodgepodge of entreaties, threats and arguments" (op. cit., p. 239) seems to deal less than generously with a province confronted by very real difficulties. We of a later generation have all been brought up on the view that all proposals to issue paper currency are suspect; that at the bottom is the desire of debtors to defraud creditors. That a currency is necessary to the efficient working of an exchange economy is a truth I have seen no economist deny. That today no advanced country manages on a specie currency is well known. Why then should the efforts of the American colonies to supplement their meagre supply of specie be always suspect, even when they had the support of some of the ablest men of the time and men that did not belong to the debtor class?

the matter was referred to the Board of Trade for consideration. In February, 1754, Partridge and his counsel and "also several persons trading to and interested in" the province appeared on behalf of the bill. Robert Hunter Morris, the New Jersey chief justice and long-time opponent of the assembly's loan office projects, was in London at the time. Later in the month he appeared before the Board and discussed the bill.[99] The Board immediately drew its representation. The following passages will serve to indicate the Board's current thought concerning paper currency:

> We are inclined to believe, [it stated,] that a moderate quantity issued on proper security and having a proper Fund for its redemption within a limited time, may operate to the advantage of a trading Colony, and serve to improve and extend the Settlement of it, and may also be the least burthensome method of levying money for the support of Government.

The Board, however, could not agree "that the making of such Paper money a legal tender in all Payments is either necessary or proper," but thought that, among other things, it was "contrary to the sense of Parliament expressed in the Act" of 1751. It might be observed in this connection, that if "the sense of Parliament" expressed in that act with respect to New England was to determine the policy of the crown towards paper currency in all the colonies, then loan offices them-

---

99. Board of Trade Journal, 1754-1758, January 31, February 5, 28, March 14, 18, 1754.

selves were contrary to "the sense of Parliament" since they were not allowed by the terms of the statute. The Board of Trade, however, never discovered this fact.[100]

The Board recommended that an emission of ₤60,000 be allowed provided the bills should not be declared a legal tender and provided also "that the Interest arising from the Loan of the Bills, during their continuance, be appropriated to all the established and contingent Services of Government, and be issued by Warrants from the Governor and Council only." The desire of the people of New Jersey for paper currency was to be the instrument for obtaining a permanent civil list in the province.[101]

The Privy Council issued an instruction in the form suggested by the Board of Trade, but before the governor was authorized to assent to such a bill, it was required that the draft of it must first be approved by the home authorities.[102]

When Governor Jonathan Belcher received the instruction, he wrote home that he did not believe the assembly would authorize any emission on the conditions mentioned in that instrument -- and in this he was

---

100. *N. J. Archives* (1st series), VIII (pt. 1), 196-199. Dated March 18, 1754.
101. Ibid.
102. *Acts of the Privy Council, Colonial, 1745-1766*, #224; Labaree, *Royal Instructions*, I, #333.

quite right.[103] Instead, the assembly drafted another bill, this time for ₤70,000. Of the sum, ₤60,000 were to be issued on loan, and the remaining ₤10,000 were for the use of his majesty in repelling the French. The bills, however, were made a legal tender. This the assembly contended was necessary as it apprehended that the inhabitants of the province would not mortgage "their Lands for a specie which it is uncertain that they can ever Part with," as would be the case with non-legal tender bills. Moreover, since in the course of trade the New Jersey bills had a currency in New York and Philadelphia, it was doubtful, it was urged, if the merchants of those cities would give credit to a currency not a legal tender in New Jersey. It may be that because of the force of custom non-legal tender bills would have continued to circulate much as had the legal tender ones, but this is conjectural and it can scarcely be said that the objections of the assembly were not reasonable ones. At least Governor Francis Bernard, who came over in 1758, and who has come down in history as one not over-inclined to see merit in the colonists' case where none existed, when he was confronted with the same objections on the part of the assembly to making non-legal tender bills, confessed that he was

---

103. Belcher to B. T., August 14, 1754, <u>N. J. Archives</u> (1st series), VIII (pt. 1), 13.

unable to answer them.[104]

As to the second condition imposed by the instruction -- that the interest should be appropriated to the expenses of government subject to the warrants of governor and council only -- the assembly would go but a short step towards complying. The interest money, after "the necessary charge Attending the Emission" had been met, was appropriated to the retiring of the Ł13,772 still outstanding in bills issued during the late war and the Ł10,000 appropriated to the king's use by the issuing act. As the retirement of the former sum had already been provided for in ten annual installments from the proceeds of a tax, the effect of this provision was to repeal the tax. After the bills above mentioned had been retired, the considerable sum arising annually from the interest money was made available for his majesty's use in conducting the war, subject only to future appropriations. In this way it could not be drawn upon by governor and council to meet the ordinary expenses of government.[105]

---

104. Petition of N. J. House of Representatives to King, October 17, 1754, ibid., 14-16; Bernard to B. T., August 31, 1758, ibid., IX, 134. Said Bernard: "And indeed I can't with satisfaction to myself answer one of the arguments for the present necessity of making these bills Legal Tenders." Moreover, he says that the arguments "are the sentiments of some of the most sensible men of [the] province with whom I have talkt on this subject" (p. 135).

105. Ibid., VIII (pt. 2), 15-16. The draft of

Governor Belcher looked askance at the measure, and wrote home suggesting an amendment requiring the province to make good at all times to the possessors of the bills any depreciation that they might undergo.[106]

---

the bill is printed in ibid., pp. 36-72. The loan money was to be lent out for periods of sixteen years, payable in equal installments with interest at 5 per cent. During the first eight years of the life of the act, the principal sums repaid were to be relent for the remainder of the period and were to be paid in in equal annual installments. The loans to any one person were to be from ₤12 1/2 to ₤100 (pp. 47-49). Kemmerer, op. cit., p. 243, says: "The ₤70,000 [sic] was on the face of it an attempt to bribe and threaten the Crown into surrendering on the question of paper money." I presume this to mean that the ₤70,000 bill was an attempt, &c. I do not think it of necessity either threat or bribe. It is hard to see how it could have been a threat unless it implied that unless it was assented to, there would be no funds forthcoming for the defense of the colonies. As a matter of fact, although the bill was not assented to, funds were forthcoming for defense. As to its being a bribe, this is a strange use of that term. One might just as readily say that the instruction sent over in 1754 authorizing the governor to assent to a ₤60,000 loan act provided that the bills were not made a legal tender and the interest money was appropriated to the service of government, constituted "on the face of it an attempt to bribe and threaten" the assembly "into surrendering on the question of paper money." A bribe in that the assembly might have the money if it established a permanent civil list (at least for the sixteen year period during which the bills were to circulate) and a threat in that unless it did the people of New Jersey should have no paper currency, no difference what the needs of the province. It seems to me, however, that to characterize either the bill or the instruction as "on the face of it an attempt to bribe and threaten" contributes little to our understanding of either the paper money problem or the larger problem of providing popular home rule within the framework of the Empire.

106. Belcher to B. T., November 26, 1754, ibid., p. 73. Kemmerer, op. cit., p. 243, observes that Belcher "feared the rate on New Jersey bills would be cut in half," and cites Belcher's letter referred to

Such an amendment would have proved thoroughly unworkable. The bill, however, despite Agent Partridge's efforts on its behalf was discountenanced because the assembly had not conformed to the requirements imposed in the instructions of the year before.[107]

When news of the action of the home authorities was received in New Jersey, the assembly rather than establish a loan office on such terms as were imposed upon them put aside their bill for the time being. Nevertheless, New Jersey was to have a paper currency. In fact, already in April, 1755, the assembly had issued £15,000 of legal tender bills for the prosecution of the war. Another issue in the same amount was to follow in August, and an additional £10,000 were authorized in December. These bills were issued on tax funds and were to be retired within the five year period provided by the Currency Act of 1751. The needs of the war caused the governor to assent to the various emitting acts without

---

above. What Belcher said was "... there will be a Circulation, of near double the Value, of paper Currency, to what has generally been at any one time in this Province." It is true that Belcher feared depreciation, but the history of paper currency in the Middle colonies gives no reason to believe that the emission of £70,000 would have halved the value of the bills. Nor, as is obvious from the statement quoted above, did Belcher say that it would.

107. *Board of Trade Journal,* 1754-1758, January 7, 22, 23, 28, February 18, March 18, 19, May 27, 1755; Partridge's memorial, dated March 17, 1755, *N. J. Archives* (1st series), VIII (pt. 2), 95-99; Board's representation, March 19, 1755, ibid., pp. 100-102; *Acts of the Privy Council, Colonial,* 1754-1766, #224.

requiring a suspending clause or scrupling over the fact that the bills were declared a legal tender. He did, however, insist on their retirement within five years.[108]

In June, 1756, the province appropriated the sum of ₤17,500 on terms similar to those of the issues of the year before.[109] In 1757, however, it revived its loan office project, proposing an issue of ₤89,000, of which ₤60,000 were for loan, and ₤29,000 for the king's use. The latter sum was to be retired from the interest money arising from the loan bills. But Belcher discouraged the proposal, and it was laid by.[110]

In August, Governor Belcher died. He had always insisted that the paper issues of the province should be retired within five years. His successors, however, were less insistent, and the later issues were made redeemable at distant periods, one issue remaining in circulation until 1783. These were the longest periods provided by the emitting acts of any of the colonies in placing in circulation their bills to finance the French and Indian War. The later, as well as the earlier, war issues may be followed in Table XXI, and the amount outstanding in each year, calculated according to the pro-

---

108. Report to Board of Trade, September, 1764, C. O. 323/19, L. C. P.
109. Ibid.
110. Kemmerer, op. cit., p. 250.

TABLE XXI

Part A

NEW JERSEY WAR ISSUES OF BILLS OF CREDIT, 1755-1764

Year	Issues £	To be Retired by Taxes on Real and Personal Estates (All years inclusive)
1755, Apr.	15,000	1757-1759
1755, Aug.	15,000	1758-1760
1755, Dec.	10,000	1761
1756, June	17,500	1761-1762
1757, Mar.	10,000	1763
1757, June	5,000	1763
1757, Oct.	30,000	1768-1773
1758, Apr.	50,000	1774-1778
1758, Aug.	10,000	1760
1759, Mar.	50,000	1764-1767
1760, Mar.	45,000	1768-1773
1761, Mar.	25,000	1774-1778
1762, Mar.	30,000	1779-1780
1763, Dec.	10,000	1781
1764, Feb.	25,000	1781-1783

Total £347,500

Value in sterling when issued £211,953
Value in sterling September 1764 £204,471

Note: There was system in arranging the retirements of the bills; the object was to spread them evenly over the years. The extent to which this was achieved can be seen by consulting the "Cancelled" column, Part B, this table.

Source: Report to Board of Trade, 1764, C. O. 323/19, L. C. P.

TABLE XXI

Part B

NEW JERSEY BILLS OF CREDIT ON TAX FUNDS

(calculated according to the terms of the issuing acts)

Year	Issued £	Cancelled £	Outstanding £
1753			15,302
1754		1,530	13,772
1755	40,000	1,530	52,242
1756	17,500	1,530	68,212
1757	45,000	6,530	106,682
1758	60,000	11,530	155,152
1759	50,000	11,530	193,621
1760	45,000	16,530	222,091
1761	25,000	14,030	233,061
1762	30,000	16,530	246,531
1763	10,000	16,530	240,000
1764	25,000	12,500	252,500
1765		12,500	240,000
1766		12,500	227,500
1767		12,500	215,000
1768		12,500	202,500
1769		12,500	190,000
1770		12,500	177,500
1771		12,500	165,000
1772		12,500	152,500
1773		12,500	140,000
1774		15,000	125,000
1775		15,000	110,000

Source: Report to Board of Trade, 1764, C. O. 323/19, L. C. P. Amount outstanding in 1753 and retirements of same over ten years following, New Jersey Archives (1st series), IX, 144.

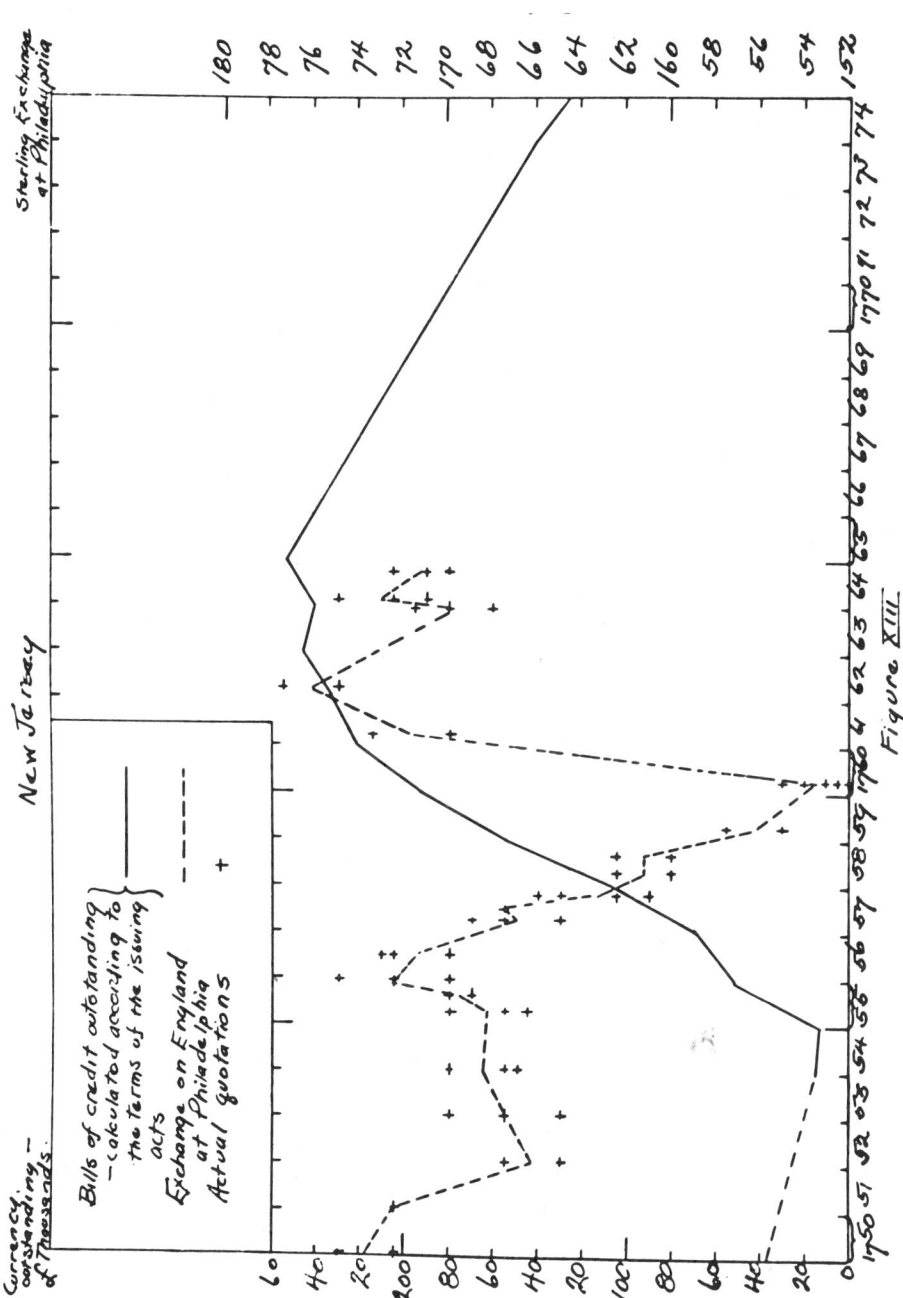

Figure XIII

visions of the emitting acts, together with the rate of sterling exchange at Philadelphia, may be followed in Figure XIII.[111] The total sum in bills of credit issued during the war was ₤347,500, equivalent to ₤211,953 sterling at the time of issue and ₤204,471 in September, 1764.[112]

Shortly after Governor Belcher's death, the assembly again revived its loan office project. A petition was sent over and Richard Partridge endeavored faithfully to secure a favorable answer. The Board of Trade, however, renewed its oft-repeated objections to the proposal: the interest was not appropriated to the use of government subject to the warrant of governor and council; and the bills were declared a legal tender. Moreover, it disapproved of the surplus interest money's being appropriated in mitigation of taxes toward the retirement of bills of credit already outstanding. A further consideration that influenced the Board, and indeed the most substantial of its objections, was that

---

111. The printed data concerning retirements have so many gaps that it is impossible to determine from them the precise number of bills of credit in circulation during these years. It was probably somewhat in excess of the amounts indicated in Figure XIII, but, by and large, the retirements appear to have been made promptly, and the calculation made according to the provisions of the emitting acts may be of some service.

112. Report to B. T., 1764, loc. cit. This, if one is inclined to measure depreciation by the rather dubious method of comparing the sterling exchange rate before and after issues, indicates a depreciation of but 2.6 per cent.

since there were already in circulation some ₤107,000 of war issues, that sum was "sufficiently large for all purposes in the ordinary Course of commercial Dealings," and consequently there was no need at this time for a loan issue to supply a circulating medium. A second representation of the Board, however, in reply to the renewed application of the agent makes it appear that this was but an ancillary objection and that the Board would have given way on it had its other objections been met. The Privy Council accepted the recommendation of the Board, and for the fourth time within a decade the favorite project of the New Jersey assembly was discountenanced in England.[113]

At the time the Board of Trade submitted its first representation on the loan office bill, it also submitted a draft of instructions for Governor Bernard, who had been recently commissioned. A new article respecting paper currency enactments was included. It was proposed that the governor be authorized to assent to such

---

113. Board of Trade Journal, 1754-1758, November 23, 1757; February 1, 8, 15, 16, 29, March 1, May 10, 30, June 6, 9, 1758. N. J. Archives (1st series), IX, 11-12, order of reference, November 16, 1756; pp. 12-14, Partridge's petition on behalf of assembly, dated November 8, 1757; pp. 34-38, representation of B. T., February 21, 1758; pp. 107-110, memorial of Partridge, February 21, 1758; pp. 113-116, representation of B. T. thereon, June 9, 1758. Acts of the Privy Council, Colonial, 1745-1766, #343. The Board of Trade Journal indicates that Robert Hunter Morris was again before the Board when the measure was under discussion.

measures without requiring a suspending clause, provided the bills of credit were issued under the wartime emergency provisions applicable to New England. The Committee of Council, however, took the position that with ₤107,000 in bills already in circulation in the province and a desire already manifest for an issue of an additional ₤60,000 on loan, "the hands of the Governor ought to be tied up in the strictest manner from accumulating any more of this paper money, if not till the whole of the large sum, now Current, shall be paid off and cancelled, yet at least for the present." The result was that the Privy Council refused to assent to the change proposed by the Board of Trade and reincorporated the old instruction requiring a suspending clause in all bills for emitting paper currency.[114]

---

114. N. J. Archives (1st series), IX, 37-38, 49-50; Acts of the Privy Council, Colonial, 1745-1766, #348.

The thinking of the Committee of Council is indicated by the following passage: The power of assenting to paper currency acts in case of emergency "the Lords of the Committee apprehend to be by no means proper to be given to the Governor, at least for the present; Not that they are willing to suppose the Governor anywise inclined to exercise power without an emergency, but they conceive as soon as it shall be come known within the Province, that the Governors hands are not tied up, but that he is at Liberty to assent to Acts for issuing more Paper money in Cases of Emergency, the Inhabitants will take advantage of it, and soon enter into measures to create some emergency or other, and the governor will, in such Case, find it difficult to execute the power so vested in him, which would be attended not only with great inconveniences but ill Consequences to the said Province, as must manifestly ap-

Bernard, however, upon arriving in the province, realized that the king's interests made it impossible for a governor to adhere to such an instruction and that the only alternatives were either the disregarding of the instruction by the governor or the changing of it by the home authorities. Bernard suggested a change in his instructions in a letter to the Board of Trade and urged that he be relieved of the necessity of insisting that no bills be made a legal tender. As a result of Bernard's appeal an instruction was issued in February, 1759, authorizing him to assent to ₤40,000 in bills of credit to be used to support the New Jersey forces. The bills were to be sunk "in the years 1764 and 1765 at farthest." No restriction was placed on their being made a legal tender. Since there seemed to be little hope that the assembly could be dissuaded from its practice of appointing commissioners to apply the funds voted, the instruction permitted the governor to assent to such bills provided he had previously had the opportunity of nominating or approving the commissioners.[115]

---

pear, when the Committee informs your Majesty, that there is actually at this time paper Bills outstanding and Current in that Colony, amounting to no less than 107,000 1." Ibid., pp. 372-373.

115. Bernard to B. T., August 31, 1758, inclosing a copy of a message from the assembly, ibid., pp. 129-131; same to same, same date, ibid., pp. 131-136; same to same, October 31, 1758, and inclosure, ibid., pp. 139-

As a matter of fact, the assembly appropriated ₤50,000 rather than the ₤40,000 allowed, and Bernard, because the assembly's action in response to the requisition of the crown had been quick and generous, felt that he would "have shown more duty than discretion to have examined [the] bill too nicely," and assented to the measure.[116] Such a permissive instruction, however, was not issued again, and later issues were passed by the governors in violation of their instructions.

New Jersey participated in the parliamentary grants and applied her share toward the retirement of her bills, at the same time reducing taxes.[117] It is impossible from the printed records to determine the amount received by the province. Her share in two of the grants is noted below.[118]

The effect upon prices of New Jersey's wartime issues of bills of credit is difficult to determine. What direct evidence is available is untrustworthy and conflicting.[119] It is probable, however, that since

---

146; representation of B. T., December 7, 1758, ibid., pp. 147-148; instruction, ibid., pp. 156-158 (also in Labaree, Royal Instructions, I, #334.

116. Bernard to B. T., March 30, 1759, N. J. Archives (1st series), IX, 171.

117. Kemmerer, op. cit., p. 280.

118. Grant of 1756, ₤5,000 sterling (Kimball (ed.), Corresp. of R. I. Gov., II, 200); of 1759, ₤9,166 sterling (ibid., p. 298). Information on the province's share in the remaining grants is lacking.

119. See Kemmerer, op. cit., p. 278.

the economy of East Jersey was bound up with New York, and that of West Jersey, with Philadelphia, prices in the two sections did not vary much from those in New York and Philadelphia, respectively.

During the period the interference of the crown authorities in the currency affairs of New Jersey was vexatious and, on the whole, productive of little good. In the early years the province was embarrased by the refusal of the home authorities to sanction the renewal of her loan office. Except under Belcher, the requirement that the war issues be retired within five years was evaded, and the crown never succeeded in preventing the bills of the province from being made a legal tender. Nor did it succeed in its attempt to use the desire of the people of New Jersey for a paper currency as the instrument to wrest control over appropriations from the assembly. From the standpoint of the probable effect upon prices of the proposed emission of ₤60,000 on loan in the later years of the war, the refusal of the Board of Trade to sanction such a measure may be defended. On the other hand, it must be remembered that the precise effect of such an issue upon prices is highly conjectural, and that the province was denied the advantages of a loan office *per se.* Moreover, it should not be forgotten that it was not the probable effect of the proposed issue upon prices and exchange rates that was the main consideration of the Board. The province could have had the issue, had the bills not been made a legal tender and had the interest money been appropriated to government subject to the warrants of the governor and council. Any effect, therefore, that the restrictive policy of the crown authorities may have had in maintaining the value of the currency by refusing a loan issue was largely fortuitous, and arose rather from the refusal of the province assembly to issue money on the Board's terms than from any wisdom on the part of the Board itself.

In the light of the later history of imperial restrictions on colonial paper currency it proved a happy circumstance that the retirement of New Jersey's war issues had been delayed. In this way she enjoyed in the years before the Revolution a legal tender paper currency that would otherwise have been denied her.

In a large degree the interference of the crown in the financial affairs of the Middle colonies during the period represents little more than officious and, in most respects, ineffective meddling. The chief architect of the policy, the Board of Trade, had once been wiser when it had expressed the opinion that "because the Circumstances of the sev^l Provinces being various & very different in ... Respect" to paper currency, each might "require a distinct Consideration."[120] But from this wisdom it had departed. Now all the colonies were to be fitted into the same mold. With feigned regard for "the sense of Parliament" as expressed in the Currency Act of 1751, the Board sought to prevent the issuance of legal tender currency in the Middle colonies and sought to impose the restriction of the five year period on the war bills issued on taxes. It did not hesitate, however, to depart from the "sense of Parliament" as expressed in the Act of 1751 whenever the provisions of that statute did not coincide with its current notions of policy. The fact is, that during the period the Board of Trade never evidenced an adequate understanding of paper currency, and in consequence was never able to work out any well-articulated currency policy. All its thinking on the matter was colored by the bias that was the legacy of its counselling with the British merchants trading to America, or at least with certain groups of such merchants. Moreover, its currency policy became entangled with another article of policy, that of securing a permanent civil list in the colonies, with the result that the colonies were frequently denied issues not objectionable in themselves unless they would establish a permanent revenue for the

---

120. Representation to House of Commons, 1741, N. J. Archives (1st series), VI, 123-124.

support of the crown officials.

Nor was Pennsylvania more fortunate with respect to proprietary restraints. Although the active proprietor, Thomas Penn, was one of the enlightened men of his generation in England insofar as his understanding of paper currency was concerned, his endeavor to use the need of his province for a paper currency as the instrument for staying the development of popular government denied the province the benefits that might under happier circumstances have accrued from the continuance of its loan office.

CHAPTER VIII

THE CURRENCY OF MARYLAND, NORTH CAROLINA, SOUTH CAROLINA, AND GEORGIA, 1751-1764.

> The plenty and scarcity of Silver and Gold in [South Carolina] is altogether Casual, and therefore not all to be relied on as a Medium of Trade.
>
> -- Resolution of the Commons House of South Carolina, December 15, 1752.

THE SECOND PHASE of the currency experiment inaugurated by Maryland in 1733 was in progress in 1751. As a result of the conversion operations of the years 1748-1749 one-third of the paper currency of the province had been retired in exchange for sterling bills of exchange at the ratio of 133 1/3 Maryland currency to 100 sterling. These bills of exchange, it will be recalled, were drawn against funds in England that had been accumulated by a 15d. tax on each hogshead of tobacco exported from the province since 1733. In the conversion operations old bills had been redeemed, one-third in sterling bills of exchange, and two-thirds in new bills of credit, which were to continue in circulation until 1764, when they in turn were to be redeemed in sterling bills of exchange at 133 1/3. The tax on tobacco was to continue and, as had been the case formerly, the funds produced by it were to be transmitted to London and there invested in the stock of the Bank of England by trustees appointed for the purpose.

Not all the old bills had been exchanged in 1748-1749, probably, since the bills could be exchanged only at Annapolis, because some had been held in such small sums as to make it unprofitable to make the journey to the province capital. There were ₤6,036 18s. of such bills unexchanged. When to these are added the ₤55,975 14s. in new bills placed in circulation during the conversion operations, the total sum outstanding is seen to be ₤62,012 12s.[1] Of this amount the sum of ₤16,247 11s. 5d. represented the amount out on loan in the year 1751. The remainder had been placed in circulation as a result of various payments from the treasury.

Shortly after the conversion operations of 1748-1749, sterling exchange, which during that time had of course been at 133 1/3, rose rapidly to 180 even though the paper currency of the province was now diminished by one-third. Over the next four years, however, exchange gradually fell until by the end of 1753 it stood at 155.[2] There is some reason to believe that the behavior of exchange during these years was influenced by the fact that the balance with Great Britain probably

---

1. Archives of Maryland, XLVI, 529; XIV, 170.
2. Report of Governor Horatio Sharpe to B. T., August 1, 1764. C. O. 323/19, L. C. P.

became more favorable for the province in the years after 1749.[3] On the other hand, the tobacco law of 1747 had authorized those that grew no tobacco to make payment of officers' fees and other public dues in paper currency at the rate of ten shillings for every hundred pounds of tobacco.[4] This fact, by increasing the use of paper currency, no doubt tended to increase its value. But it should be recalled that the law of 1747 also introduced tobacco notes on the Virginia model.[5] Henceforth, all tobacco payments were to be made by the tender of these notes. The introduction of the tobacco notes no doubt facilitated the use of tobacco as money. This fact would tend to decrease the need and hence the value of the province bills of credit. The forces affecting the value of the paper currency of the province were complex, some operating in the same directions; others not. On the whole, there is some evidence to indicate that during the years between 1749 and 1753 prices fell,[6] but the data available are so

---

3. Insofar as the exports of Maryland and Virginia may be assumed to have fluctuated together, since both were tobacco colonies, the statement above follows from the changes during these years in the figures of trade between the colonies (jointly) and Great Britain. Emory R. Johnson, et al., History of Domestic and Foreign Commerce of the United States, I, 120-121.
4. Clarence P. Gould, Money and Transportation in Maryland, 1720-1765, p. 32.
5. Vide supra, pp. 15-16.
6. Gould, pp. 99-100.

meagre that anything like an accurate or comprehensive picture is impossible.

Circulating side by side with the tobacco notes and the bills of credit was a greater or lesser amount of miscellaneous coin. But coin was not a legal tender in the payment of rates and officers' fees. These could be paid only in tobacco notes or, for those who raised no tobacco, in bills of credit. It not infrequently happened that an individual was possessed of coin, but of neither tobacco notes nor bills of credit. The complaint was made that the holders of bills of credit, particularly, took advantage of this fact to drive a hard bargain, being willing to exchange paper currency for coin only at excessive rates. To ease the situation, the assembly in 1753 provided that all those that did not produce tobacco, or those that did not produce it in sufficient quantities, might pay all or the remainder, respectively, of their rates and officers' fees in money (coin or paper) at the rate of 12s. 6d. per cwt. of tobacco. The act also rated the various coins in circulation at the values at which such coins passed in Pennsylvania. The piece of eight was valued at 7s. 6d. and other coins roughly in proportion.⁷ This valuation made the ratio to sterling 166 2/3 : 100.

The act was looked upon by the proprietary authorities in England as a violation of the Act of Queen Anne, as indeed it would appear to be. But the governor of the province, Horatio Sharpe, took the opposite view, and seems to have succeeded in quieting the objections that had been raised against it.⁸

The law overvalued coin. The result was that

---

7. *Archives of Maryland*, L, 303, 340-342. No. 21. An Act for amending the Staple of Tobacco, for preventing Frauds in his Majesty's Customs, and for the Limitation of Officers' Fees.
The rates fixed by the act follow:

	£	s.	d.
English Guinea	1	14	0
French Guinea	1	13	6
Moidore	2	3	6
Johannes	5	15	0
Half Johannes	2	17	6
French Milled Pistoles	1	6	6
Spanish Pistoles not lighter than 4 dwt. 6 gr.	1	7	0
Arabian Chequins	0	13	6
Other Gold Coin (German excepted) per dwt.	0	6	3
French Silver Crowns	0	7	6
Spanish Milled Pieces of Eight	0	7	6
Other good coin'd Spanish Silver, per oz.	0	8	6

8. Cecilius Calvert to Sharpe, London, April 17, 1754, *ibid.*, VI, 45; Sharpe to Calvert, August 8, 1754, *ibid.*, V, 85; Calvert to Sharpe, London, December 10, 1754, *ibid.*, p. 131; Sharpe to Calvert, March 12, 1755, *ibid.*, pp. 176-177; also editor's note, *ibid.*, L, 366-367.

"scarcely any other Money" was used in making payments of rates and fees by those that had the option.[9] Individuals, however, were not required to receive coin at the rates established by the law. Merchants and others still had the "Option in Merchandising & trading to value the several Sorts of Money as they [thought] proper & [to] require different Prices for their Commodities in proportion[;] & a wide Difference they still make," wrote Governor Sharpe in August, 1754, "between paper & Gold or Silver Cash, tho not quite so great as before [the] Law took place...."[10]

At this juncture, the French and Indian War made its demands upon Maryland as it did upon the other colo-

---

9. Sharpe to Calvert, August 8, 1754, ibid., VI, 85.

10. Ibid. Sharpe states that before the law went into effect "₤152 or a little more [in paper] Currency would purchase ₤100 [sterling, while] now from ₤155 to 160 [paper] Cur^y is required to purchase a Bill of that Value." It required from ₤162 10s. to ₤165 and "sometimes more [in] Gold and Silver valued" at the rates established by the act to purchase a bill of exchange for ₤100 sterling. The difference, Sharpe figured, between "Paper & Gold or Silver Cur^y [was] 4 or 5 p C^{t}" in favor of paper.

The fact that paper fell in value with the enactment of the law Sharpe attributed principally to "Usurers being less able to make Advantage of the necessities of the People by engrossing what was designed to be perpetually circulating [i.e., the paper currency] & delivering it out at their own price to the People who could not do without a Share of it to pay their publick Levies & Taxes...."

Gould (p. 33) says that the valuation placed upon coin by the act "was soon adopted by many business men and became widely used." This of course would not preclude the charging of different prices when payments were made in different media.

nies. Maryland's response, however, was moderate; so moderate in fact, that other colonies looked upon her as wanting in zeal. In July, 1754, ₤6,000 were appropriated for the war. No new bills of credit were issued, but, ₤4,000 8s. in bills were borrowed from the currency office, and ₤900 and ₤1,099 12s. were borrowed from the treasurers of the Western and the Eastern Shores, respectively. These sums were "in about five Years drawn into the Currency Office by means of a Duty imposed on Wine, Servants, and Negroes imported, on Wheel Carriages and on Lycences granted Tavern Keepers and Pedlars."[11]

No further sum was granted for the support of the war until 1756, when ₤40,000 was voted. To make available funds to meet this grant, ₤30,000 in new bills of credit were emitted. The remaining ₤10,000 was available out of funds already in the currency office. There were still unexchanged in the hands of the commissioners ₤4,015 6s. in the bills printed for the conversion operations of 1748-1749. These bills the commissioners were authorized to pay out. The remaining sum of ₤5,984 14s. was to be paid out from the bills in the loan office. The sums authorized by the act of 1756 "were not thrown

---

11. No. 1. An Act for his Majesty's Service (passed July 24, 1754), Archives of Maryland, L, 559-566; ibid., XIV, 169-170; Report to B. T., August 1, 1764, C. O. 323/19, L. C. P.

at once into Circulation but paid out from time to time to the Troops which were directed to be raised and Supported for the Defence of the Province." To retire the sum appropriated, a stamp tax, various excise taxes and import duties, a tax on land and one on bachelors, and a "fine" on ordinary tavern licenses were levied at the time; and later some alterations were made. By October, 1763, the sums arising from the various taxes had proved more than sufficient to retire the ₤30,000 in new bills issued by the act of 1756, together with the ₤4,015 in the unexchanged conversion bills that had been paid out. After these sums were destroyed there still remained a considerable sum in bills of the older issue in the currency office.[12]

The effect of the emitting act of 1756 was to add ₤34,015 6s. to the circulating bills of the province. The sum now outstanding was ₤96,017 18s. This sum appears to have remained extant until the ₤34,015 noted above were burned in the fall of 1763. The amounts in actual circulation (i.e., outside the currency office) between 1756 and 1763, however, were something less. In the first place, the bills issued under the act of

---

12. No. 5. An Act for granting A Supply of Forty Thousand Pounds for his Majesty's Service ... (passed May 15, 1756), Archives of Maryland, LII, 480-521; ibid., XIV, 169-170; Report to B. T., 1764, C. O. 323/19, L. C. P.; Kathryn L. Behrens, Paper Money in Maryland, 1727-1789, pp. 42-43; Gould, p. 103.

1756 were paid out only gradually; and in the second, as the taxes levied under the act were paid in, larger and larger sums in bills accumulated in the currency office. The accounts of the currency office after the early 'fifties become increasingly confusing, so that all one can say is that after 1756 the bills of credit circulating in the province increased to near ₤96,000; then as they began to accumulate in the currency office the amount in circulation decreased until on August 1, 1764, it was reported to be only ₤41,295 11s. 4d.[13] The sums out on loan for the various years, averaging around ₤14,000 during the 'fifties, may be followed in the note below.[14]

The effect of the issue of 1756 on prices seems impossible to discover. As to exchange rates, that uncertain gauge of depreciation, Governor Sharpe wrote in

---

13. Archives of Maryland, XIV, 170.
14.

Year	Amount Out on Loan		
	₤	s.	d.
1750	16,778	14	1
1751	16,247	11	5
1753	16,643	14	11 1/4
1755	14,876	8	5 3/4
1758	12,757	8	3
1765	222	0	0

Source: Reports in "Upper House Journals," Archives of Maryland, passim.

1764: "During the late war Exchange was very fluctuating, sometimes so high as Seventy [per] Centum [advance] and for some time in 1759 so low as £155 for a hundred, but for these last four Years the Exchange here hath been gradually lowering as the time when our Bills of Credit are to be sunk approaches, so that at present it is under Forty [per] Cent [advance] and will certainly be very soon at 33 1/3 ...."[15] At the same time Sharpe wrote of the bills issued in 1756 -- and with reference to their value as of that year the same would apply to all the bills outstanding -- : "Their Value was never depreciated but continued rather to increase, so that for sometime before they were sunk [1763] six Shillings in such Bills passed in all payments as a Spanish Dollar or as Six Shillings American [i.e., proclamation] Currency."[16]

During the winter of 1764-1765 virtually all of the currency of the colony was retired according to the provisions of the original issuing act, that of 1733. Sterling bills of exchange at 133 1/3 were exchanged for the bills of credit still in circulation. A report of the commissioners of the currency office, dated August 1, 1764, indicates that this sum was £41,296,

---

15. Report to B. T., August 1, 1764, C. O. 323/19, L. C. P.
16. Ibid.

while there were ₤20,717 in bills of credit and ₤9,184 in gold and silver in the currency office.[17] Since December 1, 1763, the money collected by the 15s. tobacco export duty had been paid into the currency office rather than transmitted to England.[18] The money noted above as being in the currency office had accrued from this and other tax payments and from principal and interest payments on the loans made under the act of 1733. By 1765 all the loans save a remnant of ₤222 had been repaid.[19] On June 7, 1764, the trustees in London held bank stock worth ₤50,731 sterling, or ₤66,641 Maryland currency, counting exchange at the redemption rate of 133 1/3.[20] From the ₤66,641 in bank stock and the ₤9,184 in gold and silver in the treasury -- a total of ₤75,825 -- there were to be redeemed only the ₤41,296 in bills of credit still in circulation. This left a surplus to the province of ₤34,529 Maryland currency. It is impossible to follow the conversion operations in detail, but by 1767 they were virtually complete.[21]

The testimony is unanimous that as the time for the redemption of the Maryland bills of credit approached, they were hoarded by the wealthy, who sought to profit

---

17. *Archives of Maryland,* XIV, 170.
18. Gould, p. 104.
19. Ibid., p. 109.
20. Ibid., pp. 104-105.
21. Ibid., p. 105.

by the anticipated rise in value.[22] So far had this gone by 1762 that the assembly provided that payment of taxes levied under the emitting act of 1756 might be made in gold or silver as well as in bills of credit.[23] The promissory notes of individual merchants, issued in small denominations, had by this time also made their appearance to supply the lack of small change.[24] The retirement of the paper currency of the province naturally accentuated the scarcity of currency already complained of. "Some Medium of an internal Intercourse we must have, if our old one is demolish'd another will spring up in its place," wrote Daniel Dulaney at the time.[25] Fortunately for Maryland, the fact that her bills of credit had never been made a legal tender in private transactions made it easier for her, within the restraints imposed upon the colonies by the legislation

---

22. Ibid., pp. 105-107. The Virginian, Jerman Baker, wrote at the time in the course of his argument in a letter to a friend: Consider Maryland "where they emitted a paper currency, and stipulated that it shou'd be redeemed at a medium of 33 1/3 Exchange, for which purpose there is a fund established in England, this exchange being far below the trading course. The consequence is that all this money is locked up in the chests of the Wealthy, and the trade is supported by notes issued by private people, and the little gold and silver that may find its way among them ...." To Duncan Rose, London, February 15, 1764, William and Mary Quarterly, XII (1903-1904), p. 240.

23. Behrens, p. 46.

24. Ibid.; also extract from Rose's letter, note 22, above.

25. Quoted in Gould, p. 111.

of the British Parliament in 1764, to supply her need for a circulating medium than it was for those colonies where paper currency had customarily been endowed with the legal tender quality in transactions between man and man. Because the people had been accustomed to using non-legal tender paper in commercial transactions, there were not the fear that such currency would fail to circulate that existed in the colonies where the practice had been otherwise. In 1765 it was proposed to issue bills of credit against the bank stock remaining in the hands of the trustees in London. Such bills were to remain in circulation for a period of ten years. This was done the next year. In issuing the new bills, the monetary unit was changed to the Spanish milled dollar, and $173,733 in bills of credit were emitted. They were equivalent to current money at 7s. 6d. the dollar and to sterling at 4s. 6d.[26] In 1765 the assembly had directed that the money remaining in the currency office and in the hands of the treasurers should be invested in bank stock. The sum so purchased added to that already held amounted at par to ₤26,800 sterling. As the stock was currently selling at considerably above par, bills of credit equivalent to ₤39,089 18s. 6d.

---

26. The $173,733 at these rates equalled ₤65,149 17s. 6d. current money of Maryland or ₤39,089 18s. 6d. sterling.

sterling were issued against the holdings of the province. Since a deadlock between the upper and the lower house of the assembly had for seven years prevented the payment of the "journal of accounts," as the annual charges of government were called, most of the new issue ($150,769) was used to satisfy the accumulated demands on the province. The remainder, after deducting the expenses of the issuing office, which amounted to a little over $3,300, was left for further appropriation.[27]

The history of the second phase (1749-1765) of the Maryland experiment with a paper currency shows improvement over the first phase (1733-1749) largely because the amount of currency in circulation had been reduced by a third at the beginning of the period, and to a lesser extent, because the use of bills of credit had been extended. The provision of the tobacco act of 1747 that made rates and taxes payable in paper currency when tendered by those not growing tobacco contributed to this latter aspect. But much more important in this respect was the fact that Maryland was growing into her currency as her trade and population increased. On the

---

27. Behrens, pp. 48-52. In deference to the Currency Act passed by the British Parliament in 1764, the law provided that "nothing herein contained shall extend or be construed or taken to make any tender of the said bills of credit in discharge of any contract whatsoever, lawful except such contracts as shall or may be made expressly and specifically for, or for the delivery of such bills of credit." Quoted in ibid., p. 52.

other hand, the introduction of tobacco notes in 1747 doubtless added to the efficiency of tobacco as a monetary competitor of the bills of credit. Moreover, the rating of foreign coin in public payments at the high ratio of 166 2/3 to 100 sterling appears to have been unfortunate in its effect upon the value of paper and added another confusing element to the already exceptionally confused state of the Maryland currency. In fact, conversion from one medium to another in Maryland appears more difficult than perhaps anywhere else. The war issue of ₤34,000 in 1756, which constituted the only addition to the paper currency of the province during the period, seems to have caused a minimum of disturbance. It is true that later during the war, exchange rose to new heights, but the factors responsible for this were complex, and the rôle of the new issue was probably a minor one.

While Maryland has been praised for redeeming the entire issue of ₤90,000 of 1733 in sterling bills of exchange at 133 1/3, this was perhaps but a dubious virtue. Notwithstanding the redemption provisions, the bills depreciated between redemption dates -- during the first phase very considerably, for exchange rose to 200. The result was that as the bills fell in value, creditors and those in whose hand the bills depreciated suffered; and as they retrieved their value with the approach of a redemption date, debtors (and in most cases another set from those that originally profited) in their turn found themselves the losers. As the bills increased in value both hoarders and creditors gained. It would seem then, that contrary to the usual view, the redemption of the bills of credit of the province at 133 1/3, instead of undoing the injustice to creditors or holders of bills occasioned by their original depreciation, merely added a second series of injustices by now causing losses to a new set of debtors and providing gains for a new set of creditors and those (mostly hoarders) in whose hands the bills appreciated.[28] This example should lay the fallacy that the way to maintain the value of bills of credit was to issue them on "ample" funds. Actually, this was accomplished by limiting the amount and extending the use of the bills issued. It is doubtful whether the Maryland bills, had they been issued on no funds at all, would have depreciated much more than they did in the years after 1733 and again after 1749. In Maryland the original issue was relatively large, and the use circumscribed. It is true that Maryland did not add to the ₤90,000 author-

---

28. This is not a new view. It was well known to so staunch an opponent of paper currency as Thomas Hutchinson at the time he was battling for the return of Massachusetts to a silver currency (1748). Vide supra, p. 251.

ized in 1733 until the French and Indian War. But it is also true that her sheltered position largely relieved her of the necessity of war issues in the early years; and when the French and Indian War finally brought the scene of hostilities nearer home, her contributions to the struggle were, one is almost forced to say, but niggardly. Maryland's monetary virtues were that after the issue of 1733 she refrained from further peace-time emissions and that she managed her loan office with reasonable efficiency.[29]

In North Carolina, as in Maryland, the years 1751-1765 found the colony's paper currency experiment in its second phase.[30] North Carolina, where, it will be recalled, the first bills of credit were issued in 1712, had put out successive issues. After 1722 no bills appear to have been retired by taxes. The result was a steady depreciation in the value of the paper medium. In 1748 the outstanding issues had been redeemed in bills of a new tenor at the ratio of seven and one-half

---

29. In the light of the foregoing comments, together with the record of the other colonies as detailed herein, the statement of Clarence P. Gould, usually a judicious commentator, that "it is hardly too much to say that [the Maryland issue of 1733] was the most successful paper money issued by any of the colonies," seems scarcely deserved. Gould, p. 111.

30. The currency history of Virginia during the period, which logically might be expected to be treated here, will be discussed in a separate chapter (ix) because of the bearing it had upon the passage by the British Parliament of the Currency Act of 1764.

to one. But advantage had also been taken of the opportunity to issue thrice as many new bills as were needed to retire those already in circulation. The amount of bills of credit now in circulation was ₤21,350 proclamation currency, as the new tenor bills were called. Although the new bills had been issued at the proclamation rate of 4__s.__ North Carolina currency to 3__s.__ sterling, they did not hold at that figure. As one might expect when the paper currency of the colony was in effect trebled, their value, measured by the price of sterling exchange, soon fell by one-fourth.[31]

The emitting act of 1748 had laid a tax of one shilling annually on each rateable until such time as the bills should be retired. Contrary to former custom, the tax was made payable in "Gold, Silver, or Bills of Credit," rather than in bills of credit or the rated commodities, as had been the case theretofore. This marked an advance in the colony's fiscal practices. Nevertheless, the amount of bills retired by the tax was modest. By February, 1754, only ₤3,439 had been retired leaving ₤17,911 still in circulation.[32] While this marks an improvement over the days when

---

31. Mr. Stewart writing to the secretary of the S. P. G. in 1767 stated that in 1754 about ₤50 of North Carolina currency equalled ₤30 sterling. North Carolina Colonial Records, VII, 493.

32. Ibid., VIII, 215.

North Carolina retired no bills at all, the retirements were still so moderate that it would have taken nearly thirty-seven years to retire the whole issue at this rate.

Although the tax levied by the act of 1748 abolished the practice of paying taxes in the rated commodities, the custom continued in private transactions. In 1754, and again at the close of the period in 1764, the assembly passed legislation aimed at removing one of the standing objections to a commodity currency -- the practice of debtors to tender their most inferior stock in satisfaction of their obligations. North Carolina, as had Maryland in 1747, took a leaf from the Virginia book of experience and inaugurated a system of commodity warehouses. Commodities were no longer to be tendered directly in payment of debts, but were to be deposited in public warehouses, where they were inspected and graded, after which notes were issued against them "equal to the value of the commodities at official ratings." These notes were made a legal tender for private debts and for certain public taxes with some restrictions as to time. The notes came to have a wide circulation in the tidewater counties, in which the warehouses were located. But in the remote frontier areas their importance appears to have been negligible.[33]

The effects of the introduction of the commodity notes upon the colony's currency rates were mixed. The notes were an improvement insofar as they brought about a standardization of the commodities tendered in payments. And viewed without regard to its effect upon the value of the colony's bills of credit, the issuing of the notes, which could readily be passed from hand to hand, doubtless facilitated the use of commodities as money. But by this very token, the commodity notes tended to depreciate the bills of credit. Since the colony was committed to the use of bills of credit, and since the necessities of the times made their use almost imperative, it would have been wiser to have suppressed the use of commodity currency altogether. But the prevailing temper in North Carolina probably made this a political impossibility.

The same year that witnessed the introduction of commodity notes witnessed the emission of an additional Ł40,000 in bills of credit. The occasion for the issue was the outbreak of the war with the French and Indians. The circumstances attending the issue, however, lend credence to the charge that the friends of paper money in the colony improved the opportunity to add to the

---

33. Charles J. Bullock, *Essays on the Monetary History of the United States*, pp. 157-158.

432

amount outstanding. Only Ł12,000 of the sum issued was applied immediately to aid Virginia in her expedition against the French. The sum of Ł4,000 was appropriated for the building of forts; another Ł6,000 for the building of public schools, which it was later alleged had no patrons; Ł6,200 for the building of churches and the purchase of glebe land; Ł2,000 for the erection of public buildings; Ł1,000 for Anson and Rowan counties; Ł4,000 for the payment of public debts; Ł2,800 for contingencies of government; and Ł800 to cover the expenses of issuing the bills. It is indicative of the temper of the times that the lower house also wished to establish a loan office for the issuance of Ł80,000. The act was passed during the administration of the president of the council, Matthew Rowan. The assembly, it appears, took advantage of the necessities of the times to force Rowan to assent to the measure, either with or without the accompanying use of a bribe, as has been charged.[34] No one has suggested how the money necessary for defense could have been raised except by the issuance of bills of credit, but that this was not the compelling cause for the entire issue seems equally clear. Moreover, the inadequacy of the tax levied to retire the bills lends credit to the charge that a

---

34. Ibid., pp. 158-160.

prime object in the passing of the bill was to increase the currency in circulation. The annual one shilling tax on each rateable levied in 1748 was continued and to supplement it, a duty of 4d. per gallon on spiritous liquors imported into the colony was imposed.[35]

At first there seems to have been a reluctance on the part of the people in the northern counties to circulate the bills, although they seem to have had a ready circulation elsewhere. By 1756, however, their circulation was general.[36] The Spanish milled dollar, worth 6s. at proclamation rates was passing, apparently, at above 8s., and it was said that the gold pistole, equal to 22s. at proclamation rates could not be had for 30s.[37] These figures indicate an exchange rate of about 175-180. Exchange in 1754 had been near 167.

Shortly after the issue of 1756, Arthur Dobbs, the new governor, arrived in the province, bringing with him schemes to rehabilitate the paper currency of the colony and at the same time ingratiate himself with the people. The essence of his scheme was to establish a loan office after the assembly had voted a tax adequate to retire the outstanding bills "in a short time." In

---

35. Laws of N. C., 1754 (c. 1), State Records of North Carolina, XXIII, 395.
36. Bullock, pp. 161-162.
37. John Rutherford, the N. C. receiver general, to B. T., North Carolina, June 19, 1756. N. C. Col. Rec., V, 586.

this way Dobbs thought soon to have the currency of the colony at par. From the governor's observations, it is evident that he, along with many others of his time, was a subscriber to the fallacious belief, that if the funds supporting a currency were ample, it would maintain its value, at least within wide limits, regardless of the amount in circulation. As a final measure of currency reform, the governor thought to introduce a copper coinage issued in small denominations by the mint in England.[38]

For one reason and another, however, all of the governor's plans came to naught, and the next event of consequence in the currency history of North Carolina was the issuance in 1756 of ₤3,400 in interest bearing non-legal tender notes for the defense of the western frontier. Governor Dobbs was restrained, as was customary, from assenting to any law issuing bills of credit unless the act contained a suspending clause. The governor, it appears, felt bound to adhere to his instructions as to legal tender non-interest bearing bills. But considerations of colonial defense impelled him to risk the displeasure of the home authorities in

---

38. Dobbs to B. T., Newbern, November 9, 1754, ibid., V, 148-149; speech of Dobbs to lower house, December 14, 1754, ibid., pp. 234-235; Dobbs to B. T., December 19, 1754, ibid., pp. 154-155; Dobbs' "Proposal for a Copper Coinage," ibid., pp. 324-325.

the case of the treasury notes. The notes were to bear interest at six per cent for one year, at the end of which time they were to be retired from the proceeds of a 2s. poll tax and a duty of 2d. per gallon on all liquors imported. The levying of a tax adequate to retire the issue within the year marks a departure from former practice.[39]

Further emissions of treasury notes on the same plan followed: ₤5,306 in May, and ₤9,500 in November, 1757; and ₤7,000 in April, and ₤4,000 in November, 1758. In each case the notes bore interest at six per cent for one year and a substantial tax was laid for their retirement at the end of the period.[40] The expenditures of the year 1759 were met by "reuttering" the sum of ₤5,500 in notes of the earlier issues that had been drawn into the treasury in the course of tax payments. A tax was levied to draw them in during the ensuing three years.[41]

In 1760 and 1761, the colony returned to issues on the old footing and for longer terms. During these

---

39. Bullock, p. 162; N. C. Col. Rec., VIII, 213-215; VI, 1309. The issues of 1754 and 1756, although they were sufficient to cause the bills to depreciate, did not satisfy some sections of the colony. Petitions setting forth a "great want of currency" and praying for relief were received in the spring of 1757. "Lower House Journal" (May 23, 1757), ibid., V, 851.
40. Ibid.
41. Ibid., VI, 1309.

years Ł12,000 and Ł20,000, respectively, were issued in legal tender bills. Moreover, the modest taxes levied to retire them insured that they would remain in circulation for a considerable period.[42]

The issues of the period may be followed in Table XXII, and the retirements and sums outstanding in Tables XXIII, XXIV, and XXV. The amounts outstanding in each year may also be followed in graphic form in Figure XIV. In November, 1764, it was reported that, beginning with the conversion issue of 1748, there had been issued during the period the sum of Ł93,350 in legal tender bills, of which Ł68,063 were still in circulation; and the principal sum of Ł29,406 in interest notes, upon which interest in the amount of Ł1,370 had accrued, making the whole sum, Ł30,776, of which there were still Ł6,969 in circulation.[43]

At the beginning of the war, sterling exchange was said to be at about Ł167 North Carolina currency to Ł100 sterling. The bills of credit, however, began to depreciate with the war issues. By October, 1755, they had fallen in value sufficiently to occasion a resolve by a committee of the Lower House, "That some method be fallen upon to Support the Credit of our Currency and to prevent Exchanging it for Gold and Silver so much

---

42. Ibid., VIII, 214.
43. Ibid., VI, 1308-1309.

TABLE XXII

An Estimate of Monies emitted and raised in the Province of North Carolina from the year 1748 — Showing to what purposes the same was applyed, by what Taxes sunk, &c.

TIME OF EMISSION & GRANT.	SUMS EMITTED IN PROCLAMATION BILLS.	SUMS EMITTED IN INTEREST NOTES.	TO WHAT PURPOSES APPLIED.	TAXES TO SINK THE SAME.
April 1748	£21350		£ 2000 For a Fort at Ocacock Inlet 1500 do at Topsail Inlet 500 do at Bar Inlet 2000 do at Cape Fear River 15350 For publick debts & contingencies of Gov^t £21350	One shilling Poll Tax to be collected until the whole sum is paid into the Treasury and burnt.
February 1754	40000		12000 For the Virginia expedition 2000 Fort Johnston 2000 Fort Granville 1000 Anson and Rowan Counties 4200 The payment of Public Debts 6000 Public Schools 7200 Churches and Glebes 2000 Public Buildings 2800 Contingencies of Government 800 To Com^{rs} for stamp^g & pay^g out the money £40000	The above Tax continued and 4d. per gallon on all spirituous liquors imported to be collected until the whole sum is paid in and burnt.
Septr 1756		£3400	For the Western Frontiers	2s. Poll Tax for the year 1757 and 2d. per gallon on all liquors imported in one year, surplussage to be applied to the contingent charges of Government
May 1757		5308	For the assistance of South Carolina	4s. 6d. Poll Tax for the year 1757; and Tax on suits at Law to raise a sum to discharge this emission.
Novem^r 1757		£9500	£7000 For three Companies for the Service of this Province 2500 For payment of Public Debts	6s. 6d. Poll Tax for the year 1758, surplussage to be applied to contingent charges of Government.
April 1758		7000	For the assistance of General Forbes	4s. 6d. Poll Tax for the year 1759 and 2d. p^r. gallon on all liquors imported in four years, surplussage to be applied to contingent charges of Government.
Novem^r 1758		4000	For two Companies for Forts Granville and Johnston	3s. 1d. Tax for 1760. Surplussage to be applied to contingent charges of Government.
June 1760	£12000		7000 For the Cherokee Expedition 2000 Premium to persons killing Indians 3000 Payment of Public Debts	1 shilling Poll Tax to commence January 1763 and continue till the whole is collected and paid.
March 1761	20000		For raising 500 men for the service of Virginia and South Carolina	2 shillings Poll Tax to commence January 1764 and continue till the whole is collected and paid.

TABLE XXIII

NORTH CAROLINA PROCLAMATION BILLS

Year	Amount Issued ₤	Amount Cancelled ₤	Amount Outstanding ₤
1748	21,350		21,350
1749		190	21,160
1750		514	20,646
1751		527	20,119
1752		1,091	19,028
1753		739	18,289
1754	40,000	338	57,951
1755		1,897	56,054
1756		1,809	54,245
1757		1,987	52,258
1758		1,701	50,557
1759		1,143	49,414
1760	12,000	1,479	59,935
1761	20,000	106	79,829
1762		3,769	76,060
1763			
1764		8,312	67,748
1765			
1766		3,786	63,962
1767			
1768		7,774	56,188

N. C. Col. Rec., VIII, 213-214, 215.

TABLE XXIV

NORTH CAROLINA INTEREST NOTES

Year	Amount Issued ₤	Interest ₤	Amount Cancelled ₤	Amount Outstanding Inc. Interest ₤
1756	3,600			3,600
1757	14,806	131	2,540	15,997
1758	11,000	542	7,843	19,696
1759		403		20,099
1760		147	4,374	15,872
1761		147	513	15,506
1762			6,244	9,262
1763				9,262
1764			3,632	5,630
1765				5,630
1766			1,712	3,918

N. C. Col. Rec., VI, 1308-1311; VIII, 213-215.

TABLE XXV

NORTH CAROLINA
PAPER CURRENCY OUTSTANDING

Year	Proclamation Bills ₤	Interest Notes (inc. int.) ₤	Total ₤
1748	21,350		21,350
1749	21,160		21,160
1750	20,647		20,647
1751	20,119		20,119
1752	19,028		19,028
1753	18,289		18,289
1754	57,951		57,951
1755	56,054		56,054
1756	54,245	3,600	57,951
1757	52,258	15,997	68,255
1758	50,557	19,696	70,253
1759	49,413	20,099	69,512
1760	59,934	15,872	75,806
1761	79,829	15,506	95,335
1762	76,060	9,262	85,322
1763			
1764	67,748	5,630	73,378
1765			
1766	63,963	3,918	67,880
1767			
1768	56,188	3,918	60,106
1769			
1770			
1771			
1772			

N. C. Col. Rec., VIII, 213-215; VI, 1308-1311.

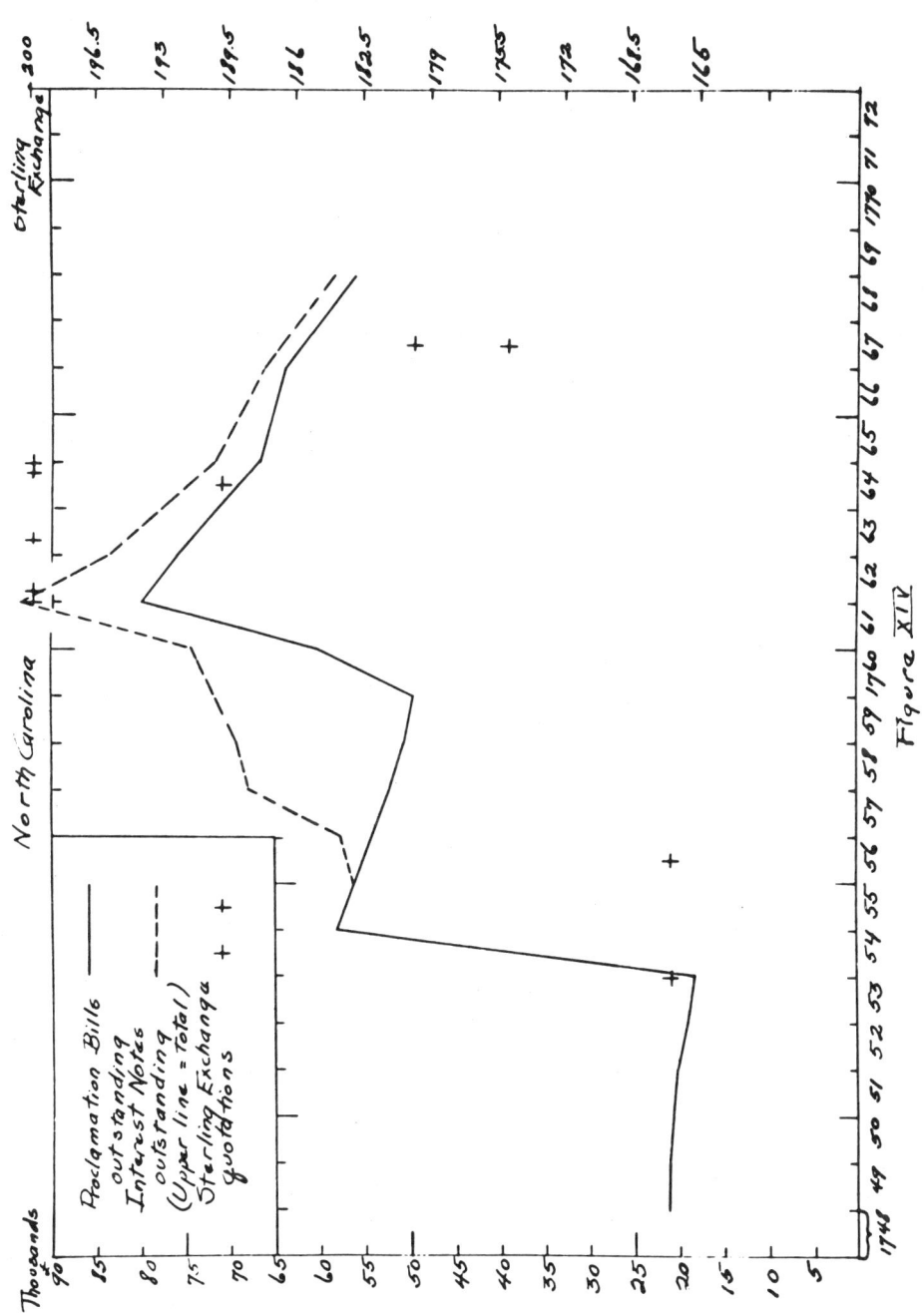

Figure XIV

above the Legal Parr."[44] In 1756 exchange was at 175-180; in 1759 at 190; and by 1761 at 200, at which figure it remained until 1764. Thereafter, as the currency of the colony was retired, the trend was downward, until in 1767 exchange was quoted at 175 to 180.[45]

North Carolina was apportioned ₤7,789 sterling out of the parliamentary grants of ₤50,000 to Virginia and the Carolinas in 1757, and the general grant of ₤200,000

---

44. "Lower House Journal" (Oct. 11, 1755), ibid., V, 549.
45. NORTH CAROLINA: PRICE OF STERLING EXCHANGE.

Year	Rate	Ref.: N. C. Col. Rec.
1754	166 2/3 ("about")	VII, 493
1756	175-180	V, 586
1759	190	VI, 17
1761	200	VI, 615
1761, Dec.	200 (about)	VI, 598-599
1762, Apr. 30	200 ("near")	VI, 712
1763, May 16	200	VI, 988
1764, Nov. 22	200	VI, 1245, 1304
1764, Dec. 8	200 (about)	VI, 1057
1767, June	175	VI, 493
1767, June 29	180	VI, 491

On June 19, 1756, John Rutherford, the North Carolina receiver general, wrote to the Board of Trade: "Proclamation money tho it is not very plenty & a great demand for it for cheating of Creditors paying of Taxes & Quit Rents yet a Pistole in gold [worth] 16^s 6^d [sterling] which ought to be equal to 22^s [North Carolina currency at the proclamation rate] cannot be purchased for 30^s[;] a [Spanish] Dollar worth 4^s 6^d [sterling] cannot be purchased for 8^s ...." N. C. Col. Rec., V, 586.

In December, 1761, Governor Dodd, in reply to queries of the Board of Trade, stated: "What bullion can be procured is bought up at [100 per cent] above Sterling Money, a Guinea above 45 Shillings, a pistole above 30, and a Dollar above 9 shillings ...." Ibid., VI, 612.

in 1759. The money, however, had not yet been received in the colony in 1762. The delay grew out of an altercation between the assembly and the governor, each of whom wanted to gain exclusive control of the grant. The colony's London agent, James Abercromby, recommended that the money be brought over in specie and used to retire an equivalent amount of bills of credit. The assembly wished to adopt this course.[46] But the governor opposed the plan, charging that the real objective of the leaders in the assembly was a scheme whereby they, in collusion with the treasurer, could buy up the outstanding paper at the rate it currently passed, i.e., £200 currency for £100 sterling, and then exchange it at the treasury to their own considerable advantage at the proclamation rate of £133 currency for £100 sterling. The governor proposed that the funds from the grants be made available in the colony through the sale of bills of exchange on the agent in London. He argued that if the grants were brought "over in specie it would be immediately bought up to send over again to

---

46. Bullock, p. 166, thinks that the proposal of the assembly "to use the Parliamentary grant in redeeming a part of the outstanding paper" was "certainly a singular thing for a colonial assembly to wish to do." He was apparently unaware that this very thing was done by various colonial assemblies; and that during the French and Indian War, where it was not done, the grants were applied to finance the further conduct of the war in lieu of additional issues of bills of credit, which amounts to much the same thing.

pay debts or Purchase Goods in Britain."[47] But the argument did not appeal to the Board of Trade, which felt that "the remitting the money in specie which being substituted in the place of paper notes, [would] occasion a Circulation of Cash, the want whereof has ever been the plea for a paper currency, that having no intrinsic value in itself has constantly depreciated to the great prejudice and loss of the British merchant." Nor did the method proposed by the governor appear to the Board of Trade to be "less liable to fraud than the other."[48] How the controversy was terminated does not appear; nor is there any indication of the extent to which the colony shared in later grants.[49]

The depreciation that the North Carolina bills of credit underwent during the decade of the 'fifties brought the colony under attack by the British merchants. The issues of both 1748 and 1754 had been declared "a lawful Tender, in all Payments whatsoever, as Proclamation Money, or as Sterling Money, at the proper

---

47. Dobbs to B. T., Brunswick, December, 1761, ibid., p. 599.
48. B. T. to Dobbs, June 10, 1762, ibid., p. 725.
49. On the controversy, beside the specific references cited in the two preceding notes, see: Bullock, p. 166. N. C. Col. Rec., VI, xi. Letter Book of James Abercromby, Virginia State Library: A. to Dobbs, March 4, 1758, pp. 77-78; same to same, March 13, 1758, pp. 83-84; A. to Ja: Swann, March 17, 1758, pp. 88-90; A. to Col. Innis, March 26, 1758, pp. 90-92; A. to Samuel Swann [the speaker of the N. C. House], April 19, 1758, pp. 95-96.

Difference ... between Proclamation Money and Sterling; that is ..., at Four Shillings Proclamation Money for Three Shillings Sterling."[50] The effect of such a provision upon sterling creditors during a period in which the North Carolina currency was depreciating is obvious. By 1759, with exchange at 190, the British merchants with sterling debts due them in the colony were being paid in bills of credit on the basis of ₤133 1/3 currency for each ₤100 sterling. When they went to convert the bills into sterling exchange at the prevailing rate in order to place their money in England, they found that their ₤133 1/3 currency would purchase only ₤70 sterling. Thus, in effect, a ₤100 sterling debt was commuted into one of ₤70, and the creditor lost thirty per cent of the sum due him.

This was the state of affairs that was set out by a group of London merchants trading to North Carolina, with whom were joined certain "Gentlemen and Merchants in and from that Colony," in a petition to the Board of Trade in March, 1759.[51] The petitioners prayed that the governor might be instructed to secure an amendment to the acts of 1748 and 1754 to the purpose that all

---

50. Laws of N. C., 1748 (c. x), State Records of N. C., XXIII, 294. The act of 1754 contained a similar provision. Laws of N. C., 1754 (c. 1), ibid., pp. 392-393.

51. N. C. Col. Rec., VI, 16-17.

sterling debts due the merchants of Britain and elsewhere, as well as all debts to the crown, when paid in bills of credit should "be paid Ad Valorem"; and that in the future such a proviso should be included in all issuing acts.

The merchants presented their petition at a propitious time, for the way had been prepared for them by the efforts of the merchants trading to Virginia to bring about a change in the currency practices of that colony.[52] The result was that the Board of Trade was willing to grant more than the petitioners asked, and in due course an instruction in the same form as one lately sent to the Virginia governor was sent to the governor of North Carolina.[53] In it, he was directed to use his endeavors to procure an amendment to the acts complained of to the effect that sterling debts should be payable in "bills of credit if the creditor be willing to accept the same and not otherwise, not according to their nominal value ..., but according to the real difference in value between such paper bills and sterling money at the time of discharging such debts," and in the future to require that such a clause

---

52. This is discussed in detail in the chapter following.
53. Board of Trade Journal, 1759-1763, March 16, 28, April 3, 10, May 23, 1759; Acts of the Privy Council, Colonial, 1745-1766, #386; Representation of B. T. (April 10, 1759) is in N. C. Col. Rec., V, 22-24.

be included in all issuing acts.[54] This instruction, had it been acted upon, would in effect have deprived the bills of their legal tender quality with respect to sterling debts, for that cannot be deemed a legal tender which the creditor is at liberty to refuse. One can find justice in the prayer of the merchants' petition that sterling debts be paid only _ad valorem_ in bills of credit, but to allow the creditor to refuse to receive bills of credit even when tendered _ad valorem_ gave it into his power to determine, in effect, the rate of exchange at which such payments should be made.[55]

The Board of Trade was likewise quick to act with respect to the payments of obligations due the crown, for the problem was an old one, and one that had frequently given rise to complaints.[56] The governor was further instructed "to take especial care" that the act to be passed amending the acts of 1748 and 1754, as well as all future emitting acts, should include a clause "declaring that the paper bills of credit already issued or thereby to be issued shall not be a lawful tender in payment of [the] quit-rents or of any debts of what

---

54. Leonard W. Labaree, _Royal Instructions to British Colonial Governors_, I, #337.

55. This ground was fought over in the dispute between the merchants trading to Virginia and the House of Burgesses and is fully discussed in the next chapter.

56. See for example, John Rutherford, the North Carolina receiver general, to B. T., June 19, 1756, _N. C. Col. Rec._, V, 586-589.

nature soever due or to become due" to the crown.[57]
The matter of quit-rent payments was a thorny problem, and one not likely to be solved by such an instruction, even if acted upon. So scarce was specie, that the only medium in many cases in which payments to the crown could be made was bills of credit. One with any appreciation of realities could scarcely expect a back-country farmer owing a few shillings in quit-rents to the crown to procure a sterling bill of exchange in which to make payment. The crown was, in fact, fortunate if he made payment at all. The collectors, then, found themselves forced to take payment in whatever form offered. This would have been possible under the policy contemplated in the instructions, but it would have left to the collectors the determination of the value at which the bills of credit would be accepted. Such discretionary power lodged with them would have left the way open to abuse, and would in any event, have proved a fruitful source of complaint.

The governor appears not to have succeeded in securing the passage of an act amending the laws of 1748 and 1754 in accordance with his instructions. Nor did he secure the inclusion of the desired clause in future emitting acts. The best that could be done was to se-

---

57. Labaree, *Royal* Instructions, I, #337.

cure the omission of the clause specifically making the bills a legal tender for sterling debts at proclamation rates. Both the act of 1760, placing £12,000 in circulation, and that of 1761, emitting £20,000, contained a legal tender clause providing that the bills of credit to be issued should be "a lawful Tender in all Payments whatsoever as Proclamation Money."[58]

The meaning of this provision is far from clear. It appears that the courts in cases involving sterling debts for long granted judgments in bills of credit at the rate of £133 1/3 currency for £100 sterling. We learn, however, from a letter written by Governor William Tryon to the Board of Trade, July 15, 1767, that this practice "was overruled in the superior court of justice" sometime before Tryon arrived in 1766, and that it had "ever since been constantly the practice to allow the merchant upon recovery of his debt *ad valorem* and not according to the legal tender" rate of £133 1/3 to £100.[59] The substance of the prayer contained in the merchants' petition of 1759 was thus realized, and the determination of the rate of exchange was placed in the hands of the courts, where it appears rightfully to

---

58. Laws of N. C., 1761 (c. 1), State Records of N. C., XXIII, 540; the act of 1760 contains the same phraseology save that the word "money" is omitted after "proclamation," Laws of N. C., 1760 (c. 1), ibid., p. 516.

59. N. C. Col. Rec., VII, 511.

belong. The colony had now arrived at the method for some years in use in Virginia, but where it had been the subject of bitter complaints emanating from the merchants trading to that colony. Apparently the merchants trading to North Carolina and those trading to Virginia were not of one mind as to what methods of handling sterling debts protected their interests. The former group prayed for the method that the latter group protested as destructive of their property.

The paper currency outstanding in North Carolina, which had amounted to ₤20,119 in 1751, reached its peak in 1761, when the amount in circulation, proclamation bills and interest bearing notes together, was ₤95,335. From that time the trend was downward. In 1764, the amount was ₤73,378; and by 1768, it had been reduced to ₤60,106. During the period from 1751 to 1764 the population of North Carolina had perhaps quadrupled, if the increase in "taxables" in the colony be an indication.[60] Taking into consideration this increase in population, the amount of bills in circulation in 1764 scarcely appears excessive in comparison with the amount in circulation in 1751; and certainly by 1768, the colony had grown into its currency then out-

---

60. Greene and Harrington, American Population before 1790, pp. 157-158. There were 9,437 taxables in 1751; 40,576 in 1764; and 46,701 in 1768.

standing.

The year 1751 found South Carolina with her finances in good order. Her paper currency in circulation totaled perhaps Ł154,000, which was made up of Ł106,500 in legal tender bills issued in 1731 without period set for their redemption, Ł12,600 of the non-legal tender public orders issued in 1742,[61] and perhaps Ł35,000 in tax certificates.[62] Exchange on London usually fluctuated between 700 and 725,[63] and the Spanish milled dollar passed at

---

61. Governor James Glen to B. T., July 15, 1751. Public Records of South Carolina, MS, XXIV, 352. Historical Commission of South Carolina, Columbia, S. C.

62. The precise amount of tax certificated outstanding in each year is not ascertainable before 1753. But it is possible to reach a close approximation, since the annual issues are known, and since tax funds were available to draw them in within the ensuing year.

The tax certificates issued annually from 1746 to 1751 follow:

Year	Ł	Year	Ł
1746	182	1749	13,848
1747	1,837	1750	23,848
1748	2,296	1751	31,901

South Carolina Commons House Journal, MS, XXVIII, 505 (April 17, 1753). Historical Commission of South Carolina.

63. Sterling exchange quotations appearing in the South Carolina Gazette:

Year		Rate of Exchange
1749	(March 6 - May 29)	725-730
	(June 5 - 26)	700-725
	(July 24 - Oct. 16)	700-715
	(November 27)	715-725
	(December 18 to	
1750	January 15)	725
	(Feb. 19 - May 26)	700-715
	(June 18 - Sept. 24)	700

31s.[64]

Besides the three forms of paper in circulation in South Carolina, there was a varying amount of specie. The account of the provincial treasurer in December, 1752, indicates that of the ₤27,000 balance in the treasury, about one-half was in pistoles and Spanish dollars.[65] Nevertheless, there was then, and for some years had been, the feeling that the currency of the province was inadequate to the needs of commerce. And this lack, it was held, could only be supplied by a further paper issue, since "the plenty and scarcity of Silver and Gold in [the] Province [was] altogether Casual, and therefore not at all to be relied on as a Medium of Trade."[66] Consequently, for a decade and a half the province had been endeavoring to obtain the royal approval for a bill to increase its legal tender bills.

During the early 'twenties the South Carolina merchants had bitterly opposed additions to the paper currency of the province: so bitterly, in fact, that they had for a short time been committed to "gaol" for con-

---

64. Account of Jacob Motte, Treasurer, S. C. Commons House Journal, MS, XXVIII, 96. The 31s. rate at which the dollar was accounted was, neglecting shipping charges and insurance, equivalent to an exchange rate of 677.
65. Ibid.
66. Resolution of Commons House, December 15, 1752, S. C. Commons House Journal, MS, XXVIII, 141.

tempt of the assembly because of the "scandalous and defamatory" nature of their memorial.[67] In 1730, however, merchants of the province joined with planters in representing to the crown "the absolute necessity that some paper money should be allowed to have a currency" in South Carolina "under proper regulations, as well for carrying on the annual services of ... government there as for the daily circulation of trade amongst the inhabitants."[68] In consequence, an instruction was issued (1730) to the South Carolina governor empowering him to give his "assent to an act or acts for the establishing a new paper currency upon such a foot as may best answer the necessities of the province and be most conducive to the public utility thereof," always taking care that any such act should contain a suspending clause.[69]

In 1736 the assembly sought to take advantage of

---

67. "Memorial of the Merchants and other Inhabitants of Charles City & Port in behalf of themselves and several Merchants of Great Britain who trade to & have considerable Effects in this Province" (December, 1722), S. C. Public Records, MS, IX, 178-189. Petition to Governor, Council, and House to accompany same, ibid., pp. 189-190. Proceedings in the S. C. Commons House respecting the above, ibid., pp. 191-204.

68. As summarized in the instruction issued in 1730. Leonard W. Labaree, Royal Instructions to British Governors, 1670-1776, I, #340. See Calendar State Papers, America and West Indies, 1730, #83, for a suggested scheme for a new currency for South Carolina (February 28, 1730).

69. Labaree, Royal Instructions, I, #340.

the liberty granted in the instruction and passed an
act providing for ₤210,000 in bills of credit, of which
₤100,000 were to be exchanged for bills of the issue of
1731, and the remaining ₤110,000 were to be placed out
on loan on land "or other sufficient security" at eight
per cent interest. The bills were to be a full legal
tender in all transactions. As one of the objects of
British policy was to secure a fund for the issue of
1731, an ingenious device for supplying this deficiency
was hit upon. It was provided that the annual interest
on the money placed on loan should be paid in gold and
silver, and that five-eighths of the money so received
should be lent out until such time as the whole principal out on loan should amount to ₤210,000, at which
time the debt of ₤100,000 (really ₤106,500) owing by
the public as a result of the issue of 1731 would "be
entirely paid off and discharged." As the issue of
1731 would still be in circulation, it is evident that
what is meant was that the bills of 1731 would now be
backed by landed security and would no longer rest
solely upon the credit of the colony, or in other
words, the debt would now be one of the borrowers
rather than of the province.[70]

The law was unique in one other feature. Since a

---

70. *Statutes at Large of South Carolina*, III, 423-430 (#597, passed May 29, 1736).

main object of the act was to furnish a circulating medium as well as a revenue to the government from the interest money no provision was made for the repayment of the principal of the loans. This in some respects appears ill-advised. The better way to have accomplished the same result, that is, a circulating medium constant in amount, would have been to require the loans to be repaid in annual installments over a reasonable period of years and then to relend the money to new borrowers. But with the desire to keep the amount of bills out on loan from diminishing, one can have little quarrel.

The act contained a suspending clause, as was required by the instruction of 1730. Upon consideration by the authorities in England, the act was found to be "agreeable to" the instruction of 1730, and "to contain many good clauses and provisos." Two matters, however, were objectionable: (1) the clause directing the treasurer to allow a ten per cent reduction "on all duties inwards which shall be paid in silver and gold" in order "to encourage the bringing of silver and gold into [the] Province" was found contrary to the Act of Queen Anne; and (2) the failure of the assembly to include a clause "to oblige the borrowers to repay any part of the principal towards the sinking of the ... bills, which ought to have been provided for by gradual payments annually and should have commenced at least upon the acquisition of a sufficient fund for the discharge of the old debt," i.e., the bills of 1731. In consequence, an instruction was issued in 1739 directing the governor to recommend "the passage of another act for the same purpose not liable to the aforementioned objections." This act was also to contain a suspending clause.[71]

In 1746 the South Carolina assembly passed such an act.[72] The new law was in most respects similar to the old one, but the clause directing the treasurer to remit ten per cent of all duties inward when paid in specie was omitted, the principal of the loans was made payable in ten annual installments to begin at the time the principal sum out on loan should equal ₤210,000, and bills equivalent in amount to the annual payments were to be burned. The act contained a suspending clause.

Despite the fact that the act of 1746 was passed in a form that met the objections of the Board of Trade to the earlier act, South Carolina was again to be denied a loan office. Times had changed and so had the Board of Trade. The foes of paper currency were in the ascendant at Whitehall, and the new doctrine was

---

71. Labaree, Royal Instructions, I, #341.
72. S. C. Statutes, III, 671-677 (#738, passed June 17, 1746).

the "destruction of all Paper Currency." Beginning with the year 1748, South Carolina's ₤210,000 act, together with certain matters relating to the financing of the province's participation in the King George's War, was before the Board of Trade until the measure was finally represented for disallowance in 1753. During the period Governor James Glen and the assembly, through its London agents Peregrine Furye and James Crokatt, attempted to prevail upon the Board to grant favorable consideration to the act. The correspondence of the Board with Governor Glen and its "misrepresentation" to the Privy Council in 1753 reflect little credit upon it. The Board misread the report on the currency of the province sent over by the assembly in 1749 in response to the resolution of the House of Commons, and, in consequence, questioned its candor; it misunderstood Governor Glen's plainest arguments, and cast doubt on his integrity because in giving his own views in his letters to the Board, he spoke in a tone different from the one he had used earlier in opposing the projects of the assembly, when as a matter of fact, in the earlier instances he had, in pursuance of his instructions, merely been repeating the arguments that the Board of Trade had urged upon him; and, lastly, it misread and misrepresented the act itself when it recommended its disallowance to the Privy Council. It would be tedious to review the controversy in detail. Suffice it to say that if there were valid reasons why the act should have been disallowed, they were not those stressed by the Lords Commissioners for Trade and Plantations.[73]

It is difficult to form a judgment as to whether the issue was needed or not. The failure of the sizeable issues of public orders during the French and Indian War noticeably to affect prices or exchange, however, would indicate that the province could doubtless have absorbed the loan issue; and the new bills might conceivably have quickened trade by making it less necessary to do business on credit. Moreover, the

---

[73]. The provision of the Act that silver should be received in payments of interest at 37s. 6d. per oz. was doubtless contrary to the policy embodied in the Act of Queen Anne and was, not without some reason, noted by the Board of Trade. However, the earlier Board had not objected to the same provision in the act of 1736. Actually, the Board's fine scruples on the matter of violations of the policy embodied in the Act of Queen Anne (the act itself was not violated, vide supra, p. 148) had more regard to form than substance. Strictly speaking, the policy, which had never been made effective, was violated whenever silver rose above proclamation rates in any of the paper money colonies -- and there was no paper money colony in which this had not happened. But since South Carolina merely placed the prevailing value on silver (and gold), it could by this provision scarcely have drawn coin from the other colonies. And this was the evil that the Act of Queen Anne really sought to prevent. In fact, the establishing by statute of the value at which gold and silver should be received in interest payments at the figure prevailing before the new issue, might conceivably have retarded a rise in the price of specie should the new issue prove excessive. But members of the Board of Trade did not concern themselves with considerations of this kind. (See next note for references.)

availability of loans would no doubt have encouraged settlement and enabled many to procure estates for themselves. Certainly, the prevailing opinion among all classes in the province was that the issue was needed; and the bumbling, inept, and procrastinating manner in which the Board of Trade dealt with the matter could not but prove vexatious, and left the province sensitive to future efforts of the imperial authorities to regulate the paper currency of the colonies.[74]

When the Board of Trade had sent up its representation in 1753, it had not been content with recommending the disallowance of the act of 1746, but it had further recommended the issuing of a new instruction respecting paper currency in South Carolina. Such an instruction was issued in 1755. The policy embodied in the instrument not only sought to prevent further additions to the legal tender bills of the province, but also sought

---

74. Board of Trade Journal, 1741/2-1749, May 15, July 12, 13, 22, October 26, December 8, 1748, April 30, 1750, July 3, 1752, June 6, November 2, 1753. Peregrine Furye to John Pownall, January 27, 1747/8, S. C. Public Records, MS, XXIII, 53-55; Glen to B. T., July 27, 1748, ibid., pp. 177-182; enclosure in Glen to B. T., October 10, 1748, ibid., pp. 211, 225-227; Glen to B. T., December 23, 1749, ibid., pp. 426-430; B. T. to Glen, November 15, 1750, ibid., XXIV, 158-168; Glen to B. T., July 15, 1751, ibid., pp. 346-364; Representation of B. T. to Privy Council, 1753, ibid., XXV, 233-290. Report of 1749, S. C. Council Journal, MS, XVII, 766-770 (Historical Commission of South Carolina). Acts of the Privy Council, Colonial, 1745-1766, #213, #256.

to provide for the retirement of those already in circulation. The governor was directed to recommend the passage of a law establishing a fund to retire the Ł106,500 issued in 1731 "within a reasonable limited time"; for the future he was required to withhold his assent from any bill issuing bills of credit until after provision had been made for retiring the bills already in circulation; even then issues were limited to "sudden and extraordinary emergencies of government in the cases of war and invasion"; and in every case the prior leave of the crown was necessary. The bills issued in such emergencies were not to be a legal tender in private transactions and were to be retired "within a reasonable time, not exceeding five years." Moreover, the governor was restrained from assenting to any bill prolonging the periods of any public orders that might then be in circulation.[75] It is evident that a policy more severe even than had been applied to New England by the Currency Act of 1751 was to prevail in South Carolina.

In the years from the close of King George's War until the opening of the French and Indian War, during which there were no new paper issues and the last of the old public orders were retired, the province was

---

75. Representation, S. C. Public Records, XXV, 233-290; Labaree, *Royal Instructions*, I, #342.

forced to place greater reliance upon specie to circulate its trade. At the beginning of the period specie appears to have been relatively scarce. Certain groups of individuals raised the rates at which they would accept coin, with a view to keeping it in the province.[76] In 1752 the assembly directed the provincial treasurer to receive coin at a higher rate, the piece of eight being raised from 3l$s.$ to 3l$s.$ 10$d.$, and other coins in proportion. Nevertheless, it apparently had little faith in the measure, for it resolved at the same time "that the plenty and scarcity of Silver and Gold in this Province is altogether Casual, and therefore not at all to be relied on as a Medium of Trade."[77]

Throughout the period between the wars there were some years in which South Carolina's balance of trade with Great Britain was favorable, and others when it was not. On the average, however, the advantage appears

---

76. See, for example, the notice in the South Carolina Gazette, December 11, 1749: "As Gold and Silver is now become scarce here, and what little we have likely to be wholly drained from us by the petty Traders from the Northern Colonies, who generally come here this Time of Year, with their Beer, Apples, Chesnuts, &c. picking up all the Gold and Silver they can, by giving more for the same than it here at present passes for: To remedy in part such an Evil, we hear, the Gentlemen of the Law have unanimously agreed to take in Satisfaction of their Fees, Spanish Pistoles at 6 l. each, Doubloons at 24 l. each, and mill'd Dollars at 32s. & 6d. each."

77. S. C. Commons House Journal, MS, XXVIII, 64-97, 141-143.

to have been with the province.[78] But even so, this fact could not be relied on to build up a stock of specie in South Carolina adequate to the province's currency needs. The reason was simple. The specie that accrued to the province from this source was spent for slaves, because, as Governor Glen computed, it would yield an annual return of from sixteen to twenty-five per cent when so invested, but if invested within the province would not yield more than eight, or considering risks, perhaps only six.[79] Even so, all of the specie coming into the province does not seem to have been spent for this purpose. By the middle of the decade the stock must have increased somewhat over that in the province at the close of the last war, for in 1755 Governor Glen wrote: "Gold and silver begin to take up their abode with us, two thirds of all Payments being now made in those Metals."[80]

The outbreak of the French and Indian War, however, made reliance upon an uncertain specie currency less necessary. The province met the expenses of government during the war by issuing public orders totaling

---

78. Johnson et al., History of Domestic and Foreign Commerce of the United States, I, 120-121.
79. Glen to B. T., July 15, 1751, S. C. Public Records, MS, XXIV, 353-354.
80. Glen to Arthur Dobbs, governor of North Carolina, February 20, 1755, Colonial Records of North Carolina, V, 378-379.

£816,358 for the years 1755-1763. The public orders, all of which were in the nature of bills of credit, were made receivable for all taxes and duties at the treasury. Provision was made for their redemption from tax funds, usually over a period of five years.[81] The governors seem to have considered the emergencies of the war sufficient reason for not holding up such issues until the prior leave of the crown had been obtained. Thus in South Carolina as elsewhere the instructions gave way before the needs of defense. The ordinary expenses of government, as well as a not inconsiderable part of the military expenses of the war, were met by the issuance of tax certificates. Custom had changed little in the quarter of a century since Alexander Cumings had written that in South Carolina, "pay, after twelve Months, was reckoned as ready Money." The method employed by the assembly in meeting ordinary public obligations was annually to compute the sum owing to those that during the preceding year had performed services for, or supplied goods to, the public; ascertain the balance on the various funds in the treasury; and lay a tax for the difference on the estates in the

---

81. Of the acts authorizing the issuance of public orders, those of 1760 are printed in full in S. C. Statutes (III, #897, #899). The orders authorized by the first act were of denominations of £25 and £50; those of the second, of £20.

province to be paid during the ensuing year. In the meantime, that the public creditors might not be kept waiting longer for their money, the treasurer was authorized to issue tax certificates to them in satisfaction of the debts of the province. Such certificates were customarily issued in denominations of from ₤5 to ₤50 and were receivable at the treasury during the year following their issuance. Actually, however, some of each year's issue usually remained outstanding for a longer period, simply because many people paid their taxes in other forms of money and the holders of the certificates, since they readily passed as money, could not be induced to bring them to the treasury for exchange.[82]

The public orders likewise circulated freely.[83] The issuance of the public orders and tax certificates

---

82. The tax act of 1760 is printed in full, ibid., #898.

83. The provincial treasurer, in a newspaper advertisement in 1761 urging the holders of certain orders and tax certificates to bring them in for exchange, observed that he apprehended that "the chief occasion of the ... certificates, remaining so long outstanding is the great facility with which, they do pass in lieu of money ...." S. C. Gazette, June 13, 1761 and following issues.

In the Petition of the South Carolina Commons House to the King in 1766, it is stated that the public orders and tax certificates, "tho not legal tender, ... had as much Credit and passed as freely ...." S. C. Commons House Journal, MS, XXXVII, 216-220 (November 27, 1766).

As to the tax certificates, Governor William Bull wrote earlier in the same year, that "these circu-

greatly increased the paper circulation of the province during the war years. At the close of 1754, there was in circulation in legal tender bills, public orders, and tax certificates combined, the sum of ₤156,000. In 1761, the peak year, the sum was ₤868,000; by 1764, it had been reduced to ₤585,000; and by 1765, to ₤472,000. (The issues of tax certificates can be followed in the note below,[84] while the issues of public orders may be followed in Table XXVI. The sums annually outstanding in lawful bills, public orders, and tax certificates are given in Table XXVII, and are set forth graphically in Figure XV.)

The war issues appear to have had no observable effect upon the rate of exchange. Sterling exchange was contemporaneously reported to be at 721 to 100 in October, 1763, and at the same figure in the fall of

---

late readily." Bull to B. T., May 3, 1766, S. C. Public Records, MS, XXXI, 32.

84. South Carolina Issues of Tax Certificates

Year	₤	Year	₤
1753	42,322	1762	88,692
1754	42,077	1763	--
1755	64,104	1764	93,834
1756	85,159	1765	48,045
1757	96,626	1766	37,742
1758	129,381	1767	86,420
1759	74,167	1768	105,000
1760	77,656	1769	70,000
1761	180,571		

Source: S. C. Commons House Journal, MS, XXXVIII, 350 (March 27, 1770).

TABLE XXVI

SOUTH CAROLINA ISSUES OF PUBLIC ORDERS, 1751-1764

Year	Issues £	Purpose	Funds	Ref.: S. C. Statutes, IV
1755	33,600	"Defence of North America"	Taxes on estates real and personal, 4 yrs.	#835[x]
1756	50,000[y]	"Fortifications"	?	#856[x]
1757	160,000	"Howarth's Regiment"	do., 5 years	#866[y]
1757	44,300	"Fortifications"	do.	#866[x]
1757	25,000	"Fortifications"	do.	#865[x] #866[x]
1760	246,693	"Lyttleton's Regiment"	£70,000 sunk immediately; "remainder to be sunk in regular proportions" 1761-64, inc., by taxes as above	#897
1760	125,000	"Middleton's Regiment"	Taxes as above, 1761-65, inc.	#898
1762	15,000[z]	"Cherokee Trade"		#920 #925?[x]

[x] Printed by title only in Statutes.
[y] Not given in Report of 1764, but referred to in various reports in Commons House Journal, MS. Later in the reports in the CHJ, it is consolidated with the orders of 1757.
[z] Not given in Report of 1764.

Source: Report to Board of Trade, 1764, C. O. 323/19, L. C. P.; S. C. Statutes; S. C. Commons House Journal, MS, Hist. Com. of S. C.

TABLE XXVII

SOUTH CAROLINA
PAPER CURRENCY OUTSTANDING

Year	Lawful Bills £	Public Orders £	Tax Certificates £	Total £
1750	106,500			
1751	106,500			
1752	106,500			
1753	106,500	3,500	42,322	152,322
1754	106,500	2,800	46,856	156,156
1755	106,500	35,779	79,080	221,359
1756	106,500	84,959	120,357	311,816
1757	106,500	288,755	147,582	542,837
1758	106,500	275,078	213,989	595,567
1759	106,500	235,845	179,024	521,369
1760	106,500	619,085	138,232	863,827
1761	106,500	519,016	242,228	867,744
1762	106,500			
1763	106,500	326,810	151,606	584,916
1764	106,500	295,010	183,736	585,246
1765	106,500	204,310	161,568	472,378
1766	106,500	171,080	169,093	446,673
1767	106,500	119,942	117,705	344,147
1768	106,500	130,128	245,370	481,999
1769	106,500	112,153	279,000	497,654
1770	136,226 x	85,304	202,624	424,154
1771	136,226 x			
1772	136,226 x			
1773	123,945 x	124,276	143,261	391,391
1774	113,443 x	69,580	75,948	258,971

x In 1769 South Carolina passed an act to reissue the province's £106,500 of legal tender bills (S. C. Statutes, IV, #000). The law, however, was disallowed; but not until after some of the new bills were in circulation and £7,504 10s. of the old bills had been destroyed, leaving £98,995 10s. still outstanding. After the disallowance of the act, the new bills were destroyed as they came into the treasury, but no more of the old ones were burned. The sums above indicated by an (x) are arrived at by adding the new bills outstanding to the £98,995 10s. in old bills. These sums were "outstanding," but not necessarily all of them were "in circulation," i.e., outside of the treasury. During these years reports on the condition of the treasury contained notations similar to the following, that there was the sum of "about

(Note to Table XXVII, **continued**.)

₤35,000 of the old Lawful Bills ... laying in the Treasury, being torn, obliterated and impassable." (S. C. Commons House Journal, MS, XXXIX, 108, March 3, 1774.)

Source of table: Committee Reports appearing in S. C. Commons House Journal, MS, for these years, *passim*. Historical Commission of South Carolina, Columbia, S. C.

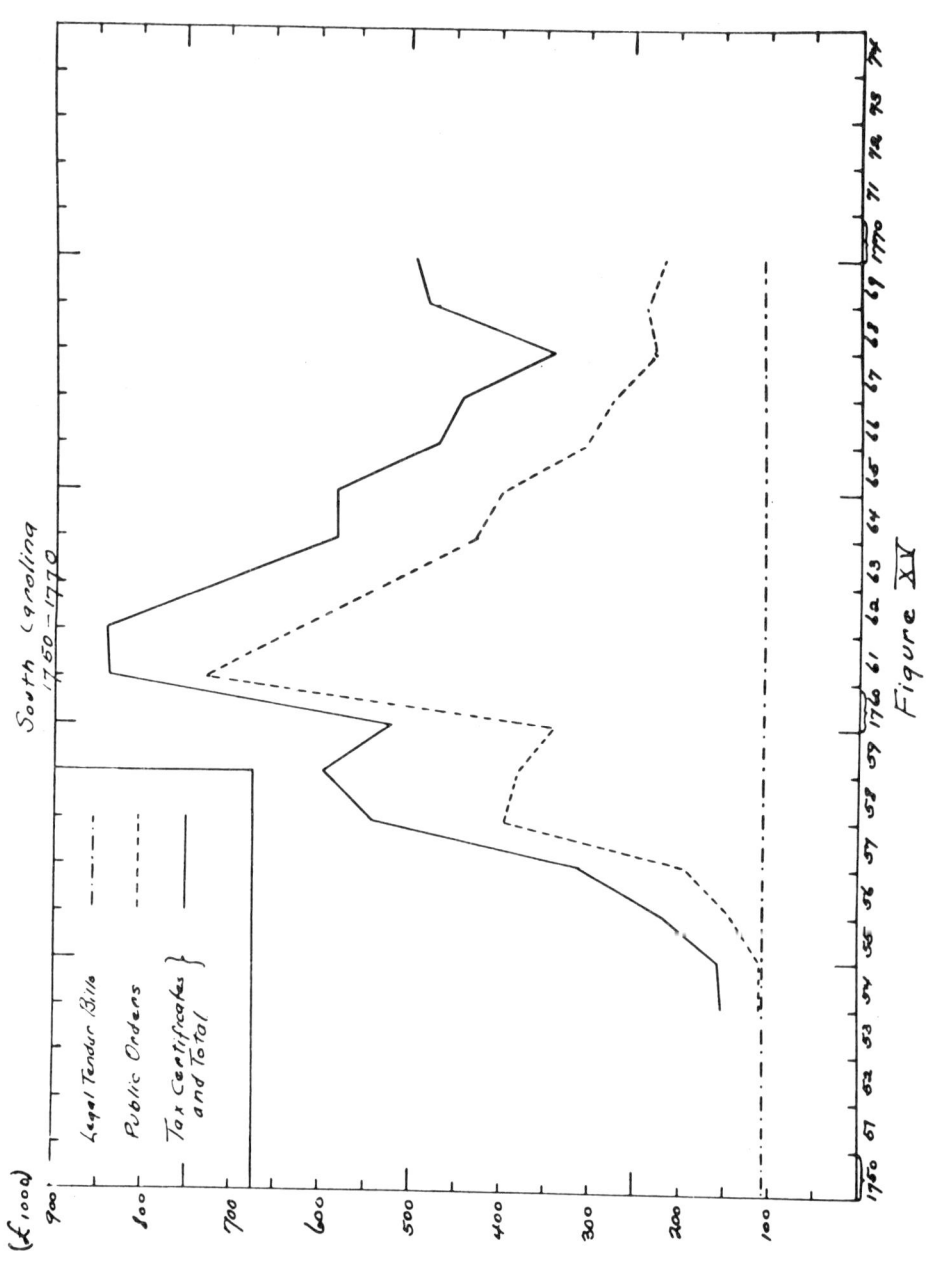

Figure XV

1764.[85] The petition to the king in 1766 states that exchange was not "in the least affected" by the sizeable sums in public orders and tax certificates outstanding during the war.[86] Nor does the behavior of such price indices as we have indicate that the increase in the paper circulation of the province was the important factor in price determination.[87] The indices, however, are made up largely of export commodities, whose prices are determined for the most part by conditions on the world market, and consequently are not well adapted to measuring the effects of changes in the money supply.

Data concerning the extent of South Carolina's participation in the parliamentary grants have not been discovered.

The diminution of the amount of public orders and tax certificates outstanding after 1760 tended to accentuate the currency problem. The period ends with the assembly ardently desiring an addition of ₤40,000 to its legal tender to relieve in some measure the

---

85. S. C. Public Records, MS, XXX, 49-50 (October 18, 1763); Letter Book of Henry Laurens, MS, South Carolina Historical and Genealogical Society, Charleston.
86. S. C. Commons House Journal, MS, XXXVII, 217.
87. George Rogers Taylor, "Wholesale Commodity Prices at Charleston, South Carolina, 1732-1791," Journal of Economic and Business History, IV, 356-377 (February, 1932); Arthur H. Cole, Wholesale Commodity Prices in the United States, 1700-1861, I, 50-64 (based on Taylor's work).

stringency that it felt would develop as a result of further reductions in the public orders and tax certificates extant. In fact, the province was the first to lodge a protest against the Currency Act of 1764,[88] and resentment against the restraint did not abate with the years.

Georgia, which came under royal government in 1754, established a loan office in the following year and authorized the emission of Ł7,000 sterling to be lent out on good security at six per cent interest. The reasons given for the enactment were that "Gold and Silver being frequently carried out" of the colony, the people were laid under "many Inconveniences and Hardships" and were "rendered incapable of raising Money to pay" their taxes. A loan issue was thought the proper remedy. Although the act contained a suspending clause and there is no record of its being approved in England, the "Account" transmitted to Parliament in 1764 states that Ł2,987 were issued under the act, all of which had been retired prior to that year.[89] In the summer of 1757 an issue of Ł738 sterling was authorized "to be

---

88. S. C. Commons House Journal, MS, XXXVI, 231 (August 14, 1764); S. C. Committee of Correspondence to Charles Garth, the London agent, September 4, 1764, Robert W. Gibbes, *Documentary History of the American Revolution*, 1855, I, 1-6.

89. *Georgia Colonial Records*, XVIII, 48-65 (act passed, February 17, 1755); "Account" of 1764, C. O. 323/19, L. C. P.

applied in discharge of the public debts"; and in the spring of 1759 the sum of ₤799 sterling was emitted "to defray the Expence of repairing the Church in Savannah[,] for building a Public Magazine [in] Savannah[,] for securing the Light House on Tybee and to make good a Deficiency of the last Public Tax destroy'd by an Accident of Fire." These acts likewise contained suspending clauses, and although never affirmed in England, the sums authorized by them were placed in circulation and are reported to have been retired prior to 1764.[90]

On May 1, 1760, ₤1,100 sterling; on December 10, 1761, ₤180 sterling; and on March 25, 1762, ₤540 sterling were authorized in "certificates" to meet outlays occasioned by the war. Provision was made to retire each of the sums from tax funds over a period of five years. Of the ₤1,830 authorized by the three acts, ₤827 8s. were reported still in circulation on September 29, 1764.[91]

An act of a different nature, which authorized the emission of ₤7,410 sterling, was passed on May 1, 1760.[92] This is the loan act referred to by Governor James Wright in his letter to the Board of Trade of November

---

90. Ga. Col. Rec., XVIII. 235-240 (act passed, July 28, 1757), 308-313 (act passed, March 27, 1759); "Account," loc. cit.
91. "Account," loc. cit.
92. Ga. Col. Rec., XVIII, 435-455 (act passed, May 1, 1760); "Account," loc. cit.

15, 1764.[93] The act carried a suspending clause and was confirmed by the crown on June 23, 1761.[94] The bills authorized by it bore the date of February 17, 1762, and the entire issue was in circulation in 1764. This sum, added to the "certificates" still outstanding, made a total circulation of Ł8,237 sterling in that year[95] in a colony whose population consisted of 6,800 whites and 4,500 blacks.[96]

By 1764, although Georgia's experience with bills of credit had been but of short duration, the paper issues of the colony had come to be looked upon as indispensable to its trade and prosperity. Governor Wright, in his letter transmitting the "Account" of 1764, indicated the feeling of the colony when he besought the Lords of Trade to interest themselves, should the occasion arise, in preventing a repeal of the colony's loan act. "If we lose that," he wrote, "be assured my Lord's t'will Reduce us to the Greatest Distress, for its Scarce Possible to Carry the Common

---

93. C. O. 323/19, L. C. P.
94. Acts of the Privy Council, Colonial, 1745-1766, p. 802.
95. "Account" of 1764, loc. cit. It will be noted that all issues were in sterling terms, a practice that probably grew out of the fact that the sterling sola bills had long formed an important ingredient in the colony's currency supply (vide supra, p. 128).
96. Greene and Harrington, American Population before 1790, p. 181. The legal tender currency of South Carolina with perhaps 40,000 and 80,000 to 90,000 blacks (ibid., p. 175), was the equivalent of only Ł15,000.

Occurances in Life, even with what Cash money we now have[;] and if we Lose any of that it will near Ruin us, and hurt the Province Exceedingly."[97]

---

97. Wright to B. T., December 15, 1764, C. O. 323/19, L. C. P.

CHAPTER IX

THE INTRODUCTION OF PAPER CURRENCY IN VIRGINIA; THE BRITISH AND SCOTTISH MERCHANTS' PROTESTS; THE CURRENCY ACT OF 1764

Money, the acknowledged Sinews of War was necessary, immediately necessary; Troops could not be levied and supported without it; of Gold and Silver, there was indeed some ... in the Hands of Individuals, but the Publick could not command it. Did there not result from hence a Necessity, an absolute Necessity of our having Recourse to a Paper Currency, as the only Resource from which we could draw Relief?

-- Robert Carter Nicholas on the introduction of paper currency in Virginia in 1755.

The bad Effect and pernicious Operation of the legal Tender annex'd to Paper Bills of Credit are universally admitted, and have been severely felt in most of your Majesty's American Colonies; and to shew the Sense of the Merchants of the principal Cities of Great-Britain upon the Subject, we beg leave to subjoin their Memorials ..., complaining of the Losses they have sustained, and the Confusion that has arisen from the Introduction of this impolitic, as well as fraudulent System into the Colonies of Virginia and North-Carolina.

-- Representation of the Board of Trade, 1764, recommending the adoption of the Currency Act of 1764.

From and after the first day of September, 1764, no act, order, resolution, or vote of assembly, in any of his Majesty's colonies or plantations in America, shall be made, for creating or issuing any paper bills or bills of credit of any kind ..., declaring such ... to be legal tender in payment of any bargains, contracts, debts, dues, or demands whatsoever.

-- Currency Act of 1764.

> Virginia Money has fallen a little, and what then, has not War evil Effects all the World over. See the Stocks & Credits at Home where Thousands of Innocents suffer under faith or having faith in Government, more than a few Pedlars do, trading to Virginia, that makes such a mighty disturbance, as to shake all the Northern Colonys; the Loss on Virginia Paper was honestly acquired, by the Governments exerting itself in the common cause, had it looked on tamely as Maryland did, like an unnatural Offspring, it had not been blamd, perhaps Commended.
>
> -- John Watts, New York merchant, to General Robert Monckton, April 14, 1764.

VIRGINIA was the last of the thirteen colonies to have recourse to a paper currency. Such exchange of commodities as her rural, slave-labor economy necessitated, devoted as it was to the production of a staple crop that could be exported directly to England, had been effected through the media of book credit, bills of exchange, tobacco notes, and the limited amount of gold and silver that circulated in the colony. Moreover, the necessity of financing a war against a foreign enemy, which, both north and south, had been the cause of the introduction of paper currency in so many other colonies, had not confronted Virginia until in 1753 the French encroached upon land claimed by her in what is now western Pennsylvania.

Nor did Virginia on this occasion emit paper currency until other means of raising the funds necessary had failed. The truth is, that in a struggle of the magnitude of the French and Indian War, the colonies' only means of timely and adequate exertion was the issuance of bills of credit. No colony succeeded in supplying the funds by any other method. This was obvious to men in all classes at the time, but has been lost sight of since because later writers, filled with the enthusiasm of those embarked in a sacred crusade for "sound" money, have found it more convenient to write the history of colonial currency everywhere from the well-publicized happenings at certain periods in New England, and more particularly in Rhode Island, than to examine the facts elsewhere.[1]

On February 14, 1754, after the return of Major George Washington from his trip to the French on the Allegheny, Governor Robert Dinwiddie convened the House of Burgesses in order that they might take steps to combat the encroachments of the French, now presenting such a formidable menace. The Burgesses voted ₤10,000 and authorized the treasurer to borrow that sum at six per cent interest pending the raising of the money by a tax.[2] It was one thing, however, to authorize the treasurer to borrow, but another thing to raise the

---

1. When we substitute reflection for emotion, we find that the answer to the question, What is sound money? is far from simple. See for instance the observations of the Board of Governors of the Federal Reserve System on the objectives of monetary control, Federal Reserve Bulletin, XXIII, 827-828 (September, 1937).

2. William A. Hening, Statutes at Large of Virginia (1819 ed.), VI, p. 418 (27 Geo. II, c. 1).

money by such means. On March 18, Governor Dinwiddie wrote to Colonel Joshua Frye, who was in charge of the Virginia forces: "Money is scarce, and I have been much disappointed by the Treasurer, who says he has none, nor can he borrow any."[3] A little later Dinwiddie induced the council to borrow ₤2,000 from the fund arising from the tax of two shillings per hogshead on all tobacco exported. This was but a temporary expedient; money was scarce and continued hard to raise.[4]

The defeat of the Virginia forces under George Washington at Fort Necessity in mid-summer indicated that a greater exertion was necessary to defend the frontiers and expel the French. In October the Burgesses voted ₤20,000 to be raised by a tax.[5] This was supplemented by aid from England.[6] With the coming of

---

3. "Official Records of Robert Dinwiddie," I, 110, in Virginia Historical Society, Collections (new series), Vol. III. Hereinafter cited as Dinwiddie.

4. D. to Col. Fairfax, June 27, 1754, Dinwiddie, I, 224.

George Hume, of Culpepor County, in writing on August 27, 1754, to his brother, Captain Jno. Hume, who was serving in the British Navy, makes some interesting comments on the scarcity of money. "Money is so scarce," he writes, "that it is a rare thing to see a dollar, and at publick places where great monied men will bet on cock fights, horse races, etc., the noise is not now as it used to be -- one pistol[e] to 2 or 3 pistoles to one -- it is now common [to] cry 2 cows and calves to one or 3 to one or sometimes 4 hogshead tob^o to one and y^t gives no price, so I do not know how we shall maintain a war, the French [have] very much the advantage of us." William and Mary Quarterly (1st series), XII (1903-1904), 240.

5. Hening, VI, 435-440 (28 Geo. II, c. 1).
6. Dinwiddie to B. T., November 16, 1754, Dinwiddie,

the British forces under General Braddock early in 1755, and the need of Virginia support, the Burgesses were again convened. They voted ₤6,000 to be raised by a lottery, and then, in order that the funds provided by the taxes levied the autumn before might be made immediately available, authorized the treasurer to issue ₤20,000 in legal tender treasury notes bearing five per cent interest.[7] Robert Carter Nicholas, a member of the House of Burgesses at the time and later the treasurer of the colony, but never an exponent of paper currency as such, later expressed the logic of the circumstances in these words: "Money, the acknowledged Sinews of War was necessary, immediately necessary; Troops could not be levied and supported without it; of Gold and Silver, there was indeed some, what Quantity I do not know, in the Hands of Individuals, but the Publick could not command it. Did there not result from hence a Necessity of our having Recourse to a Paper Currency, as the only Resource from which we could draw Relief?"[8]

The disaster that befell the expedition under

I, 401. "His M'y has been graciously pleas'd to order [₤]10,000 in Specie and a C't to draw for [₤]10,000 more."

7. Hening, VI, 453-461 (28 Geo. II, c. 1); 467 (c. 2).

8. Letter from Nicholas to Messrs. Purdie and Dixon, publishers of the Virginia Gazette, dated September 22, 1773, and appearing in the issue of September 30, 1773. Nicholas was then treasurer of the colony. William and Mary Quarterly (1st series), XX, 246-247.

General Braddock made necessary the raising of increased funds to retrieve what had been lost. Governor Dinwiddie immediately (July) called the Burgesses together and that body voted an additional ₤40,000 in treasury notes similar in form to those authorized earlier in the year, but to remain current until 1760.[9]

When the Burgesses again met in October, they discussed the possibility of erecting a loan office to provide a revenue to carry on the war. A bill authorizing the emission of ₤200,000 to be current on loan for eight years passed that body, but the Governor opposed the project, and the council rejected the bill. Dinwiddie, seeing that the Burgesses had broken into factions and were disputing among themselves, dissolved the assembly and took "his Chance of new Members."[10]

The newly elected Burgesses voted sums of ₤25,000 and ₤30,000 in March, 1756, to be made available through the issuance of the familiar treasurer's notes bearing five per cent interest, and made provision for retiring

---

9. Ibid., pp. 528-529 (29 Geo. II, c. 1).
10. Journals of the House of Burgesses, 1752-1758, pp. 319-332 (October 27 to November 8) passim. (Hereinafter cited as JHB.) The bill was entitled a bill, "For supplying the Deficiencies of the several Funds for the Protection of this Colony against the Encroachments and Depredations of the French and Indians, and for advancing and securing the public Credit"; Legislative Journals of the Council of Colonial Virginia, III, 1156 (November 8, 1755); Dinwiddie to Gov. Arthur Dobbs, November 13, 1755, Dinwiddie, II, 266; D. to B. T., November 15, 1755, ibid., 269-270.

them by June 30, 1760, from the proceeds of taxes levied in the issuing acts.[11] There was one other issue at this session; the sum of ₤10,000 was authorized (₤12,000 seems to have been issued) to indemnify the owners of tobacco lost when certain of the public tobacco warehouses were burned. These notes bore no interest, but had the same legal tender quality as did the notes of former issues. They were to be retired by December 15, 1757.[12]

The various sums in treasurer's notes issued on tax funds were not voted, however, without a consideration of the alternative of establishing a loan office. Specie was scarce in Virginia at the very outset of hostilities. And the situation was not improved by the fact that what little there was was collected and sent northward by the practice of the army paymasters of selling sterling bills of exchange in Virginia to provide funds for the army stationed in New York.[13] It is not surprising, then, to find the March session of the House of Burgesses in 1756 opening with petitions urging the scarcity of cash and praying for a loan office. "The Freeholders and Merchants of the County of

---

11. Hening, VII, 18 (29 Geo. II, c. 1); p. 32 (c. 2).
12. Ibid., p. 49 (29 Geo. II, c. 9); Report to Board of Trade, 1764, C. O. 323/19, L. C. P.
13. Dinwiddie to Henry Fox, May 24, 1756, Dinwiddie, II, 415.

Caroline,"[14] "sundry Inhabitants of the Counties of Goochland, Hanover, Henrico, Chesterfield, and Charles-City," and "the Inhabitants of the County of Halifax,"[15] all petitioned for relief in this form. An issue of Ł300,000 or more on loan was suggested. The proposal was referred to a committee with instructions to bring in a bill,[16] and on April 20, Richard Bland for the

---

14. JHB, 1752-1758, p. 339-340 (March 26, 1756): "A Petition of the Freeholders and Merchants, of the County of Caroline, setting forth, That by Reason of the great Scarcity of Cash, occasioned by the Shortness of this and the two preceeding Crops, a proper Medium is wanting to support the necessary Occasions of Trade; whereby they are rendered unable to Support their Families, and pay those Taxes which the Incursions and Depredations of a bloody and faithless Enemy, make so necessary at this Time; and praying that this House would apply a proper Remedy, whereby the great Inconvenience of the Want of Specie may be prevented either by erecting a Bank and Loan-Office, or such other Method as this House shall think fit, the Charge of which they would support, was presented to the House and read."

15. Ibid., p. 357 (April 6, 1756). "A Petition of sundry Inhabitants of the Counties of Goochland, Hanover, Henrico, Chesterfield, and Charles-City, setting forth, that great Inconveniencies have arisen to most of the Inhabitants of the Colony, and are like to continue, for Want of a proper Circulation of Credit, insomuch that Business is obstructed and many Families are likely to be ruined, by having their Goods sold for less than half the Value, thro' the great Scarcity of Cash, and praying that a Loan Office may be established, and Paper Currency may issue, to the amount of Ł300,000 or any greater Sum that may answer the present Exigencies."

"Also a Petition of the Inhabitants of the County of Halifax to the same Purpose, were severally presented to the House and read ...."

16. At the time of the presentation of the Caroline petition, Edmund Pendleton, Peter Hedgman, Richard Bland, and John Baylor were appointed a committee to bring in "a Bill or Bills ... pursuant to the Prayer of the ... Petition." Ibid., p. 340 (March 26). After

committee brought in a loan office bill bearing the same title as the one negatived by the council the year before.[17] The bill was considered on several occasions by the committee of the whole. In the meantime, the several issues of treasurer's notes on tax funds were voted, and before the house had come to any determination of the loan office bill, it was prorogued by the governor.[18]

When a year later in April, 1757, the House of Burgesses again met to consider the matter of voting war supplies, it again received several loan office petitions. But by this time the sentiment of the Burgesses seems definitely to have crystalized against such an expedient and the petitions were uniformly rejected by the committee to which they were referred.[19] The committee's action on one of the points in the Albemarle petition, however, indicated the direction that things were to take. This petition prayed "that no more of the last Ł40,000 Paper Currency," which bore interest, might "be issued, and that the Paper Money" thereafter to be issued might "not bear Interest." By

---

the other petitions were received, Archibald Cary and William Samuel Harris were added to the committee.
17. Ibid., p. 372.
18. Ibid., pp. 383, 384-385, 386, 394, 397.
19. Petitions from the "Freeholders and Housekeepers of Albemarle County," the "Freeholders and Merchants of Louisa County," and "the Inhabitants of the County of Stafford" were received. Ibid., pp. 427-428.

this time the charge on the colony was so great and the task of raising further large sums so formidable, that the Burgesses, on a hint, it was said,[20] from Lord Loudoun, the newly appointed commander in chief in America and the governor in chief of Virginia, decided that further issues of treasurer's notes should not bear interest. Moreover, new non-interest-bearing notes were to be issued in exchange for the interest-bearing notes already in circulation. In consequence of this decision, the act of June 8, 1757, voting Ł80,000 in non-interest-bearing notes for the further support of the war also provided for issuing Ł99,962 10s. in similar notes to retire the older interest-bearing notes still in circulation. The new notes were to be drawn in by tax funds by March 1, 1765.[21]

Later issues were of a similar nature. From 1755 to 1762, inclusive, Ł440,000, exclusive of the exchange issue of 1757, were issued to finance the colony's contribution to the war. These issues, together with their

---

20. Jerman Baker to Duncan Rose, London, February 15, 1764, William and Mary Quarterly (1st series), X (1903-04), 240. Baker was a Virginian. The Virginia government was immediately under a lieutenant governor. The position of governor was a sinecure. Loudoun was the absentee governor. The lieutenant governor in the colony at the time was still the bluff Scotchman, Robert Dinwiddie.

21. Hening, VII, 69-87 (April session, 1757, 30 Geo. II, c. 1); JHB, 1752-1758, p. 491, assented to June 8, 1757.

periods of circulation and the tax funds provided for their redemption, may be followed in detail in Table XXVIII. Some idea of the sums outstanding may be obtained from Figure XVI.

Robert Carter Nicholas later described the introduction and use of bills of credit in Virginia as follows:

> Paper Currencies, I believe, had obtained in several other Colonies on this Continent long before an Introduction of such a species of Money amongst us was thought of here. Our Assembly had so little Inclination to it, that, at the first Commencement of those Hostilities, which were introductory to the late War, when they were called upon for Aids, they preferred borrowing the Sum desired, even at an advanced Interest. In the Progress of the War, many and earnest Requisitions from the Crown were made of our Assembly; the Sums required, from Time to Time, were so very considerable, that there was no Prospect of borrowing them; could they have been had, the Interest would have proved so enormous a Burthen, that the Country could not have borne it, without distressing the People amazingly. Hence arose an absolute necessity of having Recourse to a Paper Currency. The Sums voted, at different Times, were upon proper Estimates; and Funds, the most ample and unexceptionable, were established for the Redemption of the Treasury Notes; indeed, I can say with great Truth, that the Assembly was so scrupulous in this Matter, that, rather than there should be the smallest Doubt of their Sufficiency, they valued the funds at much less, than those, who were best acquainted with them, were persuaded they would yield. The demand of large Sums was almost annual for several successive Years; the Periods of Redemption of the different Emissions were various, [because] it would have been too burthensome to the People to have been obliged to sink an entire Emission by Taxes to be collected within the year. 22

---

22. Letter in Purdie and Dixon's Virginia Gazette, July 29, 1773: reprinted in William and Mary Quarterly, XX, 232-233.

There is no reason to believe that this is other than the honest account by an honest and exceptionally well-informed man of the reasons for the introduction of paper currency into Virginia. It was a measure of war-time finance dictated by inexorable circumstance, and not, as some have thought, the result of a debtor-creditor struggle.

Virginia's load was eased by her participation in the several parliamentary grants. The precise sum is not ascertainable, but such scanty information as has come to light may be seen in the note below.[23] None of the money so received was applied to the redemption of the outstanding treasurer's notes. It was, however, applied in lieu of additional issues to the further conduct of the war.[24]

The effect of the introduction of paper upon prices and exchange rates is not easily untangled. There were other disturbing elements. Short crops influenced the price of Virginia's staple commodity, tobacco. The sale by the representatives of the crown of bills of exchange drawn upon the treasury in England doubtless in-

---

23. Of the ₤50,000 sterling voted Virginia and the Carolinas in 1757 (30 Geo. II, c. 26), Virginia received ₤32,269. George L. Beer, British Colonial Policy, 1754-1765, p. 55, n. 3. Information concerning the colony's share of later grants is lacking.
24. Report of the Treasurer, John Robinson, to B. T., 1764. C. O. 323/19, L. C. P.

TABLE XXVIII

VIRGINIA BILLS OF CREDIT

Year	Act (in Hening)	Issued £	Redeemable on or before	Purpose	No.
1755	(May)[x] 28 Geo. II, c. 2	20,000[z]	1756, June 30	War	1
1755	(Aug.) 29 Geo. II, c. 1	40,000[z]	1760, June 30	War	2
1756	(Mar.) 29 Geo. II, c. 1	25,000[z]	do.	War	3
1756	(Mar.) 29 Geo. II, c. 2	30,000[z]	do.	War	4
1756	(Mar.) 29 Geo. II, c. 9	12,000	1757, Dec. 15	Tobacco burnt in public warehouses	5
1757	(Apr.) 30 Geo. II, c. 1	80,000	1765, Mar. 1	War	6
1757	do.	99,962	do.	To redeem issues (2), (3), (4)	7
1758	(Mar.) 31 Geo. II, c. 1	32,000	do.	War	8
1758	(Sept.) 32 Geo. II, c. 1	57,000	1766, Sept. 14	War	9
1759	(Feb.) 32 Geo. II, c. 1	52,000	1768, Apr. 20	War	10
1759	(Nov.) 33 Geo. II, c. 1	10,000	1769, Oct. 20	War £5,000 re-issued out of (5), (6); £5,000 new issue	11

(continued)

TABLE XXVIII

(continued)

VIRGINIA BILLS OF CREDIT

Year	Act (in Hening)	Issued ₤	Redeemable on or before	Purpose	No.
1760	(Mar.) 33 Geo. II, c. 1	20,000	1768, Oct. 10	War	12
1760	(May) 33 Geo. II, c. 1	32,000	1769, Oct. 20	War Cherokees	13
1762	(Mar.) 2 Geo. II, c. 1	30,000	do.	War	14

Total ₤539,962 or ₤440,000 exclusive of exchange issue of 1756 (7).

---

   x Month session began
   z Bore 5 per cent interest

The taxes levied to retire the several issues were varied and defy summation in the space available. They were taxes on land, white tithables, negro tithable, negroes imported, and tobacco exported.

Source: Hening, Statutes; JHB; Report to B. T., 1764, C. O. 323/19, L. C. P.

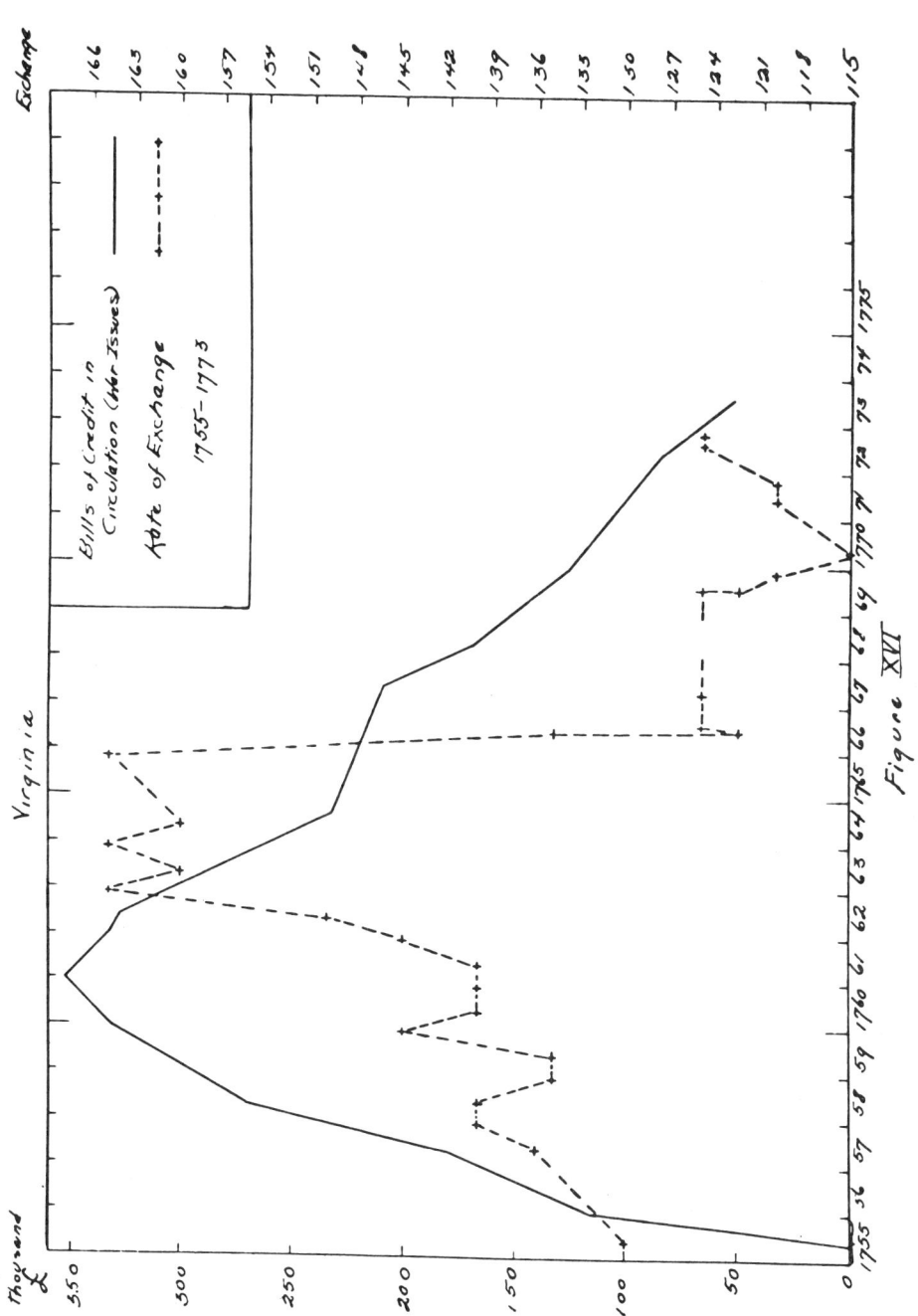

Figure XVI

fluenced both prices and exchange rates. It tended to retard the rise of prices by carrying off specie to the northern colonies and thus diminishing the amount of money that would otherwise have been in circulation in Virginia. Moreover, the increase in sterling bills offered in the market by this activity and, more latterly, by the drawing of bills of exchange upon the parliamentary grants tended to keep the price of exchange from rising. This in turn tended to keep prices from rising as fast as they otherwise would have. The greatest rise in exchange rates did not come until near the end, and after the close, of the war. Some idea of the behavior of exchange rates may be gained by reference to Figure XVI.

These fluctuations in exchange, however, had serious repercussions in England. It will be recalled that in 1728 Virginia valued Spanish silver at a rate slightly below that allowed by the Proclamation of Queen Anne. As a result of this enactment Ł125 Virginia currency were equivalent, at par, to Ł100 sterling. For three decades exchange had fluctuated about this figure. In 1749, six years before the introduction of paper currency, in order that disputes might be prevented, an act was passed authorizing the sheriffs in executing judgments for sterling debts after June 10, 1751, to levy the sums due in Virginia currency at the rate of Ł125 Virginia currency to £100 sterling.[25] In due course the law was confirmed by the crown with no one raising objection.[26] In November, 1751, however, the merchants of Liverpool and Bristol trading to Virginia each presented a memorial to the Board of Trade, praying that the law might be disallowed.[27] The substance of the memorials was the same. It was urged that the rate of exchange in Virginia for many years past had scarcely ever been as low as 125, the figure set in the act, "but generally much higher and sometimes Forty p^r. Cent and Upwards and upon an Average for Seven Years past [had] been at about thirty three and 1/3^d p^r. Cent and [that] there [was] no prospect of its being lower." As a result, the merchants represented that they were "laid under great hardships" and that they would "be considerable sufferers" if they were forced to receive their sterling debts at the figure established by the law.[28] As the law had already been confirmed, the Board of Trade informed the merchants that it "could not entertain the petition[s]," but recommended that they should "apply

---

25. Hening, V, 540 (October session 1748, 22 Geo. II, c. 12); passed May 1, 1749, JHB, 1742-1749, p. 400.
26. *Acts of the Privy Council, Colonial, 1745-1766*, #159.
27. *Board of Trade Journal, 1749/50-1753*, p. 230 (November 19, 1751).
28. Memorial of the Bristol Merchants. C. O. 5/1328, Library of Congress Transcripts; Memorial of Liverpool Merchants, **ibid.**

in the first instance to his Majesty," whereupon the petitions were withdrawn.[29]

It appears from the records of the Privy Council that the memorials from the Liverpool and Bristol merchants, together with a petition of similar tenor from the London merchants trading to Virginia, were presented to the Privy Council and referred to its Committee on the same day that they were withdrawn from the Board of Trade. Two weeks later, they were referred, as was customary in such cases, to the Board of Trade.[30] There is no indication, however, that the body gave the matter attention. The Journal is silent, and it was not until three years later, that the matter again came up. Certainly the hardships suffered by the merchants could not have been great, or the matter would not have been allowed to languish so long. The result of the renewed examination of the matter was that on August 27, 1754, an instruction was sent to the Virginia governor directing that he "earnestly recommend ... to the assembly" of his colony that it pass another act similar to that passed in 1749, but taking care that no clause "for regulating the rate of exchange to the prejudice" of the British merchants should be inserted.[31]

---

29. Board of Trade Journal, 1749/50-1753, p. 233 (November 26, 1751).
30. Acts of the Privy Council, Colonial, 1745-1766, #159.
31. Ibid., Board of Trade Journal, 1754-58, pp.

When the House of Burgesses convened on May 1, 1755, Governor Dinwiddie transmitted his instruction to that body, and it forthwith set about amending the law complained of. The result was that the act of 1749 was altered so as to provide that sterling debts should be discharged in current money at such difference of exchange as the courts should think just.[32] This amendment, unless it were abused by the courts, would appear calculated to do justice to both Virginia debtors and British creditors and was in accord with the practice elsewhere, in New York and Pennsylvania, for example.

Nothing further was heard from the British merchants until news was received in England of the passage in the summer of 1757 of the Virginia act for emitting ₤80,000 in non-interest-bearing bills for the support of the war and ₤99,962 10s. in similar bills to be exchanged for the older interest-bearing issues. These bills, as had been the older issues, were made a legal tender for all debts except the king's quit rents, which remained payable in sterling. Sterling debts if paid in bills, however, were subject to the provisions of the act of 1749 as amended in 1755, whereby a sum in

---

62-64 (August 6, 1754); Labaree, Royal Instructions, I, #236.
  32. JHB, 1752-1758, pp. 232, 248, 293; Hening, VI, 478-483 (May session, 28 Geo. II, c. 7); passed July 9, 1755, JHB, 1752-1758, p. 293.

Virginia currency sufficient to satisfy the full sterling value of the debt was collected. In the fall of 1757 the colonial agent, James Abercromby, wrote that the London merchants were alarmed over the legal tender clause in the new act (although it was the same clause that had been incorporated in the issuing acts of the preceeding two years), and that they were resolved to apply to the crown to have the act disallowed. Abercromby's letters indicate that at various times throughout the ensuing winter and spring he tried to defend the Virginia enactment in his discussions with the merchants.[33]

The arguments of Abercromby and those of Governor Dinwiddie, who had returned to London, were to no avail, however, and in June, 1758, the London and the Bristol merchants presented memorials that as thoroughly misrepresented the case in Virginia as one may well conceive to be possible. The act of 1749 was still complained of as being in force. The whole argument centered around the assumption that by the provisions of the act of 1749 and the legal tender provisions of the emitting act of 1757 the British merchants would be forced to receive their sterling debts in bills of

---

33. James Abercromby to Governor Dinwiddie, London, November 3, 1757; Abercromby to Richard Corbin, March 8, 1758; Abercromby to John Blair, March 31, 1758; Abercromby Letter Book, MS, Virginia State Library, Richmond.

credit at only 25 per cent advance, although sterling, they alleged, had risen to 45 per cent.[34] The merchants asked that an instruction might be given directing the governor of Virginia to procure an amendment to the acts of 1749 and 1757 providing that all debts contracted before their passage should be payable in sterling money only, and "that all debts that have been heretofore contracted, or that may hereafter be contracted in the course of ... Trade or otherwise between his Majesties subjects in Great Britain & Virginia if not otherwise expressly stipulated shall be deemed Sterling debts & made payable according to Sterling or lawfull money of Great Britain," and that current money of Virginia, bills or specie, should not be deemed a legal tender in the satisfaction of such debts unless the creditor should consent to receive it as such at the real difference of sterling exchange.[35] Through the inefficiency of the Board of Trade, which on October 29, 1755 had received a copy of the amending act of 1755; the delinquency of the agent, James Abercromby, who had been instructed by Governor Dinwiddie to press for the confirmation of the acts passed in 1755; and the apparent haziness of Dinwiddie's own memory; the all-im-

---

34. Board of Trade Journal, 1754-1758, p. 410 (June 21, 1755); London Merchants Memorial, C. O. 5/1329, L. C. T.
35. Ibid.

portant amending act of 1755 seems not to have been called to the attention of the Board.[36] The result of this misrepresentation and ineptitude was that on February 9, 1759, an instruction in the form prayed for by the merchants was issued.[37]

On July 14, 1759, Francis Fauquier, who had succeeded Dinwiddie as lieutenant governor of Virginia, in a letter to the Board of Trade acknowledged the receipt of the instruction, which he promised to transmit to the assembly at its next meeting; and which, he wrote,

> I apprehend will meet with no Difficulty of any sort; as I am sure it is the Desire and Design of the Legislature to give the Merch^{ts}. full Security in their property here. This they supposed was effectually done by the Laws now in force, and I cannot help thinking that if the Merch^{ts}. had paid due Attention to their present Situation in Regard thereto they would have been of that Opinion themselves.[38]

On November 1, at the opening of the fall session of the assembly, Governor Fauquier, as he had promised,

---

36. Board of Trade Journal, 1754-1758, p. 181 (October 29, 1755); Dinwiddie to Abercromby, September 6, 1755, Dinwiddie, II, 197.

37. Board of Trade Journal, 1754-1758, July 5, 6, 12, 1758; Acts of the Privy Council, Colonial, 1754-1766, #360; Labaree, Royal Instructions, I, #344. It is interesting to note that on January 24, 1759, the day after it had drafted the new instruction pursuant to the order of Council, the Board of Trade took up the Virginia laws of 1755, among which was the act amending the act of 1749. About two weeks later (February 8) "the merchants trading to Virginia" made application for a copy of the act, which was granted them. After this date they certainly could not plead ignorance of its existence. Board of Trade Journal, 1759-1763.

38. C. O. 5/1329, L. C. T.

transmitted the new instruction to the Burgesses. That body, however, was not so amenable to the suggestion of new legislation as Fauquier had hoped. On the contrary, the Burgesses, being under the impression that four years earlier they had remedied the evil complained of, not unreasonably resolved, that by the amending act of 1755

> the Security of the Merchants of Great Britain in the Recovery of Sterling Debts due to them from this Colony is provided for, and their Property secured in the fullest and amplest Manner; and that they have not any just Cause of Complaint on that Head. 39

It was felt by the assembly that Abercromby, the agent, had been remiss, as indeed he had, in not calling the attention of the merchants to the amending act of 1755. In fact, the dissatisfaction of the Burgesses with Abercromby, who was joint agent for governor, council, and house, antedated this time. In the spring of 1759 they had appointed an agent of their own, one Edward Montagu of the Middle Temple, by an act drawn after the example of a South Carolina act. Abercromby, however, continued on as the agent of the governor and council. A committee of the assembly had been appointed to correspond with the new agent. On December 12, it wrote him concerning the matter complained of by the merchants. He was to inform them of the provisions of the amending act of 1755 and to point out to them that

---

39. JHB, 1758-1761, p. 134 (November 8, 1759); p. 141 (November 8).

they were better off in being allowed a sum in current money sufficient to buy a bill of exchange for the sterling sum in question than they would be if they were paid in sterling coin, if such were available; for the former method of payment would place their funds in England without loss, while by the latter method they would lose the freight and insurance, which in wartime were considerable. Moreover, it was pointed out that the merchants had nothing to fear from the courts, for it was "notorious" that they had always fixed the exchange allowed at the very highest rate prevailing. The merchants had feared that the Virginia paper currency would not retain its credit. In answer to this it was pointed out that exchange was now ten per cent lower than it had been in the late war, when nothing but gold and silver had circulated.[40]

Whether as a result of Montagu's efforts or not, quiet prevailed for a period of three years and no further complaints were heard from the British merchants

---

40. Committee of Correspondence to Montagu, December 12, 1759, Virginia Magazine, X, 342-353: Instructions to Montagu, same date, ibid., XI, 1-5. The argument with respect to the loss that the British merchants would suffer in transfering sterling money to England is not as explicitly stated in this instruction as it is in later documents. But this is what they were getting at. For the sake of clarity I have given a more explicit statement of the reasoning than was contained in this correspondence. The defense here hinted at was more fully developed later.

until late in 1762. No further treasurer's notes had been issued in 1761, but in 1762 an additional £30,000 were emitted. Moreover, throughout 1761 and 1762 exchange had risen from 140 to 165. These facts caused the merchants to renew their complaints. The London merchants trading to Virginia delivered in a memorial "complaining of the pernecious effects of the large emission of paper bills of credit" in Virginia. Complaints were also received from another quarter. Richard Corbin, the deputy receiver of the quit rents in Virginia, sent over a memorial to the treasury. He urged that although the treasurer's notes were not made a legal tender in payment of the quit rent, yet their issuance had banished gold and silver from the colony and he was forced to receive the notes for want of other money. Since he received them at only 25 per cent advance, and since exchange had risen to 60 per cent, his majesty's revenue was by so much the loser.[41] Corbin's memorial was referred to the Board of Trade shortly after that body had received the memorial of the London merchants.[42]

The receipt of these complaints was the signal for a re-examination of the question, and as soon as Montagu's

---

41. C. O. 5/1330, L. C. T.
42. Board of Trade Journal, 1759-1763, December 16, 1762.

health would permit, two days were given over to a hearing and determination of the matter. Montagu and Abercromby represented the colony; memorials were delivered in for the Glasgow and the Liverpool merchants by Edward Athawes and Sir Ellis Cunliffe, respectively; and the agents and several of the merchants, attending, were heard. The result was favorable to the merchants at every point. The Board resolved that the amending act of 1755 did "not give security to the ... merchants, in the recovery of sterling debts due to them ..." and threatened Virginia with an extension of the Currency Act of 1751 if she should any longer persist in denying to the merchants the justice she had been instructed to grant by the instruction of 1759.[43]

Nor did the Board stop here. It went on to the consideration of an act passed in the colony in 1761. The treasurer's notes issued in 1757 and the spring of 1758 had been made redeemable by 1765. The periods of the later issues, as was the custom in the colonies in such cases, were extended, in this case to 1766, 1768, and 1769. This gave rise to a problem. People, instead of paying their taxes in the notes of the particular issue to be retired by the tax, paid them in whatever notes they happened to have on hand. The result

---

43. *Ibid.*, December 22, 1762; January 17, 25, 31, February 1, 2, 4, 5, 7, 1763.

was that notes of the later issues accumulated in the treasury, while those of the earlier issues, which alone could be destroyed according to the provisions of the issuing acts, remained in circulation. Efforts to have the people bring in the earlier issues in exchange for the later ones were of no avail. In order to make it possible to destroy the notes accumulated in the treasury, the legislature had in 1761 passed a law extending the circulation of all issues until 1769, but providing that all issues, as they were drawn into the treasury in payment of taxes, might be destroyed. The sole aim of the act was to facilitate the seasonable retiring and burning of the notes. Technically, however, it constituted a lengthening of the periods of the notes of the earlier issues, and the governor was not permitted to assent to such a bill without a suspending clause. Throughout the whole period, the governors had broken through their instructions in assenting to the various issuing acts without requiring a suspending clause and had justified themselves on the plea of necessity. Since, however, the same degree of necessity could scarcely be pleaded in the case of the act under discussion, the governor had insisted on a suspending clause and one was included in the act. It was unfortunate that the act came before the Board of Trade at a moment when the Board was in an ill humor towards Virginia. The act was given short shrift; it was resolved "to be liable to great objection and to contradict the tenor" of the resolutions so lately adopted, and was laid aside. This was most unfortunate, for the failure of the colony to secure the approval of the act in large measure made it possible for the Virginia treasurer, John Robinson, to misapply the colony's funds as he did. Had the act been approved, the treasurer's notes that Robinson lent out to his friends would have been destroyed by the committee of assembly, and to a great extent the loss resulting from the treasurer's malfeasance would have been prevented.[44]

The resolutions of the Board of Trade upon the merchants' memorials had been sent over with dispatch, and when the Burgesses met in May, Governor Fauquier laid them before the assembly. The Burgesses, who were of the opinion that they had done the strictest justice to all creditors, and who, since they had heard nothing from the British merchants for three years, had, not without reason, thought them satisfied with the provisions of the amending act of 1755, felt "very sensibly" the reproach contained in the resolutions of the Board of Trade. None the less, they diligently set about ex-

---

44. Hening, VII, 465-466 (November session, 1761, 2 Geo. II, c. 2); Board of Trade Journal, 1759-1763, February 4, 1763.

amining the complaints contained in the merchants' memorials and in a memorial sent over by certain members of the Virginia council.[45]

The chief complaints were: (1) that the treasurer's notes had been issued on insufficient taxes; (2) that the notes had been made a legal tender; (3) that the act of 1749 permitting the payment of sterling debts in current money at 25 per cent advance was still in force, it having received the royal approbation; while the amending act of 1755 making such debts payable in current money at the actual difference of exchange, not having received such approval, was not; and (4) that, inconsistent as it may appear, since exchange had sometimes risen between the time that judgment was given at the prevailing rate and the time a bill of exchange could be purchased, the merchants were the loser, and such provision was inadequate.[46]

The Burgesses, after a full investigation and consideration of the points of complaint, presented with considerable eloquence what to the unbiased observer

---

45. _Legislative Journals of the Council of Colonial Virginia,_ III, 1281. On April 6, 1762, on the passage of the emitting act of that year, four members of the council, William and Thomas Nelson, Richard Corbin, the deputy receiver of the quit rents, and Phillip Ludwell Lee, dissented and drafted certain resolutions which were sent over to the Board of Trade by Governor Fauquier. _Board of Trade Journal,_ 1759-1763, p. 339 (March 2, 1763).

46. _Acts of the Privy Council, Colonial,_ 1745-1766, pp. 641-645.

would appear a full answer: (1) A committee had investigated the sufficiency of the taxes to retire the treasurer's notes according to their periods. These funds were pronounced adequate, although it appeared that the sheriffs, who collected the taxes in the various counties, had been delinquent in turning them in. That this might be corrected, the assembly directed that the delinquents should "be prosecuted on their Bonds." The Burgesses insisted, however, that "this Neglect in the Officers is very distinguishable from an Insufficiency in the Taxes." Although they believed the funds sufficient, as indeed they were, yet in order that their good faith might be made manifest, the Burgesses resolved, "... that if, by an Accident, [the funds] shall happen to fail, any Deficiency ought to be supplied by a new and adequate Tax." (2) As regards having made the notes a legal tender, it was urged with considerable reason, that since emissions of paper bills were the only means of defending the colony and obeying the requisitions of the crown, to have forced them as money upon the army and those that furnished supplies, while at the same time leaving their creditors at liberty to refuse the bills when they were in turn tendered them "would have been very unjust." Moreover, to have terminated the legal tender quality once the notes were in circulation would have been unjust to those who found themselves possessed of them in consequence of having received them as such. (3) That if the merchants believed the amending act of 1755 was not in force even though the Virginia courts considered it to be, the Burgesses conceived that "it would have been more for the interest of the merchants to have solicited his Majesty's approbation of that Law, if they thought it necessary [to its being in force], than to have founded Objections on its not being in Force." (4) As to the sufficiency of the method of satisfying sterling debts actually in force under the act of 1749 as amended in 1755, the Burgesses contended, that "as the Courts have constantly ... allowed the highest Rate of Exchange, as settled by the general Consent of all the Traders, at which Bills of Exchange upon Great Britain were sold at the Time, ... Sterling Debts are virtually paid in Treasury Notes, not according to their nominal Value, but according to the real Difference of Exchange between them and Sterling Money." Concerning losses occasioned by a rise in exchange between the time a judgment was given and a bill of exchange could be purchased, there was no way to prevent this. Moreover, if the merchants lost in such cases when exchange rose, they would gain when it fell, as it was then doing.[47]

---

47. <u>JHB,</u> 1761-1765, pp. 171-192, <u>passim.</u>

In summation, the House of Burgesses embodied its position in the following resolution:

> Resolved, That as the present Possessors of the Treasury Notes have received them under the Faith of a Law making them a legal Tender in all Payments, except for his Majesty's Quitrents, to alter the essential Quality of them now would be an Act of great Injustice to such Possessors; and that as the British Merchants have constantly received, and under the present Regulations of our Laws will continue to receive, such Notes for their Sterling Debts, according to the real Difference in Exchange between this Colony and Great Britain, at the Time of Payment, their Property is so secured as to make such Alteration unnecessary with Respect to them. 48

Lest it be suggested that no difference how plausible its reasons, the House of Burgesses was embarked upon some devious design of defrauding the British merchants from which it could not be dissuaded, it should perhaps be pointed out that concurrently with its deliberations discussed above it carried through an act repealing "An Act for relief of insolvent debtors, for the effectual discovery and more equal distribution of their estates," of which the merchants had complained. The repeal was effected before the merchants succeeded in having the law disallowed by the crown.[49]

The representation drafted by the Burgesses, to-

---

48. Ibid., p. 192.
49. Hening, VII, 549-563 (November session, 1762, 3 Geo. III, c. 8); 643 (May session, 1763, 3 Geo. III, c. 2); JHB, 1761-1765, pp. 171-197, passim; repealing act assented to, May 31, 1763, ibid., p. 196. The act repealed was disallowed because of the opposition of the merchants, July 20, 1763, Acts of the Privy Council, Colonial, 1745-1766, #511.

gether with the committee report as to the sufficiency of the taxes to retire the treasurer's notes and other relevant material, was sent by Fauquier to the Board of Trade. The merchants, upon application, were given copies of the various items, and after having perused them they asked to be heard.[50] In the meantime, as against this day, the Virginia committee of correspondence had written to Montagu, putting him in possession of the arguments upon which the Burgesses relied to demonstrate the justice of their action. They also transmitted a list of judgments granted since April, 1757, in the general court of Virginia in favor of persons residing in Great Britain, together with the rates of exchange allowed. The rates of exchange allowed in such actions from 1757 to 1764 may be followed in Table XXIX. A comparison of the judgments granted dur-

---

50. Board of Trade Journal, 1754-1763, October 14, November 24, 1763.

TABLE XXIX

Rates of exchange allowed in actions for sterling money.

		% advance			% advance
1757,	April	37 1/2	1761,	April	40
	October	40		October	45
1758,	April	40	1762,	April	50
	October	35		October	65
1759,	April	35	1763,	April	60
	October	45		October	65
1760,	April	40	1764,	April	60
	October	40			

Reference: C. O. 323/19, L. C. P.

ing the period, 1757-1763, with the names of the signers of the London merchants' petition of 1762 reveals that many of them had received judgments at the advanced rates indicated in the table above. Certainly these signers had little reason for believing that the amending act of 1755 was not in force.[51]

---

51. The following signers of the merchants' petition, seven out of a list of eighteen, sued and received judgment at a higher exchange than 125 from April, 1757, to April, 1763, inclusive. The number following the name indicates the number of judgments obtained.

Edward Athawes	1	
W. Bowden (or Bowder)	4	
Capel Hanbury	1	
Cary, Moorey, and Welch	7	
Lyon(el) Lyde	1	
James Buchanan	1	
Bosworth and Griffith	1	(Gabriel Griffith)

(Continued, notes, next page.)

The Board of Trade gave over December 8, 1763, to a hearing at which the merchants and Montagu, the Virginia agent, presented their respective cases. "It was declared on the part of the merchants, that, if the paper currency was so regulated, that judgments for sterling debts due to the merchants of Great Britain should not be discharged, but in sterling money in Virginia or Great Britain, they would be well satisfied." After consideration, the Board "approved this proposition of the merchants, and were of opinion, that any further neglect of the Legislature of Virginia to give redress to the complaints of the merchants would be neither just [n]or equitable." The merchants and the agent were then informed that if Virginia "any longer refused doing justice to the British merchants, and did not comply with what was now proposed, the Board should think it their duty to advise his Majesty to lay the matter before Parliament." The merchants expressed themselves as "well satisfied" with this determination, and the Board ordered a letter embodying this direction drafted to Governor Fauquier.[52]

The letter did not reach Virginia until after the January session of the Burgesses had adjourned. In

---

References: Merchants' Petition, Acts of the Privy Council, Colonial, 1745-1766, p. 643; Virginia Magazine, XII, 1-5.

52. Board of Trade Journal, 1759-1763, p. 418.

consequence, it was not until October, 1764, that the threat of the Board of Trade was presented to the assembly. By this time, however, Parliament had already passed the Currency Act of 1764, so that whatever action the Burgesses might take was of little moment insofar as its effect upon paper currency regulation was concerned. The Burgesses did, however, review the matter once again, but adhered to their former position, expressing their reasons with clarity:

> [We] are [they resolved] still of Opinion no Injury can happen to British Creditors from receiving their Debts in the Paper Money (except of a small and accidental Nature, which cannot be provided against) since they are to be paid, and are paid, so much Paper as will place their Money in Britain without Loss, which method is preferable to the Payment in Sterling Specie here (if such we had) as that Specie would not be remitted to Britain without a loss of Freight and Ensurance. But as we have not such Specie, which the Merchants themselves well know, we can [not] suggest any Means, consistent with natural Equity, by which Sterling Debts can be secured to be paid here in Sterling Money. 53

Although from the tenor of the Board of Trade's resolution of December 8, 1763, respecting Virginia, one would have been inclined to believe it had no intention of invoking the aid of Parliament unless Virginia refused to act, such was not the case. Two days later, Thomas Penn wrote to the governor of Pennsylvania: "Our disputes with the assembly about paper money will

---

53. JHB, 1761-1765, p. 241 (November 8, 1764). See also Address to the Governor, ibid., pp. 249-250 (November 9, 1764).

soon be at an end, as a bill is to be brought into Parliament to put the colonies in that respect on the same footing with New England."[54] Sure enough, a month later to the day, the Board of Trade began a consideration of the state of the paper currency in those colonies that had been left unrestrained by the Currency Act of 1751. On January 19, the colonial agents and "several of the principal Merchants trading to" the colonies under consideration were heard on the Board's proposal to extend to the other colonies the restraints imposed upon New England in 1751. The Glasgow merchants sought to improve the opportunity and two days later presented a petition and memorial respecting the currency of Virginia, in which they uncovered certain new objections. The memorial analyzed with more suspicion than judgment the representation of the House of Burgesses and the committee report on the sufficiency of the taxes, which had been received in England late the year before. As was inevitable when a prejudiced group sought to order the financial affairs of a colony at long range, they distorted the picture. The petitioners did, however, bring forward a new argument against the sufficiency of the Virginia method of protecting British creditors. Their debts in Virginia, they urged,

---

54. To John Penn. Quoted in Root, Relations of Pennsylvania, p. 216.

rather than being contracted in sterling, "for the greatest part were contracted to be paid in Currency upon the faith of the former Low Exchange." They then proposed a set of measures looking in most part to the preventing of further issues and the retiring of those already in circulation. This complaint, in the minds of the Board of Trade, doubtless added weight to the objection against legal tender bills.[55]

The agents and the merchants having been heard, the available colonial governors and ex-governors, seven in all,[56] together with Thomas Penn, the Pennsylvania proprietor, Richard Jackson, the Pennsylvania agent, and William Allen, the Pennsylvania chief justice, who at the time happened to be in England, were called in. They severally presented their views, after which, so the Journal of the Board records, "it was agreed on all hands, that the putting a stop, by Act of Parliament, to all further Emissions of paper bills of credit as a legal tender, the declaring all bills now existing not to be a legal tender, after the periods fixed for their redemption, and the fixing a period for

---

55. Board of Trade Journal, 1764-1767, January 10, 19, 21, 23, 1764; Glasgow merchants' petition and memorial are in C. O. 5/1330, L. C. T.

56. In attendance were "the present and late Governors of New York and the late Governor of New Jersey, ... the late Governors of Massachusetts Bay, South Carolina and Nova Scotia, the late Lieutenant Governor of Virginia...," Board of Trade Journal, 1764-1767, p. 15.

the legality of the tender of such as have no fixed period of redemption,[57] would be highly expedient and proper." Thomas Penn and Richard Jackson, however, thought "that such an Act should not pass until next session, in order to give the provinces an opportunity of transmitting their sentiments upon it."[58]

The next day the agents for New York, New Jersey, Virginia, North Carolina, South Carolina, and Georgia attended and were heard. They repeated Penn's request of the day before, but the Board, "having urged the inconveniencies which would arise from any further delay, desired to be informed, whether the agents would or would not give opposition to any bill, which might be moved for in Parliament upon this subject." The agents asked that they might be given a few days to consider their reply. On February 7, the agents returned, and

---

57. South Carolina had ₤106,500 of legal tender bills with no period.

58. Board of Trade Journal, 1764-1767, February 2, 1764. On February 10, 1764, Thomas Penn wrote to John Penn, describing his part in this meeting: "I gave it as my opinion that a regulation was necessary, but whether a small fixed quantity would not be necessary, I was not certain, and proposed that the consideration of this Affair might be put off to another Session, in order that the Assembly might have time to propose some mode, of substituting it, if it should be necessary, a sort of Bills for a longer time than was allowed by the Act relating to New England, and declared my opinion that in all such Cases where the Colony was concern'd, they should have time to offer their objections, which indeed they had been allowed when other Affairs had come before Parliament." Penn Letter Book, MS, VIII, 22. Hist. Soc. of Pennsylvania.

through their spokesman, Robert Charles, who represented New York, they informed the Board that they could not agree to the proposed bill, but "that it was their unanimous opinion that a certain quantity of paper currency ought to be allowed in each colony, to be a legal tender in all contracts and dealings within the colonies, and that time should be allowed for each colony to consider and report what the sum should be."[59]

A week later, Charles Garth, representing South Carolina, and William Knox, representing Georgia, being before the Board on other business, took the opportunity to offer certain compromise suggestions in the matter of currency legislation. It was suggested (1) that no American paper currency should be deemed a legal tender in the satisfaction of any debt owing directly or indirectly to anyone residing in Great Britain or Ireland, and (2) that no paper currency that should thereafter be issued should be deemed "a lawful tender in discharge of any Debt whatsoever" until such act had received the royal approbation.[60]

The proposals offered by Garth and Knox, while of

---

59. *Board of Trade Journal*, 1764-1767, February 7, 1764.
60. *Ibid.*, February 13, 1764. There is among the Knox Papers in the William L. Clements Library the rough draft of a paper in which the various proposals of the Board of Trade are examined and which concludes with the two proposals presented by Knox and Garth.

importance as indicating a spirit of accommodation on the part of the agents of South Carolina and Georgia, were too late to influence the recommendations of the Board. Four days earlier, it had drafted its representation to the Privy Council. Therein it had stated the paper currency policy that was to find embodiment in the Currency Act of 1764, and which with but slight modification was to determine the attitude of the imperial authorities towards paper currency throughout the remainder of the colonial period. In fact, so highly did the authors of the representation value themselves on it, that, when later the tide of protest rose against the enactment of 1764, Lord Hillsborough, who as president of the Board of Trade had been largely responsible for the representation, produced it as a sufficient answer to all complaints.

The matter was very clear to the Lords of Trade. The representation [61] recited the currency history of New England and the various official expressions, culminating in the Currency Act of 1751, of the imperial authorities relating thereto. Then in much the same light, the experience elsewhere was discussed. The issuance of legal tender bills of credit was, we are led to believe, simply the result of a gigantic and all-

---

61. The representation is printed in N. J. Archives (1st series), IX, 405-414.

pervasive conspiracy of debtors bent upon defrauding their creditors. "Upon Pretence either of discharging public Debts, defraying public Services, or establishing a Medium of Commerce," the colonies left unrestrained in 1751 had issued legal tender bills of credit. These bills had depreciated. In consequence, the effects of their having been declared a legal tender were "fraudulent" and "pernicious." Moreover, such bills banished from the colonies gold and silver, "the Materials fittest" for a medium of trade. Nor were legal tender bills necessary instruments of wartime finance. Witness the case of Massachusetts, where during the late war, as a result of the restraints of the Currency Act of 1751, "larger Supplies were raised, and with more Satisfaction and Facility than was ever known before."

The difficulty with the Board's statement of the case is that at best it is an over-simplification and at worst it is inconsistent or false. In the colonies from New York to Georgia, with the possible exception of the somewhat dubious case of North Carolina, it is simply not true that the issues of bills of credit since 1751, the year in which New England was restrained, were placed in circulation for the purpose of defrauding creditors "upon Pretence ... of discharging public Debts, defraying public Services, or establishing a Medium of Commerce." They were issued as a necessary and reasonable means of financing the French and Indian War -- little more or little less. If they tended to drive gold and silver from a province, it was not necessarily because of their legal tender quality. Non-legal tender bills, issued in like amounts and in like circumstances, would, if they circulated as money, likewise tend to drive specie out of the province. As to financing wars by the Massachusetts method, a detailed examination of its effects, it will be recalled, has revealed them not so different from the effects of war financing by the use of legal tender bills as the Board of Trade sanguinely assumed.

While a critical examination raises grave doubts in the minds of the modern investigator as to either the adequacy of the Board's case or the wisdom of its remedy, it was fully convinced of the correctness of its views. It believed that it was the "Circumstance of declaring [the] Bills to be a legal Tender, which ... constitutes all the Fraud and Abuse attendant upon this Practice, and that if this was not allowed, the Colonies, whenever they should find it necessary to make use of their public Credit, would be constrained to do it in a just and equitable Manner." In consequence, the Board recommended an act of Parliament (1) that should thereafter prevent the issuance of any legal tender bills in America and (2) that should provide for the retiring of all such issues already outstanding at the end of their respective periods.

The proposals of the Board of Trade found favor with the Privy Council, and on March 9, they were "approved and ordered to be laid before Parliament, when his Majesty shall judge proper."[62] Even this determination of the Privy Council might not have led to immediate action, however, had not one of the merchants trading to North Carolina agitated the question in Parliament. Charles Garth, the South Carolina agent, was of this opinion.

> I have reason to believe [he wrote at the time], we should have heard no more of it this year had it not been for a Mr. Anthony Bacon (a North Carolina merchant) who had mooted that point with us before the Board of Trade; since that time he has procured himself to be elected for Aylesbury, and on 29th March started the question in the House.[63]

On April 4, Bacon moved for permission to bring in a bill. He was seconded by George Rice of the Board of Trade. There was opposition, however. Peregrine Cust, a London merchant, and Sir William Meredith, M. P. for Liverpool, opposed the motion. They had been supplied with arguments and material by Garth.[64]

---

62. *Acts of the Privy Council, Colonial,* 1745-1766, p. 623.
63. Garth to S. C. Committee of Correspondence, March, 1764. Quoted in L. B. Namier, *England in the Age of the American Revolution,* p. 293, from a copy of Garth's "letter book in possession of his descendent, Mr. William Godsal, of Haines Hill, Berks."
64. Namier, *op. cit.,* p. 293.

After a debate for some time [Garth reported] the Commissioners for Trade propos'd to Sir William Meredith and our friends that the present Bill should be confin'd to the single point of preventing the Colonies for the future from passing acts issuing paper bills with the clause of legal tender, but not to affect or set a period to any at present subsisting: Sir William Meredith came to me in the gallery to acquaint me with the proposition made and as the sense of the House was strong in favour of restraining the provinces of this power we [Garth and some other colonial agents] thought it better to close with the proposition. 65

After this understanding as to the scope of the proposed restriction was reached, leave was granted to bring in the bill, and George Rice and Soame Jenyns of the Board of Trade, together with Anthony Bacon, Mr. Townshend, Sir William Baker, and Sir William Meredith, were appointed to prepare and bring in the same.[66] The next day such a bill was introduced and passed to a second reading. On this same day, the Commons also adopted a resolution requesting his majesty to order accounts prepared of the tender and amount of bills of credit issued in the colonies since 1749, together with the taxes to retire them, the amounts now outstanding, and the value of the bills in sterling, as well now as when issued. This information was to be laid before the House at its next session.[67] Such had been the procedure when Parliament had been asked to act in 1739

---

65. Garth to S. C. Com. of Corresp., quoted, ibid., p. 293.

66. *Journals of the House of Commons, 1761-1764* (vol. 29), 4 Geo. III, 4° die Aprilis, [1764].

67. Ibid., 5° die Aprilis [1764].

and again in 1749. In both cases it had waited until it had full information before acting. But this wise course was now departed from; Parliament acted first and gathered information later.

The next day (April 6), Charles Montagu, the agent for the Virginia assembly, appeared before the Board of Trade "and had some discourse with their lordships on the subject of the Bill" introduced the day before in Parliament. Edward Athawes, one of the London merchants, was also before the Board, where he "delivered ... a paper containing an article which he thought might properly be inserted in the ... Bill, and had some conversation with their lordships thereupon."[68] On April 7 and 10, the bill was debated in the Committee of the Whole, where it underwent amendment. The committee amendments were severally agreed to by the House the next day and several further amendments were made by the House itself. The bill passed its third reading on April 12. The Lords on April 18 agreed to the bill without amendment, and on April 19 the act received the royal assent.[69]

The Currency Act of 1764 declared that after Septem-

---

68. *Board of Trade Journal,* 1764-1767, April 6, 1764.

69. *Journals of the House of Commons,* 1761-1764 (vol. 29), 4 Geo. III, 7°, 10°, 11°, 12°, 18°, 19°, die Aprilis [1764].

ber 1, 1764, any action of a colonial assembly issuing bills of credit and declaring them in anywise a legal tender, or any action prolonging the legal tender of the bills already in circulation should be "null and void," and that any governor assenting to such an act should, "for every such offence, forfeit and pay the sum of ₤1,000, and [should] be immediately dismissed from his government, and for ever after rendered incapable of any public office or place of trust." It was explicitly provided that nothing in the act should "extend to alter or repeal" the Currency Act of 1751.[70] Thus the status of New England was left unchanged. The British merchants had at last prevailed. As an American merchant, the New Yorker John Watts, phrased it, "a few pedlars ... trading to Virginia" (and, one may add in the interests of accuracy, to North Carolina) had succeeded in laying a restraint on the legal tender currency of the colonies. But in doing so they had also succeeded in making "such a mighty disturbance, as to shake all the Northern Colonys."[71]

Paralleling the conflict over Virginia's bills of credit was a conflict that arose over the colony's legislation respecting another element in her monetary

---

70. Danby Pickering, *Statutes at Large*, 4 Geo. III, c. 34.
71. Watts to General Monckton, April 14, 1764, John Watts, *Letter Book*, p. 243.

system -- tobacco. It will be recalled that tobacco notes were an important medium of trade in the colony. Moreover, certain public dues, officials' fees, and the salaries of the clergy were payable in tobacco notes. Conditions developed, which in the '50's led to various commutations of tobacco payments into payments of money. As the colony expanded, settlers pushed out into sections where tobacco raising was not profitable. Obviously, to require the inhabitants of these areas to make payments in tobacco was apt to work a hardship. In view of this fact, the inhabitants of Frederick, Augusta, and Hampshire counties had sometime prior to 1753 been allowed to pay the annual salaries of the clergy, which were set at 16,000 pounds of tobacco, in money at three farthings per pound. This had been found insufficient and an act of 1753 established annual salaries of £100.[72] This was equivalent to valuing tobacco at 1 1/2$\underline{d}$. per pound. Two years later, because "the low situation of the counties of Princess Anne and Norfolk rendere[d] many of the inhabitants thereof incapable of making tobacco, whereof they [were] subject to great imposition in discharging their tobacco debts," the assembly enacted that the justices of the county courts should in October of each year fix a price on tobacco,

---

72. Hening, VI, 369-370 (Nov. 1753, 27 Geo. II, $\underline{c}$. 8).

which should not be less than 10s. per cwt. (equivalent to 1½d. per pound), at which all tobacco obligations might be satisfied.[73] So far the acts had been local in their nature. The year 1755, however, was one of drought, with the result that "a very small quantity of tobacco [was] made." In consequence, the inhabitants of the colony were given the option of paying all tobacco obligations in money at the rate of two pence per pound. The act did not apply to the counties where tobacco payments had already been commuted to money payments by former acts and was to remain in force for ten months, that is, until the next crop should be gathered.[74]

The passage of the act of 1755 was the occasion for complaints on the part of the Virginia clergy, who found themselves adversely affected by the law. The matter, however, did not come to a head at the time.[75]

Three years elapsed before "unseasonable" weather again affected the tobacco crop. But such was the weather in 1758 as to occasion a "prodigious diminution" in the staple crop of the colony. As a result, an act famous in Virginia history as the "Two-Penny Act" was passed. All tobacco obligations were made payable in

---

73. Ibid., p. 502 (May 1755, 28 Geo. II, c. 17).
74. Ibid., p. 502 (May 1755, 28 Geo. II, c. 17).
75. The memorial of the Virginia clergy to the Bishop of London, 1756, is printed in JHB, 1761-1765, pp. xlii-xlvi.

money at the rate of 16*s.* 8*d.* per cwt. (equivalent to 2*d.* per pound). The act did not apply in those counties where money payments were already authorized and was to be in force for one year. The price fixed by the act was the one that had prevailed in the market before the prospects of a short crop had begun to make themselves felt. Such, however, were the results of the shortage, that the price soon rose to 27*s.* per cwt., an advance of 62 per cent. The act provided that in cases where tobacco had been contracted for at a rate higher than the 16*s.* 8*d.* per cwt. established by the law and the money or its equivalent in goods already paid over, the contract might at the option of the payer be discharged either in tobacco "or in money according to the price really given for such tobacco, together with the lawful interest arising" on the sum advanced to the time of payment.[76]

Two problems were entangled in the act. They arose out of the dual function of tobacco, which was at once the colony's staple commodity of commerce and a standard of value and of deferred payments. The act has more often been condemned than defended. One later writer

---

76. Hening, VII, 240-241 (Sept. 1758, 32 Geo. II, *c.* 6); Memorial & Petition of the Merchants of London complaining of an act passed in Virginia in October, 1758 (read by the Board of Trade, July 25, 1758[9]), C. O. 5/1329, L. C. T.

has, in fact, gone so far as to characterize it as no more than "unadorned rascality."[77] But it was scarcely that. It is a fundamental requirement that "sound" money should, other things being equal, vary as little as possible in value. An appreciating currency works hardships on debtors no less than a depreciating currency does on creditors. The price of tobacco that prevailed before the short crop of 1758, and which was adopted by the act of that year, was not one that would of itself in the ordinary course of things have caused undue complaint from either debtors or creditors. But in the 62 per cent rise that took place largely, perhaps entirely,[78] as a result of the short crop of the year 1758, creditors saw a handsome windfall, which they were denied by the "Two-Penny Act." If the price set by the act was an average one, and so it appears to have been, there is no more reason why tobacco obligations should be paid in a medium that had appreciated

---

77. Moses Coit Tyler, quoted in Beer, British Colonial Policy, 1754-1765, p. 183, n. 4.

78. Part of this rise in the price of tobacco in the years 1758-1759 has sometimes been attributed to Virginia's issues of bills of credit. The part played by the paper issues was probably small. The price of tobacco was determined in the foreign markets. This being so, the price in Virginia would have risen as a result of the colonies paper issues only if exchange had also risen. Exchange, however, fell in the latter part of 1758 and remained down until the middle of 1759. This would seem to indicate that it was the smaller supply that caused the rise in the price of tobacco.

by a 62 per cent rise in value, than that they should be paid in a medium that had depreciated proportionately. It makes a difference, however, whose ox is gored. Creditors looked upon the payment of tobacco obligations in money at the ordinary value of tobacco as payment in a depreciated currency, rather than looking at their payment in high priced tobacco as payment in an appreciated currency. The clergy, with an eye to the things of Caesar as well as to the things of the Lord, raised a great clamor against the injustice of the act and sought its disallowance at home. If they were required, they argued, to receive their salaries in tobacco when the price was low, they were entitled to receive them in tobacco when the price was high. This may be the way to look at it, but, on the other hand, it may be urged that it was something less than Christian for the clergy to have insisted on an enrichment out of the colony's calamity. Governor Francis Fauquier's observations at the time are in point. On July 14, 1759, he wrote to the Board of Trade:

> This Colony would be in a perfect State of Tranquility if the Conduct of the Clergy was as temperate as it ought to be. Their provision is of such a Nature and on such a footing that I fear there will be constant Animosities between the Clergy and Laity in every Scarce Year of Tobacco. If the Clergy were to receive their full Quota of Tobacco in a year when the planter makes small crops, Their Gains would encrease in proportion to the Distress of the planter; Then the Laity would murmur. If the Legislature set a price to ease the Country of Distress, then the Clergy murmur. The

situation is very different in England; where by means
of Tythes, the Clergy have a certain proportion of the
Crop be it great or small, and the price makes amends to
both Parson and Farmer, in Scarce Years. This law at
which the Clergy are so incensed, is a general Law respecting all payments in Tobacco of whatever Nature they
may be; and all were content but themselves. I am confident if the Clergy had applyed to the Legislature,
which they ought to have done, they would have had a
better price, tho' a price would have been set. 79

But there were others besides the clergy who were not content. These were the British merchants trading to Virginia. Here the problem was a little different. Many of the merchants had purchased tobacco for future delivery at the price of 16s. 8d. per cent before it became evident that the crop of 1758 would be short. When in the course of developments tobacco rose to 27s. per cwt., they saw themselves the losers of a 62 per cent windfall profit as a result of the act of 1758, which, by abrogating their contracts, had forced them to buy tobacco to laid their ships at the enhanced price. It is true that they lost nothing but prospective profits, but they were as sensitive to such a loss as to any other. Here the dual nature of tobacco as a commodity of commerce and as a monetary commodity complicated the situation. All that has been said above concerning paying debts in an appreciated currency applies here insofar as the tobacco debts owing from the planters to the merchants resulted from old transactions.

---

79. C. O. 5/1329, L. C. T.

However, where the merchants had within the year bought tobacco for future delivery, another element entered the problem. Here tobacco was to a large extent, although not necessarily completely, simply a commodity of trade. Commercial dealings have ordinarily been organized on the principle that in such cases those that make fortunate contracts should profit and those that make unfortunate ones should be content with their loss. But if there is such a thing as natural equity, there appears to be no inherent reason why the merchants should be entitled to profit by the planters' calamity. The times were exigent; the staple crop had failed; the war on the colony's borders called for the utmost exertion. Who would say that in such a case it is unreasonable and inconsonant with natural equity that the British merchants should be asked to forego their opportunity to profit at the expense of the planters? For be it remembered that they lost nothing but prospective profits. If they had already paid for tobacco more than the price set in the act, they were repaid in full plus lawful interest. On questions such as these, men have been wont to divide; but to characterize the provisions of the act as "unadorned rascality" does less than justice to the motives of the legislature. The act may have fallen short of providing ideal justice, but to many reasonable men it would appear, when all things were considered, that even though the act may have been to the advantage of many of those that enacted it, it was founded in an attempt to do essential justice by preventing the calamity of the many from being the opportunity of the few.

The merchants joined the clergy in their efforts to have the act disallowed, but not until after the clergy had already prevailed. On August 3, 1759, an order in council disallowed the four acts referred to above, the local acts of 1753 and 1755, and the general acts of 1755 and 1758.[80]

News of the disallowance of the acts did not reach Virginia until the next year. In the meantime, the clergy had been paid their salaries in money at 2d. the pound of tobacco. Many now brought suit for the difference between what they had received and the value of the tobacco at its market price. One of these suits, that of the Reverend James Maury, was the famous "Parson's Cause," which "furnished the occasion for the entrance of Patrick Henry into political life." Henry, who had been employed by the vestrymen of Fredericksville parish against Maury, finding the law against him, attacked the disallowance of the act by the king as a gross

---

80. Board of Trade Journal, 1759-1763, July 3, 4, 25, 31, 1759; Acts of the Privy Council, Colonial, 1745-1766, #394; Order of Disallowance, dated August 3, 1759, C. O. 5/1329, L. C. T.

instance of misrule, which forfeited "all rights to his subjects obedience." So eloquent was Henry, and so appealing were his arguments to the jury, that instead of awarding Maury the sum for which he sued, the jury gave him damages of only one penny.[81] After the trial Henry confessed to Maury, so the latter wrote at the time, "that his sole view in engaging in the cause, and in saying what he had said, was to render himself popular."[82] Thus did the pertinacity of the clergy in pursuing the things of Caesar, the desire of the home authorities to strike down any legislation that could be construed as an attack upon the creditor-interest, and the popularity-seeking of a Virginia back country lawyer-politician conspire to strike one of the first sparks from the anvil of revolution.

Late in 1762 the Virginia assembly passed an act reducing the rate at which the gold coin of the German Empire should pass within the colony. Since the passage of the act of 1714, German gold along with other gold had been rated at 5s. the dwt. It was discovered that the German gold was of a baser alloy, being "worse than Spanish doublons at least fifteen per cent." In

---

81. Edward Channing, A History of the United States, III, 5-8; George Louis Beer, British Colonial Policy, 1754-1765, pp. 184-186.

82. J. Maury to Rev. John Camm, December 12, 1763, JHB, 1761-1765, p. 1111.

consequence, it was by the act of 1762 rated at 4s. 3d. the dwt. for the future. Provision was made, however, that all inhabitants of Virginia that were in possession of such coin at the time of the passage of the act should be indemnified the difference between the new and the old valuations by payments from the colonial treasury.[83]

The act was objected to by the Board of Trade's legal adviser, Matthew Lamb, chiefly because it was an amending act without a suspending clause. He recommended repeal because of the technical defects of the act, even though the object of the law was a desirable one.[84] Despite the fact that the Board was at the moment ill disposed towards Virginia's currency policy, it deferred action on Lamb's recommendation and wrote Governor Fauquier for further information. Fauquier's reply throws light on the problem. The information he conveys was obtained from "some of the oldest and ablest Members of the House of Burgesses" and transcribed in their own words as follows:

> The greatest part of the German Coin circulating in the colonies was brought by the palatines who came from Germany to settle Pennsylvania and other northern Colonies. The people of Pennsylvania discovered the Money to be of base alloy and made it current amongst

---

83. Hening, VII, 575-576 (3 Geo. III, c. 11, November, 1762); assented to, December 23, 1762, JHB, 1761-1765, p. 164.
84. Lamb's report, C. O. 5/1330, L. C. T.

them at something less than its real Value for they made the German Caroline which weighs 6 dwt. 6 g^r. equal only to the English Guinea.

The Act of Assembly pass'd in the first year of [King George II, (1714)] made the gold Coin of the Empire current at the rate of 5s. the dwt. The Merchants of Virginia soon found out that great proffit might be made by buying this money in the northern Colonies and bringing it to Virginia, and they sent great Quantities of Gold, and Bills of Exchange to purchase this base money. The Consequence seem'd very obvious, that in time all our valuable Specie would be carried off, and this base one left in Exchange for it. The Assembly therefore, some Years since designed to put a Stop to this Evill, and a Bill was brought into the House for that purpose. But the Merchants unwilling to lose the great profits they gained by this Trade made a party against it, and threw it out at the third reading. The late War having put a Stop to this pernicious Traffick: and swept away with the other circulating Specie the greatest part of this base Coin, the Assembly thought it a proper time to settle it at its real Value; and accordingly pass'd the Act now under Consideration of their Lordships for regulating the Gold Coin of the German Empire. By this Act it is to pass at the rate of 4sh^{gs}. and three pence the dw^t. so that the Caroline above mentioned will pass in Virginia at one pound six Shill^{gs}. and six pence three farthings, which is six pence three farthings more than the Guinea goes for: tho' it must be observed the Guinea passes here for three pence less than its real Value. Very exact Experiments have been made on this money, and it is found fifteen p^r C^t. worse than the Spanish Doublons and the taking off nine pence in the dw^t. brings it as nearly to its true Value as can be done. It must be submitted whether it may not have very dangerous Consequence to oblige the people of this Colony to receive a Specie which they cannot remit to any other place but with the Loss of 15 p^r. C^t. and from what has been said this must certainly be the Case if the Act under the Consideration of their Lordships should be repealed. 85

These reasons seem to have been convincing, for the law was allowed to stand.

The French and Indian War had far reaching results

---

85. Fauquier to B. T., Williamsburg, November 19, 1764, C. O. 5/1331, L. C. T.

in its effects upon imperial currency policy. Most of the colonies from New York southward had in greater or lesser degree had recourse to legal tender paper currency as a means of financing their contributions to the conduct of the war against the common enemy. The evidence seems conclusive that, with the possible exception of the case of North Carolina, the controlling factor in the issuance of bills of credit had been the necessities of wartime finance. Any benefits that accrued to debtors as a result of the depreciation of the wartime bills appear to have been incidental and not the result of design. In fact, the period is noteworthy for the absence of protests arising from the creditor-interest within the colonies. Here and there a voice was raised against bills of credit on general principles or because of some special interest or pique of the individual, but generally the issues were acquiesced in overwhelmingly as <u>bona fide</u> wartime measures.

It was where the introduction of paper currency had been delayed longest that its use as an instrument of war finance caused the greatest protests from creditor groups in the mother country. It is unfortunate that the introduction of legal tender paper currency in Virginia came at a time when the action of the colony in making sterling debts payable in Virginia currency had called forth protests from the British merchants. Despite the fact that Virginia's first response to the complaints of the merchants and the direction of the crown pursuant thereto had been one of compliance, whereby they had protected British creditors by passing an amending law in 1755 providing that henceforward sterling debts might be satisfied in Virginia currency only at the real equivalent of sterling money as determined by the current rate of exchange upon England as ascertained by the courts, rather than at the par of exchange, 125 to 100, as had been the case since the passage of the act of 1749, the merchants uncovered fresh complaints when in 1757 new legal tender issues were emitted. The Virginia assembly, believing that it had removed all just cause for complaint by the amending act of 1755, took pains to explain its position in the hope of convincing the merchants that their interests were already fully protected. Although the Virginia legislature, believing that full justice was accomplished by the amending act of 1755, refused to grant the relief sought by the British merchants, namely, the declaring that sterling debts might be satisfied only by the tender of sterling money except by the consent of the creditor, they had reason to feel that the British merchants had been satisfied of the justice of the policy adopted in 1755, because for a period of three years no further complaints were forthcoming. In 1762, however, further paper issues in Virginia were the occasion for renewed protests from the British merchants. Henceforth events moved rapidly: the merchants trading to North Carolina added their timely protest; meanwhile, the war was ended, thus in the eyes of the home authorities removing the necessity for additional paper issues. Just as the years following the previous French war had been found propitious for imposing restraints upon the currency of New England, so now, with far less reason and far less examination, the imperial authorities thought the time propitious for extending the restraints of New England to the other colonies. Precipately, without gathering information or without granting the colonies a hearing, the Currency Act of 1764 was rushed through Parliament. It is true that such opposition as the colonial agents were able to improvise had led to some modifications of the bill. None the less, the result was the proscribing of all further legal tender issues in the colonies and the requiring that all such issues already extant should be retired at the end of their periods. The British merchants had at last prevailed in their quarter-of-a-century effort to remove the legal tender quality from colonial paper currency.

But they had overshot the mark. The fact is that the British authorities had been led into a cardinal blunder, which later the British merchants themselves realized, even though the Board of Trade remained unmoved. Paper currency was something more than a means of paying debts or financing wars; it was a means of carrying on that commerce from which the merchants, British and colonial alike, drew their life blood. Moreover, it was necessary to the colonies if the inflow of specie from the West Indian and the Southern European trade was to be made available for transmitting to England to pay the balances owing the merchants there. If the colonies were to be denied a legal tender paper currency as a medium of trade, then it would become necessary for them to retain, for a time at least, such supplies of specie as found their way into the colonies. They could do this only by buying fewer of England's products from English merchants or by failing to pay their debts to English merchants. Neither of these methods, the merchants readily realized, when they finally perceived the implications of their action, was to their advantage. Moreover, a cutting off of the supply of British manufactured goods would inevitably lead to the development of American manufactures -- a result that ran entirely counter to established British colonial policy. All these possibilities were heightened by the fact that, coincident with the imposing of restraints upon the legal tender currency of the colonies, the trade from which the colonies derived their specie had also been subjected to restraints.

While the Currency Act of 1751, because of the peculiar conditions obtaining in New England, had not been an unreasonable extension of imperial regulation, there was little reason for the passage of the Currency Act of 1764 save the importunate pleas of the British merchants trading to Virginia and North Carolina and the apparently ineradicable bias of the Board of Trade since it had come under the influence of the British merchant-creditor interest in the early '40's, and there was no reason at all for the precipitate way in which the law was enacted without first gathering information or allowing the colonies a hearing. Only Virginia and North Carolina had been complained of, and both with but little justification. None the less, all the colonies hitherto unrestrained were without notice included in the restraint. The merchants of New York and Pennsylvania (who, be it remarked, represented the creditor-interest within the colonies) were quick to realize the implications of the act. Without a medium to circulate it, trade must decline. In other words, the policy of the British government embodied in the Currency Act of 1764 would inevitably produce a deflation that would accentuate the natural post-war depression. It is small wonder that the act raised "such a mighty disturbance, as to shake all the Northern Colonies."[86] And there were repercussions in the Southern colonies as well.[87] Finally, when after two or three years the currency stringency occasioned by the retiring of the war issues at the end of their periods had begun to make itself felt; and when the Stamp Act, which in the meantime had occupied the center of the stage, had been repealed in 1766; the colonies to the southward of New England, with the exception of Maryland and the Three Lower Counties, united in a general effort to secure the modification of the Currency Act. But without avail.

In fact, the imperial authorities, far from being convinced of the unwisdom of the restraint, adopted an interpretation of the act that seems unexplainable except as a manifestation of sheer wrong-headedness. The obvious object of the law, it would seem, was to prevent creditors from being forced to receive payment of

---

86. That is, the northern colonies of those affected by the act, namely, New York, New Jersey and Pennsylvania.

87. It is an interesting fact that the Currency Act of 1764 aroused much less resentment in Virginia than it did in New York, New Jersey, or Pennsylvania, or in North Carolina, South Carolina, or Georgia. In 1763 the House of Burgesses had declared that there were "no warm Advocates for Paper Money [in the assembly] further than to preserve the Credit of what hath been issued and to prevent the evil Consequences of stopping its circulation at [that] Time." (JHB, 1761-1765, p. 189.) The later course of events in the colony does much to attest the truth of this assertion.

the sums owing them in a depreciated currency. But the imperial authorities were not content with such a reasonable interpretation of the restraining clause of the act. The restraint applied also to the making of bills of credit issued by a colonial treasury in anticipation of taxes a legal tender in payment of the taxes at the treasury, or the making of bills issued on loan a legal tender at the loan office in payment of the loan. It is difficult to see any useful purpose served by such an interpretation. Its effect, however, was unfortunate and did much to heighten the resentment against the act. As a means of alleviating the currency stringency resulting from the act, some of the colonies appear to have been willing to give trial to loan office issues that were not a legal tender between man and man; but they were deterred by the fact that they were unable to make such issues a legal tender at the loan office in payment of principal and interest. It was feared that people would be unwilling to borrow and to receive in trade a currency that it was uncertain would be received by the issuing office in satisfaction of obligations incurred when it was borrowed. It was not until 1769 in the case of New York, and not until 1773 in the case of the colonies generally, that the restrictions imposed by this interpretation were removed by acts of Parliament[88] and the colonies were permitted to supply their currency needs by loan office or treasury issues that, while not constituting a legal tender between man and man, were yet a legal tender for obligations owing the issuing office. But, with the exception of the special case of New York, it was only on the eve of the Revolution that this unexceptionable method of supplying the currency needs of the colonies was made available for their use. In several of the colonies it was used beneficially, but by this time the mischief had been done -- the resentment aroused by the restraints of the Currency Act of 1764 had already added itself to the forces operating to widen the breach between mother country and colonies.

In sum, the largely baseless clamorings "of a few pedlars" trading to Virginia and North Carolina had occasioned the adoption, and the obduracy of the imperial authorities had prevented the modification, of a vexatious policy unnecessary to the protection of creditor-interests, either in the mother country or the colonies, and obstructive to the trade of the colonies and England. The unwisdom of the policy added by so much to the cup of grievance of the colonies during those critical years when England was losing an empire.

---

88. Statutes at Large, XXVIII, 306 (10 Geo. III, c. 35 (1769)); ibid., XXX, 113-114 (13 Geo. III, c. 57 (1773)).

CHAPTER X

CONCLUSIONS

>'Tis Romantick to suppose we can keep Specie on this side of the Water when the Ballance is so evidently against us, nor is it the interest of the Mother Country we should when nothing but parsimony & shifts can effect it, which must of Course affect her Manufactorys. And yet the Use of Paper Money is abolished as an Evil, when properly treated, it is the only Medium we have left of Commerce & the only Expedient in an Exigency. Every Man of Estate here abominates the Abuse of Paper Money, because the Consequences fall upon himself, but there is just the same difference in the Use & Abuse of it, as there is in food itself, or in every one necessary Convenience or pleasure of Life.
>
> -- John Watts, New York merchant, to General Robert Monckton, April 16, 1765.

> We apprehend the late Act of Parliament [the Currency Act of 1764], prohibiting the further Emissions of Paper Money from being lawful Tender, is particularly oppressive on our Trade, and injurious to Great-Britain; For your own experience must convince you, that Commerce cannot be carried on to any beneficial Extent, without a sufficient Medium of circulating Cash; destitute of which, Trade must rest in and be confined to, the narrow Bounds of Barter amongst ourselves only.
>
> -- To the Merchants of Great-Britain; The Memorial of the Merchants and Traders of the City of Philadelphia, 1765.

FIRST AND FOREMOST among the conclusions arrived at in the course of this inquiry is the inadequacy of the traditional debtor-conspiracy explanation of colonial currency practices.[1] Much more was involved than a conflict between "farmer-debtors" and "merchant-

---

1. Perhaps this view owes most to the baleful influence of the contemporary generalizations of Dr. William Douglass, who wrote particularly of Rhode Island, Massachusetts, and New Hampshire in their worst period. "All our paper-money-making legislatures," he said, referring to these colonies during the 'thirties and 'forties, "have been legislatures of debtors, the representatives of people, who for incogitancy, idleness, and profuseness have been under the necessity of mortgaging their land." (Summary, I, 310.) "Sound-money" historians, their wariness overcome by their zeal, have applied this generalization to the whole colonial experience. See, for example, the part of that remarkable chapter (iii) in Horace White, Money and Banking, first published in 1895 (new edition, 1935, revised and enlarged by Charles S. Tippetts and Lewis A. Froman, cited), dealing with colonial bills of credit (especially pp. 47-48). White following Douglass's view, says (p. 51), "The landholders controlled the legislative assemblies everywhere. Thus the emission of bills of credit on loan was, in effect, a conspiracy of needy landowners against the rest of the community." (Italics mine.) Again he says (p. 48), "The usual course of events where bills of credit were issued was as follows: emissions; disappearance of specie; .... depreciation; repudiation of early issues in part and the emission of others, called 'new tenor'." (Italics mine.) A completely inaccurate statement of the "usual course." In fact, White's celebrated account of colonial bills of credit is most amazing, there being scarcely a whole truth in it.

Colonial bills of credit come off little better at the hands of Charles J. Bullock, Essays on the Monetary History of the United States, 1900. In his general chapter (iv) on "Colonial Paper Money" he presents substantially the same view as White. He refers to the New England experience culminating in the issues of King George's War as "this carnival of fraud and coruption" (p. 43). And, apparently referring to the whole colonial experience, says (p. 56): "This chapter of our monetary history presents a sufficiently dark and disgraceful picture." And again (pp. 56-57), "For eighty years the people of the colonies were schooled in the belief that bills of credit furnished a proper and convenient means of defraying public expenditures, ordinary as well as extraordinary. Such issues of paper would depreciate,

creditors." However neat and appealing a formula this explanation may provide, it breaks down both on logical

---

and could ultimately be wholly repudiated, or could be redeemed at a fraction of their face value. Under such circumstances, there was a strong disinclination to permit taxation to be practiced on any scale commensurate with public needs." (Italics mine.) I know of no issue "wholly repudiated" during colonial times. And the generalization, viewed in the sense that Bullock obviously means it, concerning redemption "at a fraction of their face value" is of limited application at all times, and of practically no application at all during the last twenty-five years of the colonial period, during which time there were more bills of credit issued than during the whole preceding period.

One other quotation from Bullock (p. 52) will suffice. "The advocates of paper currency always claimed that it was the only means by which a sufficient circulating medium could be secured, and many historians have accepted this plea with discreditable complacency." Presumably those creditor-elements, the merchants of the colonies and of England also made the "plea with discreditable complacency," for make it they did on occasion. One should perhaps refrain from remarks concerning the "discreditable complacency" with which other historians have accepted the sufficiency of the debtor-conspiracy explanation of colonial currency practices.

We owe much to the recent researches of Curtis P. Nettels (The Monetary Supply of the American Colonies Before 1720, 1934); but when dealing with the later period (in The Roots of American Civilization), he appears unwarrantedly to have embraced the "farmer-debtor," "merchant-creditor" conflict explanation. Says he (p. 530): Of importance "was a series of dramatic conflicts over currency -- contests to determine the prices which farmers should receive for their produce. Such prices in turn determined whether debtors should remain in a dependent state and perhaps eventually lose their improved lands through foreclosure or whether they should achieve financial independence and security." By limiting his discussion to those instances which may most readily be fitted into the Procrustean bed of the debtor-creditor formula, he succeeds, I am afraid, in leaving the reader with the notion that here is the whole explanation of colonial paper currency. Whether Professor Nettels intends to leave this impression, I cannot say. But I find no stressing of the other fac-

analysis and when confronted by historic fact. In the first place, it is not easy to group colonial society into creditors and debtors. The same colonial merchants, who appear in a creditor rôle when viewed with respect to the farmers, assume a debtor rôle when viewed with respect to the merchants of Britain. Then again, there were in colonial society, as there are in any society, a great many who were neither debtors nor creditors.

But an even more powerful objection to the sufficiency of the debtor-creditor conflict formula arises from another consideration. To provide a standard of deferred payments is but one of the functions of money.

---

tors involved.

Later, when discussing the financing of the French and Indian War (pp. 596-697), he writes: "Contests over the currency illustrate the wartime tactics of the assemblies. Unwilling to tax themselves to meet the immediate costs of the war the colonists again issued paper money in large amounts and the resulting depreciation increased the old tension between debtors and creditors [unwilling, or perhaps unable?]. Virginia now became the principal scene of conflict; there the struggle over currency and debts bore witness to the impending bankruptcy of the tobacco planters, caught as they were in the grip of British merchant capitalism." That a controversy between the Virginia legislature and British merchant-creditors did arise is quite true; but that it arose as a result of Virginia debtor-planters' attempting to ease their debts to British merchants is something else -- and a thesis not supported by the evidence, if the analysis developed in the preceding chapter be valid.

Other writers might be cited, but the evidence is merely cumulative, and the footnote already overlong.

More important is its function as a medium of exchange. One of the necessary steps in the evolution of the colonial economy was the substitution of a money for a barter economy. The need of the colonies for a currency sufficient to circulate their trade goes a long way towards providing an explanation for many colonial monetary practices. Few, I presume, would deny the advantages of a money over a barter economy. Implicit, then, in the argument of those that have condemned the resort of the colonists to paper currency is the assumption that the alternative was a specie currency adequate to their needs. But such an assumption is unwarranted. In ordinary times, the supply of specie was at best meagre and uncertain, and was not infrequently wanting altogether. As a result of these facts, the suppression of a colony's paper currency necessitated either: (1) the readjustment of its price level to the stock of specie available and a greater or lesser measure of deflation and consequent depression; (2) the supplementing of specie by a resort to commodity currency or rated commodities; or (3) the complete relapse into a commodity-currency, barter economy. Thus the advantages of a money economy could often be purchased only at the cost of assuming the risks attending the use of a paper currency, which all will admit could be abused. None the less, both the colonial and the English merchants frequently thought it a good bargain.

But as important as are the effects of colonial currency practices upon the relation of debtors and creditors and upon the trade and prosperity of the colonies, they cannot be judged by these criteria alone. The paper issues of the colonies were also instruments of governmental finance, and as such must be viewed in the light of governmental exigencies. And these were often great. Over the three-quarters of a century from the first issue of bills of credit in Massachusetts in 1690 until the passage of the Currency Act of 1764, the colonies were at war during thirty-four years, not to mention the excursions and alarms between times. Nor were the demands of the wars slight when one takes into consideration the strength of the colonies. Consider, for example, the case of New York during the French and Indian War. The New York merchant, John Watts, indicated the nature of the problem and the response of the colony when he wrote: "All our great Expences and Emissions have proceeded from a hearty desire of shewing ourselves dutiful Subjects, by Conforming to all requisitions of the Crown; for two or three Campaigns the levees amounted to every fifth Man in the Province & failing of Volunteers the number was to be made up out of the Inhabitants, & the Man detach'd and oblig'd to go on pain of Death or get another in his Room, which fell grievously heavy, even Quakers were not exempt ...."[2] And there were other colonies where the burden fell more heavily than in New York. During the emergencies of war, bills of credit provided the only means of an "immediate exertion."[3] And the English needed to be encouraged in timely exertion. Had not the French at Venango told George Washington in 1753, just before the French and Indian War broke out, "that it was their absolute Design to take Possession of the Ohio, and ... they would do it; For altho' they were sensible the English could raise two Men for their one; yet they knew their Motions were too slow and dilatory to prevent any Undertaking of theirs"?[4]

A summary view of the evolution of colonial currency practices will bring out the foregoing considerations more clearly. The common practice at the beginning of the eighteenth century of raising the value of coin was aimed at supplying the want of a currency sufficient to circulate the trade of the colonies. Any advantages arising from an easing of debt payments as a consequence of price rises resulting from the practice appear to

---

2. W. to Moses Franks, New York, June 9, 1764, John Watts, Letter Book, p. 263. Levying one man in five would be roughly equivalent to raising an army of 6,000,000 today (on the basis of the male population 20-60, census of 1930).

3. See the discussion of this point, pp. 469, 475, above, for example.

4. John C. Fitzpatrick (ed.), The Diaries of George Washington, 1748-1799, I, 55 (December 4, 1753).

have been largely incidental and not the motivating forces. This is particularly evident in the Middle colonies and New England. It was the merchants of Boston who raised the value of silver from seven to eight shillings an ounce in 1705. This action on the part of the Boston merchants determined the price for all New England and New York. And because of the influence of their policy on New York's conduct, the Boston merchants indirectly influenced the action of New Jersey and Pennsylvania. It was the merchants of New York who, because the Boston merchants maintained the rate of eight shillings per ounce, petitioned against the enforcement of the Proclamation of Queen Anne in that colony. In Pennsylvania the people "resolved by general Compact to receive all fformer dues in coine under the same denomination off value that it passed ffor [at] the time of the contract ..., and for new Bargains they [were] perticular in their agreement" as to the value at which coin should be received. In New Jersey coin passed as it did in New York and Pennsylvania. Certainly there is little here to indicate a debtor movement. Nor is there reason to believe that the motives were otherwise in the Carolinas.

With the introduction of bills of credit, the legal valuation placed upon coin became of less importance. In the paper money colonies the value of coin followed the fortunes of the paper issues. The paper issues in their inception in New England, New York, New Jersey, and the Carolinas, and, at a later time, in Virginia were governmental finance measures dictated by the needs of defense. Depreciation was most severe in the early years in the Carolinas; but those were exigent times on the southern frontier, and one is doubtless nearer the truth if he views the depreciation of their currency at that time as resulting from the demands of defense rather than from the inflationist tendencies of debtors.

The factors are more complex in New England. There the economy was different. Trade, particularly with the West Indies, brought in a supply of silver. Although much of this went to Britain annually to redress the balance of trade with the mother country, at least the trading towns of the seaboard had been able to accumulate a stock of specie. During the course of Queen Anne's War, however, much of this was exported and its place taken by the war issues of bills of credit. With the war over, the silver in most part gone, and the bills of credit yearly decreasing, the shadow of depression fell upon New England. In Massachusetts, which was the leader in the business, "farmer-debtors" and "merchant-creditors" alike were agreed upon the need for a new paper issue to supply the want of a circulating medium,

537

and upon the form that it should take, that of a loan issue. They differed only as to whether the issue should be put out by a public bank, with the profits inuring to the province, or a private bank, with the profits inuring to the merchants. There may have been a farmer-merchant controversy, but it was not a debtor-creditor one.

The proponents of a public bank carried the day, and in 1714 Massachusetts began her land bank issues. Rhode Island, following Massachusetts' example, established her first land bank the next year. In 1716 Massachusetts put out her second loan issue, and in 1721 Rhode Island set up her second bank. By 1721 the price of silver in New England had risen by about fifty per cent.

Thenceforward the bills outstanding in Massachusetts and Rhode Island multiplied, and sooner or later paper money parties developed. The value of the currency depreciated from year to year. Here the course of events best supports the debtor-creditor struggle theory. But even here there are factors that cast doubt on the sufficiency of this explanation. Did the successive bank issues of Rhode Island flow solely from the fact that they enabled borrowers and other debtors to pay their debts in a depreciated currency;[5] or was

---

5. Since the loan bills of Rhode Island were re-

the fact that they enabled the colony to levy tribute, as it were, on Connecticut and Massachusetts because the bills enjoyed a currency there on the same terms as the bills of the colony in which they circulated a considerable factor in the issues? And why, it may be asked, did the inhabitants of Connecticut and Massachusetts receive and circulate such depreciating and "fraudulent" bills? The Rhode Island bills were never a legal tender in the neighboring colonies, and those that received them in Connecticut and Massachusetts could not in turn compel their creditors to take them. The answer is, that the inhabitants of Connecticut and Massachusetts could not overlook the immediate advantage of a sale at a good price because the currency tendered was a depreciating one. Depreciation was not so rapid that the bills could not be passed on before they fell perceptibly in value. And who were these sellers? The farmer-debtors of the back country? Did the merchants of Boston eschew such opportunity of gain? Governor Shirley tells us, that in the early 'forties, when he attempted to stop the circulation within Massachusetts of the bills of the neighboring colonies, he succeeded

---

ceivable in interest and principal payments at the loan office, they were a legal tender in satisfaction of these obligations. It usually stated, however, that they were not a legal tender in private transactions, though it is further stated that the local courts usually found means to make them so.

in the country districts but failed among the merchants of Boston![6]

The merchants of Boston contributed to the depreciation of the currency of the province in other ways than by circulating the bills of Rhode Island. The issue of Merchants' Notes in 1733, and the notes of the Silver Bank in 1740, regardless of what the merchants intended of them, insomuch as they added to the supply of currency, contributed to its depreciation. And when the merchants issued them, what was the relative strength of the motives arising from a desire to supply a currency (chiefly for their own use)[7] that would maintain, or, in the latter case, even increase, its value and from the thought that the notes could profitably be lent out at interest?

Nor were issues by the merchants confined to Massachusetts. Connecticut's first loan issue in 1733 resulted from the colony's taking over a note issue of a group of New London merchants.

With respect to the interests of the New England merchants in the matter of a depreciating currency, there is a provocative statement by Dr. Douglass in his

---

6. S. to B. T., December 23, 1743, John G. Palfrey, History of New England (1859 ed.), I, 106n.

7. They agreed to receive their own note issues, while refusing those of Rhode Island in the first case and of the Land Bank in the second.

Discourse.[8] He writes that "the Merchants of Great Britain Adventurers to New England, because of their largest Dealings have suffered most" from the depreciation of the currency. "Their Goods," he continues, "are here generally sold at a long Credit, while the Denomination of the Money in which they are to be paid, continues depreciating ...." If these statements be true, it would seem that the merchants in New England, insofar as they dealt in British goods, were protected against loss, because, while they might be paid in a depreciated currency, they likewise paid their creditors in the same currency. That this was not always the case, however, is indicated by a further statement of Douglass.[9] He speaks of factors being "obliged to give an extra Quantity of [paper currency] to purchase Silver and other Returns; which can be exported, to satisfy Debts"; and that "in this Shape also the Merchant [i.e., the colonial merchant] becomes a Sufferer."

Another practice difficult to reconcile with the debtor-conspiracy theory was that of providing penalties for selling at different prices for specie than for paper. And among the colonies that from time to time enacted provisions of this sort was Rhode Island. Such enactments have usually been thought but another nefarious

---

8. In Colonial Currency Reprints, III, 329.
9. Ibid., p. 330.

scheme of the debtor-conspirators.[10] But perhaps the opposite is true. The commonly accepted gauge of depreciation of New England bills of credit was the rise in the price of silver. If silver did not rise in price, that is, if a new issue of bills continued to be worth the same in terms of silver as bills had been worth before the issue, the bills would undergo no depreciation. What could be more logical, then, for those who wished to prevent depreciation, than to lay penalties on those who depreciated the bills; that is, on those who valued silver at rates higher than they valued bills? Maintaining the parity of specie and paper through the device of interconvertibility has now long been regarded as an orthodox practice of preventing the depreciation of paper.[11] Why should the attempt of a

---

10. Horace White, op. cit., p. 48, says: "In addition to legal-tender acts there was a great variety of laws to compel people to sell their property at the same price for bills of credit as for silver. The 'debtor class' were not satisfied with forcing depreciated paper upon creditors for past obligations, but insisted that they ought to be able to buy as much property with paper as with specie." This last sentence is one of the most amazing sentences from White's whole amazing account of colonial bills of credit. If the paper was depreciated, it was not equal to silver; if it was equal to silver, it was not depreciated (more than silver). It would require, one would think, considerable legerdemain to depreciate the currency so as to pay debts in it, while at the same keeping it from depreciation so that one could purchase more with it.

11. Depreciation of both specie and paper is perfectly possible under conditions of parity maintained through interconvertibility. Prices, measured either in specie or paper, may rise as the amount of money increases.

colonial legislature to accomplish the same result by other, albeit futile, means be suspect? Such measures might be evidence of the legislature's lack of understanding of monetary phenomena, but they are scarcely evidence of fraudulent intent. The indispensable element, one would think, in defrauding creditors by means of a depreciating currency was a currency that depreciated. Measures to maintain its value are not consonant with the debtor-conspiracy theory, unless it be urged that the debtor-depreciators, being subtle rogues, knew that their apparent measures would fail and only adopted them to obscure their roguery.

A further assumption of the debtor-conspiracy theory is that the creditors were defenseless against a depreciating currency. Such in many instances was not the case. In Massachusetts between 1712 and 1742 the courts followed the settled rule that all debts contracted in terms of bills of credit or lawful money due on bonds or mortgages were understood as payable in bills of credit "according to their _nominal_ Value, whether such Bills should rise or fall in their real Value, between the Time of contracting the Debt and the Payment of it." This practice of the courts, we are told,

influenc'd and govern'd Men in their Dealings, Contracts & Dispositions of their Estates at their Death during the above-mention'd thirty Years: As to the Creditor, who plac'd out his Money at Interest, and consequently chose what Kind of Security his debtor should give him; if he made his Election to have his Debt ascertain'd and not to stand the Chance of the Rise or Fall of the Bills in their Value, he took his Bond or Mortgage with Condition for the Payment of so many Ounces of Silver, or a Sum certain in Sterling Money, or in Proclamation Money only; If on the other Hand he had an Opinion, that the Bills of Credit were more likely to rise than fall in their Value, he took a Bond or Mortgage with Condition for the Payment <u>of Bills of Credit.</u> 12

The means were evidently at hand by which long-term creditors could protect themselves against depreciating bills of credit. If, as debtor-conspiracy historians have not infrequently urged, these creditors were "the more intelligent part of the community,"[13] it would be a reflection to suggest that they did not have the wit to use them. And what has been said of Massachusetts applies generally.

From 1742 until Massachusetts returned to silver in 1750, creditors were protected by the requirement that the tender of bills of credit in satisfaction of an obligation must be in sufficient sum to equal the value of the debt when contracted. On the other hand, the full measure of this protection was not always realized, because the administration of the law was

---

12. "An Enquiry Into the State of the Bills of Credit of the Province of Massachusetts-Bay ...," 1743, in <u>Colonial Currency Reprints</u>, IV, 183-184.

13. The phrase is from Elisha R. Potter, "A Brief Account of Emissions of Paper Money, Made by the Colony of Rhode Island," in Henry Phillips, <u>Historical Sketches of the Paper Currency of the American-Colonies,</u> I, 105.

such that a sufficient sum was no always allowed to make up the depreciation.

Increasingly during the 'twenties and 'thirties the sums outstanding in Massachusetts resulted from the neglect of the tax collectors and the failure of the legislature to apportion the taxes provided by the issuing acts. There seems no way of determining the relative importance of the desire of debtors to maintain the circulation of bills of credit, and of the natural reluctance of legislatures to tax and of constituents to be taxed, in occasioning this accumulation of bills. But the latter motive doubtless operated as well as the former.

The motive for the Land Bank issue in 1740, if one neglects the direct interest that the issuers had in the profit to be derived from lending the bills out at interest, appears to have been resistance to deflation rather than promotion of inflation, for the prospects then were that the province bills would all be retired by 1742.

Of the last years of the period, an anonymous pamphleteer, who was hostile to a depreciating currency, wrote in 1749: "Upon the breaking out of [King George's War], all Hopes of putting a period to the Paper Currency [of Massachusetts] vanish'd; for the Defence of the Four Governments of New-England, lays in a manner, tho' very unreasonably, upon the Massachusetts Province, and such large Sums were necessary for carrying on the War, especially for the Charge of the successful Expedition against Cap Breton, that the Taxes for drawing in the Bills issued for those Charges were greater than it was possible for the People to pay before 1746; and so the Funds for the future Emissions were necessarily laid upon more distant Years. The Bills being thus multipli'd sunk in their Value faster than usual; so that 56 or 58s now [1749] will purchase no more silver than 30s would do five or six Years ago." [14] This was the "great inflation," and here is recognition by a contemporary observer hostile to a depreciating currency that its essential cause was the exigencies of war.

During the period from the close of Queen Anne's War to the middle of the century, the relative influence upon the currency history of New England of the interest of debtors in a depreciating currency and of the other factors involved is perhaps imponderable. But the other factors -- the threat of deflation and depression following Queen Anne's War; the willingness of the inhabitants of the several New England colonies, "farmer-debtors" and "merchant-creditors" alike, to

---

14. "A Brief Account of the Rise, Progress, and Present State of the Paper Currency of New-England ...," Boston, 1749, in Colonial Currency Reprints, IV, 385.

circulate the bills of their neighbors because they quickened trade and made possible advantageous sales, even though the practice permitted one colony to levy tribute on another; the reluctance of legislators to tax, and of constituents to be taxed, which contributed to the accumulation of bills in Massachusetts; the fact that it is not easy to divide the people of New England into clearly defined classes made up of those favorably, and of those adversely, affected by a depreciating currency; that long-term creditors were not so defenseless against a depreciating currency as has usually been supposed; that the loss from depreciation resulting to those "in whose hands the bills were constantly dying" fell upon creditors and debtors alike in proportion to their average holdings of bills;[15] and, lastly, that the essential cause of currency issues during the years of the "great inflation" was the demands of defense -- are of sufficient weight to cast doubt on the adequacy of the debtor-conspiracy explanation of even this period of colonial monetary history.

If doubts arise as to sufficiency of the debtor-conspiracy theory with respect to the New England experience during the period just surveyed, the course of events elsewhere is such as to make one even more skep-

---

15. That is, insofar as debtors did not use the bills they held to pay debts contracted before.

tical of the adequacy of the debtor-conspiracy formula as an explanation of colonial currency history generally. It is true that currency practices outside of New England at times brought protests from creditor groups, but these, insofar as they emanated from colonial groups, became more infrequent with the passage of the years, until in the period after 1764 we find the merchants of the Middle colonies taking the lead in the effort to secure the relaxation of the restrictions imposed on legal tender bills of credit by the Currency Act of 1764. Opposition to bills of credit in the years after 1751 came chiefly from British merchants, who, as a matter of historic fact, at best had usually but little understanding of the problems confronting the colonists, and at worst not infrequently based their case on little more than suspicion and misunderstanding.

By 1722, the depreciation of the bills of South Carolina brought a protest from merchants both in the province and in England. But by 1730 the colonial merchants were willing to join with the planters in allowing that a quantity of paper was necessary to circulate the trade of the province. In later decades there is no evidence of opposition to the province's loan office bill by merchants resident in South Carolina. And the opposition of the English merchants was a doctrinaire one, since by the 'forties the English merchants most active in their opposition to paper currency had come to think of every colony as but another Rhode Island. After 1764 the merchants of South Carolina heartily joined in the protest against the Currency Act of 1764.

The course of events in North Carolina, next to that in Rhode Island, perhaps best fits the debtor-creditor formula. Certainly the colony showed little zeal for retiring her bills. But here again there is an imponderable. How much did this result from the general laxness in all fiscal affairs that seemed to be indigenous to North Carolina during this period (and which is not necessarily the same thing as a debtor-conspiracy, even though it might contribute to a depreciating currency); and how much did it result from the wilful measures of debtors? The question unfortunately does not admit of answer.

But when one comes to the Middle colonies, the picture assumes a different aspect. The introduction of bills of credit in New York and New Jersey resulted from wartime demands. It is true that a group of New York merchants protested that colony's emission of 1717, but the chief question at issue was not the likelihood that the bills would depreciate; and so ill-founded did the protests of the merchants appear, that they received the rebuke of the Board of Trade. New York's one loan issue, that of ₤40,000 in 1737,[16] seems unexceptionable. It caused no observable rise in prices; it provided a revenue for the government; it appears to have facilitated the settlement of the colony and stimulated trade. Indeed, the figures of imports from England before and after the issue are extremely interesting. In 1737, the value of imports rose abruptly from ₤86,000 sterling the year before to ₤125,833 sterling. And the increase was sustained. The average of the five years beginning with 1737 shows an increase of 65 per cent over the average of the preceding five years.[17] The extent to which the relation of the loan issue to this increase in imports was causal, or merely casual, is another imponderable; but it could scarcely have been entirely casual.

The later issues of the colony (within the period of this study) were war issues; they were emitted on

---

16. The sum of ₤48,350 was emitted at this time, but ₤8,350 were for the use of government. Colonial Laws of New York, III, c. 745.

17. Emory R. Johnson, et al., History of Domestic and Foreign Commerce of the United States, I, 120-121.

New York Imports from Great Britain

Year	₤ Sterling	Year	₤ Sterling
1732	65,540	1737	125,833
1733	65,417	1738	133,436
1734	81,758	1739	106,070
1735	80,405	1740	118,777
1736	86,000	1741	140,430

sufficient funds and for reasonable periods; and they were, on the whole, promptly retired. They had been, as the New York merchant, John Watts, observed, the colony's "only means of an immediate exertion." When after the French and Indian War "the Trade ... swept off all [of New York's] Gold and Silver for remittances," paper was all that was left to circulate the colony's trade. And it was yearly sinking. Realizing their reliance upon a paper medium, the merchants of the colony were in the forefront of the movement to secure the repeal of the Currency Act of 1764. Nor did British merchants suffer from the rise in exchange after the war; for if they were paid in colony bills, it was in a sum equivalent to the sterling value of the debt. The debtor-conspiracy theory had no validity when applied to New York.

The introduction of paper currency in Pennsylvania and Delaware resulted from the depression of the early 'twenties. The specie of these colonies had been swept off, and trade was virtually at a standstill. Since a circulating medium no longer existed, the colonies had either to fall back on simple barter; monetize commodities by rating them and making them a tender in payments; or provide a paper currency. Considering the later monetary history of the two colonies, one is inclined to say that they wisely chose paper issues.

These not only supplied a circulating medium, but were issued in such form as to provide legitimate debtor relief at the time and to yield a revenue throughout their life. The spirit in which Pennsylvania and Delaware introduced paper currency is indicated by the observation of Francis Rawle in 1725 concerning the Delaware currency:

> ... due Care ought to be had [he wrote] to preserve the Value of our Paper-Currency ... continuing the Care already taken in the Security, and also restricting the Sum in a due Proportion to the Trade of this River: for a great Excess in that Respect will inevitably debase the Value of it, tho' a reasonable plenty is advantageous in encreasing Trade and Navigation, which cannot thrive without it. 18

And this spirit prevailed throughout the colonial period.

It is true that the early issues of Pennsylvania and Delaware were opposed by the merchants of those colonies. Their opposition resulted from the depreciation that bills of credit had undergone elsewhere, chiefly in South Carolina and New England, and persisted throughout the 'twenties. But when it became apparent that moderate issues of bills did not depreciate and that they were of service as a circulating medium, their antagonism subsided. And even at the mid-century, when

---

18. Francis Rawle, *Ways and Means for the Inhabitants of Delaware To Become Rich*, Philadelphia, 1725, as quoted in Richard A. Lester, "Currency Issues to Overcome Depressions in Delaware, New Jersey, New York and Maryland, 1715-37," *Journal of Political Economy*, XLVII, 185 (April, 1939).

the merchants of England were opposing colonial paper currency generally, the London merchants trading to Pennsylvania were willing to testify to the advantages arising from the bills of credit of that province.

The men of Pennsylvania perceived that a currency should be elastic, and should vary in amount with trade. The desire of the province for a modest increase in its loan issues in the 'fifties was dictated by this consideration and by that of the legitimate advantage arising from the aid a moderate loan issue rendered in settling the province. It is an indication of the cautious temper of the Pennsylvania assembly that more than once during these years, when the amount of a proposed addition to the loan issues was under consideration, the sum sanctioned was less than that proposed in the first flush of enthusiasm for a new issue. There is every indication that the members of the assembly were honest men, who wished to avail themselves of the benefits of moderate loan issues, while avoiding the abuses of immoderate ones.

The issues of Pennsylvania during the decade and a half before 1764 were all war issues; and, with the exception of the fact that Delaware renewed her loan issue in 1759, the same was true of that colony. What depreciation ensued may rightly be attributed to the war. Certainly there was no debtor-creditor struggle, for there were no more eloquent protests against the restrictions of the Currency Act of 1764 than those that came from the pens of the Pennsylvania merchants. The plain fact is "that Commerce cannot be carried on to any beneficial Extent, without a sufficient Medium of circulating Cash"; and such were the conditions that obtained in Pennsylvania (and it was not otherwise in Delaware, or for that matter, in New York or New Jersey) at the close of the French and Indian War that the "merchant-creditors" of the province believed that the provisions of the Currency Act of 1764 "prohibiting the further Emissions of Paper Money from being lawful Tender, [were] particularly oppressive to [the] Trade [of the Province], and injurious to Great-Britain."[19] Nor is there record of protests from the British merchants trading to Pennsylvania that they suffered as a result of Pennsylvania's paper issues, for the practice was to allow payment of sterling debts in colonial currency only when bills were tendered in quantity equivalent to the sterling value of the obligation.

New Jersey, as had Pennsylvania and Delaware, felt the depression of the early 'twenties; and following Pennsylvania's example, she too established a loan

---

19. To the Merchants of Great-Britain; The Memorial of the Merchants and Traders of the City of Philadelphia, 1765.

office. In the 'thirties there were two additional loan issues. The New Jersey bills maintained their value, facilitated trade, and for long returned a revenue sufficient to make taxation unnecessary.

Throughout the 'forties and 'fifties, the province ardently desired a further loan issue, although she was never successful in obtaining it. There is little reason to believe that this demand arose from "debtor-depreciators." It seems more likely that it grew out of a consideration of the manifest advantages of the former loan issues, which had shown little tendency to depreciate. What would have been the future of bills of credit in New Jersey, however, had she been unrestrained, there is no way of knowing. The fact that her bills circulated in New York and Pennsylvania made it possible for her to put out larger issues without depreciation than would otherwise have been possible. But by this very token, her position was such that she could have become the Rhode Island of the Middle colonies. Whether she would have or not, had she been unrestrained by the crown, can only be speculated upon.

The chief object in introducing paper money in Maryland in 1733 was to provide a currency that would obviate the necessity of reliance on tobacco. For a variety of reasons, however, tobacco retained many of its monetary functions. The bills authorized in 1733 were issued on adequate funds and were all redeemed at the end of their periods in sterling bills of exchange at the rate at which they were originally emitted. Nevertheless, they depreciated between redemption dates. This was due to two factors: the size of the issue; and the fact that the bills of credit did not supplant, but rather supplemented, the tobacco currency.

The tender laws of Maryland were not such as to indicate a debtor-conspiracy.[20] Nor does the history of the loan office established by the act of 1733 support in any remote degree the view that "the emission of bills of credit on loan was, in effect, a conspiracy of needy landowners against the rest of the community."[21] Throughout most of the life of the province loan office, borrowers were not sufficient to absorb the available bills. And Clarence P. Gould has found in the list of borrowers in 1755 "the names of the most prominent men in the colony, including a surprising number of those engaged in mercantile affairs."[22]

Maryland's currency history does not support the debtor-conspiracy thesis.

Virginia and Georgia introduced bills of credit at the beginning of the French and Indian War. The meagre

---

20. See Clarence P. Gould, Money and Transportation in Maryland, 1720-1765, pp. 114-115.
21. See note 1, this chapter.
22. Gould, p. 109.

evidence available contains no indication of a debtor movement in Georgia; and on the face of the record one is inclined to think the needs of the war a sufficient explanation.

On the other hand, a debtor-creditor struggle has been seen by some in the Old Dominion. "Virginia," writes Curtis P. Nettels, "now became the principal scene of [debtor-creditor] conflict; there the struggle over currency and debts bore witness to the impending bankruptcy of the tobacco planters, caught as they were in the grip of British merchant capitalism."[23] But if the analysis developed in the preceding chapter be correct, this judgment is not supported by the evidence. A sufficient explanation is to be found in the demands of the war. This view finds further corroboration in the fact that the supposed "debtor-conspirators" of Virginia mildly acquiesced in the restraints of the Currency Act of 1764, in contrast to the vigorous protests of the "merchant-creditors" of New York and Philadelphia. All things considered, it seems probable that the Virginia Burgesses spoke but simple truth when they said: "There are no warm Advocates of Paper Money among us."[24]

When one examines the paper currency of the American

---

23. See note 1, this chapter.
24. **JHB**, 1761-1765, p. 189 (May, 1763).

colonies in detail, colony by colony, and period by period, he finds that bills of credit were much more than instruments "for cheating creditors." Rather, they provided variously: the colonies' "only expedient in an exigency"; a circulating medium in lieu of, or in supplement to, specie; the means of facilitating the settlement of the country through loans on land; and a revenue in support of government. "There is just the same difference in the Use & Abuse" of paper money, wrote the New York merchant, John Watts, in 1765, "as there is in food itself."[25] If some colonies abused it, others used it, and drew sustenance from its use. Some, in fact, were conspicuously successful in their management of their bills of credit. And if further evidence of this fact is desired, let one cast his eye over the graph in Arthur H. Cole's Wholesale Commodity Prices in the United States, 1700-1861,[26] showing wholesale prices at New York and Philadelphia, and he will perhaps be surprised to see how much more stable prices were during the colonial period than during the period from the adoption of the Constitution to the Civil War. And the same would hold for New Jersey and Delaware.[27]

---

25. John Watts, Letter Book, p. 348.
26. Vol. I, pp. 107-108.
27. One could develop at length an interesting comparison of conditions in the colonies during the paper money period with conditions during various periods of our national history: with the period of wildcat banking;

The currency policies of the colonies were frequently influenced by the regulations of the imperial authorities at Whitehall and Westminster, no less than by considerations of defense or economic advantage on the American side of the Atlantic. Until the early 'forties, it may be said that, on the whole, the attitude of the Board of Trade towards the bills of credit of the colonies was reluctantly sympathetic and essentially reasonable. It acknowledged their use as an instrument of governmental finance and as an aid to trade. It conceded that a paper currency in the colonies permitted the sending of specie to Britain to the enlargement of British manufactures. It realized that in their circumstances the several colonies were "various & very different," and that each might "require a distinct Consideration" in respect to bills of credit. It confined its restraints chiefly to Massachusetts, New Hampshire, and the Carolinas, colonies where depreciation had been marked (it was without power in the charter colony of Rhode Island).

But after the early 'forties, as the Board came under the influence of the London merchants, whose predominant interest was a creditor one, it lost its power

---

or, more latterly, with the period since 1914, with its wartime price rise and its great depression, accompanied by a subsidence of prices and a collapse of the banking system.

to discriminate. Paper currency came to be weighed solely, one is almost inclined to say, with respect to its effect, actual or potential, on creditors. The merchants were countenanced in their efforts to secure the suppression of colonial paper currency by act of Parliament. But King George's War intervened. Once the war was over, however, both merchants and Lords of Trade returned to the attack. In the later stages they received aid from Massachusetts and from certain merchant groups in Rhode Island. The result was the suppression of New England's legal tender bills by the Currency Act of 1751. The act, however, was a compromise measure, since the desire had been to make the restraint general.

But the Board of Trade was not to acknowledge defeat. Since the "sense of Parliament" had been obtained with respect to paper currency in America, so the Board viewed it, the restraints imposed on New England should be extended to the colonies to the southward through the instrumentality of the royal instructions, even though Parliament had deliberately exempted these colonies from the provisions of the act. Its attitude towards bills of credit became more and more the doctrinaire one of those who viewed all paper issues as the instruments of debtor-conspirators. While during the French and Indian War the Board did not, in most instances, formally abandon its policy of extending the restraints of the Currency Act of 1751 beyond New England, it was forced to connive at the breaking of instructions and the issuing of legal tender bills as instruments of war finance. It did, however, have considerable success in enforcing the five year periods required for war bills by the act applying to New England.

But such concessions as the Board of Trade made to bills of credit during the war were concessions to expediency; fundamental principles remained unchanged. Legal tender bills were instruments of debtor-depreciators. Come the peace, they must go. The result was the Board's crowning blunder -- the Currency Act of 1764.

The Currency Act of 1751 restraining, in particular, the charter colony of Rhode Island, which was beyond the reach of the royal instructions, had been not without reason. It had, moreover, come at a time when the payment of the large parliamentary grants for the Cape Breton and intended Canada expeditions eased the transition from paper to specie. And it had been desired by Massachusetts as protection against the depreciating issues of her smaller neighbor.

But there was nothing similar in the situation in 1764. Almost without exception, the colonies affected had in good faith issued their bills of credit (on adequate funds) in response to the requisitions of the crown. After the close of the war their specie was swept off for remittances and their chief reliance in trade was their paper, which was yearly sinking. Such was their situation when the Board of Trade, supported by the British merchants, without giving the colonies a chance to be heard, impugned their motives by charging a debtor-conspiracy and rushed through the Currency Act of 1764, prohibiting further issues of legal tender bills and providing that the periods of those already outstanding should not be extended. And to compound the blunder, the act was interpreted not only to prohibit issues that were declared a legal tender between man and man, but also those that were made a legal tender at the treasury or loan office.

The whole mischief resulted from the debtor-conspiracy view that the Board, mislead by the misrepresentations of the British merchants trading to Virginia, took of colonial bills of credit. But the colonists viewed them, to use the language of John Watts, as their "only Expedient in an Exigency" and "the only Medium ... of Commerce" they had left. If they were to be denied paper, they reasoned, they would need specie. But their supply of specie had been curtailed by the trade regulations that followed the peace of 1763. If they were forced to retain what specie still came into the colonies, they would, for a time at least, have to do without British manufactures. And British policy did not permit them to develop their own. It is little wonder that the Currency Act of 1764 proved a fertile source of resentment in the crucial years that followed.

Had the imperial authorities been content after the French and Indian War to relie upon the royal instructions for effecting such restraints as were necessary to prevent the currency policy of one colony from injuring another (or the merchants in Britain), there is no reason to believe that the means would not have been sufficient. But men at Whitehall capable of a better understanding of the realities of colonial bills of credit and of the views, or even prejudices, if you will, of the colonists respecting them, would also have been needed to permit the use, while preventing the abuse, of paper currency.

One indictment of the policy of Britain respecting colonial currency remains. Restraints were never lacking, but in the whole course of colonial history never once did the imperial authorities attempt any positive contribution to the solution of the colonial monetary problem. By imposing restraints increasingly doctrinaire and undiscriminating, and by failing to make any positive contribution to solving the problem of an adequate currency for the colonies after having denied them recourse to their own measures, the imperial authorities added by so much to the forces loosening the hold of the mother country on her American provinces.

BIBLIOGRAPHY

BIBLIOGRAPHY

MANUSCRIPTS

Library of the American Philosophical Society.

    Benjamin Franklin Papers.

William L. Clements Library.

    George Clinton Papers.

    Franklin-Galloway Letters.

    William Knox Papers.

    Shelburne Papers.

Library of Congress.

    British Public Record Office, Transcripts and Reproductions.

        C. O. 5 / 65-69, 1063-1088, 1097-1106, 1131-1132, 1141, 1280-1286, 1296, 1301, 1327-1334, 1344-1353, 1366-1369, 1375. Relates chiefly to Virginia and New York.

        C. O. 5 / 323 contains the reports of the several colonies to the Board of Trade in 1764 relative to bills of credit issued since 1749, photostats of which were obtained from London through the courtesy of the Library of Congress.

    House of Lords Library, Reproductions.

        225, 227, 228, 300, 315.

    Benjamin Franklin Papers.

    Force Transcripts, I, contain correspondence of the Committee of Correspondence of the Georgia Assembly with the London agents,

William Knox and Charles Garth, 1762-1771.

Historical Society of Pennsylvania.

    Board of Trade Papers, Transcripts from the British Public Record Office.

        Proprieties, XVIII (1748) - XXIV (1776).

        Plantations General, XIV (1748) - XXXI (1775).

    Chaloner & White, Philadelphia Merchants, MSS, 1744-1777.

    Pemberton Papers, 1765-1775.

    Penn Letter Books, II (1748) - X (1775).

    Penn Official Correspondence, 1748-1771.

    Thomas Wharton MSS, 1765-1768.

Pennsylvania Archives.

    Provincial Papers, 1764-1769.

Virginia Historical Society.

    Lee Papers.

Virginia State Library.

    Letter Book of James Abercromby, 1751-1773. Contains letters from Abercromby only.

    Allason Letter Book, 1757-1772. Merchants letters.

Historical Commission of South Carolina.

    South Carolina Commons House Journal, 1748-1775.

    South Carolina Council Journal, 1748-1775.

    Public Records of South Carolina, Transcripts of the South Carolina material in the British Public Record Office.

Selected items before 1848. 1848-1875.

Letter Book of Charles Garth, 1766-1775. Contains letters between Garth and the Committee of Correspondence of the South Carolina Assembly. The Garth letters published in the South Carolina Historical and Genealogical Magazine are from this source.

South Carolina Historical and Genealogical Society.

Letter Books of Henry Laurens.

BROADSIDES

Library of Congress.

Massachusetts, 1750-1775.

New York, 1750-1775.

North Carolina, 1750-1775.

Pennsylvania, 1755-1775.

South Carolina, 1750-1775.

Virginia, 1750-1775.

United States, 1750-1775.

NEWSPAPERS

The Boston Evening Post. 1750-1762.

The Boston News Letter. 1748-1763.

The Newport Mercury, Newport, R. I. 1758-1769.

The New London Summary, New London, Conn. 1758-1763.

The New York Journal, or General Advertiser. 1766-1769 (incomplete file).

The New York Mercury. 1760-1768.

The Pennsylvania Chronicle and Universal Advertiser, Philadelphia. 1767-1770.

The Pennsylvania Gazette, Philadelphia. 1760-1770.

The Pennsylvania Journal; and Weekly Advertiser, Philadelphia. 1764-1766.

The Virginia Gazette (Purdie and Dixon), Williamsburg. 1766-1772 (incomplete file).

The Virginia Gazette (Rind), Williamsburg. 1768-1771 (incomplete file).

The South Carolina and American General Gazette, Charleston. 1748-1775.

The South Carolina Gazette; And Country Journal, Charleston. 1765-1775.

PRINTED MATERIAL - CONTEMPORARY

[Balch, Thomas (ed.)], Letters and Papers relating chiefly to the Provincial History of Pennsylvania, with some Notices of the Writers. Philadelphia, 1855.

Ballagh, James C. (ed.), The Letters of Richard Henry Lee, 2 vols. New York, 1911, 1914.

Belcher, Jonathan, "The Belcher Papers," 2 vols., Massachusetts Historical Society, Collections (sixth series), VI, VII. Boston, 1893, 1894.

[Borden, William], An Address To the Inhabitants of North-Carolina; occasioned By the difficult Circumstances the Government seems to Labour under, for Want of a Medium, or something to answer in lieu of Money; for the Encouragement of the People, In regard to Business: To which is added, A Proposition for a Paper-Currency, whereby the Possessors of the Soil may in a very honorable Manner, and with cheerful Hearts, discharge their Quit-rents and publick Taxes: And whereby, also, new Life may be given to Trade and Commerce, so far as is necessary; which will be a natural Inducement to the fair Trader to settle and reside in the Government, as well as the only Means to propogate Navigation (that necessary Branch of Business) in all its proper Parts. Williamsburg, 1746. (American series; photostat reproduction by the Massachusetts Historical Society, no. 218, Boston, 1928.) Also reprinted in Boyd (ed.), below.

Boyd, William K. (ed.), Some Eighteenth Century Tracts concerning North Carolina. Raleigh, 1927.

Contains:

"William Borden's Address to the People and Burgesses (1746)."

"A Table of North Carolina Taxes, 1748-1770."

Brigham, Clarence S. (ed.), "British Royal Proclamations Relating to America, 1603-1783," American Antiquarian Society, Transactions and Collections, XII. Worcester, Mass., 1911.

Browne, William H. (ed.), "Correspondence of Horatio Sharpe," Archives of Maryland, VI, IX, XIV. Baltimore, 1888, 1890, 1895.

Belknap, Jeremy, A History of New Hampshire, 3 vols. Second edition, Boston, 1813, cited. First published, 1784-1792. Also a one volume edition published at Dover, 1831.

Chalmers, George, An Introduction to the History of the Revolt of the American Colonies ..., 2 vols. Boston, 1845.

Chalmers, George, Opinions of Eminent Lawyers, on Various Points of English Jurisprudence, Chiefly Concerning the Colonies, Fisheries, and Commerce of Great Britain, 2 vols. London, 1814.

Colden, Cadwallader, "The Letters and Papers of Cadwallader Colden," 9 vols. New York Historical Society, Collections, L, LI, LII, LV, LVI, LXVII, LXVIII. New York, 1917, 1918, 1919, 1922, 1923, 1934, 1935.

CONNECTICUT

Connecticut Historical Society, Collections. Hartford.

XI (1907), XIII (1911), XV (1914) "The [Gov. Jonathan] Law Papers, 1741-1750."

XVI (1916) "The [Gov. Roger] Wolcott Papers, 1750-1754."

XVII (1918), XVIII (1920) "The [Gov. Thomas] Fitch Papers, 1754-1766."

XIX (1921) "The [Gov. William] Pitkin Papers, 1766-1769."

Public Records of the Colony of Connecticut, 1636-1776, edited by Charles J. Hoadly, 15 vols. Hartford, 1850-1890. Consists of the "Assembly Journals."

Davis, Andrew McF. (ed.), "Colonial Currency Reprints," 4 vols., Publications of the Prince Society, XXII-XXV. Boston, 1919-1911.

Davis, Andrew McF. (ed.), Tracts relating to the Currency of Massachusetts-Bay. Boston, 1902.

DELAWARE

Laws of the State of Delaware from [1700 to 1797], 2 vols. New-Castle, 1797.

De Bert, Dennys, "Letters of Dennys De Bert, 1757-1770," Colonial Society of Massachusetts, Publications, XIII (Transactions, 1910-1911). Boston, 1912.

Dickinson, John, The Writings of John Dickinson, edited by Paul Leicester Ford, Historical Society of Pennsylvania, Memoirs, XIV. Philadelphia, 1895.

Dinwiddie, Robert, "The Official Records of Robert Dinwiddie, Lieutenant-Governor of Virginia, 1751-1758," 2 vols., edited with an introduction and notes by R. A. Brock. Virginia Historical Society, Collections (new series), III-IV. Richmond, 1883-1884.

Douglass, Dr. William, A Discourse concerning the Currencies of the British Plantations in America. London, 1739; Boston, 1740. Reprinted in American Economic Association, Economic Studies, II. New York, 1897. Also in Colonial Currency Reprints, III.

Douglass, Dr. William, A Summary, Historical and Political, of the First Planting, Progressive Improvements, and Present State of the British Settlements in North-America, 2 vols. London, 1755, edition cited. First published in Boston, 1749-1751.

"An Enquiry Into the State of the Bills of Credit Of the Province of Massachusetts-Bay ...." [Boston] 1743, Colonial Currency Reprints, IV.

Fitzpatrick, John C. (ed.), The Diaries of George Washington, 1748-1799, 4 vols. Boston and New York, 1925.

Foulke, Samuel, "Fragments of a Journal Kept by Samuel Foulke, of Bucks County, While a Member of the Colonial Assembly of Pennsylvania, 1762-3-4," Pennsylvania Magazine of History and Biography, V, 60-73. Philadelphia, 1881.

Franklin, Benjamin, The Writings of Benjamin Franklin, edited by Albert H. Smyth, 10 vols. New York, 1907.

Franklin, Benjamin, The Works of Benjamin Franklin, edited by Jared Sparks, 10 vols. Boston and Milwaukee, 1856. Several later editions.

Fries, Adelaide L. (ed.), Records of the Moravians in North Carolina, 1752-1783, 4 vols. Raleigh, 1922-1930.

Fry, Richard, A Scheme for a Paper Currency, Together with Two Petitions written in Boston Gaol in 1739-1740, with an introduction by Andrew McF. Davis. Providence, 1908.

Garth, Charles, "Correspondence of Charles Garth," South Carolina Historical and Genealogical Magazine, various volumes. Charleston.

GEORGIA

    The Colonial Records of the State of Georgia, edited by Allen D. Chandler. Atlanta.

        XIII-XV (1907) Contain "Journal of Commons House of Assembly," 1755-1782.

        XVI (1907), XVII (1908) Contain "Journal of

the Upper House of Assembly," 1755-1774.

    XVIII (1910), XIX, Pt. I (1911) Contain "Statutes," 1754-1773.

Gibbes, Robert W., Documentary History of the American Revolution [relating chiefly to South Carolina], 3 vols. New York, 1855.

GREAT BRITAIN

    Acts of the Privy Council of England, Colonial Series, edited by James Munro, under the general supervision of Sir Almeric W. Fitzroy, Clerk of the Privy Council, 6 vols. London, 1908-1912.

    "British Royal Proclamations Relating to America, 1603-1783," edited by Clarence S. Brigham. American Antiquarian Society, Transactions, XII. Worcester, Mass., 1911.

    Calendar of State Papers, Colonial Series, America and West Indies, edited by Cecil Headlam and Arthur P. Newton. The 23 volumes covering the period 1700-1733, published, London, 1910-1939, were consulted.

    Journal of the Commissioners for Trade and Plantations from April 1704, to May 1782, Preserved in the Public Record Office, 14 vols. London, 1920-1938. The earlier "Journals" are published in Calendar of State Papers, Colonial Series, America and West Indies, above.

    The Journals of the House of Commons. Vols. XIII-XXXIV cover the period, 1699-1776. London.

    Journals of the House of Lords. Vols. XXVII-XXXIV cover the period, 1701-1776. London.

    The Manuscripts of the House of Lords (new series), VII (1706-1708), VIII (1708-1710) consulted. London, 1921, 1923.

    The Parliamentary History of England from The Earliest Period to The Year 1803. (Cobbett and Hansard.) Vols. V-XVIII cover the period, 1688-1777. London, 1807-1819.

The Statutes at Large, edited by Danby Pickering, 109 vols. London.

Stock, Lee Francis (ed.), Proceedings and Debates of the British Parliaments respecting North America, 4 vols. published. Vols. II-IV cover the period 1689-1739. Washington, 1924-1937.

Hening, William W. (comp.), The Statutes at Large; Being a Collection of all the Laws of Virginia from the First Session of the Legislature in the Year 1619, 13 vols. Richmond, 1819-1823.

Hutchinson, Peter Orlando (ed.), The Diary and Letters of His Excellency Thomas Hutchinson, Esq., 2 vols. Boston, 1884.

Hutchinson, Thomas, The History of the Colony and Province of Massachusetts-Bay, 3 vols. First published 1765-1828. Edition edited by Lawrence S. Mayo (3 vols., Cambridge, Mass., 1936) cited.

Kimball, Gertrude S. (ed.), The Correspondence of the Colonial Governors of Rhode Island, 1723-1775, 2 vols. Boston, 1903.

Kimball, Gertrude S. (ed.), Correspondence of William Pitt, when Secretary of State, with Colonial Governors and Military and Naval Commissioners in America, 2 vols. New York and London, 1906.

Labaree, Leonard W. (ed.), Royal Instructions to British Colonial Governors, 1670-1776, 2 vols. New York, 1935.

Lee, Richard Henry, The Letters of Richard Henry Lee, edited by James C. Ballagh, 2 vols. New York, 1911, 1914.

Lee, Richard Henry, "Extracts from the Lee Papers," Southern Literary Messenger, XXVII-XXX. Richmond, 1858-1860.

McMurtrie, Douglas C. (ed.), Rates of Exchange in Pennsylvania, MDCCVI, With a facsimile of a printed Act "for the better proportioning the rates of Money in Payments," not represented in any American Collection; reproduced from the only known original in the Public Record Office, London. Chicago, 1935.

Macpherson, David, Annals of Commerce, Manufactures, Fisheries, and Navigation ... of the British Empire and Other Countries from the Earliest Accounts to ... 1801, 4 vols. London, 1805. Vol. III covers the period, 1708-1782.

MARYLAND

Archives of Maryland, 56 vols. Baltimore, 1883- Various volumes reproduce the "Proceedings and Acts of Assembly" to 1761.

The General Public Statutory Law and Public Local Law of the State of Maryland, ... 1692 to 1839 ..., edited by Clement Dorsey, 3 vols. Baltimore, 1840.

Sharpe, Horatio, "Correspondence of [Gov.] Horatio Sharpe," 1753-1771, Archives of Maryland, VI, IX, XIV. Baltimore, 1888, 1890, 1895.

MASSACHUSETTS

The Acts and Resolves, Public and Private, of the Province of the Massachusetts Bay, edited by Albert C. Goodell, A. S. Wheeler, and W. C. Williamson, 20 vols. Boston, 1869-1918.

Belcher, Jonathan, "The Belcher Papers," 2 vols., Massachusetts Historical Society, Collections (sixth series), VI, VII. Boston, 1893, 1894.

"Broadsides, Ballads & c. Printed In Massachusetts, 1639-1800," Massachusetts Historical Society, Collections, LXXV. Boston, 1927.

Davis, Andrew McF. Davis, Tracts relating to the Currency of Massachusetts Bay. Boston, 1902.

"An Enquiry Into the State of the Bills of Credit Of the Province of Massachusetts-Bay ...." [Boston] 1743, Colonial Currency Reprints, IV.

Fry, Richard, A Scheme for a Paper Currency, together with two Petitions written in Boston Gaol in 1739-1740. Providence, 1908.

Hutchinson, Peter Orlando (ed.), The Diary and Letters of Thomas Hutchinson. (See full entry under editor.)

Hutchinson, Thomas, History. (See under author.)

"Land-Bank and Silver-Bank Papers," Colonial Society of Massachusetts, Collections, IV. Boston, 1910.

Mather, Cotton, Diary, 1709-1724. (See under author.)

Mauduit, Jasper, "Jasper Mauduit, Agent in London for the Province of the Massachusetts-Bay, 1762-1765" (letters and accounts). (See under author.)

Rowe, John, Letters and Diary of John Rowe, Boston Merchant, 1759-1762, 1764-1779, edited by Anne Rowe Cunningham. Boston, 1903.

Sewall, Samuel, "Letter Book of Samuel Sewall," Massachusetts Historical Society, Collections (sixth series), I, II. Boston, 1886, 1888.

Shirley, William, Correspondence of William Shirley ..., 1731-1760, edited by Charles H. Lincoln, 2 vols. New York, 1912.

Mather, Cotton, "Diary of Cotton Mather, 1709-1724," Massachusetts Historical Society, Collections (seventh series), VII, VIII. Boston, 1911, 1912.

Mauduit, Jasper, "Jasper Mauduit, Agent in London for the Province of the Massachusetts-Bay, 1762-1765" (letters and accounts), Massachusetts Historical Society, Collections, LXXIV. Boston, 1918.

To The Merchants and Manufacturers of Great-Britain; The Memorial of the Merchants and Traders of the City of Philadelphia. [Philadelphia, 1765.]

NEW HAMPSHIRE

Belknap, Jeremy, A History of New Hampshire. (See under author.)

Documents and Records Relating to the Province of New Hampshire (cited as New Hampshire Provincial Papers), compiled by Nathaniel Bouton, 7 vols. Concord, N. H., 1867-1873.

Laws of New Hampshire (The Province Period), edited by Albert S. Batchellor, 3 vols. Manchester, N. H., 1904-1915.

A List of Documents in the Public Record Office in London, England, relating to the Province of New Hampshire ... with Notes and Indexes, edited by Albert S. Batchellor. New Hampshire Historical Society, Collections, X. Manchester, N. H., 1893.

"Provincial Taxes in New Hampshire, 1753-1766," New Hampshire Historical Society, Collections, III, 152. Concord, N. H., 1832.

NEW JERSEY

An Analytical Index of the Colonial Documents of New Jersey, in the State Paper Offices of England. Compiled by Henry Stevens; edited with notes, and references to printed works and manuscripts in other depositaries, by William A. Whitehead. New York, 1858.

Documents relating to the Colonial History of the State of New Jersey (Archives of the State of New Jersey), 40 vols. Newark, 1880- Vols. I-X contain the correspondence of the governors and allied items; Vols. XIII-XVIII, the "Journals of the Governor and Council."

Morris, Lewis, "The Papers of Lewis Morris Governor of the Province of New Jersey from 1738 to 1746," New Jersey Historical Society, Collections, IV. New York and Newark, 1852.

NEW YORK

The Colonial Laws of New York from the Year 1664 to the Revolution, 5 vols. Albany, 1894.

The Documentary History of the State of New York, under the direction of Christopher Morgan, 4 vols. Albany, 1849-1851.

Documents relating to the Colonial History of New York, edited by E. B. O'Callaghan, 15 vols. Albany, 1853-1887.

Journal of the Legislative Council of the Colony of New York, 1691-1775, 2 vols. Albany, 1861.

Journal of the Votes and Proceedings of the General Assembly of the Colony of New-York, 3 vols. Vols. I, II, New York, 1764, 1766; III, Albany, 1820.

Smith, William, The History of the late Province of New-York from its discovery to ... 1762, 2 vols. New York, 1829.

State of New York. Messages from the Governors comprising Executive Communications to the Legislature and Other Papers Relating to Legislation from ... 1683 to ... 1906, edited by Charles Z. Lincoln. Albany, 1909. Vol. I covers the colonial period.

Watts, John, "Letter Book of John Watts, Jan. 1, 1762-Dec. 22, 1765." (See under author.)

Nicholas, Robert C., "Paper Money in Colonial Virginia," William and Mary Quarterly, XX, 227-262. Williamsburg, 1911-1912. Reprint from the Virginia Gazette of three letters of Nicholas, the colonial treasurer, July 16, 20, Sept. 22, 1773.

NORTH CAROLINA

Boyd, William K., Some Eighteenth Century Tracts concerning North Carolina. (See under author.)

The Colonial Records of North Carolina, edited by William L. Saunders and Walter Clark, 30 vols. Raleigh and Goldsboro, 1886-1906. Vols. I-X contain the "Journals of the Assembly" and the correspondence of the governors and other officials, 1662-1776. Vols. XXIII, XXV, The State Records of North Carolina, contain laws, 1715-1790.

Fries, Adelaide L. (ed.), Records of the Moravians in North Carolina, 1753-1783, 4 vols. (See under editor.)

Williamson, Hugh, The History of North Carolina, 2 vols. Philadelphia, 1812.

Palfrey, John G., History of New England from the Revolution of the Seventeenth Century to the Revolution of the Eighteenth, 5 vols. Boston, 1859-1890. The footnotes reproduce much contemporary material.

Pargellis, Stanley (ed.), Military Affairs in North America, 1748-1765. Selected Documents from the Cumberland Papers in Windsor Castle. New York and London, 1936.

PENNSYLVANIA

    Dickinson, John, *The Writings of John Dickinson*, edited by Paul Leicester Ford, Historical Society of Pennsylvania, *Memoirs*, XIV. Philadelphia, 1895.

    Hazard, Samuel (ed.), *The Register of Pennsylvania* (later *Hazard's Register of Pennsylvania*), 16 vols. Philadelphia, 1828-1835.

    McMurtrie, Douglas C., *Rates of exchange in Pennsylvania, MDCCVI* .... (See under author.)

    To The Merchants and Manufacturers of Great-Britain; The Memorial of the Merchants and Traders of the City of Philadelphia. [Philadelphia, 1765.]

    Minutes of the Provincial Council of Pennsylvania, 1683-1776, 10 vols. Usually cited as *Pennsylvania Colonial Records*. Harrisburg, 1838-1852.

    Pennsylvania Archives (first series), 12 vols. Philadelphia, 1852-1856.

    Pennsylvania Archives (second series), 19 vols. Harrisburg, 1874-1893.

    Pennsylvania Archives (eighth series), edited by Gertrude MacKinney and Charles F. Hoban, 8 vols. Cited as *Votes and Proceedings of the House of Representatives of the Province of Pennsylvania, 1682-1776*. Harrisburg, 1931-1935.

    Statutes at Large of Pennsylvania from 1682 to 1801, compiled by James T. Mitchell and Henry Flanders, 13 vols., II-XIV, published. Harrisburg, 1896-1909.

    Thomson, Charles, "The Thomson Papers, 1765-1816," New York Historical Society, *Collections*, XI. New York, 1878.

Pickering, Danby (ed.), *Statutes at Large*, 109 vols. London.

Pitkin, Timothy, *A Statistical View of the Commerce of the United States of America* .... Hartford, 1816.

This edition contains statistics relative to colonial trade.

Pitt, William, *Correspondence ... with Colonial Governors ...*, edited by Gertrude S. Kimball. (See under editor.)

Pownall, Thomas, *The Administration of the British Colonies*, 2 vols. Fifth edition, London, 1774.

Ramsay, David, *The History of the American Revolution*, 2 vols. Philadelphia, 1789. Several editions have been published.

Ramsay, David, *The History of the Revolution of South Carolina, from a British Province to an Independent State*, 2 vols. Trenton, 1785.

RHODE ISLAND

Cooper, T. R., *A letter to the common people of the Colony of Rhode-Island, concerning the unjust Designs, and actual Attempts, of a Number of Misers, and Money Jobbers, (particularly such of that Character as are in Place and Power,) to compel all the Old Tenor Debtors in this Colony to pay near three Times as much as they owe.* Providence, 1763. (American series; photostat reproductions of the Massachusetts Historical Society, no. 97.)

Kimball, Gertrude S. (ed.), *The Correspondence of the Colonial Governors of Rhode Island, 1723-1775*, 2 vols. Boston, 1903.

Records of the Colony of Rhode Island and Providence Plantations, in New England, edited by John R. Bartlett, 10 vols. Providence, 1856-1865.

Riddell, William R., "Benjamin Franklin and Colonial Money," Royal Society of Canada, *Proceedings and Transactions* (third series), XXIII, sec. ii, 105-114.

Rowe, John, *Letters and Diary of John Rowe, Boston Merchant, 1759-1762, 1764-1779*, edited by Anne Rowe Cunningham. Boston, 1903.

Sewall, Samuel, "Letter Book of Samuel Sewall," Massachusetts Historical Society, *Collections* (sixth series), I, II. Boston, 1886, 1888.

Sharpe, Horatio, "Correspondence of Horatio Sharpe," 1753-1771, edited by William H. Browne, 3 vols. Archives of Maryland, VI, IX, XIV. Baltimore, 1888, 1890, 1895.

Sheffield, John Lord, Observations on the Commerce of the American States .... Sixth edition, enlarged, London, 1784.

Shirley, William, Correspondence of William Shirley ..., 1731-1760, edited by Charles H. Lincoln, 2 vols. New York, 1912.

Smith, Adam, An Inquiry into the Nature and Causes of the Wealth of Nations. Everyman edition, 2 vols. London and New York, 1910. First published, 1776.

Smith, William, The History of the late Province of New-York from its discovery to ... 1762, 2 vols. New York, 1829.

Smyth, Albert H. (ed.), The Writings of Benjamin Franklin, 10 vols. New York, 1907.

SOUTH CAROLINA

"An Account of the Rise and Progress of the Paper Bills of Credit in South Carolina ...," Statutes at Large of South Carolina, IX, Appendix.

An Essay on Currency, Written in August 1732. Charlestown: Printed and Sold by Lewis Timothy, in Church-Street. 1734. Reprinted in facsimile, Columbia, S. C., 1935.

Garth, Charles, "Correspondence of Charles Garth," South Carolina Historical and Genealogical Magazine, various volumes. Charleston.

Gibbes, Robert W., Documentary History of the American Revolution, 3 vols. (See under author.)

Ramsay, David, The History of the Revolution [in] South Carolina ..., 2 vols. (See under author.)

The Statutes at Large of South Carolina, edited by Thomas Cooper and David J. McCord. Vols. II-IV, IX, deal with the period of this study. Columbia, S. C., 1836-1841.

Sparks, Jared (ed.), The Works of Benjamin Franklin, 10 vols. Boston and Milwaukee, 1856. Several later editions.

Spotswood, Alexander, "The Official Letters of Alexander Spotswood, Lieutenant-Governor of the Colony of Virginia, 1710-1722," edited by R. A. Brock, 2 vols. Virginia Historical Society, Collections, I, II. Richmond, 1782, 1785.

Stiles, Ezra, Extracts from the Itineraries and other Miscellanies of Ezra Stiles, D. D., LL. D., 1755-1794, with a selection from his Correspondence, edited by Frank B. Dexter. New Haven, 1916.

Stock, Lee Francis (ed.), Proceedings and Debates of the British Parliaments respecting North America, 4 vols. published. Vols. II-IV cover the period 1689-1739. Washington, 1924-1937.

Thatcher, Oxenbridge, Considerations on Lowering the Value of Gold Coins, Within the Province of the Massachusetts-Bay. [Boston, 1762.] (American series; photostat reproductions by the Massachusetts Historical Society, no. 103. Boston, 1923.)

Thomson, Charles, "The Thomson Papers, 1765-1816," New York Historical Society, Collections, XI. New York, 1878.

VIRGINIA

    Calendar of Virginia State Papers and Other Manuscripts, edited by William P. Palmer. Vol. I covers the period, 1652-1781. Richmond, 1875.

    Dinwiddie, Robert, "The Official Records of Robert Dinwiddie, Lieutenant-Governor of Virginia, 1751-1758," edited by R. A. Brock. (See under author.)

    Journals of the House of Burgesses of Virginia, edited by John Pendleton Kennedy, 13 vols. Richmond, 1905-1915.

    Lee, Richard Henry, The Letters of Richard Henry Lee, edited by James C. Ballagh, 2 vols. New York, 1911, 1914.

    Lee, Richard Henry, "Extracts from the Lee Papers," Southern Literary Messenger, XXVII-XXX. Richmond, 1858-1860.

Legislative Journals of the Councils of Virginia, edited by H. R. McIlwaine, 3 vols. Richmond, 1918-1919.

Nicholas, Robert C., "Paper Money in Colonial Virginia," *William and Mary Quarterly*, XX, 227-262. (See under author.)

Spotswood, Alexander, "The Official Letters of Alexander Spotswood ...," edited by R. A. Brock. (See under author.)

The Statutes at Large of Virginia, compiled by William W. Hening. (See under compiled.)

The Virginia Magazine of History and Biography. Richmond. As cited.

William and Mary College Quarterly. Williamsburg. As cited.

Washington, George, *The Diaries of George Washington, 1748-1799*, edited by John C. Fitzpatrick, 4 vols. Boston and New York, 1925.

Watts, John, "Letter Book of John Watts, Jan. 1, 1762-Dec. 22, 1765," *New York Historical Society, Collections*, LXI. New York, 1928.

Williamson, Hugh, *The History of North Carolina*, 2 vols. Philadelphia, 1812.

Wright, John, *The American Negotiator; or, The various Currencies of the British Colonies in America; as well the Islands, as the Continent* .... London, 1765, edition.

PRINTED MATERIAL - NON-CONTEMPORARY

Andrews, Charles M., *The Colonial Period of American History, England's Commercial and Colonial Policy* (Vol. IV). New Haven, 1938.

Andrews, Charles M., "Current Lawful Money of New England," *American Historical Review*, XXIV, October, 1918.

Arnold, Samuel G., *History of the State of Rhode Island*

and Providence Plantations, 2 vols. New York, 1859.

Baker-Crothers, Hayes, Virginia and the French and Indian War. Chicago, 1928.

Baldwin, Alice M., The New England Clergy and the American Revolution. Durham, 1928.

Bayse, Arthur H., The Lords Commissioners of Trade and Plantations Commonly Known as the Board of Trade 1748-1782. New Haven, 1925.

Beer, George L., British Colonial Policy, 1754-1765. New York, 1907.

Behrens, Kathryn L., "Paper Money in Maryland, 1727-1789," John Hopkins University Studies in History and Political Science, series xlI, no. I. Baltimore, 1923.

Bell, H. C., "West Indian Trade before the Revolution," American Historical Review, XXII, January, 1917.

Besanzon, Anne, Robert D. Gray, Miriam Hussey, Prices in Colonial Pennsylvania. Philadelphia, 1935.

Bolles, Albert S., Financial History of the United States from 1774 to 1879. New York, 1879.

Bradbeer, William W., "New Jersey Paper Currency, 1709-1786," New Jersey Historical Society, Proceedings (new series) VII, 185-194. Newark, 1923.

Bronson, Henry, "A Historical Account of Connecticut Currency ...," New Haven Historical Society, Papers, I. New Haven, 1865.

Bullock, Charles J., Essays on the Monetary History of the United States. New York, 1900.

Carey, Lewis J., Franklin's Economic Views. Garden City, 1928.

Chalmers, Robert, A History of Currency in the British Colonies. London, 1893.

Channing, Edward, A History of the United States, II, III. New York, 1908, 1912.

Clark, W. A., The History of Banking Institutions organized in *South Carolina Prior to 1860.* Columbia, S. C., 1922.

Cole, Arthur H., *Wholesale Commodity Prices in the United States, 1700-1861,* 2 vols. Cambridge, 1938.

Crane, Verner W., *Benjamin Franklin, Englishman and American.* Baltimore, 1936.

Crane, Verner W., *The Southern Frontier, 1670-1732.* Durham, 1828.

Crittenden, Charles C., *The Commerce of North Carolina, 1763-1789.* New Haven, 1936.

Davis, Andrew McF., *Currency and Banking in the Province of Massachusetts-Bay,* 2 vols. New York, 1901.

Davis, Andrew McF., "The General Court and Quarrels between Individuals arising from the Land Bank," American Antiquarian Society, *Proceedings,* XI. Worcester, Mass., 1898.

Davis, Andrew McF., "The Merchants' Notes of 1733," Massachusetts Historical Society, *Proceedings,* second series, XVII. Boston, 1903.

Derby, Elias H., *The History of Paper Money in the Province of Massachusetts before the Revolution.* Boston, 1874.

Dickerson, Oliver M., *American Colonial Government, 1696-1765; A Study of the British Board of Trade in its relation to the American Colonies, Political, Industrial, and Administrative.* Cleveland, 1912.

Diffenderfer, Frank, R., "Our [Pennsylvania] Early Currency and Its Value," Lancaster County Historical Society, [*Publications*], XIV, no. 5. Lancaster, 1910.

Dodd, Agnes F., *History of Money in the British Empire and the United States.* London and New York, 1911.

Douglas, Charles H. J., "Financial History of Massachusetts Bay from the Organization of the Colony to the American Revolution," *Columbia University Studies in History, Economics and Public Law,* I, no. 4. New York, 1892.

Essays in Colonial History Presented to Charles McLean

Andrews by his Students. New Haven, 1931. Contains Lawrence H. Gipson, "The Taxation of the Connecticut Towns, 1750-1775" (pp. 284-294), which, together with an additional essay, is reprinted as "Connecticut Taxation, 1750-1775," Connecticut Tercentenary Commission, Publications. New Haven, 1934.

Fay, Bernard, Bernard Fay's Franklin, the Apostle of Modern Times. Boston, 1929.

Feavearyear, Albert E., The Pound Sterling; a History of English Money. Oxford, 1931.

Felt, Joseph B., An Historical Account of Massachusetts Currency. Boston, 1839.

Fisher, Edgar J., "New Jersey as a Royal Province, 1738 to 1776," Columbia University Studies in History, Economics and Public Law, XLI, whole no. 107. New York, 1911.

Fisher, Irving, The Purchasing Power of Money. New York, 1911.

Fisher, W. C., "The Tabular Standard in Massachusetts History," Quarterly Journal of Economics, XXVII, May, 1913.

Gipson, Lawrence H., The British Empire before the American Revolution, III. Caldwell, Idaho, 1936.

Gipson, Lawrence H., "Connecticut Taxation, 1750-1775," Connecticut Tercentenary Commission, Publications. New Haven, 1934.

Gordon, Thomas F., The History of New Jersey, from its discovery by Europeans, to the Adoption of the Federal Constitution. Trenton, 1834.

Gordon, Thomas F., The History of Pennsylvania, from its discovery by Europeans, to the Declaration of Independence in 1776. Philadelphia, 1829.

Gouge, William H., A Short History of Money and Banking in the United States, including an account of Provincial and Continental Paper Money. Philadelphia, 1833. Second edition, New York, 1835.

Gould, Clarence P., "Money and Transportation in Maryland, 1720-1765," Johns Hopkins University Studies in *History and Political Science,* series xxxiii, no. 1. Baltimore, 1915.

Greene, Evarts B., and Virginia D. Harrington, *American Population before the Federal Census of 1790.* New York, 1932.

Harrington, Virginia D., "The New York Merchants on the Eve of the Revolution," *Columbia University Studies in History, Economics and Public Law,* no. 440. New York, 1935.

Haseltine, John W., *Description of the Paper Money issued by the Continental Congress of the United States and the several Colonies.* Philadelphia, 1872.

Hawks, Francis L., *History of North Carolina,* 2 vols. Fayetteville, N. C., 1858-1859.

Heath, William E., "The Early Colonial Money System of Georgia," *Georgia Historical Quarterly,* XIX, June, 1935.

Hepburn, A. Barton, *A History of Currency in the United States.* Revised and rewritten edition, New York, 1915.

Hickcox, John H., *An Historical Account of American Coinage.* Albany, 1858.

Hickcox, John H., *A History of the Bills of Credit or Paper Money issued by New York from 1709 to 1789.* Albany, 1866.

Hinkhouse, Fred J., "The Preliminaries of the American Revolution as Seen in the English Press, 1763-1775," *Columbia University Studies in History, Economics and Public Law,* no. 276. New York, 1926.

Johnson, Emory R., et al., *History of Domestic and Foreign Commerce of the United States,* 2 vols. Washington, 1915.

Keith, Charles P., *The Chronicles of Pennsylvania,* 2 vols. Philadelphia, 1917.

Kemmerer, Donald L., "The Colonial Loan-Office System in New Jersey," *Journal of Political Economy,* XLVIII, December, 1939.

Kemmerer, Donald L., *Path to Freedom, The Struggle for Self-Government in Colonial New Jersey*. Princeton, 1940.

Labaree, Leonard W., *Royal Government in America, A Study of the British Colonial System before 1783*. New Haven, 1930.

Lester, Richard A., "Currency Issues to Overcome Depressions in Delaware, New Jersey, New York, and Maryland, 1715-37," *Journal of Political Economy*, XLVII, April, 1939.

Lester, Richard A., "Currency Issues to Overcome Depressions in Pennsylvania, 1723 and 1729," *Journal of Political Economy*, XLVI, June, 1838.

Lester, Richard A., *Monetary Experiments, Early American and Recent Scandinavian*. Princeton, 1939.

Macfarlane, Charles W., "Pennsylvania Paper Currency," *Annals of the American Academy of Political and Social Science*, VIII, no. 1. Philadelphia, 1896.

McCrady, Edward, *The History of South Carolina under Proprietary Government, 1670-1719*. New York, 1897.

McLeod, Frank F., "The History of Fiat Money and Currency Inflation in New England from 1620 to 1789," *Annals of the American Academy of Political and Social Science*, XII, no. 2. Philadelphia, 1898.

Monroe, Arthur E., *Monetary Theory before Adam Smith*. Cambridge, Mass., 1923.

Namier, Lewis B., *England in the Age of the American Revolution*. London, 1930.

Namier, Lewis B., *The Structure of Politics at the Accession of George III*, 2 vols. London, 1929.

Nettels, Curtis P., "The Beginnings of Money in Connecticut," Wisconsin Academy of Sciences, Arts and Letters, *Transactions*. Madison, Wisc., 1927.

Nettels, Curtis P., "The Money Supply of the American Colonies before 1720," *University of Wisconsin Studies in the Social Sciences and History*, no. 20. Madison, Wisc., 1934.

Osgood, Herbert L., *The American Colonies in the Eight-*

eenth Century, 4 vols. New York, 1924.

Palfrey, John G., History of New England from the Revolution of the Seventeenth Century to the Revolution of the Eighteenth, 5 vols. Boston, 1859-1890.

Pargellis, Stanley McC., Lord Loudoun in North America. New Haven, 1933.

Parker, R. Wayne, "Taxes and Money in New Jersey before the Revolution," New Jersey Historical Society, Proceedings, January, 1883.

Pension, (Miss) L. M., "The West Indies and the Spanish American Trade, 1713-1748," Cambridge History of the British Empire, I, chap. xl. Cambridge, 1929.

Phillips, Henry, Jr., Historical Sketches of the Paper Currency of the American Colonies, 2 vols. Roxbury, Mass., 1865.

Phillips, Henry, Jr., An Historical Sketch of the Paper Money Issued by Pennsylvania, together with a Complete List of all the Dates, Issues, Amounts, Denominations, and Signers. Philadelphia, 1862.

Potter, Elisha R., A Brief Account of the Emissions of Paper Money made by the Colony of Rhode Island. Providence, 1837. Reprinted by Henry Phillips, Jr., in Historical Sketches, 1865, without correction.

Potter, Elisha R., and Sidney S. Rider, "Some Account of the Bills of Credit or Paper Money of Rhode Island from the First Issue in 1710, to the Final Issue, 1786," Rhode Island Historical Tracts, first series, no. 8. Providence, 1880.

Price, R. B., and John B. Miller, "Paper Money in Colonial Pennsylvania," Historical Society of Gettysburg College [Publications], n. d.

Ricardo, David, The Principles of Political Economy and Taxation. Everyman edition, London and New York, 1911. First published 1817.

Ripley, William Z., "The Financial History of Virginia, 1609-1776," Columbia University Studies in History, Economics and Public Law, IV. New York, 1893.

Rodney, Richard S., Colonial Finances in Delaware. Wilmington, 1928.

Root, Winfred T., *The Relations of Pennsylvania with the British Government, 1696-1765.* Philadelphia, 1912.

Salley, Alexander S., Jr., "The Introduction of Rice Culture into South Carolina," Historical Commission of South Carolina, *Bulletins,* no. 6. Columbia, S. C., 1919.

Schlesinger, Arthur M., "The Colonial Merchants and the American Revolution, 1763-1776," *Columbia University Studies in History, Economics and Public Law,* LXXVIII, whole number 182. New York, 1918. Reprinted, New York, 1939.

Sellers, Leila, *Charleston Business on the Eve of the American Revolution.* Chapel Hill, 1934.

Smith, W. Roy, *South Carolina as a Royal Province.* New York, 1903.

Stillé, Charles J., "The Life and Times of John Dickinson," Historical Society of Pennsylvania, *Memoirs,* XIII. Philadelphia, 1891.

Sumner, William G., *A History of American Currency.* New York, 1874.

Sumner, William G., "The Spanish Dollar and the Colonial Shilling," *American Historical Review,* III, July, 1898.

Tanner, Edwin P., "The Province of New Jersey, 1664-1738," *Columbia University Studies in History, Economics and Public Law,* XXX. New York, 1908.

Taylor, G. R., "Wholesale Commodity Prices at Charleston, S. C. [1732-1791], *Journal of Economic and Business History,* IV, no. 2, February, 1932.

Van Doren, Carl, *Benjamin Franklin.* New York, 1938.

Wallace, David D., *The History of South Carolina,* 4 vols. New York, 1934.

Wallace, David D., *The Life of Henry Laurens.* New York and London, 1915.

Weeden, William B., *Economic and Social History of New England, 1620-1789,* 2 vols. Boston, 1890.

Wetzel, W. A., "Benjamin Franklin as an Economist," *Johns Hopkins University Studies in History and Political Science*, series xiii, no. 9. Baltimore, 1895.

White, Horace, *Money and Banking illustrated by American History*. Boston and London, 1896. Revised and enlarged edition by Charles S. Tippets and Lewis A. Froman, Boston and New York, 1935, cited.

White, Horace, "New York's Colonial Currency," *Sound Currency*, V, no. 5. New York, 1898.

Wismer, D. C., *New York Descriptive List of Obsolete Paper Money*. Federalsburg, 1931.

Wood, George A., "William Shirley, Governor of Massachusetts, 1741-1756; a History," *Columbia University Studies in History, Economics and Public Law*, no. 209. New York, 1920.

APPENDIX

TABLE II (Revised)

Part B

NEW ENGLAND BILLS OF CREDIT OUTSTANDING

Year	*Mass. ₤	R. I. ₤	Conn. ₤	N. H. ₤	Total ₤	Including Boston Merchants' Notes ₤
1703	6,431				6,431	
1704	17,675				17,675	
1705	29,455				29,455	
1706	31,124				31,124	
1707	40,825				40,825	
1708	57,003				57,003	
1709	66,364			3,000	69,364	
1710	86,648	7,000	13,739	5,500	112,887	
1711	103,426	13,300	18,687	7,500	142,913	
1712	169,022	13,300	23,637	8,000	213,959	
1713	173,970	13,300	24,178	8,000	219,448	
1714	152,126	12,198	22,876	9,200	196,400	
1715	171,760	51,948	22,490	8,335	254,533	
1716	157,062	51,948	23,681	8,335	241,026	
1717	231,875	50,225	20,433	8,335	310,868	
1718	217,510	48,837	20,080	22,435	308,862	
1719	200,660	47,685	19,822	22,345	290,512	
1720	189,906	46,826	17,828	22,299	276,859	
1721	182,194	86,541	17,487	21,381	307,603	
1722	235,100	85,854	17,499	24,993	363,446	
1723	260,087	85,211	16,832	24,635	386,765	
1724	289,984	84,726	14,663	26,314	415,687	
1725	325,188	84,403	12,198	24,611	446,400	
1726	358,140	84,247	7,975	27,567	477,929	
1727	338,658	82,387	10,274	28,353	459,672	
1728	356,388	129,370	9,220	27,375	522,353	
1729	344,423	128,861	6,738	27,308	507,330	
1730	335,323	128,063	4,381	27,155	494,922	
1731	327,786	186,065	4,667	27,155	545,673	
1732	310,520	192,729	2,554	26,200	532,003	
1733	290,640	292,197	52,024	25,207	660,068	770,068
1734	352,588	289,669	52,459	24,840	719,556	829,556

*In circulation end of May.

(Continued)

TABLE II (Revised)

Part B

(Continued)

Year	*Mass. ₤	R. I. ₤	Conn. ₤	N. H. ₤	Total ₤	Including Boston Merchants' Notes ₤
1735	339,054	287,618	52,799	22,783	702,254	812,254
1736	359,211	285,021	51,228	21,783	717,243	794,243
1737	360,000	280,979	55,714	27,319	724,012	801,012
1738	375,815	280,979	54,226	24,989	736,049	813,049
1739	365,237	376,202	50,883	22,985	815,307	859,307
1740	326,412	370,035	160,137	23,677	880,261	924,261
1741	359,919	466,061#	153,098	23,677	1,002,755	1,046,755
1742	383,118	455,435	149,450	38,760	1,026,763	1,070,763
1743	447,564	454,797	146,381	43,880	1,094,365	
1744	456,427	609,082	204,405	142,277	1,412,191	
1745	818,143	642,258	322,623	250,277	2,033,301	
1746	1,581,910	684,295	511,943	488,879	3,267,027	
1747	2,142,725	723,053	507,917	480,439	3,854,134	
1748	2,323,225	736,047	500,128	475,480	4,034,880	
1749	2,456,678	620,600	480,855	475,480	4,033,613	
1750	2,304,394	579,891	476,672	475,480	3,836,437	
1751	160,144	795,811	379,844	475,480	1,811,279	

*In circulation end of May.

#From 1741 to 1751, the sum outstanding on the Loan of 1733 (₤49,925 O.T.) and of 1740 (₤77,000 O.T. terms) was estimated, using the Massachusetts experience in drawing in the ₤100,000 O.T. Loan of 1716 as a guide with some alterations in the case of the two instalments of the Loan of 1740.

Sources. Massachusetts: Annual Treasurers' Accounts, Massachusetts Archives and Public Record Office, Microfilms, Library of Congress. <u>Microfilm Collection of Early State Records</u>, Mass., D.24, Reels 1-3; ACLS, <u>British Manuscripts Project (1941-1945)</u>, CHECKLIST (L.C., 1955), p. 53, D722, D723, D724 [being C.O. 5/853-855]; P.R.O., Accounts of 1720-21 (C.O. 5/868); 1723-24, 1725-26 (C.O. 869); 1732-33, C.O. 5/875; 1739-40, 1740-41, C.O. 5/883; 1742-43, C.O. 5/855.

(Continued)

Wheelwright Report, 1739 (issues and burnings, with some omissions, 1703-1739), Boston, Sept. 10, 1739, C.O. 5/881. <u>Mass. Acts and Resolves</u>, I-XIV, <u>passim</u>, for issuing acts, and resolves, summaries of treasurers' accounts, burning committee reports, etc.

Rhode Island: John B. MacInnes, "<u>Rhode Island Bills of Public Credit, 1710-1755</u>," unpub. Ph.D. diss. (Brown, 1952), Table XIV, pp. 588-590. Issues less burnings.

Connecticut: Henry Bronson, "Historical Account of Connecticut Currency ...," (<u>Papers of the New Haven Historical Society</u>, New Haven, 1865); <u>Connecticut Public Records</u>, V-X (1706-1757), <u>passim</u>; Conn. Archives, Finances, II, Treasurer's Accounts, 1737-1752 (State Library, Hartford), Auditing Committee Reports, 1737-1752, burnings from taxes, pp. 17, 48, 72, 92, 132, 164, 190, 220, 225, 309, 360. Report, Sept. 16, 1752, also has loan bills and bills from sale of bills of exchange drawn on Cape Breton Reimbursement burned. Conn. Hist. Soc., <u>Collections</u> (Papers of the Governors, 1724-1754), IV, V, XI, XIII, XV, XVI, <u>passim</u>.

New Hampshire: Charles J. Bullock, <u>Essays on the Monetary History of the United States</u> (New York, 1900), pp. 207-259; <u>Laws of New Hampshire</u>, II-III (1702-1774), <u>passim</u>; <u>New Hampshire Provincial Papers</u>, III-VI (Assembly Journals, etc.); N. H. Assembly Journals, I-IV (N. H. Hist. Soc., Concord), for burnings - some omitted in <u>Provincial Papers</u>, Bullock's source.

Note: All sums in Table II are in Old Tenor terms.

* * * * *

Note on the Computation of Massachusetts
Bills of Credit In Circulation

Given the requisite data, the ordinary way of computing the annual sum of bills of credit "Outstanding" is to deduct the cumulative burnings from the cumulative issues, for new bills were printed for each issue and burned when again received in payment of taxes or loan principal.

This method, however, cannot be used for Massachusetts. Many of the bills paid in were in good condition; only the "worn and torn" bills were burned and the others were reissued, new bills being printed only as needed. Thus, another method of computation is required. The data in the Treasurers' Accounts enable one to compute the annual sums "In Circulation." The cumulative sum of bills printed less the cumulative sum of bills burned gives the annual sum "Outstanding." By subtracting the bills remaining in the Treasury at the end of the year from the sum "Outstanding," one can determine the sum "In Circulation."

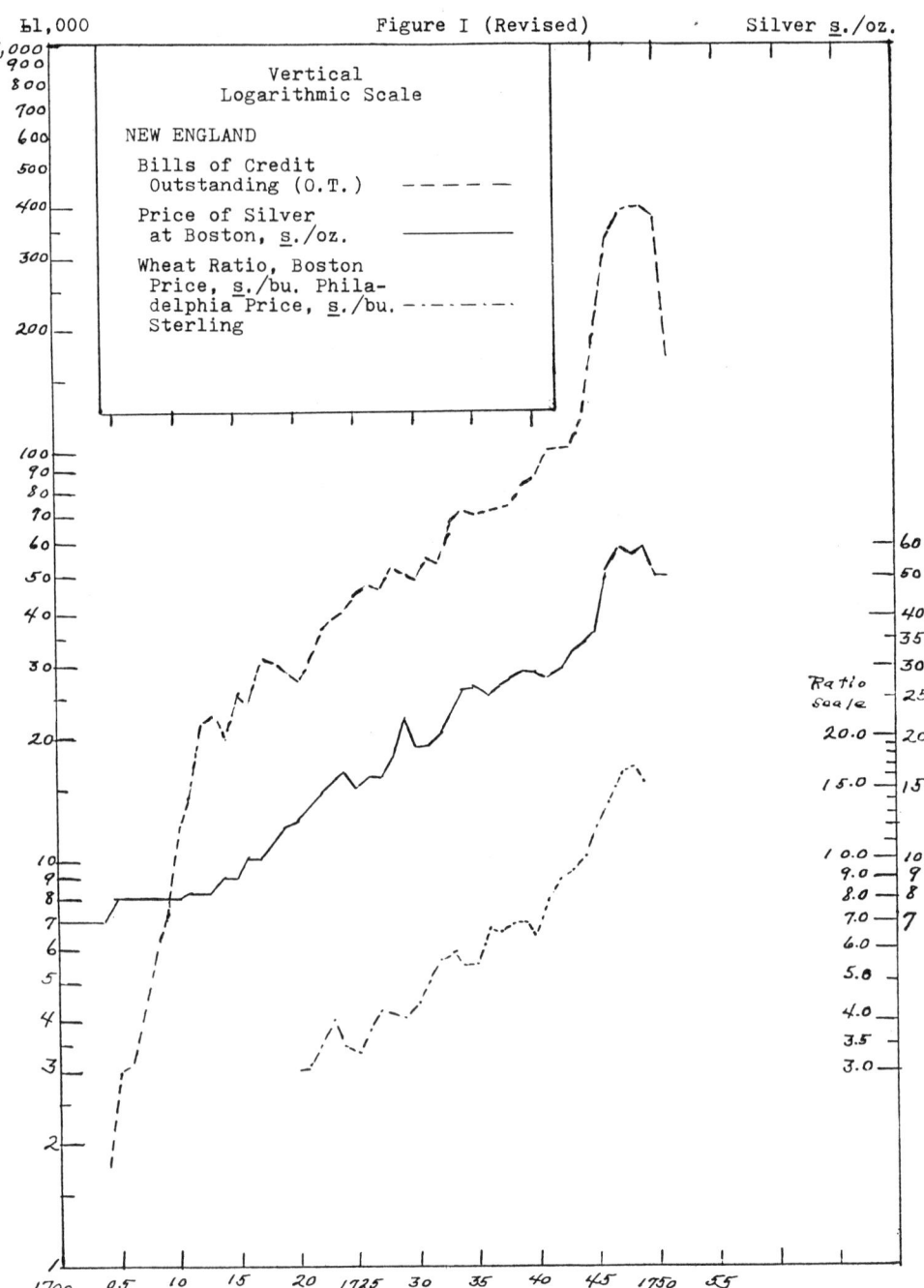

Figure I (Revised)

Notes to Figure I (Revised)

Sources:

Bills of Credit Outstanding, Table II, Part B (Revised).

Silver Price, Table III.

Wheat Price Ratio.

Wheat was a commodity, the price of which fluctuated greatly from year to year, even with a stable currency, because the crop coming to market varied as a result of the weather, infestations of "the fly" and "the rust," and plantings, and also because it was the staple export commodity in the chief producing colonies. Thus its domestic price was determined by the supply, the demand at home and abroad, and the prevailing exchange rate.

To relate changes in the price of wheat as a result of a sustained depreciation of the domestic currency (inflation), it is necessary to iron out fluctuations in price resulting from the factors indicated above.

Pennsylvania was the chief colonial producer and exporter of wheat, flour, and bread. New England, on net balance, imported wheat, Massachusetts being the chief importer. One can correct the Pennsylvania price for the depreciation its currency underwent, as measured by the exchange rate, and also for the annual fluctuations in the exchange rate from non-monetary factors, by dividing the Philadelphia price by the Sterling exchange rate, thus obtaining the Sterling price. If the Boston price in Old Tenor is divided by the Philadelphia Sterling price, the result is a ratio that reflects, rather accurately, the effect of the sustained depreciation of the Massachusetts (and New England) currency during the years for which the ratio can be computed, 1720-1749. Of course, the ratio does not iron out the effect upon the Massachusetts exchange rate and price of silver resulting from non-monetary causes, such as the sudden rise in 1729, and fall in 1730, when "the usual Returns to Great Britain turned to bad Account" in 1729, but recovered in 1730. (Vide supra, p. 64a, n. 71a.)

One should note the extent to which the Wheat Ratio line parallels the Silver Price and Bills of Credit lines on the graph.

Sources:

Philadelphia, annual average wheat price and exchange rate, Anne Bezanson, et.al, Prices in Colonial Pennsylvania, Tables 10 (p. 422-24) and 18 (p. 432), respectively.

Boston wheat price (O.T.) compiled by Ruth Crandall, in Arthur H. Cole, Wholesale Commodity Prices in the United States, 1700-1861, Appendix A, Table 36 (p. 117).

TABLE IX (Revised)

MASSACHUSETTS TREASURER'S CERTIFICATES
(Lawful Money)

Year Ending Last of May	Issued (Sums Borrowed) ₤	Cancelled (Burned) ₤	Outstanding ₤	Redeemed and in Treasury End of Year ₤	Held by Lenders ₤
1750	18,400		18,400		
1751	9,000		27,400		
1752	18,614		46,014		
1753	956	24,828	22,142		
1754	9,332	13,946	17,528	4,606	12,922
1755	36,508	5,181	48,855	13,068	35,787
1756	121,194	14,076	155,973	20,598	135,375
1757	94,181	24,121	226,033	88,186	137,847
1758	118,644	132,187	212,490	+(35,726)	176,764
1759	150,106	77,554	285,042	+(26,013)	259,029
1760	211,346	44,882	451,506	87,539	363,967
1761	210,597	156,838	505,265	52,837	452,428
1762	209,866	*233,799	481,332	*27,015	454,317
1763	124,873	*116,024	490,181	*45,065	445,116
1764	72,334	175,506	387,009	56,862	330,147
1765	131,063	181,654	336,418	57,129	279,289
1766	12,385	87,774	261,029	70,535	190,494
1767	197,000	247,029	211,000	41,307	169,693
1768	157,000	203,123	164,877	17,991	146,886
1769	125,850	160,978	129,749	18,094	111,655
1770	100,000	129,468	100,281	6,020	94,261
1771	88,158	102,543	85,896		
1772	75,091	84,648	76,339		
1773	909		77,248		
1774	16,000	**37,078	56,170		

*New Form Notes, less Old Form Notes exchanged for New.
**Burning Committee Report, Jan. 31, 1774. Massachusetts Acts and Resolves, XVIII, 744.
+Treasury balance not indicated as Treasury Certificates as preceding and succeeding ones, but presumed to be.
Sources: Annual Treasurer's Accounts, Massachusetts Archives and Public Record Office, Microfilms, Library of Congress. Microfilm Collection of Early State Records, Mass., D. 24, Reel 3; ACLS, British Manuscripts Project (1941-1945), Checklist (L. C., 1955), p. 53, D722, D723, D724, as described therein [being C. O. 5/852-855]. MA&R, XIV, 692-3, 723-4; XV, 111; XVIII, 496-7, 551-2, 576, 653-4, 740-1, 744.

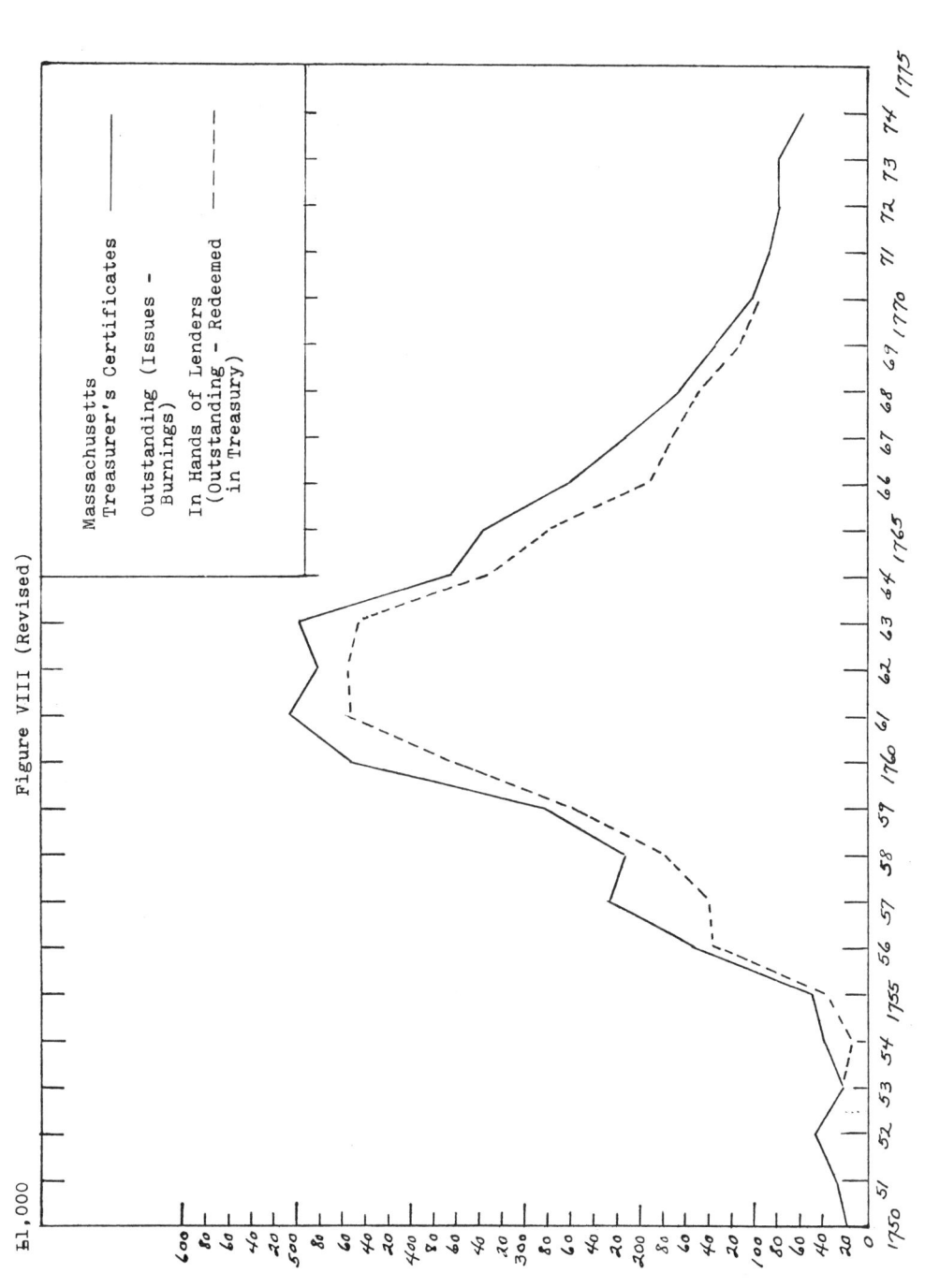

Figure VIII (Revised)

*CONNECTICUT

Bills of Credit Issued on Taxes
1740-1751
(3½ O.T. = 1 N.T.)

Year	Old Tenor Ł	New Tenor Ł	Old Tenor Terms Ł	Yearly Totals Ł	Reference; Conn. Pub. Rec.
1740, May	4,000		4,000		VIII, 295-6
1740, May		8,000	28,000		VIII, 318-21
1740, July	10,000		10,000		VIII, 322
1740				42,000	
1744, May		4,000	14,000		IX, 43
1744, Oct.		**14,000	49,000		IX, 66-7; 80
1744				63,000	
1745, Mar.		20,000	70,000		IX, 99-100
1745, July		20,000	70,000		IX, 151
1745				140,000	
1746, May		20,000	70,000		IX, 217
1746, May	3,000		3,000		IX, 217-8
1746, June		35,000	122,500		IX, 234-5
1746				195,500	
Total				Ł440,500	

*Correction of list, p. 46 n. 45. The total sum outstanding on taxes (O.T. terms), Sept. 6, 1751, was Ł340,219. Report of Auditing Committee, Conn. Hist. Soc., Collections, XVI, 101-102.

**Issue for Ł15,000, of which Ł1,000 were later diverted to exchange for bills "not fit for further service."

PARTIAL ERRATA

p.3, 1.19, between "provisions" and "to," insert "to Southern Europe in return for specie or bills of exchange on England or."

p.38n.26, for "Bank" 9, the "Year" is 1751 (Mar.), and the "Sum in Old Tenor," ₤237,000, as the ₤25,000 in a second new tenor, originally valued at 1 to 8 O.T., were revalued in Aug., 1751, at 1 to 9.48 (64s. O.T. = 6s. 9d. 2nd. N.T.). RICR, VI, 335.

MacInnes, op. cit., p.590, indicates the total lent by the nine Banks as ₤863,971 O.T. (Table XIV, pp.588-590).

p.43, 1.10, for "₤200,000," read "₤237,000."

p.46n.45. Note should be disregarded. The amount of Connecticut bills of credit outstanding on taxes given in Gov. Law to Bedford, Oct., 1749 (not 1750) is erroneous.

Subsequent consideration of Bronson's figures for the sums out on loan suggests that he misunderstood his data, and they should be neglected.

The list of bills of credit issued on taxes is incomplete. A corrected list is given in the Connecticut table in the Appendix (q.v.).

p.49. For revised figures on New Hampshire bills of credit outstanding, see Appendix, Table II (Revised) - Part B.

p. 54, 11.1-2, for "Coleman," read "Colman."

p.72, 11.3-4. The New York Report to the Board of Trade in 1739 indicates the sum then outstanding as ₤79,754. Leo F. Stock, Proceedings and Debates of the British Parliaments respecting North America, V, 36n.63.

pp.91-92. New Jersey - Table VI. The ₤4,670 issue listed under 1716, belongs under 1717.

p.202, 1.11, for "Charles Townshend," read "Chauncy Townshend, a London merchant interested in American affairs."

p.204n.73, for "Gov. Lewis," read "Gov. (Lewis) Morris."

p.206n.74, for "Gov. Lewis's," read "Gov. Morris's."

p.215, 1.21, et passim, for "Ferdinand John Paris" - the first name is spelled variously in the documents - read "Ferdinando John Paris."

p.245, 1.5, for "in May," read "on June 17" (the capitulation of Louisbourg).

p.249n.8 (con.), for "II, 466-467," read "I."

p.281. Table X (Massachusetts Parliamentary Grants). Sources now available indicate Massachusetts' share totaled ₤354,436 Sterling, yielding the colony ₤451,779 L.M.

p.284, l.15, for "Charles Alpthorp and Son," read "Apthorp"; also p.304, l.18.

p.299, l.6, add "O.T." after ₤4,132.

p.319, l.21, for "₤259,000," read "₤359,000."

p.320. Connecticut. The tax granted to retire the issue of 1758 was 8d./₤, not 3d.

p.331n.144, for "*Ibid.*, pp.335-336," read "*Ibid.*, V, 335-336."

pp.345-346. New York - Table XVI (con.). The actual "Cancellations" for 1766 J, 1766 N, and 1767 J are ₤20,037, ₤12,433, and ₤14,567 (*N.Y. Assembly Journals*, PRO). The cancellations in the Table are estimates. The corresponding "Outstanding" sums are ₤146,465, ₤134,032, and ₤119,465. The "Outstanding" sums for 1767 N *et seq.* are ₤37 less than those in the Table.

pp.348-349. Table XVII - New York Parliamentary Grants. Sources now available indicate the total sum received was ₤136,668 Sterling, not all of which was received in the province by 1764.

pp.390-391. Table XX - Pennsylvania Parliamentary Grants. Pennsylvania participitated in only the grants for the services of 1758, 1759, and 1760. Sources now available indicate the net Sterling sum received by Pennsylvania (including Delaware) was ₤75,305. Pennsylvania's share of the Grant of ₤29,993 for 1758, was ₤26,902; Delaware's, ₤3,091. (Franklin, *Papers*, IX, 241.) The net yield of Pennsylvania's share was ₤108,247 (Penna. Currency).

p.393, l.5, for "six," read "eight"; last l., for "₤4,588," read "₤3,961."

p.394, l.1, for "₤15,302," read "₤17,850."

p.407, l.12. New Jersey. After "bills" and before "," insert, "and the support of government."

p.425, l.13-p.426, l.9. Delete the passage "Fortunately for Maryland ... had been otherwise." Maryland bills of credit (1733) possessed a qualified legal tender quality. For the complicated legal tender provisions of the Act of 1733, see *Archives of Maryland*, XXXIX, 95-97.

p.432, ll.13-14. Between "The" and "act," insert ₤40,000.

pp.460-461. Table XXVI - South Carolina Issues of Public Orders. 1757, for "Fortifications," read "St. Michaels Church and State House." 1760, for "₤246,963," read "₤316,693."

p.475, ll.9-11 and n.23. Parliamentary Grants - Virginia. Sources now available indicate the total sum received by Virginia was ₤99,175 Sterling.

p.485n.4, l.3, for "Montagu," read "Montague" (his spelling); also p.496, l.2. Both spellings appear in the documents.

p.506, ll.16-17. "Mr. Townshend" is Charles Townshend.

p.510, l.2, for "1.2$\underline{d}$.," read "1$\frac{1}{2}\underline{d}$."

p.511, l.8, for "27$\underline{s}$.," read "45-50$\underline{s}$."; l.9, for "62," read "170-200."

p.514, l.17, for "27$\underline{s}$.," read "45-50$\underline{s}$."; l.18, for "62," read "170-200"; l.21, for "laid," read "lade."

p.540, ll.1-7. Here Douglass is speaking of British merchants trading to New England on their own account, not selling to colonial merchants whose obligations were in sterling and were thus the losers by inflation, which increased the price of sterling exchange and of silver for returns.

l.18. Omit "[i.e., the colonial merchants]," as it was the British merchant that is referred to.

Thomas Hutchinson indicates that during "the first thirty years" of paper currency in New England, "the greatest part of the goods imported from England were shipped by merchants and tradesmen there upon their own account, and by the depreciation of the medium, while their debts were outstanding, lost a great part, many times one half, of their principal." (Boston Evening Post, Jan. 11, 1762, p. 3, col. 1.) Later the practice changed, the colonial merchants importing on their account, as above explained. Thus the incidence of depreciation was in large measure transferred to the colonial merchants.

p.557, ll.11-22. See the comments in the Preface respecting colonial price indices.

p.562, l.7, for "relie," read "rely."

Dissertations in American Economic History
An Arno Press Collection

Adams, Donald R., Jr.   **Wage Rates in Philadelphia, 1790-1830.** (Doctoral Dissertation, University of Pennsylvania, 1967). 1975

Aldrich, Terry Mark.   **Rates of Return on Investment in Technical Education in the Ante-Bellum American Economy.** (Doctoral Dissertation, The University of Texas at Austin, 1969). 1975

Anderson, Terry Lee.   **The Economic Growth of Seventeenth Century New England:** A Measurement of Regional Income. (Doctoral Dissertation, University of Washington, 1972). 1975

Bean, Richard Nelson.   **The British Trans-Atlantic Slave Trade, 1650-1775.** (Doctoral Dissertation, University of Washington, 1971). 1975

Brock, Leslie V.   **The Currency of the American Colonies, 1700-1764:** A Study in Colonial Finance and Imperial Relations. (Doctoral Dissertation, University of Michigan, 1941). 1975

Ellsworth, Lucius F.   **Craft to National Industry in the Nineteenth Century:** A Case Study of the Transformation of the New York State Tanning Industry. (Doctoral Dissertation, University of Delaware, 1971). 1975

Fleisig, Heywood W.   **Long Term Capital Flows and the Great Depression:** The Role of the United States, 1927-1933. (Doctoral Dissertation, Yale University, 1969). 1975

Foust, James D.   **The Yeoman Farmer and Westward Expansion of U. S. Cotton Production.** (Doctoral Dissertation, University of North Carolina at Chapel Hill, 1968). 1975

Golden, James Reed.   **Investment Behavior By United States Railroads, 1870-1914.** (Doctoral Thesis, Harvard University, 1971). 1975

Hill, Peter Jensen.   **The Economic Impact of Immigration into the United States.** (Doctoral Dissertation, The University of Chicago, 1970). 1975

Klingaman, David C.   **Colonial Virginia's Coastwise and Grain Trade.** (Doctoral Dissertation, University of Virginia, 1967). 1975

Lang, Edith Mae.   **The Effects of Net Interregional Migration on Agricultural Income Growth:** The United States, 1850-1860. (Doctoral Thesis, The University of Rochester, 1971). 1975

Lindley, Lester G.   **The Constitution Faces Technology:** The Relationship of the National Government to the Telegraph, 1866-1884. (Doctoral Thesis, Rice University, 1971). 1975

Lorant, John H[erman].   **The Role of Capital-Improving Innovations in American Manufacturing During the 1920's.** (Doctoral Thesis, Columbia University, 1966). 1975

Mishkin, David Joel. **The American Colonial Wine Industry:** An Economic Interpretation, Volumes I and II. (Doctoral Thesis, University of Illinois, 1966). 1975

Oates, Mary J. **The Role of the Cotton Textile Industry in the Economic Development of the American Southeast:** 1900-1940. (Doctoral Dissertation, Yale University, 1969). 1975

Passell, Peter. **Essays in the Economics of Nineteenth Century American Land Policy.** (Doctoral Dissertation, Yale University, 1970). 1975

Pope, Clayne L. **The Impact of the Ante-Bellum Tariff on Income Distribution.** (Doctoral Dissertation, The University of Chicago, 1972). 1975

Poulson, Barry Warren. **Value Added in Manufacturing, Mining, and Agriculture in the American Economy From 1809 To 1839.** (Doctoral Dissertation, The Ohio State University, 1965). 1975

Rockoff, Hugh. **The Free Banking Era: A Re-Examination.** (Doctoral Dissertation, The University of Chicago, 1972). 1975

Schumacher, Max George. **The Northern Farmer and His Markets During the Late Colonial Period.** (Doctoral Dissertation, University of California at Berkeley, 1948). 1975

Seagrave, Charles Edwin. **The Southern Negro Agricultural Worker:** 1850-1870. (Doctoral Dissertation, Stanford University, 1971). 1975

Solmon, Lewis C. **Capital Formation by Expenditures on Formal Education, 1880 and 1890.** (Doctoral Dissertation, The University of Chicago, 1968). 1975

Swan, Dale Evans. **The Structure and Profitability of the Antebellum Rice Industry:** 1859. (Doctoral Dissertation, University of North Carolina at Chapel Hill, 1972). 1975

Sylla, Richard Eugene. **The American Capital Market, 1846-1914:** A Study of the Effects of Public Policy on Economic Development. (Doctoral Thesis, Harvard University, 1968) 1975

Uselding, Paul John. **Studies in the Technological Development of the American Economy During the First Half of the Nineteenth Century.** (Doctoral Dissertation, Northwestern University, 1970) 1975

Walsh, William D[avid]. **The Diffusion of Technological Change in the Pennsylvania Pig Iron Industry, 1850-1870.** (Doctoral Dissertation, Yale University, 1967). 1975

Weiss, Thomas Joseph. **The Service Sector in the United States, 1839 Through 1899.** (Doctoral Thesis, University of North Carolina at Chapel Hill, 1967). 1975

Zevin, Robert Brooke. **The Growth of Manufacturing in Early Nineteenth Century New England.** 1975